Spartanburg District

Conveyance Book
AA
1848-1850

&

Conveyance Book
BB
1850-1852

Transcribed by Betty Jean Foster Dill
From SC Archives Microfilm C 609 (UP)
&
Edited by Joseph R. Gainey
For
The Piedmont Historical Society
1999

Please Direct All Correspondence and Book Orders to:

Southern Historical Press, Inc.
PO Box 1267
375 West Broad Street
Greenville, SC 29602-1267
or
southernhistoricalpress@gmail.com

----

southernhistoricalpress.com

ISBN #0-89308-717-3

Printed in the United States of America

INTRODUCTION

Spelling used in the deed book was kept in this transcription. Most misspellings are underlined. Names are underlined where there is a difference in how they are usually spelled.

Many deeds for property in the Town or Village of Spartanburg were recorded in Conveyance Books AA and BB, 1848-1852.

The name of the district and town was spelled both ways: "Spartanburgh," in some of the older records and "Spartanburg," throughout these records for 1848-1852.

Though not repeated after every record in this transcript, this statement was at the end of each one in the Conveyance Books:
Registered, Examined and certified the [date, almost always filled in].
Original delivered to [mostly not filled in].

OVERVIEW

Although the volumes abstracted here are technically "deed books", that is a totally insufficient description of their content and character. While it must be admitted that deeds for real estate comprise the lion's share of Spartanburg County Deed Books "AA" and "BB", that is not their total scope. They contain a plethora of mortgages, bills of sale, contracts, apprenticeships, slave sales and other personal property transactions, agreements, and other types of records. Unfortunately, with the exception of the deeds *per se*, none of these documents are indexed in the present set of indices available at the Spartanburg County R. M. C. Office and on microfilm at the S. C. Department of Archives and History in Columbia, SC, the Spartanburg County Public Library, the LDS Family History Library in Salt Lake City, Utah and elsewhere. To remedy this situation, Betty Jean has prepared a comprehensive index which includes not only names and places but provides access points to geographical features (such as creeks and rivers), churches, named roads, business and corporation names, slaves, and even family cemeteries. This feature widens the usefulness of this volume to local and regional historians, demographers, and sociologists in addition to genealogists—its primary intended audience.

Certainly, there are gaps in the record. But, this is due not to clerical errors—although it must be admitted that there are some very obvious scrivener errors in these books—as much as to the poor record keeping countenanced by South Carolina law at the time. (Not until the 1870s was it a statutory requirement to record deeds and other instruments to file them in the county where the property was located and this law had no requirement demanding retrospective recording on older records. Georgia made recording of such documents mandatory starting in 1785.) Simple, physical possession of a validly executed legal document was sufficient to secure an owner's legal right to property. Unfortunately, far too few family papers from this era containing unrecorded legal documents survive to even begin to fill this gap in the public record. So, the researcher must do the best s/he can with the existing documentation.

Deeds are basic to genealogical and historical research on the local level. The era covered by this volume was one when many Spartans migrated westward. Clear evidence of the relocation of both whites and blacks appear here. The passing of land from father to son (or son-in-law) is also represented. Changes in slave ownership is another aspect of these documents which was inaccessible to the researcher prior to the publication of this volume—unless the researcher had the time to sit down with the original books and go through them page by page. For these and many other reasons, this publication is a very welcome boon to anyone researching Spartanburg District in this period, and I am glad to have had a part in making it more readily available. I want to thank Betty Jean Dill for her dedication and excellent job in preparing the original abstracts and the index.

Joseph R. (Joey) Gainey
April 16, 1999

Book AA

p. 1-2.   5 Jan 1848. Mortgage. **J.B. Powell** bound unto **James McMakin** & **Mary McMakin,** his wife, for $2,000 conditioned for the payment of $1000. As security for debt and bond, **J.B. Powell** sold to **James McMakin & Mary R. McMakin**, 40 acres on the branches of the South fork of Tyger River and on the north side of the road leading to **McMakin**'s Factory, part of Lot N° 8. It is agreed between the two parties, that **J.B. Powell** is to occupy the premises until default of payment. Wit: **Anna P. Fleming, Benjamin R. Allender.**   Signed **J.B. Powell.**   Witness oath, 1 May 1848: Signed, **Anna P. Flemming** to **J.B. Tolleson,** Clerk & Mag. Registered, examined & certified 1st May 1848.

p. 2-3.   29 Nov 1847. Deed of Conveyance. **John C. Hoyt** of Greenville Dist, for $20 paid by **James Tucker** of Greenville Dist, sold 814 acres in Spartanburg Dist on some of the head waters of Motlows Creek and both sides of Goodgion Road; bordering **Benjamin Pruitt.** Wit: **L.P. Corruth [Cornith?], John Lankford.** Signed, **John C. Hoyt.** Witness oath, 29 Nov 1847: Signed, **John Lankford** of Greenville Dist to **R.P. Goodlett,** M.G.D. Registered Examined & certified 1st May 1848. Original delivered to ~~ **James Tucker.**

p. 3-4.   1 Dec 1846. Mortgage. **Solomon Ballard** of Spartanburg Dist, for $150 paid by **Isaiah Bowling** of Spartanburg Dist, sold Three head of horses, two clay bank mares, the mare is ten years old and colt about seven months old, and the other a mare - four years old in the spring, two cows four yearlings and fifteen head of sheep, and seven bee hives, one bed and bedding, and two hundred bushels of corn Two thousand bundles of fodder, and a lot of shucks & all my interest in a yoke of Oxens and cart. If **Solomon Ballard** pays **Isaiah Bowling** $150 on or before 25 Dec 1850 sale is null & void. Witness: **James Caldwell.** Signed, **Solomon (x) Ballard.** Witness oath, 6 May 1848: Signed, **John Bowling** to **James Caldwell,** Mag. S.D. Registered examined & certified 7th May 1848. Original delivered to~~ **N.M. Bollin** 12 Augt 1838

p. 4-5.   10 Apr 1846. Mortgage. Spartanburgh District. **E.C. Leitner & George Leitner** are indebted to **John Stroble Jr.** for $800 payable in four annual installments, with interest. **E.C. Leitner & George Leitner** assign **John Stroble Jr.** forever, Ten original shares in the <u>Bivingsville Cotton Manufacturing Company</u> of the value of $100 each. Bivingsville Cotton Manufacturing Company being in Dist of Spartanburg on Lawson Fork. Wit: **James Edward Henry, D.C. Judd.** Signed & sealed, **E.C. Leitner, George Leitner.** Witness oath: **D.C. Judd** to **J.B. Tolleson** Clk & Mag. Signed, **D.C. Judd.** Registered 8th May 1848.

p. 6-7.   15 Apr 1846. Mortgage. **E.C. Leitner & George Leitner** are indebted to **J.W. Miller** for $800 payable in four annual installments with interest. **E.C. Leitner & George Leitner** assign **J.W. Miller** Ten original shares of in the <u>Bivingsville Cotton Manufacturing Company</u> of the value of $100 each. <u>Bivingsville Cotton Manufacturing Company</u> being in Dist of Spartanburg and on Lawsons Fork. Wit: **James Edward Henry, David C. Judd.** Signed & sealed, **E.C. Leitner, George Leitner.** Witness oath, 8 May 1848: **D.C. Judd** to **J.B. Tolleson,** Clk & Mag Ex officio. Signed, **D.C. Judd.** Registered 8th May 1848. Original delivered [blank]

p. 7-8. 15 Apr 1846. Mortgage for real estate. Spartanburg Dist. **E.C. Leitner & George Leitner** are indebted to **Samuel Miller** Sheriff for $1600 payable in four annual installments. **E.C. & George Leitner** assign **Samuel Miller** forever, Twenty original shares in the Bivingsville Cotton Manufacturing Company. Bivingsville Cotton Manufacturing Company being in Spartanburg Dist on Lawson Fork. Wit: **J. Edward Henry, D.C. Judd.** Signed **E.C. Leitner, George Leitner.** Witness oath, 8 May 1848: **D.C. Judd** to **J.B. Tolleson.** Signed, **D.C. Judd.** Registered May the 8th 1848.

p. 9-10. 11 Apr 1848. Sheriff's Title. **R.C. Poole,** Sheriff of Spartanburgh Dist, for $81.50 paid by **Tho⁸ Brian** sold 80 acres. Whereas **John Robertson, Elizabeth Robertson, Henry White & Margaret White, William Carver & Mary H. Carver** on or about the 17th day of Jan 1848, did exhibit their Petition to the Court of Ordinary at Spartanburg Court House setting forth that **John M⁰Lure** departed this life intestate on [no date], seized and possessed in fee 80 acres on the waters of North Pacolet River bounded by **P.S. Hunter &** others, and division of said land yet remained to be made, which they prayed might be done and whereas afterwards on the 4th of February 1848, **R. Bowden Esq** Ordinary of Spartanburg District ordered that the land be sold by the Sheriff of Spartanburg on the first Monday in March. **R.C. Poole** as Sheriff, after having duly advertised the Tract of Land for sale by public outcry, on the 5th day of March 1848, did then openly and publicly according to the custom of Auctions, sell and dispose of the Tract of land unto **J. Bryan** for **Thomas Bryan** for the sum of $81.50 being at that price the last and highest bidder for 80 acres on the waters of North Pacolet river adjoining **Peyton Hunter** and **Thomas Bryan** and **M⁰Clure & Allison.** Wit: **J.W. Quinn, J.B. Tolleson.** Signed, **R.C. Poole,** S.S.D. Witness oath, 8 May 1848: **J.W. Quinn** to **J.B. Tolleson,** Clerk & mag. Signed, **J.W. Quinn.** Registered 8th May 1848.

p. 10-11. 4 March 1848. Mortgage. **S.G. Seay** is indebted to **Henry Dodd** for $912.35 [or $912.41], payable in five equal annual payments on the 10th day of Feb in each of the five years. **S.G. Seay** sold to **Henry Dodd** all that tract or parcel of land [acres not stated] on the waters of north Pacolet river which adjoins the Land of **D. McMullin, Willy Duncan &** said **Dodd.** Wit: **R.F. M⁰Kinney, James M. Jackson.** Signed, **S.G. Seay.** Witness oath, 18 March 1848: **J.M. Jackson** to **G. Cannon,** Notary public. Signed, **Ja⁸ M. Jackson.** Registered 5th May 1848.

p. 11-12. 4 July 1846. Deed of Conveyance. **John Beason** of Spartanburgh Dist, for $12.50 sold to the Church at Antioch (adjacent cittizens) one acre and a quarter of land it being a part of the 3 acres and a quarter now owned by said Church and neighbors, with free use of the water and I will in no way prohibit or debar any one from the use of the same. Border: **John Beasons** fence on the east side of the big Road, **John Terry.** Wit: **Sampson Bobo, Silus Woodruff.** Signed & Sealed, **John Beason.** Witness oath, 5 Aug 1841: **Sampson Bobo** to **L. Lankford** Magt. Signed, **Sampson Bobo.** Registered 5th June 1848.

p. 12-13. 22 Aug 1844. Deed of Conveyance. **W.A. Rogers** of Green Co. Alabama, to **Noah Webster** of Spartanburg Dist, all my interest in 316 acres known as the **Rolin Calvert** farm lying on both sides of Dutchmans creek to mouth of a small creek called Camp branch. If I have more interest in the above stated tract than is contained in the boundary as all one note, I also convey it by this deed. Wit: **G. Nicholls, A.S. Camp.** Signed, **W.A. Rogers.** Witness oath, 5 Jun 1848: **Adam**

S. Camp to **John Linder**, Magt. Signed, **A.S. Camp.** Registered 5th June 1848.

p. 13-14. 12 Jan 1847. Deed of Conveyance. **Thomas R. Tucker** of Spartanburg Dist, for $200 paid by **Sirpaton Tinsley** of Spartanburg Dist, sold 195 acres, part of a tract of land (originally granted to **John Tucker** in 1805) Part of which was conveyed to me by **J. Tucker** in 1814 the ballance of claim for part pay went for the maintainance of **Mary Tucker** the widow of said **T. Tucker,** (and my M____); on both sides of Shoaly fork creek of North Tyger river. In addition to the above tract of land and for the above sum of money paid to me, I sell to the said **Sirpaton Tinsley**, all my interest in two lots of land, one on the east end containing 111 acres , the other on the west end of the original survey containing 48 acres, the above three lots extending from the eastern line to the western line and to the southern line of the original survey, a dividing line made by **Sirpatin Tinsley** and **John Wheeler**. Wit: **Presly Davis, William E. Ward.** Signed **Thomas R. Tucker.** Witness oath, 16 Aug 1847: **Presley Davis** to **Thomas Ballenger**, Magt. Signed, **Presley Davis.** Registered 5th June 1848. Original to [blank]

p. 14-15. 29 Jan 1848. Deed of Conveyance. **James & Darcas Hamm, Massey Peake** and **David D. Peake**, Legatees of the estate of **Benjamin & Caroline Peake**, both being Deceased, for $225, sold the real estate of **Benjamin & Caroline Peak**, three fourth[?] of one half of 150 acres, (excepting the graves), part of a tract originally granted to **Robert Cowden** in 1753 on Dutchmans Creek; bordering **John Morrow**. Wit: **Cyntha B. Hamm, Massey P. Hamm.** Signed: **James Hamm, Dorcas P. Hamm, Massey Peake, D.D. Peake.** Wit oath, 9 May 1848: Signed, **Cynthia B. Hamm** to **Harvey Wofford**, Magt. Registered 10 June 1848.

p. 15-16.   30 Jan 1833. Deed of Conveyance. **Ja' Hamm, Dorcas Hamm** and **Massey Peake**, legatees of the estate of **Benjamin Peake** Decd, of Spartanburg Dist, for $200 paid by **Thomas Peake,** of Spartanburg Dist, sold all their interest in the estate of **Benjamin Peake** deceased. Test: **Giles Bearden, Winn Bearden.** Signed & Sealed: **James Hamm, Dorcas P. Hamm, Masey (x) Peake.** Witness oath, 9 Feb 1844: **Winn Bearden** to **H. O'Shoal**, Magt. Signed, **Winn Bearden.** Registered 10th June 1848. [Massey Peake signed her name in the deed above this one; in this deed she made her mark]

p. 16-17. 9 Feb 1844. Deed of Conveyance. **D.D. Peake** of Spartanburg Dist and legatee of the estate of **Benjamin Peake**, Decd, for $100 paid by **Casandria Peake,** of Spartanburg Dist, sold all my right in the estate of **Benjamin Peake**, decd. Wit: **Giles Bearden, Winn Bearden.** Signed **David D. Peake.** Witness oath, 9 Feb 1844: **Win Bearden** to **H. O'Shoal**, Magt. Signed, **Winn Bearden.** Registered 10 June 1848.

p. 17.   19 April 1848. Deed of Conveyance. **Polly Posey** of Spartanburg Dist, in good mind and sense do relinquish the plantation I now live on to my son **Zephaniah Posey**, excepting as much of the plantation as one hand can tend as good as there is on the plantation where I shall choose. Wit: **W.N. Wofford, Osborn (x) West.** Signed **Polly (x) Posey.** Witness oath, 6 May 1848: **William N. Wofford** to **Z. Lankford**, Magt. Signed, **W.N. Wofford.** Registered 13th June 1848.

p. 18.   9 March 1848. Deed of Conveyance. **William C. Rose** of Gaston Co., N.C. late of

Spartanburg Dist, sold to [price not mentioned] **John T. Kirby,** 119 acres in Dist of Spartanburg, bounded by **Mitchell Tolleton, Thomas Wills** and others. Wit: **E.L. Huggins, T.O.P. Vernon.** Signed, **William C. Rose.** Witness oath, 2 Apr 1848: **T.O.P. Vernon** to **J.B. Tolleson,** clk & mgt. Signed **T.O.P. Vernon.** Registered 20th June 1848.

p. 19-20. 16 Oct 1847. Sheriff's Titles. **R.C. Poole** successor of **G. Nicholls,** sheriff of Spartanburg Dist. **Alfred Tolleson,** by virtue of writ issued out of the Court of common pleas, Spartanburg Dist., tested 12 Nov 1844 at the suit of **Alfred Tolleson** against **Huey?/Henry? Reily** to **G. Nicholls,** Shff, commanded [to sell?]from the goods, chattels and tenements of **Huey?Henry? Reiley** to levy the sum of $394.17 with damages and costs, has seized and taken the lands and tenements of **Huey? Riely,** all that tract containing 169 acres on waters of Packolett river and bounded by **John Easterwood, Wm B. Riely, H.H. Thomson, Walton Brown & Alfred Tolleson;** purchased by **Alfred Tolleson** of Spartanburgh Dist, for $270. Wit: **J.H. Wilson, John R. Poole.** Signed, **R.C. Poole,** successor. Witness oath, 20 Jun 1848: **J.H. Wilson** to **J.B. Tolleson.** Signed, **J.H. Wilson.** Registered 20th June 1848.

p. 20-21. 13 Nov 1847. Deed of Conveyance. **J.W. Tucker** of Spartanburgh Dist for $100 paid by **John T. Kirby** of Spartanburgh Dist sold a parcel of land in the Village of Spartanburg situated on what is called church street adjoining lots on the N and S owned by **John T. Kirby,** on the W by the public street, on the E by **R. Thomas** Decd, containing ¾ acre - which I purchased of **George Nicholls.** Wit: **J.H. Wilson, Alfred Tolleson.** Signed **J.W. Tucker.** Witness oath, 20th June 1848: **J.H. Wilson** to **J.B. Tolleson,** Clk & Magt. Signed **J.H. Wilson.** Registered 20th June 1848.

p. 21-22. 22 April 1848. Sheriff's Titles. **R.C. Poole,** Sheriff of Spartanburg Dist, to **Wm Terry** for $1150.50. All the legatees of **John Terry** deceased, on or about the 7th day Feby 1848 petitioned the Court of Ordinary at Spartanburg Court House setting forth that **John Terry** departed this life intestate [no date] 1847, possessed in fee of land containing 234 acres in two tracts on the waters of Enoree river bounded by lands of **Willis Lanford, John Beason, Dr. Benjiman F. Kilgore, David Brewton, Wm Terry** and **John W. Farrow** that division yet remained to be made. On the 14th day of February 1848, **R. Bowden Esqr** Ordinary ordered that the land be sold by the sheriff on the first Monday in March. Wit: **J.B. Tolleson, Peyton Turner.** Signed, **R.C. Poole,** S.S.D. Witness oath, 20 Jun 1848: **Peyton Turner** to **J.B. Tolleson,** Clk & Mgt Ex officio. Signed **Peyton Turner.** Registered 20th June 1848.

p. 22-23. 20 March 1848. Deed of Conveyance. **John Wingo,** son of **Abner** of the District of Spartanburg for $160 sold to **Reubin Bowden,** 80 acres on both sides of Holstons waters of Fair Forest Creek bounded by **E. Jackson, R. Bowden, Collin's** road, **J. Wingo's** spring; a store in Wingo's field; and **John Wingo,** S of A, doth bind myself, my heirs........ Wit: **Jesse Cleveland, A. Wingo.** Signed, **John Wingo.** Release of dower, 20th May 1848: **Margaret (x) Wingo** to **J.B. Tolleson,** Clk & Magt.

p. 23-24. 24 April 1848. Sheriff's Title. **R.C. Poole,** Sheriff of Spartanburg Dist, to **James Tapp.** By order of the court of common pleas held for Spartanburg Dist, tested the 14th day of February 1846 at the suit of **D.W. Moore,** commanding me that of the goods and chattels, lands and tenements of **Joshua Tapp** to levy the sum of $52.51 with damages and costs, I have seized the lands and tenements of the said **Joshua Tapp,** all that tract containing 105 acres on the waters of fair forest creek and bounded by lands of **James Tapp** and **Hiram Bullman;** sold to **James Tapp** of Spartanburg Dist, for the sum of $314, the land being sold subject to a mortgage to the Ordinary for $313. Wit: **John Golightly, R. Bowden**. Signed **R.C. Poole,** S.S.D. Witness oath, 20 Jun 1848: **R. Bowden** to **J.B. Tolleson,** Clk & Mgt.

p. 25. 19 Feb 1848. Deed of Conveyance. **D^r Ja' Bivings** to **Susan E. & J.B. Cleveland. James Bivings** of Spartanburg Dist in, for the natural good will and affection for my daughter **Susan E. Cleveland** and her husband **J.B. Cleveland** and $1 paid by the said **Susan E. & John Cleveland** of Spartanburg Dist, I release [to them] 192 ½ acres in Spartanburg Dist on the waters of Chinquepin it being a part of the **Benson** tract purchased by me of **N. Gist** and originally entered by **James Steadman,** bounded by **Thomson** tract, **Benson** tract, **Jesse Cleveland's** old field, **A.W. Bivings**. Wit: **J.S. Finch, J.W. Tucker**. Signed **Ja' Bivings**. Witness oath, 15 Feb 1848, to **J.W. Tucker,** Magt. Signed, **J.S. Finch**. Registered 22 June 1848.

p. 26.   15 April 1848. Mortgage. Spartanburg District. **Hiram Nelson** to **John Linder.** For the purpose of securing the payment of three notes to **John Linder** for $38.12½ each, due in twelve months, two years, & three years from this date; this day given for 61 acres herein mortgaged; bounded by lands of **John Linder, J. Templeman, O. Patterson** Et Al. Should I fail to make payments by the time the notes come due, I consent that the sheriff advertise the above premises twenty days and sell the above to the highest bidder and make the title to the purchaser, but should I pay the above described notes when due, this obligation shall be null and void. Wit: **A.S. Camp, He$\underline{ny}$ Cannon**. Signed **Hiram Nelson**. Witness Oath, 20 June 1848, **A.S. Camp** to **J.B. Tolleson,** Clk & mag. Eiff. Registered 20th June 1848.

p. 26-27. 15 April 1848. Deed of Conveyance. **James Cannon** to **John Linder,** for $153 sold 51 acres, adjoining **John Linder's** home tract, **James Cannon** and **Poole**'s land. Signed **James Cannon**. Wit: **Henry Cannon, A.S. Camp**. Witness oath: **A.S. Camp** to **J.B. Tolleson,** Clk and Mag Oiff. Registered 20th June 1848.

p.27-28.   6 Dec 1847. Deed of Conveyance. **G. Nicholls,** Spartanburg Dist, for $90 paid by **John Bomar Jr.,** Spartanburg Dist, sold 13 acres on fair forest creek about 2 miles South of Spartanburg village on the east side of the road leading to **Ralph Smith**'s and bounded by the fairforest on the north; beginning at a sweet gum on the south bank of said creek on the east side of the road and running along said road to **Kinsman Seay**'s line and to **J. Bomar**'s corner. Signed **G. Nicholls**. Wit: **J.M. Elford, R.E. Cleveland**. Wit oath, 20 June <u>1848</u>: **R. Easley Cleveland** to **J.B. Tolleson**. Release of dower, 29 Dec 1847: Signed **C.N. Nicholls,** wife of **George Nicholls** to **Lecil Bearden,** Magt S.D. Registered 20th June 1848.

p. 28-30. 14 Sept 1841. Deed of conveyance. **John D. Williams,** of L<u>aw</u>rens Dist, to **Maj^r Wm Eddins,** of A<u>be</u>ville Dist, for $500, "all my interest" in 560 acres in Spartanburg Dist on the waters of Broad River adjoining the Limestone Springs tract, which is one third part of the above tract purchased by **Maj^r Wm Eddins, W. Gracy** and myself on the 14th day of September 1841 as appears by a reference to a title given to us by **Maj^r H.J. Dean**, Commissioner of Equity for Spartanburg Dist. Wit: **Dr. J.A.S. Milligan, Emanuel Wiss, J.B. Eddins.** Signed, **John D. Williams.** Witness oath, 3 June 1848: **Emanuel Wiss** of Laurens Dist. to **E. Watson**, M.L.D. Wit: **Elihu Watson**, Mag Laurens Dist. Release of Dower, 3 June 1848, signed **Phebe C. Williams.** Registered 28th June 1848.

p. 30-31.   23 March 1848. Deed for two lots in Spartanburg. **H.H. Thomson**, of Spartanburg Dist, to **William Carver** of Spartanburg Dist, for $75 secured to be paid, "two lots in the Village of Spartanburg which I bought at sheriff's sale as the property of **Wm Poole** and numbered Lot 14 containing Two acres adjoining, by a street, the lot I heretofore sold to the said **Carver** and numbered 7 in a plat made by **George Nicholls** Sheriff and by which he sold also a lot on the Tanyard branch adjoining, by a street, on the east lot which belonged to the Estate of **R. Thomson** Dec^d, both of these lots buildings & boundaries will more fully appear by reference to the plot by which **George Nicholls** sold the same to the said **Wm Carver** Excepting the claim which **Jane Pool** has for wood on the said lots. Wit: **J.W. Webber, R.E. Cleveland.** Witness oath, 20 June 1848: **J.W. Webber** to **J.B. Tolleson.** Release of dower, 20 June 1848: Signed, **M.E. Thomson** to **J.B. Tolleson.** Registered 20 June 1848.

p. 32-33.   15 Dec 1846. Deed of Conveyance. **Joseph Carver** of Pickings Co, Dist of Pintleton, to **John S. Finch** of Spartanburgh Dist, sold 431 acres for $30; on branches of Greens and Meadow Creek waters of Lawsons Fork being all that tract of land which was granted to **Isham Pullum** on the 16th day of July 1795, excepting that which I deeded to **G. McFearson** in two deeds dated 2 Nov 1831, which **McFarson** sold to **John S. Finch** and this deed is to include the whole of the Land included in the **Isham Pullom** grant by including the two deeds together. Wit: **Joseph (x) Goliver, Collins Smith.** Signed **Joseph (x) Carver.** Pickens Dist, witness oath, 15 Dec 1846: **Collins Smith** to **E. Hughes**, Mag. Release of dower, 16 Dec 1846. **M^n Nancy Carver** wife of **Joseph Carver**, (release included her right of dower or claim to all the land within the **Pullam** Grant of 16 July 1795), to **Edw. Hughs.** Signed, **Nancy (x) Carver.** Registered 3 July 1848.

p. 33-34.   12 Feb 1848. Deed of Conveyance. **James Bivings** to **J. & J.D. Bivings**, all of Spartanburgh Dist, for $100 sold 24 acres on the waters of Middle Tyger it being a part of the tract purchased by me of **Thomas Collins** & where the factory now stands; bound by south side of pond or river, **Mrs. Crawford's** line. Wit: **J.S. Collins, John (x) Ralph, Stephen Ally.** Signed **Jas. Bivings.** Witness oath, 3 July 1848: Signed, **John S. Collins** to **J.W. Tucker**, Magst. Signed **J.S. Collins.** Registered 3 July 1848.

p. 34-35.   12 Feb 1848. Deed of Conveyance. **James Bivings** to **Jas D. Bivings**, all of Spartanburgh Dist; in consideration of the loss sustained in the loss of building & removing from Chinquepin to Tyger & the giving up his claims to the property on my place where we first built the factory I convey (267 acres) unto **James D. Bivings**, all that tract on the waters of the Middle Tyger it being a part of a tract purchased by me of **Thomas Collins**, the factory tract bordering the river, **J. Collins** line, **Caldwell's** line. Wit: **J.S. Collins, John (x) Ralph, Stephen Ally.** Signed **Jas Bivings.** Witness oath, 3 July 1848: Signed, **John S. Collins** to **J.W. Tucker.** Registered 3 July 1848.

p. 35-36.   7 Jan 1848. Deed of Conveyance. **John L. Ballenger** of Pickins Dist, Exo^r of **E.**

Ballenger Dec^d, sold to **William Dodd** of Spartan<u>burgh</u> Dist, at public vendue, all the real Estate of said **E. Ballenger** Dec^d, being in the district of Spartanburgh; on the south side Lawson^s Fork Creek & bounded by **S.W. High, William P. Moore** & others, containing 484 acres for the sum of $1,240, to me paid or secured to be paid by the said **William Dodd**. Wit: **S.W. High, M. Seay**. Signed, **John L. Ballenger**, Exo^r. Witness oath, 3 July 1848: signed, **M. Seay** to **J.B. Tolleson**, Clk & Mag Ex officio. Registered 3 July 1848.

p. 36.   14 Jan 1848.   Relinquishment.   Spartan<u>burgh</u> District. **Hamilton Cannon** for $37 relinquishes to **Simpson Cannon** "all my claim and Interest in the land which **William Cannon**, Deceased, willed to his wife **Lucy Cannon** during her life time." Wit: **J.J. Vandiver, Ellis Cannon**. Signed **Hamilton Cannon**. Witness oath, 15 July 1848: signed, **Ellis Cannon** to **J.B. Tolleson**. Registered 5 July 1848.

p. 37-38.   18 March 1836. Deed of Conveyance. **Robert Bullington** of Spartan<u>burgh</u> Dist, to **Samuel Bullington**, for $450, sold the parcel of land whereon he [Samuel] now lives on the south side of South Pacolet River containing 134 acres bounded by said river, **McDowell's**. Wit: **Moses Foster, John Bomar**. Signed, **Robert Bullington**. Witness oath, 20 July 1848: signed, **Moses Foster** to **Z. Lanford**, Magst. Release of dower: **Mary (x) Bullington** , wife of **Robert Bullington**, to **Z. Lanford**. Registered 22 July 1848.

p. 38-39.   21 Jan 1847. Deed of Conveyance. **Samuel Bullington** of Spartan<u>burgh</u> Dist, to **Oliver Clark** of Spartanburgh Dist, sold 134 acres for $450, where **S. Bullington** now lives; on the south side of South Pacolet River, bounded by the river, **McDowell's** line. **Elizabeth Bullington** joins her husband, **Samuel Bullington**, in the Deed and relinquishes her claim of Dower unto **Oliver Clark**. Wit: **Pinckney Hammett, [J. or] T.S. Bullington**. Signed **S. Bullington, Elizabeth (x) Bullington**. Witness oath, 20 July 1848: signed **Pickney Hammett** to **Z. Lanford**. Release of Dower: **Elizabeth (x) Bullington** to **Z. Lanford**. Registered 22 July 1848.

p. 39-40.   19 Feb 1848. Deed of Conveyance. **Simpson Bobo** of Spartan<u>burgh</u> Dist, to **W.H. Wilbanks** of Spartan<u>burgh</u> Dist; 126 acres for $125, all that tract of land in Spartan<u>burgh</u> Dist known as the **Mosley** tract bounded by **Steadman** and **Cantrell**. Wit: **O.E. Edwards, G. Nicholls.**. Signed **Simpson Bobo**. Witness oath, 8 August 1848: Signed **O.E. Edwards** to **J.B. Tolleson**, Clk & Mg Exoffo. Release of Dower: signed, **Nancy Bobo**, wife of **Simpson Bobo**, to **O.E. Edwards**, Notary Public and Magistrate ex officio.

p. 40-42.   28 Oct 1847.   Deed of Conveyance. **William Johnson** of Spartan<u>burgh</u> Dist, to **W^m H Wilbanks** of Spartanburgh Dist, for $80, sold 70 acres on the <u>Georgia Road</u>, bounded by **William Little, John Steadman, Sarah Burke**. Wit: **William Little, Henry Johnson**. Signed, **William (x) Johnson** . Witness oath, 8 Oct 1847: signed **William Little** to **P.W. Head**, Magst. Release of Dower: **Ibby (x) Johnson** to **P.W. Head**, Magst. Registered 8 August 1848.

p. 42-43.   28 Oct 1847. Deed of Conveyance. **William Johnson** of Spartan<u>burgh</u> Dist, for $250 paid by **William H. Wilbanks** of Spartanburgh Dist, sold all that tract [acres not given] lying on Buck Creek. The creek and swamp are boundaries. Wit: **William Little, Henry Johnson**. Signed,

William (x) Johnson. Witness oath, 28 Oct 1847: signed **Henry Johnson** to **P.W. Head**, Mag. Release of Dower: **Ibby (x) Johnson** to **P.W. Head**, Mag.

p. 43-44.   4 Feb 1848. Deed of Conveyance. **William Little** of Spartanburgh Dist, for $90 paid by **W.H. Wilbanks**, of Spartanburgh Dist, sold 72 acres on a branch of the waters of Buck Creek. Bordered on the Georgia Road. Wit: **Theophilus Thorn, Nathaniel Thorn**. Signed **William Little**. Witness oath, 8 April 1848: Signed, **Nathaniel Thorn** to **Elias Wall**, Magistrate. Release of Dower: **Charlotte (x) Little**, wife of **Wᵐ Little**, to **Elias Wall**. Registered 8 August 1848.

p. 44-45.   22 July 1848.   Mortgage.   **Esaw Price** of Spartanburgh Dist, to **A. Phelps** of Spartanburgh Dist, in consideration of five notes of hand bearing date with this mortgage and to fall due as follows, (Viz) One of $200 due the 1ˢᵗ Feby next, all the others $175 each to fall due Feby [each] year by Single note payable to **A. Phelps**. **Esaw Price** conveyed to the sᵈ **A. Phelps** (1) all that tract of land (464 acres) where **A. Phelps** now lives, on main Thickety Creek in Spartanburgh Dist, bounded by **F. Guthree, Jas Richards** & others. (2) Also (350 acres) all the tract or plantation whereon I, the said **Esaw Price** now lives on Turner's Creek bounded by lands of So Ca Man Co [South Carolina Manufacturing Company?] & others. Above deed void if the above notes are paid at the times specified. Wit: **Josiah McEntire, Noah Williams**. Signed **Esaw Price**. N.B. I do hereby certify that the above named **Esaw Price** is at full liberty to cancel or trade the within named premises or any part thereof so as to satisfy sd notes. This 22ⁿᵈ July 1848. Signed **A. Phelps**. Witness oath, 25 July 1848: signed **Noah Williams** to **A. Bonner**, Mag. Registered 8 August 1848.

p. 45-47.   7 Aug 1848. Sheriff's Titles.   **R.C. Poole**, Sheriff of Spartanburgh Dist, to **Samuel White**. Whereas **Isaac Crocker** and **Elizabeth Crocker** on or about the 26ᵗʰ November 1847 did Exhibit their petition in the Court of Ordinary at Spartanburgh Court House; that **Andrew Harmon** departed this life intestate on or about [no date], Seized and possessed in fee 115½ acres, bounded by **John King, Col. Bates**, the widow **Lucy Harmon** & Lot B, that part and division of said Land yet remaining to be made. On the 8ᵗʰ day of May 1848 **R. Bowden, Esq.**, Ordinary, Ordered that the land be Sold by the Sheriff. After having duly advertised the land for Sale by public outcry on the 3ʳᵈ day of July 1848 did then openly & publicly according to the custom of auctioning sell the tract of land unto **Samuel White** for the sum of $450 he being at that price the last and highest bidder for the same. Wit: **J.H. Seay, John Tuck**. Signed **R.C. Poole** {Seal}. Witness Oath, 7 Aug 1848: Signed, **John Tuck** to **J.B. Tolleson**. Registered Examined and certyfied 8 August 1848. Original delivered to ~ **Samuel White** 7ᵗʰ Oct. 1848.

p. 47.   13 Feb 1847. Deed of Conveyance. **Josiah Kilgore** of Greenville Dist, to **John T. Smith** for $400 sold 204 acres on which **Smith** now lives; on a branch of Pigeon Roost of South Tyger River, part of a tract granted to **Jesse Smith** & conveyed to **Kilgore** by **Thomas Wood** 21 April 1840. Wit: **William Smith, Phil C. Lester**. Signed **Josiah Kilgore**. Witness oath, 7 August 1848: Signed, **William Smith** to **J.B. Tolleson**. Registered, Examined and Certified the 8 August 1845. The original delivered to ~ **J.T. Smith** 1 April 1850.

p. 48.   18 Sept 1847. Deed of Conveyance. **James McMakin** of Spartanburgh Dist, to **Guilford Mason** of Spartanburgh Dist, for $224 sold 96 acres on the branches of the waters of South Tyger

River adjoining lands of **Richard Williams, Wiley D. Wood, Mason**'s line & others. Wit: **William Smith, James Thaxton.** Signed, **James McMakin.** Witness oath, 2 August 1848: Signed, **William Smith** to **Isham Wood**, Mag. Registered 8 Aug 1848.

p. 49-50. 21 Jan 1848. Mortgage. **Lucy Harmon** of Spartanburgh Dist is indebted to **William Lee** or **Samuel Harmon,** by single bill payable one day after date and dated this 21st day of January 1848 for $480.35. **Lucy Harmon,** for better securing the payment of the said sum, sells in plain and open market delivers unto **Samuel Harmon** a Negro Girl about 8 years old named **Lucindy** being the same she purchased at the sale of her deceased husband's property. If **Lucy Harmon** pays **Samuel Harmon** the sum above mentioned then this deed of bargain & sale shall is void. Wit: **James V. Turner, R. Bowden.** Signed, **Lucy (x) Harmon.** Witness oath, 7 August 1848, **R. Bowden** to **J.B. Tolleson.** Registered 8 August 1848.

p. 50-51.   3 Feb 1838. Title Bond. **James Silman** for $900 bond to **Joseph Lawrence.** The condition of the above bond is such that if **James Silman** makes **Joseph Lawrence** a title to a tract of land in the Dist of Spartanburgh on Holston Creek having such form as the plat represents Surveyed by **John Bynum** for **James Sharp** the 16th of August 1804, containing 482 acres when **Lawrence** makes the last payment which will be 25 December 1841 for the land then the above obligation to be void and of no effect. Attest: **Thomas Jackson** [only one witness named]. Signed **James Silman.** Witness oath, 13 March 1848. Personally came **Isaac West** before me & made oath that he saw **James Silman** sign the within bond for titles to **Joseph Lawrence** and that he saw **Thomas Jackson** sign it as a witness. Sworn to and subscribed before me this 13 day of March 1848. **M.D. Dickey**, Mag. Signed **Isaac West.** Registered Examined and Certified the 15 August 1848. Original delivered to~~ **Joseph Lawrence.**

p. 51-52. 11 July 1848. Deed of Conveyance. **A.B. Thomason** of Spartanburgh Dist, to **E.C. Leitner** of Spartanburgh Dist, for $300, sold 100 acres, part of the estate of the late **Robert Thomson** marked N° 9 in the plan of said division and purchased by **A.B. Thomason**, bounded by **John Turner, John Linder & The Bivingsville Cot. M. Co.** Styled in the annexed plats. Wit: **R.W. Foster, J.M. Bagwell.** Signed **A.B. Thomason.** Release of dower, 21 July 1848: **Nancy (x) Thomason,** wife of **A.B. Thomason**, to **J.W. Cooper**, Mag. {Seal. Witness oath, 14 August 1848: Signed, **J.M. Bagwell** to **John Linder**, Mag. Registered 18 August 1848.

p. 52-53. 24 July 1848. Deed of Conveyance. **E.C. Leitner** of Spartanburgh Dist, to **John Turner** of Spartanburgh Dist, for $325 sold 100 acres purchased by **E.C. Leitner** from **A.B. Thomason,** being a part of the land purchased by **A.B. Thomason** of the Estate of **Robert Thomson** deceased, marked N° 9 in the place of division of said estate, bordering **John Turner, John Linder & the Bivingsville Cotton Man. Co.** Wit: **W. Poole, John P. Fowler.** Signed, **E.C. Leitner.** Release of Dower: Signed, **Elizabeth B. Leitner**, wife of **E.C. Leitner**, to **John Linder**, Mag. Witness Oath, 7 August 1848: Signed **John P. Fowler** to **John Linder**, Mag. Registered 18 August 1848.

p. 53-54. 2 Feb 1848. Deed of Conveyance. **H.C. Young & H.J. Dean** of Spartanburg Dist, to **Simpson Bobo** of Spartanburg Dist, for $1000, sold seventeen hundred acres (1700) on Thickety Creek waters of Packolet river whereon **Hugh Moore** formerly lived bounded by **Holeman Smith,**

William Brice, So. Car. Man. Company, Samuel Otterson & others. Wit: **Tho' O.P. Vernon, O.E. Edwards.** Signed, **H.C. Young, H.J. Dean.** Witness oath, 2 July 1848: **Tho' O.P. Vernon,** to **J.B. Tolleson,** Clerk & Mag. Exfo. Release of dower, 13 May 1848: Wife of **H.J. Dean,** signed **Mary Owen Dean,** to **O.E. Edwards,** Notary Public & Mag. Ex officio. Registered 18 August 1848.

p. 55. 7 Aug 1848. Mortgage. Spartanburg District. **Wilburn Crocker** sold to **John Simpson** one clay bank horse for $66.10 with interest from the 30th November 1847, which horse I warrant and defend to the said **John Simpson** his heirs and assigns forever, Provided nevertheless and it is understood that whereas the said **John Simpson** is my security to the Bivingsville Cotton Mac. Co. for $66.10 on one day after date of the 30th November 1847. Know ye that should the said **John Simpson** have to pay the same or any part thereof to the said Company while he is my security as aforesaid then the sale to be binding and of full force and in that event he shall have the right by himself or agent to seize said horse and sell him to the highest bidder by advertising ten days at one or two public places. But should the said **John Simpson** not have to pay the said money or any part thereof then said to be null and void. Wit: **William Petty.** Signed **Wilburn (x) Crocker.** Witness oath, 7 Aug 1847: Signed **Wm Petty** to **J.W. Cooper,** Mag. Registered 18 Aug 1848.

p. 55-57. 20 Aug 1848. Mortgage. **W.A. Bishop** is indebted to **G.B. Bishop** in the sum of $500 by single Bill due the 21st June 1848 & bearing date the 20th June 1848. **W.A. Bishop** conveys to **G.B. Bishop** 315 acres where **W.A. Bishop** now lives it being the tract of land that the said **W.A. Bishop** sued & gained from **Henry Bishop** in the Court of Equity at June Term 1846. Provided **W.A. Bishop** pays to **G.B. Bishop** the $500 according to the single Bill above mentioned then these presents shall be utterly null and void. Wit: **J.W. Martin, J.B. Tolleson.** Signed, **W.A. Bishop, G.B. Bishop.** Witness oath, 23 August 1848: Signed, **J.W. Martin** to **J.B. Tolleson,** Clk & Mag Exff. Registered 23 Aug 1848.

p. 57-58. 2 Feb 1847. Deed of Conveyance. **Robert Casey** of Spartanburg Dist, for $262 paid by **Roddey Lanford** of Spartanburgh Dist, sold 93½ acres; bounded by **Roddy Lanford, Jonathan Floyd, Manly Floyd, Toliver Scott, Lecil Bearden & Dr B.F. Nicholls.** Wit: **Manley Floyd, J.B. Page.** Signed, **Robert (x) Casey.** Witness oath, 1 April 1848: **John B. Page** [Signed, **J.B. Page**] to **Z. Lanford,** Mag. Registered 4th Sept 1848.

p. 58-59. 30 Nov 1845. Deed of Conveyance. **Joseph Brown** of Spartanburg Dist, for $396.62 paid by **John S. Brown** of Spartanburg Dist, sold one half of 185 acres known as the Forge tract, lying on the north side of South Tyger river. Bounded by the river and **H. Wakefield. John S. Brown** as a contrivation of the land is to have the N.W. Corner of said tract bordering on **N. McElrath** and Forge branch, furthermore **John S.** is to have one half of the privileges [of the] shoals or shoals & waters of the river. Wit: **James McHugh, James Leonard.** Signed **Joseph Brown.** Witness oath, 23 Aug 1848: Signed, **Joseph McHugh** to **Mark Bennett,** Mag. Registered 4th Sept 1848.

p. 59-60. 7 Oct 1847. Deed of Conveyance. **Littleton Bagwell** for $10 paid by **Govan Mills** of Spartanburg Dist, sold 2 and 2/10 acres, part of the south west corner of the tract of land whereon **Bagwell** now lives, beginning at **Bagwell & Mills** corner. Attest, 7 Oct 1847: **Lowry Burnett, H. Hammett.** Signed, **Littleton (x) Bagwell.** Witness oath, 7 Oct 1847: Signed, **Lowry Burnett** to **Jas**

Smith, Mag. Registered, Examined & Certified 16th Sept. 1848, Original delivered to~~ **Govan Mills**, 10th April 1850.

p. 60-61. 23 Sept 1843. Deed of Conveyance. **Joseph Allen** of Spartanburg Dist, for $2,500 paid by **D.A. Chamblain,** sold 475 acres where **Allen** lives on Fergersons Creek. Wit: **James M. Anderson, Jared Drummond.** Signed **Joseph Allen.** Witness oath, 1st Sept 1848: Signed, **Jared Drummond** to **J.B. Tolleson,** Clk & Mag. Exiffo. Release of Dower, 30 Sept 1843: Signed, **Sarah Allen** to **John Anderson** Magt. Registered 16 Sept 1848.

p. 61-62. 16 June 1848. Deed of Conveyance. **Joseph Cooper** of Greenville Dist, for $1500 paid by **Jesse Leatherwood** of Spartanburg Dist, sold 300 acres on the north side of Enoree river, bordering on a settlement road and west side of **Arnold's** branch. Wit: **John Leatherwood, S.S. Robuck.** Signed **Joseph Cooper.** Witness oath, 16 June 1848: Signed **S.S. Robuck** to **Jonas Brewton,** Mag. Release of Dower, 16 June 1848: Signed, **Casander Cooper** to **Jonas Brewton,** Mag. Registered Examined & certified 16 Sept 1848. Original delivered to~~ **Jesse Leatherwood** 12th Oct 1848.

p. 63-63 [63 repeated]. 3 July 1848. Sheriff's Titles. **R.C. Poole,** Sheriff of Spartanburg Dist, to **John Sarratt. Frances Green** about the 30th January 1848 did Exhibit her petition in the Court of the Ordinary at Spartanburg Court House setting forth that **Edward Green** departed this life Intestate [no date] 1848 seized and possessed in fee of a certain plantation containing 147 acres in Spartanburg Dist, bounded by **D.B. Ross, John Sarratt** and others, that part and division of said land yet remained to be made. On the 19th day of May 1848 **R. Bowden** Esq Ordinary ordered that the lands be sold by the sheriff on the first Monday in July ensuing or on such other sale day as would be most for the advantage of the parties on a credit of twelve months; 147 acres sold by **R.C. Poole,** Sheriff, to **John Sarratt,** it being land deeded from **Simpson Hester** to **Edward Green** on the 15th August 1833. Wit: **R. Bowden, Simpson Linder.** Signed, **R.C. Poole,** SSD. Registered 21st Sept 1848.

p. 63-64. 5 Sept 1848. Sheriff's Titles. **R.C. Poole,** Sheriff of Spartanburg Dist, to **Ezekiel M. Spriggs.** By virtue of a writ of fieri facias issued out of the court of common pleas held for Greenville Dist tested the 14th day of April 1848, at the suit of **E.M. Spriggs** commanding me that of the goods and chattels lands and tenements of **Michael D. Dickie** of Spartanburgh Dist to levy the sum of $1394.56¼ with interest, damages and costs. I have seized and taken the lands and tenements of the said **M.D. Dickie**; 500 acres, the tract where the **Rev. John Grambling** formerly lived being in the Dist of Spartanburg on the waters of Lossons fork Creek, bounded by lands of **Adam Grambling, Ruebin Grambling, William Carver, Samuel Grentz, Morris Pollard & William Bishop** deceased; purchased by **Ezekiel M. Springs** at public vendue for $405. Wit: **J. Powell, W.W. Hastings.** Signed **R.C. Poole,** SSD. Witness oath, 22 Sept 1848: Signed **W.W. Hastings** to **J.B. Tolleson,** Clk & Mag Ex iffo. Registered Examined and Certified 23 Sept 1848. Original delivered to~~ **E.M. Spriggs** 25 Oct 1848.

p. 64-66. 14 Oct 1847. Sheriff's Titles. **R.C. Poole,** Sheriff of Spartanburg Dist, to **The President & directors of the bank of the State of South Carolina.** By writ of fieri facias issued out of the Court of Common pleas held for the Dist of Charleston tested the 3rd day of December 1845 at the suit of the president & directors of the bank of the State of South Carolina and against **Charles M. Furman** Admr. de bonis now of **Abraham Markley** Dec^d to me directed commanding me that of the goods and chattels, lands and tenements of the said **Abraham Markley** deceased to levy the sum of $28,434 with damages and costs, I have seized and taken a tract of land, 507 acres lying on Fawn branch formerly bounded by lands of **John Clements, Jefferson Rowland** and others, and sold at public vendue and purchased by the president and directors of the bank of the State of South Carolina, of the Dist and State aforesaid, for $345, the highest bid. Wit: **J.B. Cottrell, John R. Poole.** Signed **R.C. Poole.** Witness oath, 7 Oct 1848: Signed, **John R. Poole** to **J.B. Tolleson**, Clk & Magt Exff. Registered 7th Oct 1848.

p. 66-68. 14 Oct 1847. Sheriff's Titles. **R.C. Poole**, Sheriff of Spartanburg Dist, to The President & directors of the bank of the State So.Ca. Whereas by virtue of a writ of fieri facias issued out of the Court of common pleas held for the district of Charleston tested the 3rd day of December 1845 at the suit of the president & directors of the bank of the State of South Carolina and against **Charles M. Furman** Adm^r de bonis now of **Abraham Markly** deceased to me directed ... to levy the sum of $28,434 ...... I have seized a tract of land containing 419 acres on the road leading from Spartanburg C.H. to Coulters ford Bridge near **Betty Green** meeting house on the Waters of Lossons fork creek of Packolette river & bounded by lands of **James Dillard, James Cannon, Richard Thomson** deceased and others. Land exposed to sale at public vendue and purchased by the president & directors of the bank of the State of South Carolina of the District and State aforesaid, for $232, the highest bid. Wit: **J.B. Cottrell, J.R. Poole.** Signed **R.C. Poole**, SSD. Witness oath, 7 Oct 1848: Signed **John R. Poole** to **J.B. Tolleson**, Clk & Mag. Exff. Registered 7th Oct 1843.

p. 68-69. 14 Oct 1847. Sheriff's Titles. **R.C. Poole**, Sheriff of Spartanburg Dist, to The president & directors of the Bank of the state of S.C. [Same as above] sold land of **Abraham Markly** dec^d, 1,008 acres bounded by lands originally **Brown's, Hopkins, Dr. Oldright's & Abraham Markly's** but now bounded by lands of **Hugh Price, Jacob Price, Ezekiel Dobbins, Susan Williams,** the widow **Green & Silas Cash** being on the ridge between Island Creek & Thickety. Highest bid $30 by Bank of S.C. [Wit same as above]. Registered 7th Oct 1848.

p. 70-71. 14 Oct 1847. Sheriff's Titles. [Same as above] Sold land of **Abraham Markly** to Bank of S.C. For $45 sold 687 acres on the south side of North Pacolet river, waters of said river, bounded by lands originally of **Canol** and unknown lands of **John Moore's,** and **Markly's** and now lands of **Foster Jackson, William Jackson, Henry Kelso,** & others. [Witnesses same as above] Registered 7th Oct 1848.

p. 71-73. 14 Oct 1847. Sheriff's Titles. [Same as above]. Sold lands of **Abraham Markly** to Bank of S.C. for $57, highest bid for 414 acres on Waters of Thickety Creek and bounded by lands of **John Oglesby, John S. Cole,** The Rolling Mill Company & others. Colling ground mentioned. [Same witnesses]. Registered 7th Oct 1848.

p. 73-74. Sheriff's Titles. [Same as above]. Sold land of **Abraham Markly** to Bank of S.C. For $20, the highest bid, 676 acres on the south side of North Pacolet river and on the waters of said river and bounded by lands originally of **Hooper's, Moore's & Markly's** and vacant land, and now bounded by lands of **Robert Jackson, Andrew Jackson, Samuel Jackson, Robert Clark** and others. [Same witnesses as above]. Registered 7th Oct 1848.

p. 75. Mortgage. Spartanburg Dist. **Alex Flemming** is indebted to **Thomson & Tucker** for $50 bearing date 28th Augt 1847, due in six months. For better securing the payment of the above note, **Alex Flemming** mortgages title to the land which was "deeded to me by my Father **Alex Flemming** deceased on the 5th day of January 1843 lying on the Waters of the Fairforest Creek containing 43 acres adjoining lands of **John Murph, James Fleming, W.W. Harris** and others; deed void if **Alex Flemming** pays the note when due. Wit: **Hiram Mitchell, Jno. Wheeler.** Signed **Alexander Flemming.** Witness oath, 7th Oct 1848: Signed, **Hiram Mitchell** to **J.B. Tolleson**, Clk & Mag Ex iffo. Registered Examined and certified 7th Oct 1848. Original delivered to ~~ -- 19 June 1852 the mortgage Satisfied to **Thomas & Tucker.**

p. 75-76. 12 Feb 1848. Deed of Conveyance. **Wiley Hannah** of Spartanburg Dist, for $1,000 paid by **Laban Hannah** of Spartanburg Dist, sold 131 acres on the North side of the Enoree river, bordering **James Nesbitt, Robert C. Hannah** and Enoree river. Wit: **William Terry, William L. Hughston.** Signed, **Wiley Hannah.** Witness oath, 28 Sept 1848: Signed, **William Terry** to **Z. Lanford**, Magt. Registered 7th Oct 1848.

p. 77-78. 14 [month not given] 1847.Deed of Conveyance. **Ephraim Potter** of Spartanburg Dist, for $200 paid by **Abner Potter** of Spartanburg Dist, sold 200 acres on Island Creek on the East side, starting on **J. Potter's** corner, **Jesse Murry's** line, the road running from **Randol Cash's** to **B. Cash's**, along the Meeting house road to an old path that leads up to **James Potter's**, and **Jesse Scrugg's** line. Wit: **Bryant Bonner, Thomas Foster.** Signed, **Ephraim (x) Potter.** Witness oath, 23 Sept 1848: Signed, **Thomas Foster** to **William Guthrie**, Mag. Registered 7 Oct 1848.

p. 78-79. 25 Oct 1848. Deed of Conveyance. **H.H. Thomson** of Spartanburg Dist, for $50 paid by **J.W. Tucker, Esq.** of Spartanburg Dist, sold Two lots in the Town of Spartanburg, being of the **Poole** lots on the TanYard Branch, one lot 8/10 acre, bounded by Greenville road, the other lot something less than 3/4 acre, bounded by Greenville Road. Wit: **Hiram Mitchell, W.C. Bennett.** Signed, **H.H. Thomson.** Witness oath, 25 Oct 1848: Signed **Hiram Mitchell** to **J.B. Tolleson**, Clk & Mag. Ex ifffo. Registered 25th Oct 1848.

p. 79-81. 24 Oct 1848. Mortgage. **R.C. Poole** has this day bought of **H.H. Thomson** a lot in the Town of Spartanburg adjoining the said **R.C. Poole's** Hotel Lot containing 4 and 8/10 acres and boundary of said Lot will more fully appear by reference to a Deed which I this day made him. **R.C. Poole** owes $142.50 by three seals under seal Each for $47.50 Due in twelve months, 2 years and three years from this date and all bearing interest from 24th Oct 1848 and also for $1 paid to the said **R.C. Poole.** Wit: **Hiram Mitchell, R. Bowden.** Signed, **R.C. Poole.** Witness oath, 25 Oct 1848: Signed, **Hiram Mitchell** to **J.B. Tolleson**, Clk & mag. Ex iffo. Registered 25 Oct 1848.

p. 81-82. 20 Sept 1846. Deed of Conveyance. **James & John Lee, Senior** of Spartanburg Dist, for $250 paid by **William Lee,** sold 100 acres beginning at the mouth of **Pearce's** old spring where it empties into Richland Creek to within 40 yards of **John Pearche's** old spring, east side of said branch near the lane between **William** and **James Lee's** land to **Richard Thomson's** line or lands formerly belonging to said **Thomson**, to **Crocker**'s old line, and meanders of Richland Creek. Wit: **William R. Poole, Washington Poole.** Signed, **James (x) Lee, John (x) Lee.** Witness oath, 13 Sept 1846: Signed **W.R. Poole** to **B.F. Bates**, Mag. Registered 23rd Oct 1848.

p. 82-83.   31 Oct 1848. Mortgage. Spartanburg District. **A.J.W. Land to John Linder. A.J.W. Land** for the purpose of securing the payment of the purchase money, Viz, a note of $25 due to **John Linder** on 25th Decr. 1849 and bearing date 31st October 1848 as mortgage and sell to **John Linder** 2 acres of land lying on the west side of the Village of Spartanburg bounded by lands formerly owned by **John H. Shook, Richard Thomson & Dr. Bennett**, marked as N° 13 on the plat. If the above note which was given for the purchase money of said Lot is paid on time this obligation is null and Void. Attest: **W. Hunt, W.F. Cannon.** Signed, **A.J.W. Land.** Witness oath, 31 Oct 1848: Signed, **W. Hunt** to **R. Bowden**, Exoff Mag. Registered 31st Oct 1848.

p. 83-84.   31 Oct 1848. Mortgage. Spartanburg District. **Elizabeth Land to John Linder. Elizabeth Land** for the purpose of securing the payment of the purchase money of a Lot of land I Bot of **John Linder** (Viz) one note for $25 due on the 25th December 1849 bearing date on the 31st October 1848 assigned by myself & **A.J.W. Land** payable to **John Linder**, I do mortgage sell & release unto **John Linder** the certain Lot being on the west side of Spartanburg Village known by Lot N° 19, & bounded at the time of purchase by the property of **William Poole**, by Lots Bot by **Dr. William Bennett, G.W.H. Legg**, Esq & **Col. H.H. Thomson.** If the above note is paid when due, this obligation shall be of no effect. Attest: **W. Hunt, W.F. Cannon.** Signed, **Elizabeth (x) Land.** Witness oath, 31 Oct 1848: Signed, **W. Hunt** to **R. Bowden**, Ex off. Mag. Registered 31 Oct 1848.

p. 84-85.   13 Sept 1848. Deed of Conveyance. **Elizabeth Dukes**, of Union Dist, SC, for the Love, good will and affection I have and bear my beloved Daughter in law, **Penelope Dukes**, wife of my son, **William Rodney Dukes**, release unto **Penelope Dukes** and the heirs of her body; 40 acres in Spartanburg Dist, adjoining **Elias Smith**, land this day conveyed by me to my daughter **Martha Bennett, Capt. West** and **J. Win Smith**, being the tract conveyed to me by **Alexander Bennett**. To have and to hold the said tract of Land to the said **Penelope Dukes** and the heirs of her body begotten by the said **William Rodney Dukes** forever and not to be liable for the debts or subject to the contracts of the said **William Rodney Dukes** or anyone else but to remain for the use and benefit of the said **Penelope Dukes** and the heirs of her body. Wit: **J.D. Keenan, W.W. Keenan.** Signed, **Elizabeth (x) Dukes.** Witness oath, Union Dist, S.C., 13 Sept 1848: Signed, **James D. Keenan** to **W.W. Keenan**, Mag. Ex off. Registered 6th Nov 1848.

p. 85-87.   6 Oct 1848. Deed of Conveyance. **James Lawrence** of Spartanburg Dist, for $250 paid by **Daniel Johnson,** sold 150 acres where I now live, lying on Fawns Branch waters of Lawsons fork creek; Bounded by **Daniel White** on the S and W, by **Isham Clement** on the E and **Matthew Seay** on the N. Wit: **Andrew B. Bishop, G. Hicks.** Signed, **James Lawrence.** Release of dower, 1 Nov 1848: Signed, **Milly (x) Lawrence** to **Elias Wall**, Magistrate. Witness oath, 3^{d} Oct 1848 [this date earlier than date of deed]: Signed, **G. Hicks** to **Elias Wall**, Magt. Registered 6th Nov 1848.

p. 87-88.   26 Feb 1842. Deed of Conveyance. **Nathan Gentry,** for $1,300 paid by **John Gentry,** sold 5 tracts of land, Viz, One tract of 35 acres, deeded by **James Askew;** one tract of 24 acres, deeded by **Nathaniel Burton;** one deeded by said **Nathanial Burton** of 54 acres; one tract deeded by **John Fielder** of 102 acres; one tract deeded by **Ford Mason** of 132 acres. In all containing 347 acres, more or less. Lying and bounded by North Tyger river, lands of **Jonathan Crow, Toliver Scott & Bratton Thomas.** Wit: **Francis Ward, Paul Combee.** Signed, **Nathaniel (x) Gentry.** Witness oath, 26 Feby 1842: Signed, **Francis Ward** to **Jonas Brewton,** Mag. Registered 6th Nov 1848.

p. 88-89.   13 Dec 1845. Deed of Conveyance. **James Wood** of Spartanburg Dist, for $500 paid by **Jonathan Goforth** of Spartanburg Dist, sold 2 lots, N°. 1 and N°. 3, total 145 acres, bounded by **Thomason, John Brown,** a lane, spring, ford and branch mentioned but not named. One point of measurement was a cucumber tree. Wit: **Robt. W. Draper, Joshua Draper.** Signed, **James Wood.** Witness oath, 20 Dec 1845: Signed, **Robt. W. Draper** to **Joshua Draper,** Magt. Release of dower, 25 Feb 1846: Signed, **Harriet A. Wood,** wife of **James Wood** to **Joshua Draper,** Magst. Registered examined & certified 6th Nov 1848. Original delivered to~~ **Jonathan Goforth** 1 Jany 1849.

p. 90-91.   3 Dec 1845. Deed of Conveyance. **Smith Lipscomb** of Spartanburgh Dist, for $450 paid by **James Wood** of Spartanburg Dist, sold 2 Lots, N° 1 & N°. 3, total 145 acres, boundaries same as above, including the cucumber tree. Wit: **James Phillips, Joshua Draper, ?Sen.** Signed, **Smith Lipscomb Jun.** Witness oath, 13 Decr 1845: **Joseph Draper,** Mgt. Signed, **Joshua Draper,** mag. Release of Dower, 26 Dec 1845: **Sarah Lipscomb,** wife of **Smith Lipscomb,** signed, **Sally Lipscomb** to **Joshua Draper,** Magst. Registered 6th Nov 1848. Original delivered to ~~ **Jonathan Goforth** 1 Jany 1849.

p. 91-92.   3 Mar 1846. Deed of Conveyance. **Lewis Bobo** of the State of Alabama, for $100 paid by **William J. Whitmire** of Spartanburg Dist, sold that Lot of land in the Village of Glenns Springs on the North side of the branch in to which the Glenns Springs enters its waters, known as Lot N° 11, Containing 1 acre in form of one half acre in front of main street and running back in a straight line from said street, Sufficiently to make one acre which said Lot takes in all the improvements which **Bobo** made - this lot N° 11 is to have sixteen feet all round the said acre of land as a passway and to have free privilege to ways and waters on the Glenns spring tract of land especially to the mineral spring as a private family. Together with all and singular the rights, members, hereditaments and appurtenances to the said premises belonging or in anywise incident or appertaining Except and by this be it known that I Except from the privilege of boarding persons that come for the benefit of the mineral water, also the privilege of merchandise or retailing any Intoxicating Spirits to have and hold..... Wit: **R. Starnes, John Gibbs.** Signed, **Lewis Bobo.** Witness oath, Union Dist, SC, 19 Aug 1848: Signed, **John Gibbs** to **Mathias Myers,** Magt. Registered 6th Nov 1848.

p. 92-93.   [Date not filled in]. Deed of Conveyance. **W.J. Whitmire** of Spartanburg Dist, for $150 paid by **James Gillum** of Abaville Dist, sold the same 1 acre, above, in Village of Glenns Springs, with the same exceptions as above. Wit: **Laban Hannah, A.J. Graham.** Signed, **W.J. Whitmire.** Witness oath, 24th Sept 1848: Signed, **A.J. Graham** to **P.R. Bobo,** Mag. Registered 6th Nov 1848.

p. 94-95.   22 July 1844. Deed of Conveyance. Spartanburg District. **John C. Zimmerman &**

Martha Glenn & W.J.T. Glenn for $25 to us paid by **Lewis Bobo** of SC, sold that Lot of land in the Village of Glenn Springs on the North side of the branch into which the Glenn Springs enters its water; Lot Nº. 11 in above two deeds and including the same exceptions. Wit: **Alvan Lancaster, Martha W.T. Peake.** Signed, **John C. Zimmerman, Patsy Glenn, W.J. Thomson Glenn.** Witness oath, 30 Sept 1844: Signed, **Alvan Lancaster** to **Joel Dean**, Mag. Registered 6th Nov 1848.

p. 95-96. 8 Oct 1845. Deed of Conveyance. **Andrew P. Gramling** of Spartanburg Dist, for $900 paid by **Reubin Gramling,** sold 216 acres on the south side of south Pacolet river, bounded by **William Golightly,** branch above **Gramlings** spring, **Bruton,** and the river; including where the said **Gramling** resides. Tract was originally granted to **John Gowen** and sold by him to **Robert Black** and given by **Black** to his Two sons, **William** and **Samuel** and sold by them to **Archibald Nelson** and by **Nelson** to **Robert D. Tally** and by **Tally** to me. Wit: [not clear, may be **J.P.** [or **J.T.**] **Gramlin, John D. King.** Signed **Andrew P. Gramlin.** Witness oath, 10th Oct 1848: Signed, **John D. King** to **James Caldwell**, Mag. S.D. Registered 6th Nov 1848.

p. 96-97. 10 Nov 1847. Deed of Conveyance. **L. Lucus** and **W. Archer** of Spartanburg Dist, for $350 paid by **R. Gramlin** of Spartanburg Dist, sold 130 acres on the North side of South Packolette and adjoining the land of **A. Lancaster** and others; the upper end of a Lake then with the Lake to where it intersects with the River. Wit: **G.W. Green, Henry H. Gramlin.** Signed, **Lemuel Lucas, William B. Archer** by **John B. Archer.** Witness oath, 11 Nov 1847: Signed, **G.W. Green** to **S. Bullington**, Mag. Registered 6th Nov 1848.

p. 97-98. 10 Nov 1847. Deed of Conveyance. **J.R. Gramling** of Spartanburg Dist, for $100 paid by **Reubin Gramling** of Spartanburg Dist, sold 62 acres on the ridge between South Pacolet river and __?__[brias, crias, lerias?], beginning at **R. Gramlings** spring branch and along an old road, a corner on **R. Gramling & O.B. Gramling's** land. Wit: **William P. Dickson, Wm D. Holcomb.** Signed, **J.R. Gramling.** Witness oath, 11 Nov 1847: Signed, **William D. Holcomb** to **S. Bullington**, Mag. S.D. Registered 6th Nov 1848.

p. 98-99. 29 Oct 1819. Deed of Conveyance. **John Foster** of Spartanburg Dist, to The Trustees of Foster's Meeting House sold 1 acre for $10 paid by **Robert Wood, John Gramling, Andrew Gramling, David Ulmer, John L. Rast & Frederic Rast**, Trustees of Spartanburg Dist, for the purpose of Building a meeting House for the Methodist Episcopal Church — on the waters of North Tyger river. Tests: **Reubin Gramling, Thomas Crawford.** Signed, **John Foster.**   October 10th 1838 — **Sterling Bower Griffin, Harvy Finch & Willis S. Wingo** are only appointed to fill the above Vacancy of Trustees, Vis, **Robert Wood, David Ulmer, John Rast & Fredrick Rast.** Occasioned by their removal to the west. Signed, **Andrew Gramling, John Gramling.**
          Feby. 15. 1845. — **Enoch Brannon & Reubin Gramling** are only appointed to fill the Vacancy in the above bord of Trustees occasioned by the removal of **A. Gramling & S. Gregory.** Signed, A.W. Walker. Witness oath, 8th Nov 1820: Signed, **Thomas Crawford** to **John Chapman**, J.P.   Know all men by these presents that **Richard H. Golightly** is only appointed to fill the vacancy in the above board of Trustees occasioned by the removal of **Rev. John Gramling** — Feby. 20th 1846. Signed, **A.B. McGilroy**, P.C.   Registered, examined & certified 6 Nov. 1848 —

p. 100-101.   11 Oct 1848. Deed of Conveyance. Spartanburgh Dist. **Elizabeth Webb,** for $2 paid by **G.B. Palmer,** sold all that Tract of Land lying on Rocky Fork of Thickety containing 100 acres. Line on **Vinson Sprouce's** fence, old line, **Palmer's** line and meanders of the creek; the land deeded by my father **Elisha Sanders [or Landers?]** to my husband **James Webb** and by him sold to **William Guthrey** of said District without my consent or assignment; this is therefore to grant and release all my right of inheritance unto the said **G.B. Palmer.** Wit: **Daniel Webb, Charles Webb.** Signed, **Elizabeth (x) Webb.** Witness oath, Oct 30th 1848: Signed, **Daniel Webb** to **A. Bonner,** Mag.   Release of Dower, 30th Oct 1848: Signed **Elizabeth (x) Webb** to **Andrew Bonner** J.Q. [Repeated with different wording]: 30 Oct 1848. I, **Andrew Bonner** J.Q. do hereby certify that **Elizabeth Webb** formerly the wife of **James Webb** Deceased did this day appear before me; Signed, **Elizabeth (x) Webb.**

p. 101-102.   12 May 1848. Release of Dower. **Susan Hames** to **Green B. Palmer. Susan Hames** wife of **Wᵐ B. Hames,** forever relinquishes her claim of dower to 130 which was conveyed by her husband **Wᵐ B. Hames** to **Caleb Cooper** the 12th day of Nov 1842; bounded by **Elisha Sanders [or Landers?], G.B. Palmer, Holaman Smith** & others. Also another tract of 100 acres adjoining the above named Tract and bounded on the south by Rocky Fork and formerly conveyed by her husband **Wᵐ B. Hames** to **Elisha Sanders.** [the "S" in Susan's name looks exactly like the first letter in Landers/Sanders; they all look like "L"s]. Signed, **Susan (x) Hames** to **A. Bonner,** J.Q. Registered 12 Nov 1848. Original delivered to ~ **G.B. Palmer, Esq.**

p. 102-104.   18 April 1848. Deed of Conveyance. **Samuel Linder & Anna** alias **Nanna Linder** to **G.B. Palmer** for $70 paid to **Anna** alias **Nanna Linder** for her inheritance in 337 acres Lying on Rocky Fork of Thickety, bordered by **R.O. Guthrie, Sprouce's** fence, the Old line. N.B. **Samuel Linder** has assigned his right away before and does this to make his wife's Title good. Wit: **P. Quinn Camp, Olvy? (x) Bright.** Signed, **Samuel Linder, Anna A. Linder.** Witness oath, 11 May 1848: **P. Quinn Camp** to **A. Bonner,** J.Q. Release of dower, 11 May 1848: Singed, **Anna** alias **Nanna Linder** to **A. Bonner,** J.Q. [p. 104, a second release of dower]. Registered Examined & certified 15 Nov 1848. Original delivered to~ **G.B. Palmer Esq.**

p. 104-105.   29 Nov 1848. Deed of Conveyance. **Alexander Grisham** of Spartanburg Dist, for $300 paid by **Wᵐ M. Grisham** of Greenville Dist, sold 121 acres where **Alex** lives, the land I purchased as the property of **Hugh Bailey** deceased, in Spartanburg Dist, the tract known as the part of **Kendrick's** Tract on branches of Maple swamp creek waters of Tyger river. Wit: **Joseph Smith, J.B. Tolleson.** Signed, **Alexander Grisham.** Witness oath, 29 Nov 1848: Signed, **Joseph Smith** to **J.B. Tolleson,** Clk & Mag. Exffe. Registered 29th Nov 1848.

p. 105-107.   7 Aug 1848. Deed of Conveyance. **John Linder** to **Isaac McAbee** sold two tracts, one of 93 acres and the other 166 acres, for $350 [price unclear, either five, tow or t-ree hundred and fifty Dollars], on the waters of Greens Creek which **John Linder** Bot of **Wᵐ Going** adjoining lands of **Wᵐ West** Et el, it being in two adjoining tracts bounded by the spring branch, Greens Creek and **West's** field. Test: **J.W. Tucker, Wᵐ Petty.** Signed, **John Linder.** Witness oath, 13 Nov 1848: Signed, **J.W. Tucker** to **J.B. Tolleson,** Clk & Mag. Exffo. Release of Dower, 24 Oct 1848: Signed **Louisa Linder** to **J.B. Tolleson,** Mag. Exiffo. Registered Examined and certified 29th Nov 1848.

Original delivered to ~~ **Elisha McAbee** 10 Jany 1849.

p. 107-109. 3 July 1848. Sheriff's Titles. **R.C. Poole** Sheriff of Spartanburg Dist, to **John Sarratt**. Whereas **Frances Green** on or about the 30th day of January 1848 did Exhibit her petition in the court of Ordinary at Spartanburg Court House setting forth that **Edward** departed this life intestate [no date] 1848 seized and possessed in fee of 147 acres bounded by **D.B. Ross, John Sarratt** and others and that part and division of the land yet remained to be made which she prayed might be done — And whereas afterwards on the 19th day of May 1848 **R. Bowden Esq.** Ordinary ordered the land to be sold by the sheriff; sold 147 acres at public auction for $315 to **John Sarratt**; being land deeded from **Simpson Hester** to **Edward Green** on the 15th August 1833. Wit: **R. Bowden, Simpson Linder**. Signed, **R.C. Poole**, S.S.D. Witness oath, 29 Nov 1848: Signed, **R. Bowden** to **J.B. Tolleson**, Clk & magt. Ex Iffo. Registered 29th Nov. 1848.

p. 109-110. 2 Oct 1848. Mortgage. **James B. Darby** is indebted to **Tho' O.P. Vernon**, Commissioner of the Court of Equity, for $150 [to be paid] by single Bill or Bonds Each for the sum of $50, due 2nd Oct 1849, 2nd Oct 1850, & due 2nd Oct 1851; mortgage on 72 acres on the branch waters of the Enoree river and bounded by **David Halcomb & David Frazier**. Wit: **Stephen Darby, E.W. Attaway**. Signed, **Tho' O.P. Vernon**, C.E.S.D., **James B. Darby**. Witness oath, 22 Nov 1848: Signed, **E.W. Attaway** to **Z. Lanford**, Magt. Registered 1st Dec 1848.

p. 111. 25 Oct 1848. Deed of Conveyance. **Ezekiel M. Spriggs** of Lumpkin County, GA, for $800 paid by **Edward Ballenger** of Spartanburg Dist, sold 500 acres on the waters of Lawsons fork of Packolet river, where the **Rev. John Gramling** formerly lived and which he deeded to **M.D. Dickie**, bounded by lands of **Aaron Gramling, Reubin Gramling, William Carver, Samuel Gentry, Moses Pollard** and **William Bishop** deceased. Wit: **John G. Landrum, Edward W. Ballenger**. Signed **E.M. Spriggs**. Witness oath, 4 Nov 1848: **John G. Landrum** to **B.F. Montgomery**, Mag. Registered Examined & certified 4th Dec 1848. Original delivered to ~~ **E. Ballenger**, 1 Jany 1849.

p. 112. 13 Aug 1848. Deed of Conveyance. **Branson Hall, Elijah Alverson, William McDowell, John McDowell, Rice R. Ramsey** and **Diana Ramsey**, for $150 paid by **William Robbs** of Spartanburg Dist, sold 142 acres on the waters of south Packolette River, part of the land originally granted to **William Ramsey**; bounded by **Daulton, Ramsey, Bullington, Dixon & Rice R. Ramsey**. Wit: **Green R. Robbs, James Robbs**. Signed, **R.R. Ramsey, David Ramsey, W[m] F. McDowell, Branson Hall, Elijah Alverson, John McDowell**. Witness oath, 7 Aug 1848: Signed, **James Robbs** to **W.H. Wilbanks**, Mag. Registered Examined & certified 4th Dec 1848. Original delivered to ~~ **William Robbs**, 7th Jany 1850.

p. 113-114. 6 Nov 1848. Commissioner Title [mortgage]. **L.W. Mayfield** to **Tho' O.P. Vernon**, Commissioner of the Court of Equity. [**Mayfield** to pay] $195 by Three Single Bills or Bonds each of $65 one due 2nd Oct 1849, 2nd Oct 1850, and 2nd Oct 1851 with Interest from date, mortgage for 115¾ acres, Lot N° 3, a part of the real estate of **John K. Wood**, dec[d], on South fork on Tyger River bound by **Abraham Mayfield & Jesse Cannon**. Wit: **Richard Ballenger, J.S. Collins**. Signed, **Tho' O.P. Vernon**, C.E.S.D., **L.W. Mayfield**. Witness oath, 4 Dec 1848: Signed, **Richard Ballenger** to **J.B. Tolleson**, Clk & Mag Exffi. Registered 4 December 1848.

p. 114. 15 June 1848. Assignment. **John C. Harmon,** of Spartanburgh Dist, one of the heirs at law of **Andrew Harmon** Dec[d] late of Spartanburgh Dist, for Value received do assign to **John Wright,** all my Interest right title & claim to the real Estate of said **Andrew Harmon** dec[d]. Test: **E.G. Wright.** Signed, **John C. Harmon.** Witness oath, 4 Dec 1848: Signed, **E.G. Wright** to **J.W. Cooper,** Mag. Registered 4 Dec 1848.

p. 115-116. 6 April 1848. Deed of Conveyance. **Frederick Williams** of Spartanburgh Dist, for $700 paid by **James J. Foster** of Spartanburgh Dist, sold 104 acres lying on Beaver dam Creek waters of Fairforest & adjoining land of **Mr[s] Elizabeth Moss, Capt. Daniel Strobel, Hiram Rainwaters** and land formerly belonging to the Estate of **Capt. Joel Hurt,** deceased, but now owned by **Isham Hurt, James Selman & John Golightly,** originally granted to **Phanatta Wilkins** on 7th September 1784. Wit: **Elizabeth Selman, John Strobel Jun[r].** Signed, **F. Williams.** Witness oath, 7 Dec 1848: Signed, **John Strobel Jun[r]** to **J.B. Tolleson,** Clk & mag Exiffo. Release of dower, 25 Oct 1848: Signed, **Martha (x) Williams** to **J.B. Tolleson,** Clk & mag Exeff. Registered Examined & certified 7 Dec 1848. Original delivered to ~~ **J.J. Foster,** 1 Jan 1849.

p. 116-117. 14 Feb 43. Deed of Conveyance. **Isaac W. Cooper** of Spartanburgh Dist, for $400 paid by **William Wright & Joseph Allen** of Spartanburgh Dist, sold 150 acres bounded by **Thomas Garrett** and old line. Wit: **Noel (x) Waddle, R.S. Wright.** Signed, **Isaac W. Cooper.** Witness oath, 6 Oct 1848: Signed, **R.S. Wright** to **Z. Lanford,** Magst. Registered Examined & Certified 11 December 1848. Original delivered to ~~ **W.M. Vaughan.**

p. 117-118. 8 Dec 1848. Deed of Gift or Conveyance. **Reuben Newman** of Spartanburgh Dist, to **Louisa Hughston.** Know all men by these presents that I, **Reuben Newman,** for the natural love and affection which I bear to **Louisa Hughston** my beloved daughter and also the sum of $100 to me paid, grants 100 acres beginning at a stake in the old field near the old road leading from **Emanuel Allen's** by the **Arch Bolton** old house place to where **Willis Layton** now lives this corner being near the corner of **Emanuel Allen's** cotton field and about one hundred yards South west of the place where **Bartholomew Darby** was killed, then easterly along **E. Allen's** line to a spring then down the spring branch to the fork of the branch on **Henry P. Darby's** line, bounded by lands of **Emanuel Allen, Thos Kelly, Henry P. Darby, Willis Layton** and myself. Granted to **Louisa Hughston** Provided that if my beloved wife **Sabra Newman** shall survive or outlive me that from and after my decease the said **Louisa Hughston** her heirs & assigns shall allow the said **Sabra Newman** a Support out of the said land or its products either to live on and cultivate the land or live with the said **Louisa Hughston.** Wit: **E. Allen, John H. Walker.** Signed, **Reubin (x) Newman.** Witness oath, 8 Dec 1848: Signed, **E. Allen** to **John H. Walker,** Mag. Registered Examined and certified 12 Dec 1848. Original delivered to ~~ Elisha Hughston.

p. 118-119. 7 Oct 1848. Mortgage. **James J. Boyd** is indebted to **W.L. Mitchell** for $2600 by five sealed notes falling due as follows (to wit) for $520 due 1st January each of the years 1850, 1851, 1852, 1853 and 1854. Mortgage is for a 1 acre Lot in the Village of Spartanburgh on main street bounded on the W by a Lot now owned & occupied by **Dr. R.E. Cleveland,** on the E by Estate of **Richard Thomson** deceased. Wit: **A.R. Ryan, Hiram Mitchell.** Signed, **J.J. Boyd.** Witness oath, 12 Dec 1848: Signed, **Hiram Mitchell** to **J.B. Tolleson,** Clk & Mag Exeff. Registered Examined

& certified 12 Dec 1848. Original delivered to ⁓ **Hiram Mitchell** 15 Dec 1848.

p. 119-121. 15 Dec 1848. Sheriff's Deed. **R.C. Poole** to **Drury McAbee**. Whereas **J.H. Hurt** on or about the 7th of August 1848 did exhibit his petition in the Court of the Ordinary at Spartanburgh Court House setting forth that **James Silmon** departed this life intestate on or about [no date] 1847, possessed of 90 acres on fords creek waters of Fair Forest Creek bounded by **Drury McAbee, Hiram McAbee, James H. Hurt & Eliza Selman**, that part and division yet remained to be made. On 13th Nov 1848, **R. Bowden Esq**, Ordinary ordered that the land be sold by the Sheriff on first Monday in December and was sold according to the custom of auctions for $225 to **Drury McAbee**. Wit: **Hiram McAbee, S.B. Foster**. Signed, **R.C. Poole**, S.S.D. Witness oath, 15 Dec 1848: Signed, **Hiram McAbee** to **J.B. Tolleson**, Clk & mag Exiffo. Registered 15th Dec 1848.

p. 121-122. 18 Dec 1848. Deed of Conveyance. **Mary Dodd** sold for $200 to **William High** 200 acres adjoining **Wm Dood, Nancy Pollard, Wm White** and the said **William High** being the same Tract of Land assigned to me for my Dower in the lands of **John Dood** deceased, and whereon **Kiah Johnson** resided the present year. Wit: **R.C. Poole, W.J. Poole**. Signed **Mary Dood**. Witness oath, 18 Dec 1848: Signed, **R.C. Poole** to **J.B. Tolleson**, Clk & mag Exiffo. Registered 18th Dec 1848.

p. 122-123. 6 March 1847. Deed of Conveyance. **Samuel N. Evans** of Spartanburg Dist, sold for $200 to **John S. Finch** of Spartanburg Dist, two tracts, one of 8 acres on the waters of Fairforest bounded by said **Finch, R. Bowden, Ephraim Jackson**, a road and others; the other of 7 acres bounded by said **Finch, H. McCarly**, the road and others. Wit: **Hiram Mitchell, Wm Lockwood**. Signed, **Saml N. Evins**. Release of dower, 13 Nov 1848: Signed, **E.C. Evins**, to **J.B. Tolleson**, Clk & mag. Ex iffo. Witness oath, 29 Nov 1848: Signed, **Hiram Mitchell** to **J.B. Tolleson**, Clk & Mag Ex iffo. Registered 22nd Dec 1848.

p. 124-125. 22 Dec 1848. Sheriff's Titles. **R.C. Poole** to **James Silman**. Whereas **James H. Hurt** and wife on or about the 7th day of August 1848, did Exhibit their petition in the court of the Ordinary at Spartanburg court house setting forth that **James Silman** departed this life intestate on or about the 3rd of September 1847 seized and possessed in fee of a plantation or tract of land containing 280 acres on the waters of the Packolet river bounded by **H.J. Dean, Mrs. Atkins, H. King** & others. That part and division of said land yet remained to be made which they prayed might be done and whereas afterwards To wit on the 13th day of Nov 1848 **R. Bowden Esq**. Ordinary of Spartanburg District after due Examination did order and decree that the land described in the petition be sold by the Sheriff of Spartanburg..... whereas, I, **R.C. Poole** as sheriff, after having advertised the land for sale by public outcry on 5th Dec 1848 and then openly and publicly according to the custom of auctions sell and dispose of the land described to **James Selman Junr** for $50... Wit: **Eli Jennings, Samuel Seay**. Signed, **R.C. Poole** {Seal}. Witness oath, 22 Dec 1848: **Samuel Seay** to **G.W.H. Legg**, Mgt. Registered 22 Dec 1848.

p. 125-126. 9 Aug 1848. Deed of Conveyance. **Wm Brasheres** of Spartanburg Dist, sold for $50 to **Adam McElrath** of Spartanburg Dist, 50 acres it being part of a Tract of land originally granted to **Elijah Stephens** by grant bearing date November 1794, lying on the North side of North Tyger river on small branches of the same having such shape and marks as represented by a plat upon a resurvey. Attest: **Ithia F. Brasheres, Wᵐ McElrath, Merida** (his x mark) **Besheres.** Signed, **Wᵐ (x) Brasheres.** Witness oath, 16 Aug 1848: **Merida Besheres** to **James Caldwell** Mag. S.D. Registered 23ʳᵈ Dec 1848.

p. 127. 12 Dec 1848. Deed of Conveyance. **F.H. Legg** sold for $52 to **J.S. Finch** a tract of land for a Term of Fifty Two Years, 25 acres on the North Eastern Corner of the Land **F.H. Legg** at present resides on, on Buck Branch, to the said **Finch**, his heirs and assigns for the above mentioned Term.... Wit: **R. Bowden, J.H. Vandike.** Signed, **F.H. Legg.** Witness oath, 1 Jany 1849: Signed, **R. Bowden** to **J.C. Caldwell**, Magistrate. Registered 1ˢᵗ Jany 1849.

p. 127-128. 30 Dec 1848. Deed of Conveyance. **J.S. Finch** for $50 sold to **J.H. Vandike** a tract of land for a Term of Fifty Two Years, 25 acres on the North Eastern Corner of the Land **F.H. Legg** at present resides on, on Buck Branch, to the said **Finch**, his heirs and assigns for the above mentioned Term.... Wit: **R. Bowden, Thoˢ Haynes.** Signed, **J.S. Finch.** Witness oath, 1 Jany 1849: Signed, **R. Bowden** to **J.C. Caldwell**, Magistrate. Registered 1ˢᵗ Jany 1849.

p. 128-130. 16 Dec 1848. **John S. Finch** of Spartanburg Dist, for $469.50 sold to **J.H. Vandike** of Spartanburg Dist. In case that **Bowden's** claim of 5¾ acres be not good represented by a dotted line in the plot of this land resurveyed by **M.A. Dickson** 8ᵗʰ December 1848. 234¾ acres on both sides of Buck and Buzzard branches, waters of Fair Forest Creek bounded by **John Bomar, F.H. Legg, R. Bowden** and others. Wit: **D.M. Brice, J.A. Finch.** Signed, **J.S. Finch.** Witness oath, 30 Dec 1848: Signed, **D.M. Brice** to **J.C. Caldwell**, Magistrate. Release of Dower, 30 Dec 1848: **Polly (x) Finch** to **J.C. Caldwell**, Magistrate. Registered 1ˢᵗ Jany. 1849.

p. 130-131. 4 Dec 1848. **R.C. Poole** for $26 sold to **Joseph Smith** of Spartanburg Dist. By virtue of a writ of fieri facias issued out of the court of common pleas held for the District of Spartanburg Tested the 25ᵗʰ day of Nov 1844, at the suit of **James McMakin**, to me directed commanding me that of the goods and chattels, Lands and Tenements of **David Henson** to levy the sum of $25.80½ with Interest, damages and costs, I have seized and taken that parcel containing 150 acres, on Wolfs swamp creek and bounded by **F. Clayton, F.C. Carson, John Loftis, Joseph Smith** & others...... since the seizure, said land has been exposed to sale at public Vendue and purchased by **Joseph Smith** for $26. Wit: **J. Rufus Poole, J.S. Finch.** Signed, **R.C. Poole**, S.S.D. Witness oath, 1 Jany 1849: **J. Rufus Poole** to **J.B. Tolleson**, Clk & Mgt. Effo. Registered Examined and certified 1ˢᵗ Jany. 1849. Original delivered to ~ **H.C. Collins.**

p. 131-133. 1 Jan 1849. Mortgage. **Wᵐ Goins** is indebted to **Wᵐ Carver** for $350 by four notes of hand under seal, one due 25ᵗʰ Dec 1848, one the 25ᵗʰ Dec 1849, one the 25ᵗʰ Dec 1850, and the other the 25ᵗʰ Dec 1851, being for 180 acres on the waters of Lawsons fork adjoining the **Widow Stone, Reubin Gramling** & others. Wit: **H.H. Thomson, W.H. Willbanks.** Signed, **Wᵐ Goins**, Witness oath, 1 Jan 1849: Signed, **H.H. Thomson** to **J.B. Tolleson**, Clk & Mag Ex iffo. (The foregoing mortgage was paid off and Settled in full May 1ˢᵗ 185?. **Wᵐ Carver.**) Registered 1ˢᵗ Jany. 1849.

p. 133-134. 24 March 1846. Mortgage. **Nimrod Horton** to **E.S.E. Chambers. Chambers** paid

Horton $35 for 160 acres on **Ashworth's** Creek adjoining **Henry Ruppe, Howell Westbrooks &** others. [No mention of further payment]. Test: **W.B. Turner, Isaac Horton**. Signed, **Nimrod Horton**. Witness oath, 26 Sept 1846. **Wm B. Turner** to **J.N. Covington**, Mag. Registered Examined and Certified 11th Jany. 1849. Original deliverd to **E.S.E. Chambers**.

p. 134-136.   6 Jan 1848. Mortgage. **John T. Wood** stands indebted for $370 to **Tho' O.P. Vernon** Commissioner of the Court of Equity, by three single Bills or Bonds for money due the 2nd day of October 1849, 2nd day of October 1850, and one due the 2nd day of October 1851, with Interest from the 2nd day of October 1849, each for $123.33. Mortgage on 144¼ acres bounded by Lots N°s 1 & 3,   road leading to **D.W. Moore's** factory, South fork of Tyger River. Wit: **R. Bowden, B.K. Vaughn**. Signed, **Tho' O.P. Vernon**, C.E.S.D., **John T. Wood**. Witness oath, 15 Jan 1849: **R. Bowden** to **J.B. Tolleson**, Clk & Mag Ex iffo. Registered 15th Jany. 1849.

p. 136-138.   7 Nov 1848. Deed of Conveyance. **Wm R. Poole** to **William Lee, Sen** for $975 sold 220 acres, the tract whereon **W.R. Poole** now lives, originally in two tracts, 100 acres in N° 1, N° 2, near **Pearce's** old spring, along the cross fence between **W.R. Poole** and **John Weathers** and adjoining N° 1, **James Lee, Jeremiah Lee** and others. Wit: **John Harmon, John B. Briant**. Signed, **Wm R. Poole**. Release of dower, 12 Jan 1849: Signed, **Susannah Poole**, to **J.B. Tolleson**, Clk & Mag Ex iffo. Witness oath, 8 Jan 1849: Signed, **John Harmon** to **B.F. Bates**, Not. Repub. Registered 15th Jany. 1849.

p. 138-139.   28 Dec 1848. Deed of Conveyance. **J.M. McCarley** of Spartanburg Dist, to **James McCarley** for $50 on south side of the creek called Fair Forest creek, 10 acres bordering [see next deed] **Allen Bulman**, the old field, the path going from **J.M. McCarley's** house to his spring near the shoal on said creek, and on road from the Edge of the water where a Twelve foot dam built on the highest part of the shoal near the said spring, up said creek on Road from the Eage of the water where the Twelve foot dam is full of water to where it strikes **John Keash's** line, along meanders of the creek. Wit: **James Tapp, D.F. [or T.] Smith**. Signed, **J.M. McCarley**. Release of dower, 19 Jany. 1849: Signed, **Rachel Ann E. McCarley** to **John Linder**, Mag. Witness oath, 19th Jany. 1849: Signed, **James Tapp** to **John Linder**, Mag. Registered 19th Jany. 1849.

p. 139-141.   28 Dec 1848. Deed of Conveyance. **James McCarley** of Spartanburg Dist, to **R. Bowden** of Spartanburg Dist, for $300, sold 160 acres on Fair Forest creek, beginning at a water oak on Reedy Branch, waters of Fair Forest creek SE to **Hiram Bulman's** corner, to a stake on North side of said creek, then up and crossing said creek to **Allen Bulman's** corner, running a NW course near the edge of the old field to an post oak near the path going from **J.M. McCarley's** down to his spring near the shoal on said creek, NE to just above and opposite the said spring and on Road from the Edge of the water where a Twelve foot dam is built on the highest part of the shoal near **J.M. McCarley's** spring, across said creek is full of water. Thence up said creek on Road from the ·
Edge of high water where dam is full of water to where it will intersect with **John Keash's [or Keasht's]** line, then down the meanders of the creek to the mouth of Reedy Branch to the beginning. Wit: **James Tapp, D.F. Smith**. Signed, **James McCarley**. Release of dower, 19 Jany 1849: Signed, **Nancy (x) McCarley** to **John Linder**, Mag. Witness oath, 19 Jany 1849: Signed, **James Tapp** to **John Linder**, Mag. Registered 19th Jany. 1849.

p. 141-142. 26 Aug 1848. Deed of Conveyance. **Stephen Kirby** of Spartanburg Dist, to **Reubin Briant** of Spartanburg Dist, for $100 sold 20 acres on waters of Packolet river it being a part of the old **Quinn** Tract. Beginning on a chestnut on the **Rosey West** tract. It being **James Burgess** corner of a Ten acre tract on the branch. Then NW to a white oak near the Troft Shoal branch, **Reubin Briant's** corner. Then N to the creek **Henry Harvey's** line. Thence with the meanders of the creek to **R. Briant's** line. Thence back to the white oak corner, to the spring. Thence down the **Rosey West** branch to the beginning. Wit: **James R. Briant, William Harvey.** Signed, **Stephen Kirby.** Witness oath, 22 Jany 1849: Signed, **James R. Briant** to **J.B. Tolleson,** Clk & Mag Ex iffo. Registered 22nd Jany. 1849.

p. 143-144. 29 Jan 1849. Mortgage. **Z.D. Cottrell** to **Thoˢ O.P. Vernon.** Between **T.O.P. Vernon** of the one part and **Z.D. Cottrell** of the other part, whereas **T.O.P. Vernon** with myself gave Jointly a note to **Rev Benjamin Wofford** for the sum of $1,200 more or less cash borrowed to discharge a debt contracted by us jointly for a printing press, types and fixtures thereto belonging and whereas the said **T.O.P. Vernon** after an Editorial Engagement for the space of Twelve months in conjunction with me did bargain sell and surrender to me all his interest in Press together with the assets upon the Express condition that I would assume and discharge the original note above specified and all other Notes, accounts, debts or demands subsisting against us as Co. Editors and in all other respects indemnify him against all losses as principal surety or otherwise or against them Individually where they have assumed a joint and several responsibility. Now this indenture witnesseth that the said **Z.D. Cottrell** for and in consideration of the premises do bargain sell release convey and confirm and deliver unto the said **T.O.P. Vernon** houses Lot and Lands whereon I now live containing 8 acres more or less and bounded by lands of **Wᵐ Walker, Thoˢ B. Collins** and Lands formerly belonging to the Estate of **Richard Thomson** deceased. Together with all and singular the rights ...... unto the said **T.O.P. Vernon**, his heirs, Executors & administrators forever also, my printing press with all the Types, cases, materials and fixtures of Every kind and description used therewith or thereunto belonging to have and to hold the same to him, his heirs Executors & administrators forever. — Provided always nevertheless and it is the true intent and meaning of the parties to these presents that if the said **Z.D. Cottrell** shall well and Truly pay or cause to be paid unto the holder or owner of the Notes payable to **Rev. Benjamin Wofford,** aforesaid as well as all other accounts notes debts or demands or claims now existing against us jointly then and from thenceforth these presents shall be utterly null and void any thing herein contained to the contrary thereof in any wise notwithstanding and it is the parties of these presents that the said **T.O.P. Vernon** shall have full liberty power and authority to sell the same and Execute Titles thereto to protect himself against all Losses as principal or surety upon his giving the usual Notice to the original note to **Rev. Benjamin Wofford** and all others that may have been contracted by us as Co. Editors as aforesaid prescribed by Lae in the sales of real and personal property...... Wit: **A.G. Campbell, Jno. Earl Bomar.** Signed, **Thos O.P. Vernon, Z.D. Cottrell.** Witness oath, 29 Jan 1849: Signed, **Jno. Earl Bomar** to **J.B. Tolleson,** Clk & Mag Ex iffo. Registered 29th Jany. 1849.

p. 144-145. 4 Sept 1847. Deed of Conveyance. **John Wheeler** of Spartanburg Dist, to **John Ballenger** of Spartanburg Dist, for $155 sold 124 acres on Wolf swamp creek waters of middle Tyger river, and on the Goodjoin [Rd?]. Test: **D. Ballenger, John Odam.** Signed, **Jno. Wheeler.** Witness oath, 18 Nov 1848: **John Odam** to **B.J. Montgomery,** Mgt. Registered 1st Feb 1849.

p. 145-146. 31 Dec 1847. Deed of Conveyance. **Joseph Smith** to **John Ballenger** of Spartanburg Dist, for $42.50 sold 34 acres a part of a tract originally granted to **Goin Clayton** bounded by land originally granted to **McDowell** and **Sarah Grey**. Wit: **John Odam, Jno. Wheeler**. Signed, **Joseph Smith**. Witness oath, 31 Dec 1847: Signed, **John Odam** to **Thomas Ballenger**, M.S.D. Registered 1ˢᵗ Feb. 1849.

p. 147. 22 Dec 1848. Deed of Conveyance. **Simpson Bobo**. Admr. to **Jno. Wood**. Whereas **David Dantzler** by his last will and Testament directed that his real Estate should be sold to the highest bidder and whereas the undersigned administrator with the will annexed, by virtue of the authority aforesaid Exposed 100 acres on Pigeon Roost creek, waters of S. Tyger River bounded by **Wᵐ Smith, Jaˢ A. Miller** & others known as the **Wood** place & is represented by a plat herewith annexed to sell at public outcry and **John Wood** became the high bidder at the sum of $236. Wit: **W.W. Harris, P.W. Head**. Signed, **Simpson Bobo**, Admr cum Test annexed of **David Dantzler** Deed. Witness oath, 2 Feby 1849: Signed, **W.W. Harris** to **J.B. Tolleson**, Clk & Mag Ex iffo. Registered 2 Feb. 1849.

p. 148-149. 3 April 1848. Deed of Conveyance. **John H. Wofford** of Spartanburg Dist, to **William J. Wofford** of Spartanburg Dist, for $1000 sell at my decease, no rents or charges Exacted, 197 acres on the North side of Fergusons creek the waters of Tyger River. Test: **C. Tillotson, John T.H. Wofford**. Signed, **John H. Wofford**. Witness oath, 5 Feb 1849: Signed, **J.T.H. Wofford** to **Jonas Brewton**, Mag. Registered 5ᵗʰ Feb. 1849.

p. 149-150. 22 Jan 1849. Deed of Conveyance. **C.P. Littlejohn** to **John Allen** for $1,000 sold 361 acres on the waters of Goucher creek bounded by **Francis Littlejohn, Johnathan Goforth, Widow Reid, James Lee, J.H. Lipscomb** & others. Wit: **Elijah Shippey, H. Goudelock**. Signed, **C.P. Littlejohn**. Witness oath, 22 Jan 1849: Signed, **Elijah Shippey** to **Wᵐ Lipscomb**, Mag. Release of dower, 22 Jan 1849: Signed, **Lettice W. Littlejohn** to **Wᵐ Lipscomb**, Mag. Registered 5ᵗʰ Feby 1849.

p. 150-151. 31 Oct 1846. Deed of Conveyance. **John Cunningham** and wife **Amanda C. Cunningham** both of Spartanburg Dist, to **Barba M. Pollard** of Spartanburg Dist, for $450 sold 312 acres, where we now live, beginning on the So. bank of **Green's** Creek about 200 yards from the clay ford [at] **David Golightly** corner, then SW to the Howard Gap road and down the road to **Ballenger's** and **Cothran's** corner, a stake in the head of **Mrs. Brannon's** Mill pond, **Wᵐ Brannon's** corner, up the meanders of Meadow Creek, west side at the ford of the creek..... to have and to hold except 1 acre where the graveyard is....... Wit: **Z.M. Pollard, B.M. Gramling**. Signed, **John Cunningham, Amanda Cunninham**. Witness oath, 5 Feby 1849: Signed, **Z.M. Pollard** to **J.B. Tolleson**, Clk & Mag Ex iffo. Registered Examined and certified 5ᵗʰ Feby 1849. Original delivered to ~ **B.M. Pollard** 10ᵗʰ Sept. 1850.

p. 151-153. 17 Aug 1847. Deed of Conveyance. **James Hamm** of Spartanburg Dist, to **Jesse & William J. Whitmire** of Spartanburg Dist, sold 234½ acres in two tracts for $762.12. Bound by S side of **Wofford** Road, **James Moor, Joel Dean, Perry West & John C. Zimmerman**. Wit:

W.H. Lancaster, F.S. Fergason. Signed, **James Hamm.** Witness oath, 17 Aug 1847: Signed, **W.H. Lancater** to **James Gibbs,** Mag. Release of Dower, 20 Jan 1848, Union Dist: Signed, **Dorcas P. Hamm** to **John Gibbs,** Mag. for Union Dist. Registered Examined and certified 5th Feby. 1849. Original delivered to ~~ **[I. or] J.W. Bobo** March 10th 1853.

p. 153-154.   Deed of Conveyance. **John C. Caldwell** of Spartanburg Dist, to his son **Andrew Perry Caldwell** of Spartanburg Dist, for the love & affection I bear towards my son, I have given and granted 100 acres known as the **R.N. Hadden** tract, lying on both side of Mill creek. Wit: **James H. Vandike, William K.P. Caldwell.** Signed, **John C. Caldwell.** Witness oath, 5 Feb 1849: Signed, **James H. Vandike** to **R. Bowden,** Exiffo. Mag. Registered Examined and confirmed 5 Feby. 1849. Original delivered to ~~ **A.P. Caldwell.**

p. 154-155.   16 Jany 1849. Deed of Conveyance. **John A. Linder** son of **Nathaniel Linder,** in consideration of being released by **James Templeman** from any further obligations to pay any thing towards the support of my Grand mother **Mary Wyatt,** convey unto **Jas. Templeman** all my right to a tract of land belonging to my Grand mother and authorize **Templeman** to receive any legacy rising out of said premises to me after her death. My interest is one fifth of one Eight part. The lands, 200 acres, lying on the waters of Packolet River & bounded by **John Linder, Z. Cannon & Joel Cannon.** Test: **John Turner, John Linder.** Signed, **J.A. Linder.** Witness oath, 5 Feby 1849: **John Linder** to **R. Bowden,** Exiffo Mag. Registered 5th Feby. 1849.

p. 155.   5 Jan 1849. Deed of Conveyance. **Cintha Dermid** of Spartanburg Dist. to **George A. Pike** of Spartanburg Dist, for $213.75 sold 79 acres on the south side of Packolet River, adjoining land of **Zachariah Cannon, Carter Burnett, Henry Abbott** and across Packolet River, **Henry Turner & Fielding Turner** being part of 500 acres originally granted to **Wm Dixon.** Wit: **John Eptin, Fielden Turner, James M. McAbee.** Signed, **Cintha (x) Dermid.** Witness oath, 5 Feby 1849: Signed, **John Epting** to **J.B. Tolleson,** Clk & Mag Ex iffo. Registered 5th Feby 1849.

p. 156.   12 Jun 1846.   Deed of Conveyance. **Solomon Abbot** of Spartanburg Dist., to **Lemuel Dermid** of Spartanburg Dist, for $10 sold 10 acres on Cherokee Creek waters of Pacolet River adjoining lands of **Cintha Dermid,** the Cherokee springs, **George A. Fike** and where **Solomon Abbot** now lives. Wit: **John Epting, W^m. P. Duggins, John Baber.** Witness oath, 27 June 1846: Signed, **William P. Duggins** to **H. Hicks,** Mag. Registered 5th Feby 1849.

p.157.   15 Sep 1848. Deed of Conveyance. **Solomon Abbot** of Spartanburg Dist, to **Cintha Dermid** of Spartanburg Dist, for $237 sold 79 acres on the south side of Pacolet River bounded by **Henry Abbot, Carter Burnett, Zachariah Cannon** and Pacolet River. Test: **John Epting, William P. Duggins, L.T. Dermid.** Signed, **Solomon (x) Abbot.** Witness oath, 5 Feby 1849: Signed, **John Epting** to **J.B. Tolleson,** Clk & Mag Ex iffo. Registered 5th Feby 1849.

p. 157-158.   9 April 1846. Deed of Conveyance. **Solomon Abbot** of Spartanburg Dist, to **Peyton Turner** of Spartanburg Dist, for $375 sold 125 acres on Pacolet River adjoining lands of **Jas. Bivings, Carter Burnett & Zachariah Cannon.** Wit: **John Epting, Wm P. Duggins.** Witness oath, 5 Feby 1849: Signed, **John Epting** to **J.B. Tolleson,** Clk & Mag Ex iffo. Registered 5th Feby. 1849.

p. 158-159. 15 Sept 1848. Deed of Conveyance. **Lemuel Dermid** of Spartanburg Dist, to **Geo. A. Fike** of Spartanburg Dist, for $20 sold 6 acres on Cherokee Creek of Pacolet River bounded by lands of **Geo. Fike, Solomon Abbot, Cintha Dermid** & lands belonging to the <u>Cherokee Springs Company</u> and having such form and marks as a Plot made by **John Epting** the 25th day of October 1847 annexed to this, will represent. Wit: **John Epting, Henry Turner, Wm P. Duggins.** Signed, **L.T. Dermid.** Witness oath, 5 Feby 1849: Signed, **John Epting** to **J.B. Tolleson,** Clk & Mag Ex iffo. Registered 5th Feby. 1849.

p. 159-161. 28 Feb 1848. Deed of Conveyance. **Edward W. Ballenger** of Spartanburg Dist, to **Aaron Cannon** of Spartanburg Dist, for $700 sold 283 acres on the North side of South Pacolet River and south side of **Alexander's** Creek. Test: **Hamilton Johnson, Thomas C. Wingo.** Signed, **Edward W. Ballenger.** Release of dower, 18 April 1848: **Cassy Ann Ballenger,** Signed, **C.A. Ballenger** to **M.D. Dickey,** M.S.D. Witness oath, 18 April 1848: Signed, **Thomas C. Wingo** to **M.D. Dickey,** M.S.D. Registered 5th Feby. 1849.

p. 161-162. 1 Nov 1845. Deed of Conveyance. **James Nesbitt** to **Saml. N. Evans** of Spartanburg Dist, for $1950 sold 508 acres on the waters of Tyger beginning on the wagon road, it being the Poolsville place which was sold by the sheriff & purchased by the said **James Nesbitt.** Test: **Jonas Brewton, John A. Dickie.** Signed, **James Nesbitt.** Witness oath, 1 Nov 1845: Signed, **John A. Dickie** to **Jonas Brewton,** Mag. Release of dower, 1 Nov 1845: Signed, **Caroline Nesbitt** to **Jonas Brewton,** J.Q. Registered 9th Feby. 1849.

p. 163-164. 31 Aug 1843. Deed of Conveyance. **James Peden** of Dekalb Co., GA, to **Samuel N. Evans** for $500 sold all my interest & Estate in 193 acres, being the remainder after the death of my two sisters **Mary & Margaret Peden,** on Fergason creek on which **Margaret Peden** now lives bounded by **S.N. Evans, The E.B. Peden & Mark Fowler** lands... to have and hold the said premises after the death of **Mary & Margaret Peden.** Wit: **A.W. Peden, M.A. Dickson, M.M. Anderson.** Signed, **James Peden.** Witness oath, 31 Aug 1843: Signed, **A.W. Peden** to **J. Anderson,** Magt. Release of dower, 31 Aug 1843: Signed, **Lettice Peden** to **J. Anderson,** Magt, Spartanburg Dist. Additional Release:I, **Alex W. Peden** in right of my **Aunt Polly Peden** a life interest in the within mentioned Land sell for $150 to **S.N. Evans** all my interest in said land and I, **Margaret Peden** being entitled by the will of **Elizabeth Peden** to the right of survivorship for life in the said lands in the event of **Polly Peden's** death, sell for $5 to **Col. Saml. N. Evans** all my right & interest present & prospective in the one half of said land as assigned or paid off to **Polly Peden** by the last will of **Elizabeth Peden.** Wit, 6 Jan 1844: **George Johnson, Thomas Peden, John C. Fowler.** Signed, **Alex W. Peden, Margaret (x) Peden.** Registered 9th Feby. 1849.

p. 164-166. 5 Feb 1844. Deed of Conveyance. **Alexr Miller** of Spartanburg Dist, to **Samuel N. Evans** of Spartanburg Dist, for $2,600 sell 582½ acres, all that tract of land where I now live on the North side of the North fork of Tyger river and bounded by edge of mill pond, **John Booker, Thompson** and others. Wit: **B.F. Montgomery, M.L. Thompson, B.F. Bates.** Signed, **Alexander Miller.** Witness oath, 5 Feb 1844: Signed, **M.L. Thompson** to **B.F. Bates,** Mag. Release of dower, 26 Oct 1844: <u>Salvah</u> **Miller** wife of **Alexander Miller,** signed <u>Sivah</u> **Miller** to **Thomas Ballenger,** J.Q. Registered 9th Feb 1849.

p. 166- 168.   1 Nov 1845.Deed of Conveyance. **Mark Fowler** of Spartanburg Dist, to **Samuel N. Evans** of Spartanburg Dist, for $261 sold [acres not given] beginning at the cross road below my dwelling house on Buncombe Road. Wit: **James Arnold, Mark S. Paden.** Signed, **Mark Fowler.** Witness oath, 8 Nov 1845: Signed, **Mark S. Paden** to **F.H. Legg**, Magistrate. Release of dower, 8 Nov 1845: Signed, **Rebecca (x) Fowler** to **F.H. Legg**, Magistrate. Registered 9th Feby. 1849.

p. 168-169.   22 Oct 1845. Deed of Conveyance. **George Johnson** of Spartanburg Dist, to **Samuel N. Evins** of Spartanburg Dist, for $1049 sold 347 acres on both sides of Buncomb Road and on N & south sides of Forgusan's Creek. Test: **S.L. Westmoreland**. Signed, **George Johnson.** Witness oath, 22 Oct 1845: Signed, **S.L. Westmoreland** to **J. Anderson**, Magt. Release of dower, 22 Oct 1845: Signed, **Elizabeth (x) Johnson** to **J. Anderson**, Magt. Registered 9th Feby. 1849.

p. 170-171.   22 Sept 1842. Deed of Conveyance. **William Hoy** of Spartanburg Dist, to **Samuel N. Evins** for $2,000 sold 382 acres on both sides of Forgerson's creek. Wit: **James Anderson, Nancy Anderson.** Signed, **Wm Hoy.** Witness oath, 22 Sept 1842: Signed, **James Anderson** to **John Anderson**, Magt. Registered 9th Feby. 1849.

p. 171-172.   3 Dec 1846. Deed of Conveyance. **H.F. Vernon** of Rutherford Co, NC, to **Col. Samuel N. Evins** of Spartanburg Dist, for $4,800 sold [acres not given] that tract known as the south Tyger tract, on both sides of the river. Wit: **O.E. Edwards, Tho' O.P. Vernon**. Signed, **H.F. Vernon.** Witness oath, 9 Feby 1849: Signed, **Tho. O.P. Vernon** to **J.B. Tolleson**, Clk & Mag Ex iffo. Release of dower, 8 Dec 1847: Signed **Letitia G. Vernon** to **J.H. Alley**, J.P. & **T.E. Montgomery**. Registered 9th Feby. 1849.

p. 173-174.   2 Jan 1846. Deed of Conveyance. **William H. Miller** of Spartanburg Dist, to **Samuel N. Evins** of Spartanburg Dist, for $400 sold 109 acres on the south side of the Middle Fork Tyger River, beginning on the river, along a waggon road to the Head of the Gron[?] spring branch. Wit: **A.C. Jackson, J.H. Jackson.** Signed, **W.H. Miller.** Witness oath, 23 May 1846: Signed, **A.C. Jackson** to **F.H. Legg**, Magistrate. Registered 9th Feby. 1849.

p. 174-175.   23 July 1845. Deed of Conveyance. **John C. Fowler** of Greenville Dist, to **William Leonard** of Spartanburg Dist, for $500 sold 177 acres, bordered by **Phillip Beacham's** line on N side Bens Creek, old run of the creek, **Thomas & Daniel Beacham's** Lots of their Father's real Estate on **Susannah's** line. Wit: **Silas Stone, Robert Leonard.** Signed, **John C. Fowler.** Witness oath, 23 July 1845: Signed, **Robt. Leonard** to **John Anderson**, Magt. S.D. Registered 9th Feby 1849.

p. 175-176.   15 Feb 1849. Deed of Conveyance. **Aaron Bishop** of Spartanburg Dist, to **H.H. Thomson** of Spartanburg Dist, for $56 sold 107½ acres on the waters of Sholey creek bounded as follows: Barton's branch, **Aaron & Solomon Bishop**, running NE with Furnace & Turno[??]. Wit: **David Miller, J.W. Tucker.** Signed, **Aaron Bishop.** Witness oath, 26 Feby 1849: Signed, **J.W. Tucker** to **J.B. Tolleson**, Clk & Mag Ex iffo. Registered 26th Feby 1849.

p. 176-178.   20 Nov 1848. Sheriff's Titles. **R.C. Poole** to **L.W. Hastings.** Whereas **Elvira Vaughn** on or about the 22nd of January 1848 did Exhibit her Petition in the court of Ordinary at Spartanburg Court House setting forth that **Wm H. Vaughn** departed this life Intestate on or about the [blank] of [blank] seized and possessed of a Plantation or Tract of Land containing 111 acres on the waters of the Enoree River bounded by lands of **Wm M. Vaughn** and others that part and division of said Land yet remained to be made, which she prayed might be done — and afterward to wit - on the 4th day of February 1848 **R. Bowden, Esq.** Ordinary of Spartanburg Dist after due examination did order and decree that the Lands described in the Petition be sold by the sheriff of Spartanburg; and for $261 sold to **L.W. Hastings.** Wit: **Wm Petty, R. Bowden.** Signed, **R.C. Poole**, S.S.D. Witness oath, 9th Feby 1849: **R. Bowden** to **J.B. Tolleson**, Clk & Mag Ex iffo. Registered 26th Feby. 1849.

p.178-179.   25 Dec 1847. Deed of Conveyance. **Robert Dobson** of Spartanburg Dist, to **John W. Hampton** of North Carolina, Polk County, for $81.37½ sold 245 acres, the tract whereon **Robert Dobson** now lives on the head branches of Wolf's Creek waters of North Pacolet River. Wit: **John W. Hunt, N.B. Hampton.** Signed **Robert (x) Dobson.** The condition of the above Deed is such (viz) If **Robert Dobson** pays **John W. Hampton** $81.37½ with Interest within twelve months from date the said Deed is to be null and void and of no effect. If he does not pay the above deed to remain full force to **John W. Hampton.** Wit: **John W. Hunt.** Signed, **J.W. Hampton.** Witness oath, 5th March 1849: **John W. Hunt** to **James Caldwell**, Magt. Registered Examined and certified 5th March 1849. Original delivered to ~~ **Robert Dobson** 4 March 1850.

p. 179-181.   10 Feb 1848. Deed of Conveyance. **John B. Page** of Spartanbutg Dist, to **Thomas Thomas** of Spartanburg Dist, for $450 sold 120 acres whereon I, **John Page** now live on the North side of Tyger River leaving out of the original Tract which I purchased of **Enoch Floyd** leaving out three acres which I swapped off to **Jonathan Floyd,** the dividing line made by **Jesse Pinson** and **John Gentry** and agreed to by the said **E. Floyd** and **Jonathan Floyd,** to a stone corner made by **J.T. Floyd** & myself, **John Trail's** corner, **Pinson's** line, North bank of Tyger River. Wit: **R.C. Poole, John N. Gentry.** Signed, **J.B. Page.** Witness oath, 1st April 1848: **John N. Gentry** to **Z. Lanford**, Magt. Release of dower, 28 March 1848: Signed **Frances (x) Page** to **Z. Lanford**, Magt. Registered 6th March 1849.

p. 181-182.   7 Aug 1839. Deed of Conveyance. **John Covington** of Spartanburg Dist, to **Richard Roberts** of Spartanburg Dist, for $78.50 sold 76 acres on the head of Haystack Branch bounded by state line, the road leading from the line meeting house to **Jacob Phillipse's.** Attest: **J.B. Covington, Hardy Blackwell.** Signed, **John (x) Covington.** Witness oath, 17 April 1843: Signed, **Hardy Blackwell** to **A. Bonner**, Mag. Registered 6th March 1849.

p. 182-183.   14 Sept 1839. Deed of Conveyance. **John Covington** of Spartanburg Dist, to **Richard Roberts** of Spartanburg Dist, for $60 sold 80 acres on the waters of Camp Fork bordering on camp fork below the old ford, Colter ford Road, Cowpen Road, **H. Blackwell.** Attest: **Hardy Blackwell, James Blackwell.** Signed, **John (x) Covington.** Witness oath, 17 April 1849: Signed **Hardy Blackwell** to **A. Bonner**, Magt. Registered 6th March 1849.

p. 183-184.   29 Dec 1845. Deed of Conveyance. **William Davis** of Spartanburg Dist, to **Richard Roberts** of Spartanburg Dist, for $86 sold 86 acres on the waters of Horse Creek and Suck Creek waters of Broad River, bounded by state line, the road leading from the Island ford on Broad River to the Cowpen Furnace, Colters ford Road, **Roberts, Hardy Blackwell**, the road leading from the state line meeting house to **J. Phillip's**. Attest: **C.B. Durham, E.B. (x) Durham**. Signed, **Wm Davis**. Witness oath, Dec 29th 1845: Signed, **C.B. Durham** to **J.N. Covington**, Mag. Registered 6th March 1849.

p. 184-185. 13 Oct 1834. Deed of Conveyance. **William Paris** of Spartanburg Dist, to **Richard Roberts** of Spartanburg Dist, for $45 sold 50 acres by computation, on the waters of Suck Creek, **Lidia Blackwell, Richard Roberts**. Attest: **John N. Covington, Hardy Blackwell**. Signed, **William Paris**. Witness oath, 13 Oct 1834: Signed, **John N. Covington** to **J.W. Martin**, J.P. Release of dower, 17 April 1843: Signed, **Elizabeth (x) Paris** to **A. Bonner**, Mag. Registered 6th March 1849.

p. 186.   20 Dec 1848. Mortgage. **C.C. Huggins** of Spartanburg Dist, to **R.A. Cates & Alvan Lancaster** of Spartanburg Dist. For better securing the payment of $72.97, **Huggins** mortgages 4 acres originally granted to **Dr. M.A. Moore & M. Freeninghyson[?]** lying near the Glenn Springs and adjoining **J.C. Zimmerman, Dr. M.A. Moore & Dr. D.D. Peake**. Attest: **Elias Bearden**. Signed, **C.C. Huggins**. Witness oath, 8 Mar 1849: Signed, **Elias Bearden** to **J.B. Tolleson**, Clk & Mag Ex iffo. Registered 8th March 1849.

p. 187-188.   2 Jan 1849. Deed of Conveyance. **Gainum T. Rakestraw** of Gwinnett Co., GA, to **John C. Zimmerman** of Spartanburg Dist, for $185 sold 150 acres, by estimation, lying on the waters of Fairforest creek and bounded by formerly **James Flemming's, Henry Smith, Col. Thomas Taylor**. Wit: **Elias Bearden, R.A. Cates**. Signed, **Gainum T. Rakestraw**. Witness oath, 7 Mar 1849: Signed, **Elias Bearden** to **G.W.H. Legg**, Mag. Registered 8th March 1849.

p. 188-189.   28 Feb 1849. Mortgage. **Joel B. Littlejohn** indebted to **Henry White** of Spartanburg Dist, for $21.20¾ on one note dated March 8th 1847 with interest, one note for $9.96 dated 3rd of June 1848 with interest, for better securing the payment, **Littlejohn** sells **White**, one set of smith's tools, that is to say, 1 Smith Bellows, 1 Anvil, 1 Pice, 1 shoeplate, 1 sledge Hammer, the Handhames and all the balance of the Tools — provided, if **Littlejohn** pays the sum above mentioned the 1st of October next then the above mortgage shall be null and void or otherwise in full force and Effect. Furthermore, **Littlejohn** agrees that if the sum of money be not paid on the day above written **Henry White** shall be fully authorized and Empowered to advertise the said property and sell to the highest bidder or so much as will satisfy the Debt and costs. Wit: **Henry Dodd, Robert McMillin**. Signed, **J.B. Littlejohn**. Witness oath, 5 Mar 1849: Signed, **Henry Dodd** to **W.H. Wilbanks**, Mag. Registered 8th March 1849.

p. 189-190.   28 June 1848. Deed of Gift. I, **James Bivings** of Spartanburg Dist, to **Kiddy Catherine Wingo** of Spartanburg Dist, in consideration of the natural good will and affection which I have for my Daughter, have gave and release unto her 450 acres on the waters of Chinquepin it being a part of the **Belew** Tract purchased by me from **Nath. Gist**, on the Rutherford Road. Wit: **J.W. Webber, T.J. Wingo, J.F.V. Legg**. Signed, **Jas. Bivings**. Witness oath, 14 March 1849: Signed, **J.W. Webber** to **J.B. Tolleson**, Clk & Mag Ex iffo. Registered 14th March 1849. Original delivered to ~ **A. Wingo.**

p. 190-191.   28 Feb 1849. Deed of Conveyance. **David McDowell** of Spartanburg Dist, to **James N. McDowell** of Spartanburg Dist, for $191 sold 191 acres on Branches of Lossons Fork creek waters of Packolet River, a part of a tract originally granted. Wit: **Robt. M. McDowell, Calvin McDowell.** Signed, **David McDowell.** Witness oath, 16 March 1849: Signed, **Calvin McDowell** to **J.B. Tolleson**, Clk & Mag Ex iffo.Registered 16th March 1849.

p. 191-192.   5 Feb 1849. Mortgage. **George Spencer** to **John Linder** for the purpose of securing Two Notes for $29 each given to **Edward McAbee** dated 20th Feby 1846 - one of them due 25th Decr 1848 and the other Due 25th Decr. 1849 - and Endorsed to **John Linder** by **McAbee** - and for the securing the payments to **John Linder - Jas.** [is this supposed to be **Geo.?**] Mortgages 150 acres whereon I [George Spencer?] now lives. Attest: **J.J. Vandiver, Jno. Earle Bomar.** Signed, **George Spencer.** Witness oath, 15 Mar 1849: signed, **Jno. Earle Bomar** to **R. Bowden**, Ex off. Mag. Registered 16th March 1849.

p. 192-194.   17 Feb 1849. Mortgage. **David Miller** stands indebted to **H.H. Thomson** and to him and others as the Executor of **R. Thomson** as follows, (Viz) One note under seal for $154 due 21st Nov 1847, dated 18th Nov 1847 - one note given to **Richard Thomson** for $100 under seal dated 1st Jany 1844 and due 1st Jany 1845 - one for $50 given to **R. Thomson** dated 12th Decr 1843 due 12th Decr 1844 - one for $55 payable to **R. Thomson** dated 15th Jany 1844 due 1st Jany 1845 - Note under seal one Note of hand for $100 due 1st Jany 1846 given to **H.H., J.W. & J.W. Thomson** - one note under seal for $10 given to **H.H. Thomson, J.W. & J. Waddy Thomson** dated 1st Jany 1846 due 1st Jany 1847 - **David Miller**, for the better securing of the several notes as stated above mortgages the following lot in the Town of Spartanburg Viz) The House and Lot whereon I now reside and which I bought of **David Crawford** bounded by **Andrew Houser** on one side and **Junius Thomson's** Lot on the other & on the back End by **H.H. Thomson** and the front side by the Public square. It is agreed that until defaults shall be made in payments, **David Miller** shall peacefully and quietly occupy the premises above described. Wit: **Hiram Mitchell, J.W. Tucker.** Signed, **David Miller.** Witness oath, 16 March 1849: Signed, **J.W. Tucker** to **J.B. Tolleson**, Clk & Mag Ex iffo. Registered 16th March 1849.

p. 194-196.   24 Oct 1842. Deed of Conveyance. **T. J. Linder & James A. Webster** of Spartanburg Dist, to **David Miller & Lansan Lancaster** for $1,270 sold 2⅔ acres known as **Linder's** Tan yard on the waters of Fairforest adjoining lands belonging to the estate of **Lee Linder** decd, and **Self,** beginning just above the ford of **Self** Branch. Also the right of occupying the Houses on the Right Hand side of the Road in which **Lancaster** now lives - the above tract containing the Tan Yard and all the appurtenances and all the Stock now on hand. Wit: **H.H. Thomson, Joel Dean.** Signed, **Thos. J. Linder, James A. Webster.** Witness oath, 12 Nov 1842: Signed, **Joel Dean** to **H.H. Thomson**, J.Q. Ex off.
    19 May 18[4?]3 Know all men by these presents that I, **Lanson Lancaster** for $633.50 assigned over to my copartner in the within deed, **David Miller**, all my interest in the within mentioned premises, including the Lands, buildings, Tan Yard, stock on hand and all Tools, implements and all other property connected with the same. Wit: **W[m] Trimmier, John Snoddy.**

Signed, **L. Lancaster.** Registered 16th March 1849.

p. 196-197. 15 Dec 1848. Sheriff's Titles. **R.C. Poole,** Sheriff of Spartanburg Dist., to **John T. Kirby** by writ of Fieri Ficias issues out of the Court of Common Pleas, Spartanburg Dist, 20th Oct 1840 - at the suit of **Jesse Cleveland** and others commanding that of the goods, chattels, lands & tenements of **William Tracy** to levy $1,066.71 with interest, damages & costs - the Sheiff (Viz) **George Nicholls** - have taken 515 acres on the waters of Losson's Fork and bounded by **Thomas Wells, Littleton Bagwell, J.J. Boyd, Govan Mills** & others, exposed the land to sale at public vendue and purchased by **J.T. Kirby** for $839. **J.R. Poole** successor to **George Nicholls.** Wit: **H.J. Dean, John Belton Tolleson.** Signed, **R.C. Poole,** S.S.D. Witness oath, 20 March 1849: Signed, **J. Belton Tolleson** to **J.B. Tolleson,** Clk & Mag Ex iffo. Registered 20th March 1849.

p. 197-200. 3 April 1848. Deed of Conveyance. **John T. Kirby & Marcus Kirby** to **Stephen Kirby.** Whereas **Mrs. Lovicy Kirby** did on the 8th day of June A.D. 1847, make and Execute her last will and testament which has been duly admitted of Record in the ordinary office of Spartanburg Dist in which amongst other things she made the following devise and bequest Viz My wish and devise it that my Tract of Land be divided into Two Tracts Equal so as not to injure the sales of Either and sold on a Twelve months credit and the money arising from the sale by my Executors Equally divided between my three sons **John T. Kirby, Stephen Kirby** and **Marcus Kirby** - and whereas **John T. Kirby** and **Marcus Kirby** have sold to **Stephen Kirby** all their right, title and interest to the land in said last will and testament for $1,600 sold 450 acres on the south side of Packolette River, bounded by **Henry Harvy, Reubin Briant Jun, William Reid, Reubin Brian, Sr., William Webster** and others being the land owned by the said **Lovicy Kirby** in her lifetime. Wit: **James V. Trimmier, H.J. Dean.** Signed, **Jno. T. Kirby, Marcus Kirby.** Witness oath, 18 April 1848: Signed, **H.J. Dean** to **J.B. Tolleson,** Clk & Mag Ex iffo. Release of dower, 2 March 1849: Signed, **P. Kirby** (wife of **John T. Kirby**) to **H.J. Dean,** Not. Pub. & Mag. Release of Dower, 17 March 1849: Signed, **Elizabeth J. [or I.?] Kirby** (wife of **Marcus Kirby**) to **B.F. Bates,** Not. Pub. & Mag. Ex iffo. Registered 20th March 1849.

p. 200-202. 19 Mar 1849. Sheriff's Titles. **R.C. Poole,** Sheriff of Spartanburg Dist, to **Stephen Kirby** for $450 sold 100 acres on the waters of Fair Forest creek adjoining lands of **James Quinn, Stephen Kirby** and **Zachariah Kinnett.** Whereas **Stephen Kirby** in 1848 did Exhibit his petition in the court of the ordinary at Spartanburg Court House setting forth that **Ellison Mitchell** departed this life Intestate in 1847 seized and possessed in Fee (the 100 acres above) and that part and division yet remained to be made and **R. Bowden** Esq, did order and decree that the land be sold. The highest bidder was **Amy Mitchell** and afterwards she transferred her bid to **Stephen Kirby** in writing. Wit: **J.H. Wilson, J.B. Archer.** Signed, **R.C. Poole,** S.S.D. Witness oath, 19 March 1849: **J.H. Wilson** to **G.W.H. Legg,** Mag. Registered 20th March 1849.

p. 202-203. 25 Jan 1849. Deed of Conveyance. **John J. Bullington** of Spartanburg Dist, to **Larkin Ballenger** of Spartanburg Dist, for $400 sold two parcels: 408 acres on Greens Creek waters of Pacolet River part of a tract originally granted to **Daniel Sims.** Beginning on Green's Creek at the ford about Two hundred yards below the saw mill, on the road leading from Colterans to the saw mill. Also one other piece of land on the waters of Greens creek and Meadow creek containing 75 acres, bordering Greens creek, **Wills, Wm West** and **McPhearson**. Wit: **James G. Harris, W.W. Harris**. Signed, **John J. Bullington**. Witness oath, 27 Feb 1849: **W.W. Harris** to **J.W. Tucker**, Magt. Registered 20th March1849.

p. 203-205.   21 Aug 1837. Deed of Gift. I, **Reubin Newman** of Spartanburg Dist, do this day willingly and Voluntarily give by a gift in Deed to my beloved wife, **Sabra Newman**, 114 acres of Land Lying in the West which I have a right to for services Rendered in the old War, the same I do give to her and to her heirs to use occupy and Enjoy forever with every appurtenance thereto belong or any wise Incident - the same I do warrant and forever defend all my Right and Title from me, my Heirs and assigns &c - and my Daughter **Louisa Newman**, a Daughter given to me by the second Wife, I do this day designate from all the Rest of the Heirs of my body in this way that is I do this day give and by a Gift in Deed thinking it my Indispensable duty to give the following property to my said Daughter, to wit. I Give and in plain and open market deliver to her one Negro boy named **John** and one Negro Girl named **Junet**, one feather [bed omitted ?] and furniture, Two mahogany Tables to have and to Hold to her, her Heirs and assigns from me and my heirs .... notwithstanding that if my Daughter **Louisa Newman** shall die without Issue then and in that case the above named **Junet** with all her increase if any shall be Equally divided between the Heirs of my own body and their Heirs. But all the rest of the above property I have given to her to dispose of at will forever. Wit: **John Devine, Elisha (x) Stations, Spencer B. Stations**. Signed, **Reubin Newman**. Witness oath, 22 Mar 1849: Signed, **Elisha (x) Stations** to **John H. Walker**, Mag. Registered 29 March 1849.

p. 205-206.   23 Nov 1848. Deed of Conveyance. **James Briant** of Spartanburg Dist, to **Marcus D. Briant** of Spartanburg Dist, for $200 sold 100 acres, by estimation, bounded by Poteat Creek, the spring branch, **Golightly, Tirsiding Wiatt/Wyatt** and **Turner** to contain all the land on the south side of **Poteat** as Deeded to **James Briant** by **Marcus D. Briant** and by **James Dillards, Turners, Golightlys** and others. Wit: **Reubin Briant, Jaob Briant**. Signed, **James (x) Briant**. Witness oath, 2 Apr 1849: **Reubin Briant Jun.** to **J.B. Tolleson**, Clk & Mag Ex iffo. Registered Examined and Certified 2 April 1849. Original delivered to ~ **Marcus Briant**.

p. 206-207.   14 Oct 1847. Deed of Conveyance. **Wiet McHam** of Spartanburg Dist, to **Anders Floyd** of Spartanburg Dist, for $800 sold 180 acres on the North side of Tyger River on both sides of Cane Creek and bounded by the river, **A. Pruet, McCravy** and **Thos. Betterton**'s old House place. Test: **Stephen Taylor, William H. Dehay**. Signed, **Wiott McHam**. Release of dower, 22 Oct 1847: Signed, **Elizabeth (x) Mackham** to **Sum Sumner**, Mag. Witness oath, 31 March 1849: Signed, **Stephen Taylor** to **Sum Sumner**, Mag. Registered 2nd April 1849.

p. 208-209.   7 Apr 1849. Mortgage. **Peyton Turner** stands indebted to **H.H. Thomson** for $175 with interest from this day by three sealed notes of $58.33⅓ due one, two and three years from this day. For securing the aforesaid Notes, **Peyton Turner** mortgages 7 acres which he this day bought from **H.H. Thomson** lying below the stone bridge. Meets and bounds more fully appear in the reference to the Deed made by **H.H. Thomson**. Wit: **Benj. Wofford, A.R. Bryan**. Signed, **Peyton Turner**. Witness oath, 7 Apr 1849: Signed, **A.R. Bryan** to **J.W. Tucker**, Magst. Registered 7th April 1849.

p. 209-211.   25 Dec 1848. Deed of Conveyance. **John Lofits** of Spartanburg Dist, to **David & Jacob Rudesail** for $300 sold 135 acres lying on both sides of Motlows creek. Wit: **Ephraim Bonham, W.F. King.** Signed, **John Lofits.** Witness oath, 25 Dec 1848: Signed, **Ephraim Bonhom** to **James Caldwell,** Mag. S.D. Release of Dower, 9 Jan 1849: Signed, **Jane Loftis** to **James Caldwell,** J.Q. Registered 7th April 1849. Original delivered to ~~ **David Rudesail.**

p. 211-212.   18 Nov 1848. Deed of Conveyance. **William Guthrie** of Spartanburg Dist, to **G.B. Palmer** of Cleveland Co., N.C., for $60 sold 80 acres, by computation, on Rocky Fork of Thickety Creek, two corners made and established by **Guthrie Palmer** and **Vinson Sprouse** on **Palmer's** line. Test: **J.M. Thomas, Jas. Thomas.** Signed, **Wm Guthrie.** Release of dower, 3 Apr 1849: Signed, **Clementine (x) Guthrie** to **A. Bonner,** J.Q. Witness oath, 3 Apr 1849: Signed, **James Thomas** to **A. Bonner,** Mag. Registered 15th April 1849.

p. 212-213.   24 April 1849. Mortgage. **Jonathan T. Floyd** for $100 which I owe **John N. Gentry** [mortgage] the tract of land whereon I now live containing 129 acres on both sides of the Blackstock Road bounded by **John Guinn, Thomas Aikens, Sandford Smith, George Meadows** and **Henry Steddings.** Wit: **J. Belton Tolleson, R.C. Poole.** Signed, **J.T. Floyd.** Witness oath, 24 Apr 1849: Signed, **R.C. Poole** to **J.W. Tucker,** Magst. Registered 24th day of April 1849. Original delivered to ~~ **Jonathan T. Floyd.**

p. 214-215.   4 April 1846. Deed of Conveyance. **Simpson Bobo** to **Robert D. Owens** for $125 sold 1 acre and a small fraction, in the Village of Spartanburg whereon **Robert** now lives, being one half of the Lot - Extending from the street opposite **Mrs. Mullinax** to the street opposite **W.B. Seay** The division to run North & South, Robert to have the Eastern half. Wit: **Alfred Tolleson, J.W. Quinn.** Signed, **Simpson Bobo.** Witness oath, 25 Apr 1849: Signed, **Alfred Tolleson** to **J.W. Tucker,** Magst. Release of Dower, 26 Apr 1849: Signed, **Nancy H. Bobo** to **O.E. Edwards,** Notary Public. Registered 27th April 1849.

p. 215-216.   17 Jan 1849. Deed of Conveyance. **Isaac Brown** of Spartanburg Dist, to **Berry Pearce** of Spartanburg Dist, for $150 sold 40 acres, by estimation, on the south side of Pacolette River, it being a part of a Tract of Land previously owned by my Father **Ja' Brown Senr** ~ Beginning at the mouth of Richland Creek on the south side P. River, bordering **A.T. Harmon** and **John Lee.** Wit: **Capt. Ja' H. Sloan, Fulton Brown.** Signed, **Isaac Brown.** Witness oath, 15 Mar 1849: Signed, **Jas. H. Sloan** to **B.F. Bates** Not Repub Mag Ex Offco. Registered Examined and Certified 27th April 1849. Original delivered to ~~ **Berry Pearce** 13th Mar 1850.

p. 216-217.   15 Jan 1844. Deed of Conveyance. **Richard Thomson** of Spartanburg Dist, to **David Miller** of Spartanburg Dist, for $115 sold a Lot in the Village of Spartanburg, containing something over one half acre, beginning at the corner of **Luther Lewis & David Miller's** lot running North to a stone on **H.H. Thomson's** street and to a corner of a Lot **Richard Thomson** this day sold to **H.H. Thomson,** then South to a lot I heretofore sold to **David Miller.** Wit: **H.H. Thomson, Govan Mills.** Signed, **Richard Thomson.** Witness oath, 30 Apr 1849: Signed, **H.H. Thomson** to **J.B. Tolleson,** Clk & Mag Ex iffo. Registered 30th April 1849.

p. 217-219. 15 March 1849. Deed of Conveyance. **Henry Wolf** of Spartanburg Dist, to **William F. McDowell** of the same place, for $600 sold 214 acres where **Henry** lives, known as the **Guthrie** land lying on Thomson's Creek waters of Pacolett River. Wit: **G. Cannon, Henry Dood**. Signed, **Henry Wolf.** Witness oath, 16 Apr 1849: Signed, **Gabriel Cannon** to **Elias Wall**, Magt. Release of Dower, 16 Apr 1849: Signed, **Martha (x) Wolf** to **Elias Wall** , Magistrate. Registered 8th May 1849.

p. 219-220. 13 Nov 1847. Deed of Conveyance. I, **Thomas [I. or J.] Cooley** of Spartanburg Dist, to **John Heatherington** of Spartanburg Dist, for $68 sold 35 acres on both sides of Buck Creek, bounded by lands now belonging to **John Watts,** the road that leads to where **John Watts** resides, myself and **Heatherington**. Wit: **Elias Johnson, Jeremiah Giles**. Signed, **Thomas [I. or J.] Cooley.** Witness oath, 13 Dec1847: Signed, **Jeremiah Giles** to **P. W. Head**, Magt. Release of Dower, 14 Dec 1847: Signed, **Elizabeth (x) Cooley** to **P.W. Head**, Magt. Registered 8th May 1849.

p. 221. 13 Feb 1849. Mortgage. **Simpson Bobo** to more effectually secure the payment of of $1600 to **Nathaniel Gentry** payable in Two Notes one due 20th Decr next with Interest from 20th Decr last & the other due 12 months after with Interest from 20th Decr last each for $800, mortgaged 160 acres on the South Tyger River called the old **Price** plantation, being the same tract conveyed to me this day by **N. Gentry**. Wit: **J.H. Garrison, Jesse Hollis**. Signed, **Simpson Bobo**. Witness oath, 21 Apr 1849: Signed, **Jesse Hollis** to **W.H. Willbanks**, Mag. Registered 8th May 1849.

p. 222-223.   [day not given] Jul 1848. Deed of Conveyance. **A. Phelps** to **Esaw Price** of Spartanburg Dist, for $900 sold 464 acres, part of the Tract whereon **Esaw Price** now lives Including the Plantation and Mill on Thickety Creek, bordering **Willis Smith** and **A. Phelps**. Test: **Josiah McEntire, Noah Williams**. Signed, **A. Phelps**. Witness oath, 13 Dec 1848: Signed, **Josiah McEntire** to **Wm Guthrie**, Mag. Release of Dower, 13 Dec 1848: Signed, **Ann Phelps** to **Wm Guthrie**, Mag.   Registered 8th May 1849.

p. 223-224. 30 Sept 1847. Deed of Conveyance. **Robert McMurry** of Spartanburg Dist, to **John Heatherington** of Spartanburg Dist, for $28.33 sold 28⅓ acres on Buck Creek waters of Packolet River bounded by **John Heatherington** and **Robert McMurry**. Wit: **Michael Dickson, John Heatherington Jun**. Signed, **Robert (x) McMurry**. Witness oath, 7 May 1849: Signed, **John Heatherington** to **J.B. Tolleson**, Clk & Mag Ex iffo. Registered 8th May 1849.

p. 224-225. 22 Nov 1848. Deed of Gift. I, **William Phillips** of Spartanburg Dist, to **Nancy & Josaphine Phillips** for and in consideration of the natural Love and affection which I bear to my wife **Nancy Phillips** and my Daughter **Josaphine Phillips** have given them, their Executors, administrators and assigns, one grey horse, one white cow, one black cow, one Red cow, one spotted Heifer, one black heifer and a small red bull, all my stock of Hogs, Two Bedsteads and furniture and all my Household and kitchen furniture Unto them Jointly and Equally. Wit: **James M. Sarratt, L.H. Sarratt, H.G. Gaffney**. Signed, **William Phillips**. Witness oath, 21 Apr 1849: Signed **H.G. Gaffney** to **D.B.P. Moorman**, Mag.

p. 225-226. 22 Nov 1848. Deed of Gift. I, **William Phillips** of Spartanburg Dist, to **James M. &**

W.C. Phillips, in consideration of the Natural Love and affection which I bear to my Two sons Viz ~~ **James Madison** and **William Christopher Phillips** have given them the whereon I now live to have and to hold the Tract of land Jointly and Equally, their Executors, administrators and assigns forever ~~ Except that my wife **Nancy Phillips** and Daughter **Josephine Phillips** are to live on and be supported off the land during their natural lives. Test: **James M. Sarratt, L.H. Sarratt, H.G. Gaffney.** Signed, **William Phillips.** Witness oath, 21 Apr 1849: Signed, **H.G. Gaffney** to **D.P.B. Moorman**, Mag. Registered 8th May 1849.

p. 226-227.   5 June 18496 [looks like a 6 written over a 9]. Deed of Gift. I, **Elizabeth Moore** of Spartanburg Dist, for the love and affection which I have for **Robert Moore** My Grandson, Eldest son [of] **William Moore**, I give unto the said **Robert Moore** one sorrel Mare colt Two Years old this spring and also for the love and affection which I have for my Grandson **William Davis Moore** son of the same, I do give unto him one Sorrel Mare 7 years old called Martha and the Increase of the mare if any should go to my Grand Daughter **Elizabeth Moore** Daughter of the same. I do give to the above three named children one cow and yearling & one Calf and I do give unto my Three above named Grand children all my House Hold Furniture and Kitchen furniture with the exception of one Bed & furniture which I give unto my beloved son **Hugh Moore** to Execute the above Deed of Gift. Test: **G.W. Poole, Hezekiah Willis, John Moore.** Signed, **Elizabeth (x) Moore.** Witness oath, 7 May 1849: Signed, **Hezekiah Willis** to **J.B. Tolleson**, Clk & Mag Ex iffo. Registered 8th May 1849.

p. 227-230.   6 Oct 1846. Deed of Conveyance. We, **Caleb Kimbrell** & wife **Mahaly/Mahala Kimbrell** of Spartanburg Dist, for 60 acres whereon we now live sold to us by **Henry Wolf** of Spartanburg Dist, sell to **Henry Wolf** all our interest right and Title to all the lands which belonged to **George Wolf** late of Spartanburg Dist, decd, contained in two distinct tracts, on one of which **Elizabeth Wolf** widow of **George Wolf** now resides containing 250 acres bounded by **James Burnet, Zachariah Wolf, Hugh McDowell & Wilson Cantrell** ~ The other containing about 152 acres bounded by **Henry White & Wilson Cantrell** making in the whole about 402 acres, our interest being that to which we are Entitled as one of the children and Representatives or heirs at Law of **George Wolf**, being one of Eight children of **George Wolf**. Wit: **Noah Wolf, L.P. Wolf.** Signed, **Mahala (x) Kimbrell.** Witness oath, 9 Oct 1849: Signed, **Noah Wolf** to **Elias Wall**, Magt. Release of Dower, 22 Oct 1847: Signed, **Mahala (x) Kimbrell** to **Elias Wall**, Magt. 7-day declaration, 18 Dec 1848: Signed, **Mahala (x) Kimbrell** to **Elias Wall**, Magt. Registered 15th May 1849.

p. 230-232.   14 Mar 1846. Deed of Conveyance. **H.J. Dean** of Spartanburg Dist, to **William Lockwood** of Spartanburg Dist, for $600 sold something over 2 acres, being 80 yards on the street running back 140 yards in the Town of Spartanburg on the Right hand side of the street on Road leading from the Court House to **Thomson's** Mill on Lawson's Fork bounded on the East & South by **J.E. Henry** and on the West by **A.S. Camp's** Lot & on the North by the street or Road being the same Lot conveyed by **William Walker** to **H.J. Dean**. Wit: **Alfred Tolleson, John B. Archer.** Signed, **H.J. Dean.** Witness oath, 15 May 1849: Signed, **John B. Archer** to **J.B. Tolleson**, Clk & Mag Ex iffo. Release of Dower, 14 Feb 1849: Signed, **Mary Owen Dean** to **J.B. Tolleson**, Clk of the Court of Common Pleas & Mag Ex iffo. Registered Examined & Certified 15th May 1849. Original delivered to ~~ **Henry Wolf**

p. 232-233.   12 March 1846. Deed of Conveyance. **William Walker** of the **Walker** house & District and state aforesaid, to **H.J. Dean** of Spartanburg Dist, for $600 sold something over 2 acres in the Town of Spartanburg on the Right hand side of the street or Road leading from the Court House to **Thomson's** Mills on Lawson's fork, being 80 yards on the street or Road & running back 150 yards and bounded on the East & South by **James E. Henry** on the West by **A.S. Camp's** Lot & on the North by the street or Road. Wit: **G. Nicholls, G.B. Brem.** Signed, **William Walker.** Release of Dower, 14 Feb 1849: Signed, **Mary B. Walker** to **J.B. Tolleson**, Clk & Mag Ex iffo. Witness oath, 23 Dec 1848: Signed, **G.B. Brem** to **J.B. Tolleson**, Clk & Mag Ex iffo. Registered 15th May 1849.

p. 234-235.   17 Feb 1848. An Agreement. Whereas **Amy Mitchell** purchased 100 acres that was sold as the property of **Ellerson Mitchell** deceased, adjoining lands of **James Quinn** and others and having in order to comply with the Terms of the sale consented that **Stephen Kirby** should by his giving his Note to the Ordinary of Spartanburg Dist received from the sheriff the Titles of said land on condition that if she does well and truly pay a sealed Note that she has this day given **Stephen Kirby** for $436.25 due the 7th Feby next ～ then and in that case **Stephen Kirby** is to make good and sufficient Titles to the land. Wit: **J.B. Tolleson, J.N. Murray.** Signed, **Amy (x) Mitchell, Stephen Kirby.** Witness oath, 22 May 1849: Signed, **J.N. Murray** to **J.B. Tolleson**, Clk & Mag Ex iffo. Registered 22nd May 1849.

p. 235-236.   28 Mar 1842. Deed of Conveyance. **James M. Anderson** to **David Anderson** of Spartanburg Dist, for $2000 sold 50 acres, it being the shoals on the waters of North Tyger River and on the new Road, bounded on the North by **D. Anderson**, West by **W.F. Tanner.** Wit: **James Chamblin, William W. Anderson.** Signed, **James M. Anderson.** Witness oath, 23 Nov 1848: Signed, **Jas. Chamblin** to **J.C. Caldwell**, Magistrate. Registered 22nd May 1849.

p. 236-237.   21 Dec 1847. Deed of Conveyance. **James M. Anderson** of Spartanburg Dist, to **David Anderson** of Spartanburg Dist, for $2000 sold 476 acres known as the Cross Road, Poolesville and **Drummond** land on the south side of Middle Tyger River bounded on the North by Middle Tyger, South by **S.N. Evins**, West by **Chamblain**, and Northwest by **Wingard & R. Dickson.** Wit: **S.N. Evins, William W. Anderson.** Signed, **James M. Anderson.** Witness oath, 23 Dec 1848: Signed, **S.N. Evins** to **J.C. Caldwell**, Magistrate. Registered 22nd May 1849.

p. 238-239.   3 Jan 1849. Deed of Conveyance. **Thomas Peak** of Spartanburg Dist, to **Samuel McCravy** of Spartanburg Dist, for $175 sold 50 acres, it being a part of a Tract originally granted to **John Bearden** and a part of a Tract formerly of **Jethro Osheals** lying on the west side of Blackstock Road & waters of Martey's branch & Cane Creek. Wit: **Massey Peak, E.P. Smith.** Signed, **Thomas Peak.** Witness oath, 7 June 1849: Signed, **E.P. Smith** to **J.B. Tolleson**, Clk & Mag Ex iffo. Registered 7th June 1849.

239-241.   27 April 1849. Mortgage. **W.W. Boyd** is Indebted to **Doct. Albert W. Bivings** $125.36 by sealed Notes all dated 27th April 1849 & bearing Interest from date & due 1st Jany 1851 with annual payments of $31.34 being the consideration to be paid by **Boyd** for a lot in the Town of Spartanburg conveyed this day by **Bivings,** bounded on Church street, **Benj. Wofford,** southwardly half the distance of the lot which **R.D. Owens** bought of **Simpson Bobo, Bobo,** being one half of the lot which **Owens** bought of **S. Bobo.** Wit: **R.E. Cleveland, E.L. Huggin.** Signed, **W.W. Boyd.** Witness oath, 26 Apr 1849: Signed, **R.E. Cleveland** to **J.W. Tucker,** Magst. Registered 20th June 1849.

p. 241-242. 27 April 1849. Deed of Conveyance. I, **Robert D. Owen** of Spartanburg Dist, to **Doct. Albert Bivings** of Spartanburg Dist, for $75 sold one half of the Lot which I purchased of **Simpson Bobo** and conveyed by Deed to me 4th April 1846, the half hereby conveyed is the half adjoining **B. Wofford's** Lot, running southwardly on Church street half the distance of the lot, west to **Bobo's** Line, so as to be eqidistant on said back line and equally dividing the lot. Wit: **R.E. Cleveland, E.L. Huggin.** Signed, **R.D. Owen.** Witness oath, 26 April 1849: Signed, **R.E. Cleveland** to **J.W. Tucker,** Magst. Registered 20th June 1849.

p. 242-243. 23 Nov 1848. Deed of Conveyance. The Heirs of **William Wood** of Spartanburg Dist, to **James Wood** of Spartanburg Dist, for $610 sold 59 acres on the North side of Thickety creek bounded by the creek, **Camp & Richardson.** Wit: **William Norris, James Kirby.** Signed, **James Wood, Daniel D. Draper, Caroline M. Draper, William L. Wood, John H.L. Wood, L.E.T. Wood** (pr. **James Wood**), **D.L. Wood, William Littlejohn, Lucinda Littlejohn.** Witness oath, 17 April 1849: Signed, **James Kirby** to **B.F. Bates,** Not. Repub. Mag. Registered Examined & Certified 20th June 1849. Original delivered to ~ **James Wood** 14 Sept 1849.

p. 243-245. 22 March 1849. Articles of an agreement. I, **Reubin Newman Senr** of Spartanburg Dist. do agree to rent Unto **Lecil Newman & Monroe Newman** all of my land for the Term of Three years at my death and I am to receive no Rent for the term of Three years only. For the use of the land, **Lecil & Monroe** obligate themselves to leave the Plantation in good order. I, **Reubin Newman Senr** do agree that whatever corn be in my crib also whatever meat be left in my house after my dissolution to be equally divided between my wife, **Sabra Newman, Lecel Newman & Monroe Newman.** Also, I do now while in Existence do voluntarily give unto **Lecil Newman & Monroe Newman** all my Black smith Tools to be equally divided between them for their services rendered to me while on the Bed of affliction. I do agree to sell after my death a Negro Girl, **Mary,** unto my wife **Sabra Newman** for $450 and do agree to give **Sabra** one year and six months to pay the above amount. Now let it be understood that the land I have rented to **Lecil & Monroe Newman** for three years provided the Land can be sold for its Value within the Term of three years then they are under obligation to give up the land to be sold. Agreed on by **Reubin Newman Senr,** 22nd March 1849. Wit: Signed, **Elisha (x) Stattions, E. Allen.** Signed, **Reubin (x) Newman.** Witness oath, 22 Mar 1849: I, **James J. Simons** do certify that he saw **Reubin Newman Senr & Elisha Stattions** make their respective marks to their names the 22nd of March 1849. Agreement, 22 March 1849: This is to certify that I, **Lecil Newman & Monroe Newman** do obligate ourselves to put Keep & to have the Plantation in good order for the Term of Three years as the Instrument of writing calls for. Agreed on by us both. Test: **J.J. Simons.** Signed, **Lecil Newman, Monroe (x) Newman.** Witness oath, 22 June 1849: Personally came before me **E. Allen** [and] made oath that he saw **Reubin Newman Senr** sign and as his act deliver the within Lease for the use and purposes therein contained & that **Elisha Stations** together with himself in the presence of Each other witnessed the due Execution thereof. Signed, **E. Allen** to **J.B. Tolleson,** Clk & Mag Ex iffo. Registered 22nd June 1849.

p. 245-246. 6 March 1849. Deed of Conveyance. **Jesse Foster** to **Aldridge Green** for $38 sold 30½ acres on the North side of Maple Swamp waters of south Tyger River bounded by **William Choice** and **Jesse Foster**. Test: **Joseph James, William James**. Signed, **Jesse Foster**. Witness Oath, 29 June 1849: Signed, **William James** to **Isham Wood**, Mag S.D. Registered 30th June 1849.

p. 246-248.   14 March 1849. Deed of Conveyance. **M. Beshers** to **Wm S. Mills. Meredith Brashers** of Spartanburg Dist, to **William S. Mills,** of North Carolina, for $360 sold 144 acres on Mottons creek waters of south Pacolette River, a part of a Tract originally granted to **William Brashers** bearing date August 6th 1805. Wit: **William A. Mooney, William McElrath**. Signed, **Meredith (x) Brashers**. Witness oath, 26 March 1849: **William A. Mooney** to **James Caldwell**, Mag S.D. Release of Dower, 26 March 1849: Signed, **Elizabeth (x) Brashers** to **James Caldwell**, J.Q. Registered 30th June 1849.

p. 248-250. 22 July 1849. Mortgage. **Catharine Stone** of Spartanburg Dist, to **B.F. Bates, Jacob A. Walker.** I, **Catharine Stone** am the guardian of my three children **Susan Ann, Catharine Letitia & Martha Levinia** & I have given Bond to the Commissioner in Equity for Spartanburg Dist for the faithful performance of my duties as Guardian & have given as sureties to said Bond **Col. B.F. Bates & Jacob A. Walker** Esqr..... Now, I, **Catherine Stone**, for the purpose of indemnifying & holding harmless **B.F. Bates & J.A. Walker** in the Event they should by any way put to Expense, trouble, hazard or loss, this day I conveyed unto them two tracts of land, one, 211 acres assigned to me in the division of **Moses Stones** Estate, whereon I now live joining **Robert White** and **Elias Wingo**. The other, 239 acres known as the **Zealy Stone** tract joining **Henry Harvy, Mooney Harvy, John Easterwood** and others; also six Negroes, one man named **Phil, Rhodah, Ann, Sarah, Miles & Gilbert**. If **Catherine Stone** shall well and truly discharge her duties and finally release & discharge **Bates & Walker** from all liability as Bond security this conveyance shall be utterly Void and of none effect. Wit: **J.A. Lee, J.W. Tucker**. Signed, **Catherine Stone**. Witness oath, 23 July 1849: Signed, **J.A. Lee** to **R. Bowden**. Ex off. Mag. Registered 23rd July 1849.

p. 250-252. 6 Feb 1848. Deed of Conveyance. **Maj. H.J. Dean** of Spartanburg Dist, to **John Bomar Jr.** of Spartanburg Dist, for $170 sold 50 acres on the waters of Fair Forest creek, bounded by **J.T. Kirby, D. Miller's** Tan Yard lot, said **Dean**, the heirs of **E. Bomar** deceased, and **J. Bomar,** being a part of the **Tinsley** old tract. Wit: **Maj. James Edward Henry, William A. Moore**. Signed, **H.J. Dean**. Witness oath, 25 July 1849: Signed, **James Edward Henry** to **J.B. Tolleson**, Clk & Mag Ex iffo. Release of Dower, 22 May 1849: Signed, **Mary Owen Dean** to **J.B. Tolleson,** Clk & Mag Ex iffo. Registered 23rd July 1849.

p. 252-253. 11 June 1848. Deed of Conveyance. **John H. Davis**, acting Executor of **John Black** Decd of Laurens Dist, S.C., to **Woodward Allen** of Spartanburg Dist, for $600.06 sold 243 acres adjoining **Col. Isaac Smith, Elias Wingo, Woodward Allen** & others, near the Cedar Springs it being formerly belonging to the Estate of **William E. Black & John Black,** Decd. It being the land sold by **John H. Davis** as Executor at public auction Exclusive of the Lots & Houses sold to **Elias Wingo** 6th Dec 1847, at Spartanburg Court House. Wit: **William A. Todd, J.H. Irby**. Signed, **John H. Davis**, acting Exr. Est. **J. Black,** Decd. Witness oath, 26 July 1849: Signed, **William A. Todd** to **J.B. Tolleson**, Clk & Mag Ex iffo. Registered Examined & certified 23rd July 1849. Original delivered to ~~ **Woodward Allen.**

p. 253-255. [No day] June 1848. Deed of Conveyance. **J.W. Tucker** of Spartanburg Dist, to **H.H. Thomson & J. Waddy Thomson** of Spartanburg & Union Dists, for $250 sold 59 acres called the **Neighbors** tract which I bought at Public auction from the Executors of **R. Thomson** Decd, on Lawsons Fork creek. Wit: **Govan Mills, Revd. Benj. Wofford.** Signed, **J.W. Tucker.** Witness oath, 23 July 1849: Signed, **Benj. Wofford** to **J.B. Tolleson**, Clk & Mag Ex iffo. Release of Dower, 23 July 1849: Signed, **Emily A. Tucker** to **J.B. Tolleson**, Clk & Mag Ex iffo. Registered Examined & certified 23rd July 1849. Original delivered to ~~ **H.H. Thomson.**

p. 255-257. [no day] June 1838. Deed of Conveyance. **J.W. Tucker** of Spartanburg Dist, to **J. Waddy Thomson** of Spartanburg Dist, for $1525 sold 155 acres partly within the Incorporated limits of the Town of Spartanburg being the tract I purchased at the sale of the real estate of **R. Thomson** Decd, bounded by a small branch near Chinquepin creek and Chinquepin creek. Wit: **Govan Mills, Revd. Benj. Wofford.** Signed, **J.W. Tucker.** Witness oath, 23 July 1849: **Benj. Wofford** to **J.B. Tolleson**, Clk & Mag Ex iffo. Release of Dower, 23 July 1849: Signed, **Emily A. Tucker** to **J.B. Tolleson**, Clk & Mag Ex iffo. Registered 23rd July 1849.

p. 257-260. [no day] June 1848. Deed of Conveyance. **J.W. Tucker** to **H.H. Thomson** of Spartanburg Dist, for $2931 sold (5) tracts in Spartanburg Dist and (1) in Union Dist. In Spartanburg Dist: (1) 91 acres called the **Crocker** Tract on the Wills Road, bounded by **Chapman;** (2) 180 acres called the **Bagwell** Tract N° 1; (3) 97 acres, **Bagwell** Tract N° 2 bounded by **Bagwell** Tract N° 1; (4) 131 acres, **Bagwell** Tract N° 3, bounded by **David Thomson,** a branch on the Cane Brake Track, **Bagwell** Tract N° 2; and (5) 600 acres called the **Spratt** Tract bounded by Colter's Ford Road near **Hine's** Fence, across a branch of Peter's Creek, crossing the Furnace Road and a branch of Caseys Creek. In Union Dist: 79 acres on Broad River called the **Bankhead** Tract, bounded by **Hamilton,** being the whole of the **Bankhead** tract which **R. Thomson** Decd, seized and possessed of Except one acre on the west side of Broad River including the banks & ferry known as **Howels** ferry as deeded by **Richard Thomson** to **H.H. Thomson** which deed is proven & recorded at York Court House. Wit: **Govan Mills, Benj. Wofford.** Signed, **J.W. Tucker.** Witness oath, [no day] June 1848: Signed, **Benj. Wofford** to **J.B. Tolleson**, Clk & Mag Ex iffo. Release of Dowerm 23 June 1849: Signed, **Emily A. Tucker** to **J.B. Tolleson**, Clk & Mag Ex iffo. Registered Examined & certified 23rd July 1849. Original delivered to ~~ **H.H. Thomson.**

p. 260-261. 15 Feb 1848. Deed of Conveyance. **Reubin Briant Jun.** of Spartanburg Dist., to **Joab Briant** of Spartanburg Dist, for $326 sold 270 acres on the North side of Peters creek, the land deeded to me by **John Vandiver,** bounded by **Turner,** Titiless, **Thomson.** Wit: **M.D. Briant, Enoch Chapman.** Signed, **Reubin Briant Jr.** Witness oath, 16 July 1849: Signed, **M.D. Briant** to **J.B. Tolleson**, Clk & Mag Ex iffo. Registered Examined & certified 23 July 1849. Original delivered to ~~ **Joab Bryant**

p.261-262. 7 June 1849. Mortgage. **Asail Littlefields** of Spartanburg Dist, to **Samuel Gentry** of Spartanburg Dist, for $500 sold about 75 acres NW of **John H. Walker's** school house, **Walker's** spring branch, Camp branch, bordering lands of **John H. Walker, Jesse Cooper, Willis Layton,**

J.E. Casey and **William Littlefields**. Nevertheless if **Asail Littlefieds** pays unto **Samuel Gentry** $500 on the 1st day of January 1852 this deed shall be utterly Void. Test: **John H. Walker, F.N. Walker**. Signed, **Asail Littlefields**. Witness oath, 7 June 1849: Signed, **F.N. Walker** to **John H. Walker**, Mag. Registered 23rd July 1849.

p. 262-264.   2 July 1849. Sheriff's Titles. By virtue of a Writ of Fieri Facias issued out of the court of common pleas of Spartanburg Dist, tested on the 19th of March 1836 at the suit of **John Moore & Co.** commanding me to levy $122.80 with Interest, damages and costs on the Lands and tenements of **Hugh Caldwell**. After seizure the premises exposed to sale at public vendue and sold to the highest bidder. I, **R.C. Poole**, Sheriff of Spartanburg Dist, to **James M. Nesbitt** of Spartanburg Dist, for $5 sold 100 acres on the waters of the Tyger River near Nazareth meeting House adjoining lands of **J.H. Vandike, Robert Murray, William H. Caldwell** & land where **James Cowin** Lived at time of his decease. Wit: **H.C. Poole, J.E. Wooten**. Signed, **R.C. Poole**, S.S.D. Witness oath, 2 July 1849: Signed, **H.C. Poole** to **R. Bowden**, Ex off Mag. Registered 23 July 1849.

p. 264-265.   1 Aug 1849. Deed of Conveyance. **Sabra Rodes** of Spartanburg Dist, to **Jesse Casey** of Spartanburg Dist, for $200 sold 150 acres on Two Mile creek of Enoree river bounded by **James Rodes, William Rodes** and **Sabra Rodes**, plat annexed. Test: **William W. Crow, William Watson**. Signed, **Sabra (x) Rodes**. Witness oath, 4 Aug 1849: Signed, **William W. Crow** to **John H. Walker**, Mag. Registered Examined & certified 6th August 1849. Original delivered to ~~ **Jesse Casey** June [date incomplete]

p. 265-266.   20 Sept 1848. Deed of Conveyance. **Joseph Brown** of Spartanburg District to **Hiram M. Wakefield** of Spartanburg Dist, for $260 sold 52 acres on North bank of South Tyger River. Wit: **Young Wood, James Leonard**. Signed, **Joseph Brown**. Witness oath, 21 July 1849: Signed, **James Leonard** to **Mark Bennett**, Magt. Release of Dower, 13 Nov 1848: Signed, **Mary (x) Brown** to **J.B. Tolleson**, Clk & Mag Ex iffo. Registered Examined & certified 6th August 1849. Original delivered to ~~ **H.M. Wakefield**.

p. 266-268.   6 Aug 1849. Mortgage. I, **George Horton** of Spartanburg Dist, for and in consideration of procuring Indulgence on a Note which I owe to **E.S.E. Chambers** for about $34 principle & Int for a Note my father **Nimrod Horton** owes him & also for a Deed which **Chambers** holds against the Tract of land on which I now live given to him by my father **Nimrod Horton** containing 160 acres lying on the waters of Ashworths creek bounded by **Henry Rupp** and others; and for securing the payment of the Note & Deed upon the same piece of land and whereas my father has also made me a Title to the same land, I by these presents Mortgage unto the **E.S.E. Chambers** all my right Title & Interest in the land. Wit: **John Linder, William Guthrie**. Signed, **George Horton**. Witness oath, 6 Aug 1849: Signed, **John Linder** to **J.B. Tolleson**, Clk & Mag Ex iffo. Registered Examined & certified 6th August 1849. Original delivered to ~~ **Matison Patterson**, 18th August 1850.

p. 268- 269.   6 Nov 1848. Deed of Conveyance. **Robert Dobson** of Spartanburg Dist, to **Randolph Wood** of Polk Co., N.C., for $100 sold 100 acres by estimate, on the head waters of Wolf creek waters of North Pacolet River. Wit: **James Caldwell, Arestus Callaway**. Signed, **Robert (x) Dobson**. Witness oath, 22 Dec 1848: Came **Erastus Callaway** and made oath but Signed, **A.**

Callaway to **James Caldwell** Mag S.D. Registered Examined & certified 6th August 1849. Original delivered to ~~ **Robert Dobson** by __?__ 29 Oct 1851.

p. 269-270.   28 June 1849. Deed of Conveyance.   **B.M. Gramling** and **Mary Gramling** of Spartanburg Dist, to **William White** of Spartanburg Dist, for $800 sold supposed to be about 300 acres, where **James Moore** now lives. Bordered by Howard Gap road, **Golightly, Gault & Ballenger**, north bank of Lawsons fork near **Ballengers** shop, to the mouth of **Presley Ballengers** still House branch. Wit: **J.H. Garrison, A. Gilmore.** Signed, **B.M. Gramling, Mary (x) Gramling.** Witness oath, 6 Aug 1849: Signed, **J.H. Garrison** to **J.B. Tolleson**, Clk & Mag Ex iffo. Registered 6th August 1849.

p. 271-272.   4 Aug 1849. Deed of Conveyance. **Sirpatin Tinsley** of Spartanburg Dist, to **Eber Tinsley** of Spartanburg Dist, for $200 sold 105 acres on both sides of the shoaly fork of the North fork of Tyger River part of the original grant to **John Tucker** in 1805. Wit: **James K. Dickson, William Tinsley.** Signed, **Sirpatin Tinsley.** Witness oath, 6 Aug 1849: Signed, **William Tinsley** to **J.B. Tolleson**, Clk & Mag Ex iffo. Registered 6th August 1849.

p. 272-273. 6 Aug 1849. Mortgage. I, **George Horton** for procuring Indulgence upon a Note which I owe **John Linder** for $21 it being the balance of a mortgage which my father gave to **John Linder** for 160 acres where I now live; and for securing the payment of the original Mortgage given to **John Linder** on the same land & whereas my father also made me a Title to the same land, I have mortgaged unto **John Linder** all my right Title & Interest to the land lying on the waters of Ashley's creek and I pay off the balance, all interests and costs by the 25th day of December next then this obligation to be void & of no effect. Wit: **Alberry Cannon, Edward Lipscomb.** Signed, **George Horton.** Witness oath, 6 Aug 1849: Signed, **Edward Lipscomb** to **William Guthrie**, Mag. Registered 6th August 1849.

p. 273-275.   23 Oct 1840. Deed of Conveyance. **William Page** of Spartanburg Dist, to **Joseph Foster** of Union Dist, S.C., for $400 sold 426 acres, by estimation, on both sides of Beaver Dam creek, a branch of South Pacolet River one part of which includes the farm where **William Page** lives, originally granted by patent bearing date Nov. 5th 1771 unto **Abigail Tenail** for 150 acres; the other a part of survey joining the same- granted unto me patent bearing date Nov 6th 1779 for 483 acres. Reference to the Journal conveyances will make the Title more fully appear. Wit: **Rufus W. Folger, William Smith.** Signed, **William (x) Page.** Witness oath, 7 Aug 1849: Signed, **R.W. Folger** to **J.B. Tolleson**, Clk & Mag Ex iffo. Release of Dower, 3 Nov 1840: Signed, **Elizabeth (x) Page** to **Daniel White**, J.Q. Registered 7th August 1849.

p. 275-276.   24 Aug 1849. Deed of Conveyance. **John Hall** of Forsyth Co., N.C., to **William Carver** of Spartanburg Dist, for $100 for a ½ acre lot in the Village of Spartanburg, over the Branch on south side of the main street opposite **Col. R.C. Poole** Lot. Wit: **J.V. Trimmier, J. Belton Tolleson.** Signed, **John Hall.** Witness oath, 4 Aug 1849: Signed, **J. Belton Tolleson** to **J.B. Tolleson**, Clk & Mag Ex iffo. Registered Examined & certified 24 August 1849. Original delivered to ~~ **J.V. Trimmier.**

p. 276-277. 8 Aug 1849. Deed of Conveyance. **Edward W. Ballenger** of Spartanburg Dist, to **Absolem Lancaster** of Spartanburg Dist, for $300 sold 184 acres on the south side of Alexander's creek and a public road. Wit: **J.G. Harris, William Gowen.** Signed, **Edward W. Ballenger.** Witness oath, 16 Aug 1849: Signed, **J.G. Harris** to **James Caldwell,** Mag. S.D. Registered Examined & certified 28th August 1849. Original delivered to ~ **Absolem Lancaster.**

p. 277-278. 25 Aug 1849. Deed of Conveyance. **John Bomar Jr** of Spartanburg Dist, to **John T. Kirby** of Spartanburg Dist, for $82 sold 8 acres and about 1/10 by survey made by **Col. W.W. Harris,** on the west side Road leading from Spartanburg C.H. to **Ralph Smiths;** it being a part of the land which **J.T. Kirby** sold to **G.W. Bomar** and **G.W. Bomar** sold to said **John Bomar.** Wit: **James F.V. Legg, William Petty.** Signed, **John Bomar Jr.** Witness oath, 25 Aug 1849: Signed, **James F.V. Legg** to **George W.H. Legg,** Magst. Registered 28th August 1849.

p. 279-280. 23 Aug 1849. Mortgage. **A.F. Golding** has given to **John Pickenpack** three sealed Notes each calling for $733.33⅓ due one, two & three years from the 26th December next with Interest to be paid annually. For securing payment of the notes **A.F. Golding** mortgages to **John Pickenpack** the lot bought this day from **John Pickenpack** 3 acres in the Town of Spartanburg bordered by **J. Waddy Thomson.** Wit: **W.W. Harris, H.H. Thomson.** Signed, **A.F. Golding.** Witness oath, 1 Sept 1849: Signed, **H.H. Thomson** to **J.B. Tolleson,** Clk & Mag Ex iffo. Registered 1st Sept. 1849.

p. 280-281. 10 May 1849. Deed of Conveyance. **John Thomas** of Spartanburg Dist, to **Joseph P. Thomas** of Spartanburg Dist, for $135 sold 60 acres on the long branch of Thickety creek waters of Broad river bordering **F. Guthrie, L. Linder & Stephen Bridges** old line. Wit: **Rowland Cash, William Moore.** Signed, **John (x) Thomas.** Witness oath, 10 May 1849: Signed, **Rowland Cash** to **William Guthrie,** Mag. Registered Examined & certified 3rd Sept. 1849. Original delivered to ~~ **John Thomas.**

p. 281-282. 10 May 1849. Deed of Conveyance. **John Thomas** of Spartanburg Dist, to **W.G. Thomas** for $297 sold 148 ¾ acres on the long Branch of Thickoty creek waters of Broad River. Wit: **Rowland Cash, William Moore.** Signed, **John (x) Thomas.** Witness oath, 10 May 1849: Signed, **William Moore** to **William Guthrie,** Mag. Registered Examined & certified 3 Sept. 1849. Original delivered to ~~ **John Thomas.**

p. 282-284. 4 March 1841. Deed of Conveyance. **Stephen Bridges** of Spartanburg Dist, to **John Thomas** for $200 sold 138 acres waters of Broad River Branches of Thickoty creek. Wit: **William Guthrie, James Thomas.** Signed, **Stephen (x) Bridges.** Witness oath, 28 Jan 1842: Signed, **William Guthrie** to **W.B. Turner,** Mag. Release of Dower, 2 Jan 1844: Signed, **Jane (x) Bridges** to **John Bridges,** Mag. Registered Examined & certified 3rd Sept. 1849. Original delivered to ~~ **John Thomas.**

p. 284-285. 26 March 1849. Deed of Conveyance. **Elihu P. Smith** of Spartanburg Dist, to **John N. Miller** of Spartanburg Dist, for $138 sold 23 acres on the waters of Dutchmans creek bordered by **Thomas Peak** and **James Hamm.** Wit: **Elijah Jennings, W.F. Smith.** Signed, **Elihu P. Smith.**

Witness oath, 5 May 1849: Signed, **W.F. Smith** to **H. Wofford**, Mag. Release of Dower, 5 May 1849: Signed, **Christina Smith** to **Harvy Wofford**, Mag. Registered 3rd Sept. 1849.

p. 285-287. 24 Aug 1849. Mortgage. **William Carver**, of Spartanburg Dist, made promissory notes to **John Hall** of Forsyth Co., N.C., $100 in two installments of $50 each, twelve months and two years after date, both with Interest from date; Notes annexed to this deed for ½ acre in the Village of Spartanburg over the branch on the south side of main street, opposite **Col. R.C. Poole's** lot, the SE corner and runs with the street. Wit: **J.V. Trimmier, J. Belton Tolleson.** Signed, **William Carver.** Witness oath, 5 Sept 1849: Signed, **J.V. Trimmier** to **J.B. Tolleson**, Clk & Mag Ex iffo. Registered Examined & certified 5 Sept. 1849. Original delivered to ~ **Col. W.W. Harris.**

p. 287-288. 25 May 1847. Deed of Conveyance. **Henry Howe** of Spartanburg Dist, to **William D. Howe,** Planter of Spartanburg Dist, for $50 sold 50 acres bounded per recent survey by **Henry Howe, Joseph Thomson & William D. Howe.** Wit: **William Logan, J.J. Howe.** Signed, **Henry Howe.** Witness oath, 27 Oct 1847: Signed, **J.J. Howe** to **Thomas Ballenger**, Mag. (Note in margin: Dower recorded Book M.M. page 418) Registered 5 Sept. 1849.

p. 288-290.   9 June 1848. Deed of Conceyance. **H.H. Thomson, Junius W. Thomson & J. Waddy Thomson**, Executors of **Richard Thomson** Decd, by authority of the will of **R. Thomson** and a decree of the Court of Equity for Spartanburg Dist in the case of **Govan Mills** & wife and others against **H.H. Thomson** and others, did, after duly advertising, sold the following tracts of land at public outcry: (1) A 150 acre tract called the **Cleveland** tract partly in the Incorporate limits of the Town of Spartanburg on Chinquepin Creek, sold to **J.W. Tucker** for $1525; and   (2) The **Neighbors** tract, 59 acres on bank of Lawson's [Fork?] sold to **J.W. Tucker** for $250. Wit: **Revd. Benj. Wofford, John Linder.** Signed, **H.H. Thomson, J. Waddy Thomson, J.W. Thomson,** as Executors of **Rich. Thomson** Decd. & by the Court of Equity. Witness oath, 5 Sept 1849: Signed, **Benj. Wofford** to **J.B. Tolleson**, Clk & Mag Ex iffo. Registered Examined & certified 5th Sept. 1849. Original delivered to ~ **H.H. Thomson.**

p. 290-293.   9 June 1848. Deed of Conveyance. **H.H. Thomson, Junius Thomson, W. Thomson & J. Waddy Thomson,** the Executors of **Richard Thomson** Decd, by the will of **R. Thomson** Decd, and a decree of the Court of Equity for Spartanburg Dist in the case of **Govan Mills** & wife and others against **H.H. Thomson** and others, did duly advertise and sold at public outcry the following tracts of land which were owned by **Richard Thomson** at the time of his death: (1) The **Crocker** tract, 91 acres, bounded by the Well's Road and **Chapman** Tract, sold for $171 to **J.T. Kirby** and transferred to **J.W. Tucker** of Spartanburg Dist; (2) The **Bagwell** Tract N° 1, 180 acres, which was bid off by **J.W. Tucker** for $65;. (3) The **Bagwell** Tract N° 2, 97 acres, bid off by **Jacob Zimmerman** and transferred to **J.W. Tucker,** for $37;. (4) The **Bagwell** Tract N° 3, 131 acres bounded by **David Thomson,** bid off by **J. Zimmerman** for $536 which bid was transferred to **J.W. Tucker.** The boundaries of all the above tracts, in Spartanburg Dist, will more fully appear by Plats made by **Geo. Nichols & A.S. Camp** under order of the Court of Equity. (5) The **Spratt** Tract, in Spartanburg Dist, 600 acres, bounded by South side Coulter ford Road near **Hine's** fence, crossing a branch of Peter's creek and furnace road and branch of Casey's creek, bid off by **J.W. Tucker** for $300; (6) The **Bankhead** tract in Union Dist on Broad River adjoining **Hamilton** and containing all of the **Bankhead** tract which **R. Thomson** owned, except an acre which includes the west bank of **Howels** ferry as Deeded by **Richard Thomson** to **H.H. Thomson** at York Court House, by reference to the deed will more fully appear and leaving 79 acres bid by **J.W. Tucker** for $1202. Wit: **Benj. Wofford, John Linder.** Signed, **H.H. Thomson, J. Waddy Thomson, J.W. Thomson,** as Executors of **R. Thomson** and by order of the court of Equity. Witness oath, 5 Sept 1849: Signed, **Benj. Wofford** to **J.B. Tolleson,** Clk & Mag Ex iffo. Registered Examined & certified 5 Sept. 1849. Original delivered to ~~ **H.H. Thomson.**

p. 293-294.   24 Jan 1849. Deed of Conveyance. **Elihu P. Smith** of Spartanburg Dist, to **Robert Morrow** of Spartanburg Dist, for $365.42 sold 44 acres on the East side of Dutchmans Creek branch waters of Tyger River bounded on the SW by **Robert Morrow,** NW by **Thomas Peak** and on the N & E & SE by **E.P. Smith.** Wit: **R. Bowden, William Smith.** Signed, **Elihu P. Smith.** Witness oath, 24 Jan 1849: **R. Bowden** to **H.J. Dean,** Not. Pub. & Mag. Ex off. Release of Dower, 3 Feb 1849: Signed, **Christina Smith** to **Sum Sumner,** Mag. Registered 5 Sept 1849.

p. 295-296.   19 May 1844. Deed of Conveyance. **James N. Pearson** of Spartanburg Dist, to **William Logan** as Trustee of **William Daniel Howe** & **Honoria E.M.,** his wife as per marriage settlement in the state aforesaid & recorded in Charleston Dist., sold for $340, where I now reside, 126 acres which was conveyed to me by the Commissioner in Equity for Spartanburg Dist, **H.J. Dean Esq.** on 2 Aug 1844, as per plat in clerks office in Spartanburg; bounded by **Joseph Thomson, Henry Howe** and others. Wit: **P.S. Montgomery, Peggy Montgomery.** Signed, **James N. Pearson.** Receipt of payment witnessed by **A. Davis.** Signed, **James N. Pearson.** Witness oath, 23 Oct 1845: Signed, **P. S. Montgomery, Peggy Montgomery** to **John Montgomery,** J.P. Release of Dower, 23 Oct 1845: Signed, **Rebecca (x) Pearson** to **John Montgomery,** J.P. Registered 5 Sept. 1849.

p. 296-298.   29 Aug 1849. Mortgage. **Amy Mitchell** & **J.J. Quinn** stands indebted to **Stephen Kirby** for $500 with Interest in three notes, one note for $100 due 1st February 1850, $200 due on each 1st day of January 1851 & 1852. For securing the payment of the notes they mortgage the land which they bought this day from **Stephen Kirby,** the 100 acres where **Ellerson Mitchell** lived at the time of his death. Wit: **J.B. Tolleson, N.M. Quinn.** Signed, **Amy (x) Mitchell, J.J. Quinn.** Witness oath, 29 Aug 1849: Signed, **N.M. Quinn** to **J.B. Tolleson,** Clk & Mag Ex iffo. Registered 5th Sept. 1849.

p. 298.   29 Aug 1849. Dower. **Amy Mitchell** the wife of **Ellison Mitchell** deceased, released to **Stephen Kirby** her Interest & Estate in the tract of land whereon her husband **Ellison Mitchell** lived at the time of his death, the same being sold by the Ordinary of Spartanburg Dist and she became the purchaser of the same and failing to comply with the Terms of the sale transferred her bid to **Stephen Kirby** also all her right and claim of Dower. Signed **Amy (x) Mitchell** to **J.B. Tolleson,** Clk & Mag Ex iffo. Registered 5th Sept. 1849.

p. 298-299.   11 May 1849. Sheriff's Titles. **R.C. Poole** Sheriff of Spartanburg Dist, to **H.H. Thomson** sold 70 acres for $15. A writ of fieri facias Issued out of the Court of Common pleas held 13 Oct 1849 at the suit of **Alexander Flemming,** commanding that the goods chattels & tenements of **Gilbert Flemming** be sold to levy the sum of $5 also $50 damages & costs. The Sheriff seized, advertised and sold 70 acres on the waters of Fair Forest creek bounded by **J.C. Zimmerman** and others. Wit: **T.O.P. Vernon, J.V. Trimmier.** Signed, **R.C. Poole,** SSD. Witness oath, 8 Sept 1849: Signed, **J.V. Trimmier** to **J.B. Tolleson,** Clk & Mag Ex iffo. Registered Examined and certified 8th Sept. 1849. Original delivered to ~~ **H.H. Thomson.**

p. 300-301. 3 Sept 1849. Deed of Conveyance. Executors of the last Will & Testament of **Richard Thomson, H.H. Thomson, J. Waddy Thomson & Junius W. Thomson,** in obedience to the order of the Court of Equity for Spartanburg Dist made in the case of **G. & C. Mills** and their wives against the Executors of **Richard Thomson** deceased. This day the land was exposed to public outcry for sale at the risk[?] of the former purchaser and the **Turner** tract, 86 acres on the waters of Lawson's Fork was sold to **James W. Tucker** for $366. The land adjoins **Jane Martin** and R. **Thomson's** homestead Tract. Wit: **George W.H. Legg, J.B. Tolleson.** Signed, **H.H. Thomson, J. Waddy Thomson, J.W. Thomson,** Executors of the Estate of **Richard Thomson.** Witness oath, 8 Sept 1849: Signed, **G.W.H. Legg** to **J.B. Tolleson,** Clk & Mag Ex iffo. Registered Examined and certified 8th Sept. 1849. Original delivered to ~~ **H.H. Thomson.**

p. 301-302.   20 Aug 1849. Deed of Conveyance. **Hamilton Bishop** of Spartanburg Dist, to **Pinckney Bishop** of Spartanburg Dist, for $92 sold 87½ acres on the E side of the Boiling Springs Road, bounded by **R. Moss, D. Dantzler** and W side of Howard Gap Road. Wit: **R. Bowden, J.B. Tolleson.** Signed, **Hamilton Bishop.** Witness oath, 10 Sept 1849: Signed, **R. Bowden** to **J.B. Tolleson,** Clk & Mag Ex iffo. Registered 10th Sept. 1849.

p. 302-304.   5 June 1849. Mortgage. **Simpson Bobo** is indebted to **Tho' O. P. Vernon,** Commissioner of the Court of Equity by three single bills, each for $1,165 due each 1st January 1850, 1851 & 1852, with interest, from date on each, to wit, 6th June, 1849 (total $3,495). **Bobo** mortgages 3 acres which is Lot N° 1, including the hotel house, Kitchen house, orchard &c., in the Village of Spartanburg bounded on the west by Church street, south by Main street, east by Lot N° 4, and north by Lot N° 2. Wit: **G. Nichols, J.B. Tolleson.** Signed, **Tho. O.P. Vernon,** C.E.S.D. **S. Bobo.** Witness oath, 10 Sept 1849: Signed, **J.B. Tolleson** to **R. Bowden.** Registered 10th Sept. 1849.

p. 304-305.   [day & month not given] 1849. Deed of Conveyance. **William C. Bennet** of Spartanburg Dist, to **J.W. Tucker** of Spartanburg Dist, for $17.50 sold ½ acres in Spartanburg Village on the West side of what is called the Tan Yard on Greenville branch, South side of Greenville Road, bounded by **J.B. Tolleson's** Lot and **Carver.** Wit: **James G. Harris, A.J.W. Land.** Signed, **W.C. Bennett.** Witness oath, 10 Sept 1849: Signed, **J.G. Harris** to **J.B. Tolleson,** Clk & Mag Ex iffo. Registered 10 Sept. 1849.

p. 305-306. 3 Sept 1849. Deed of Conveyance. Executors of **Richard Thomson, H.H. Thomson, J. Waddy Thomson & Junius W. Thomson,** by the authority given us under **R. Thomson's** will, advertised & sold at public outcry, the **Larcan Carden** tract to the highest bidder, **J.W. Tucker** of Spartanburg Dist, for $305. Land, 500 acres on south side of Sholey creek bounded by **Nathan Center, Guignard, Burnett,** the original line of the grant. Wit: **G.W.H. Legg, J.B. Tolleson.** Signed, **H.H. Thomson, J. Waddy Thomson, J.W. Thomson,** Executors of **Richard Thomson.**

Witness oath, 8 Sep 1849: Signed, **G.W.H. Legg** to **J.B. Tolleson**, Clk & Mag Ex iffo.Registered 10th Sept. 1849. Original delivered to ~ **H.H. Thomson**.

p. 306-308.   1 Sept 1849. Deed of Conveyance. **Robert Rakestraw** of Spartanburg Dist, to **David West** of Spartanburg Dist, for $500 sold 63 acres & 3/10 on North side of Fair Forest creek. Wit: **Alvan Lancaster, Mack D. Goodwin**. Signed, **Robert (x) Rakestraw**. Witness oath, 1 Sept 1849: Signed, **Alvan Lancaster** to **H. White**, Mag. Release of Dower, 3 Sept 1849: Signed, **Sarah (x) Rakestraw** to **Hiram White**, Mag. Registered 10 Sept. 1849. Origianal delivered to ~~ **David West**.

p. 308-309.   18 Sept 1848. Deed of Conveyance. **H.H. Thomson** of Spartanburg Dist, to **William Carver** of Spartanburg Dist, for $40 sold a Lot in the Town of Spartanburg, a 1 acre Lot lying near the Tan Yard Branch, N° 15 in the Plat under which Sheriff **Nichols** sold as belonging to the Estate of **William Poole** Decd, and sold under an Execution in favor of **H.H. Thomson** assignee vs. **Thomas Poole**. **H.H. Thomson** binds himself his heirs and all persons whomsoever Lawfully claiming the same or any part thereof (Except **Jane Poole**). Wit: **William Petty, J.W. Martin**. Signed, **H.H. Thomson**. Witness oath, 10 Sept 1849: Signed, **William Petty** to **J.B. Tolleson**, Clk & Mag Ex iffo. Release of Dower, 22 May 1849: Signed, **M.E. Thomson** to **J.B. Tolleson**, Clk & Mag Ex iffo. Registered 10th Sept. 1849. [Jane Poole for wood. See pages 30-31]

p. 309-310.   6 Aug 1849. Mortgage. **George Hannah** of Spartanburg Dist, is Indebted to **R. Bowden** Ordinary of Spartanburg Dist, for $1199.75, and mortgages 242 acres on the waters of the Enoree River, adjoining **John Lanford, James Rhodes** and others; sold on the 6th day of August 1849 as the real Estate of **Jonathan Crow** Decd by order of the Court of Ordinary for partition and division. If **George Hannah** pays before 6th day of August next, the Deed to **R. Bowden** Court of the Ordinary, the Deed is null and void. Wit: **William Lipscomb Sr, J. Belton Tolleson**. Signed, **George Hannah**. August 6th 1849, Recd. on the within bond $25.50 in part of the same (costs). Signed, **R. Bowden**, O.S.D. Witness oath, 10 Sept 1849: Signed, **J. Belton Tolleson** to **J.B. Tolleson**, Clk & Mag Ex iffo. Registered 10th Sept. 1849.

p. 311-312.   31 Dec 1847. Deed of Conveyance. **William Smith** of Spartanburg Dist, to **Wiley D. Wood** of Spartanburg Dist, for $114 sold 28½ acres on both sides of Maple swamp Creek bounded by **William Smith** and myself [?]. Wit: **James K. Dickson, Robert B. Wood**. Signed, **William Smith**. Witness oath, 6 Sept 1849: Signed, **R.B. Wood** to **Isham Wood** Mag S.D. Registered 14 Sept. 1849.

p. 312-313.   26 June 1849. Deed of Conveyance. **John Weaver & Aley Weaver** of Spartanburg Dist, to **Jeremiah Martin** for $113 sold 113 acres lying on Each side of the Road that leads from Coulters ford to Rutherford Court House, known as the land of **Shadrick Weaver**, 80 acres that's coming to his Two Grandsons, **John Weaver** and **Jacob Weaver** and 33 acres of **Sarah Weaver's** that is hers her Lifetime joining **Youngs, Cantrell's** and **Martins**. Wit: **Fielden Turner, Andrew B. Martin**. Signed, **John (x) Weaver, Aley (x) Weaver**. Witness oath, 14 Sep 1849: Singed, **Andrew B. Martin** to **A. Bonner** Mag. Registered 14th Sept. 1849.

p. 313-314.   12 Feb 1849. Deed of Conveyance. **Thomas Gist** of Union Dist, S.C., to **Jacob Price**

of Spartanburg Dist, for $132 sold 176 acres by computation, on branch of Island Creek waters of Packolet River & in Spartanburg Dist, bounded by **Henderson Cash**. Test: **Robert Scruggs, Esaw Price**. Signed, **Thomas Gist**. Witness oath, 14 Sept 1849: Singed, **Robert Scruggs** to **A. Bonner**, Mag. Registered Examined and certified 14th Sept. 1849.
Original delivered to ~ **Jacob Price** 16 Jany. 1850.

p. 314-315.   26 March 1849. Deed of Conveyance. **William Tucker** of Greenville Dist, S.C., to **James Adkins** of Spartanburg Dist, for $150 sold 130 acres on waters of Middle Tyger River, a part of the 255 acre tract granted to **Robert Spence**. Wit: **F.M. Adkins, J.M. Adkins**. Signed, **William Tucker**. Witness oath, 8 Sept 1849: Signed, **F.M. Atkins** to **James Caldwell** Mag. S.D. Registered 14th Sept. 1849. Original delivered to ~ [one name written over another] 30 Jany 1850.

p. 315-316.   7 May 1849. Deed of Conveyance. **Daniel Atkins** of Spartanburg Dist, to **James Atkins** of Spartanburg Dist, for $125 sold 130 acres, by estimation, on branch waters of Middle Tyger River on the Greenville line, bounded by **Pruit/Prewit, William Beshers,** part of a tract of land conveyed from **William Tucker** to **J.C. Martin** and **W.H. Campbell**, part of a survey granted to **Andrew Cannon** and from him to **John Spence** and from him to **William Tucker** and from him to **Jury[Iury?] H. Martin & Campbell** and from them to **James Hill** together and from **James Hill** to **Daniel Atkins** and from him to **James Atkins**. Wit: **Phillip Ross, F.M. Atkins, T.P. Atkins**. Signed, **Daniel (x) Atkins**. Witness oath, 8 Sept 1849: Singed, **F.M. Atkins** to **James Caldwell** Mag S.D. Registered Examined and certified 14 Sept. 1849. Original delivered to ~ **Francis Atkins** 30 Jany 1850.

p. 316-317.   7 April 1849. Deed of Conveyance. **Micajah C. Barnett** of Spartanburg Dist, to **Javan Barnett** of Spartanburg Dist, for $100 sold all my right Title and Interest in 200 acres on Thomson's creek, branch waters of Fair Forest, a part of the Real Estate of **Micajah Barnett** Decd, which was sold by mutual consent of all the Heirs they being of age, and bought by **Javan Barnett**, known as Lot N° 2 bounded by **J.W. Cooper** and **D. Whetstone**. Wit: **Seburn J.[or I.] Stone, Elizabeth White**. Signed, **Micajah Barnett**. Witness oath, 14 Sept 1849: Signed, **Seburn J.[or I.] Stone** to **J.B. Tolleson** Clk & Mag Ex. Iffo. Registered 14 Sept. 1849.

p. 317-318.   14 Aug 1849. Deed of Conveyance. **Elijah Barnett** of Spartanburg Dist, to **Javan Barnett** of Spartanburg Dist, for $237 sold all my Right Title and Interest in 218 acres   on Thomson's branch waters of Fair Forest it being a part of the Real Estate of **Micajah Barnett** Decd, which was sold by mutual consent of all the Heirs, they being of age, and bought by **Javan Barnett**, known as Lot N° 2 bounded by **J.W. Cooper** and **D. Whetstone**. Wit: **James F. Sloan, Seburn J. Stone**. Signed, **Elijah Barnett**. Witness oath, 14 Aug 1849: Signed, **Seburn J.[or I.] Stone** to **J.W. Cooper** Mag. Registered 14th Sept. 1849.

p. 318-319.   9 March 1849. Deed of Conveyance. **Jorial Barnett** of Spartanburg Dist, to **Javan Barnett** of Spartanburg Dist for $80 sold all my Right, Title, and Interest in 218 acres on Thomsons branch waters of Fair Forest it being a part of the Real Estate of **Micajah Barnett** Decd, which was sold by mutual consent of all the Heirs, they being of age, and bought by **Javan Barnett**, Known as Lot N° 2, bounded by **J.W. Cooper** and **D. Whetstone**. Wit: **R. Bowden, D. Scruggs**. Signed, **Jorial**

Barnett. Witness oath, 14 Sept 1849: Signed, **R. Bowden** to **J.B. Tolleson** Clk & Mag Ex. Iffo. Registered 14th Sept.1849.

p. 320-321.   13 Sept 1849. Deed of Conveyance. **Gabriel B. Styles** of Spartanburg Dist, to **S. Moury & Son** of Charleston, S.C., for $2,000 sold in all about 550 acres whereon I now live, composed of parcels purchased by me at different times, on the waters of Two Mile Creek, bounded by lands of **William Jones, John Dean, Willis Allen, James Leatherwood** and others. Wit: **John P. Smith, S.F. Styles.** Signed, **G.B. Styles.** Witness oath, 13 Sept 1849: Signed, **S.F. Styles** to **O.E. Edwards**, N.P. Registered 14 Sept. 1849.

p. 321-322.   13 Sept 1849. Mortgage. **Gabriel B. Styles** of Spartanburg Dist, mortgages for $2000 with Interest, to **S. Moury & Son** of Charleston, all my Title & interest in my Negro man slave, **Ben**, about 21 years old. **Styles** promises to pay to $500 on 1st Dec 1850, or give my order for $500 to **G. King** assignee of **C.W. Styles** before that time; $500 with the Interest which will have accrued on 1st Jan 1851; $500 plus Interest on 1st Jan 1852; and $500 plus Interest 1st Nov 1853. Wit: **John P. Smith, S.F. Styles.** Signed, **G.B. Styles.** Witness oath, 13 Sept 1849: Signed, **S. F. Styles** to **O.E. Edwards**, N.P. Registered 14th Sept. 1849.

p. 322-323.   20 June 1849. Relinquishment. **Joseph Daffron** & wife, **Nancy Daffron**, formerly **Nancy Arnold** of Walker Co., GA, to **Irvin Sarratt** for $10 sold Title and Interest which I have in right of my wife & whereof she is Entitled to as the next of kin to **Rebecca Paccal** and to all Estate whatsoever which may be due & coming to the said **Rebecca Pascal** from the Estate of **Redrick Arnold** and coming to us as the next of kin to the said **Rebecca Pascal**. Wit [one only: **H.H. Clary.** Signed, **Joseph Daffron, Nancy (x) Daffron.** Witness oath, 11 Sept 1849: Swears that to the best of his knowledge, the signature of **H.H. Clary** is genuine. Signed, **J.R. Ellis** to **D.B.P. Moorman** Mag. Registered 14th Sept. 1849.

p. 323-324.   20 Nov 1840. Deed of Conveyance. **Richard Thomson** of Spartanburg Dist, to **Zachariah J. Bates** of Spartanburg Dist, for $600 sold 195 acres on the branches of Fair Forest creek including the plantation where **John Lancaster sen**r formerly lived. Wit: **James Lancaster, Samuel White.** Signed, **Richard Thomson.** Witness oath, 17 Sept 1849: Signed, **Samuel White** to **B.F. Bates** Not. R'Pub. Ex iffo. Registered 17th Sept. 1849.

p. 324-325.   8 Sept 1849. Deed of Conveyance. **J.W. Tucker** of Spartanburg, to **H.H. Thomson** of Spartanburg, for $305 sold 500 acres on south side of Shoaly creek, bounded by **Nathan Center's** spring branch, **Guignaias** line and **Bennett.** Wit: **J.B. Archer, J.B. Tolleson.** Signed, **J.W. Tucker.** Witness oath, 18 Sept 1849: Signed, **J.B. Archer** to **J.B. Tolleson** Clk & Mag Ex iffo. Recorded 18th Sept. 1849. Original delivered to ~~ **H.H. Thomson** 24th Jany 1851.

p. 325-326.   5 Sept 1848. Sheriff's Titles. **R.C. Poole**, Sheriff of Spartanburg Dist., to **Joseph Foster** of Spartanburg Dist, for $285 sold 320 acres bounded by **Jacob Price, Thomas Evans, Richard Scruggs, James Ezell** and a survey called **Guesses** [p. 289, **Gist**] land & on the waters of Island Creek. Sold by writ of Fieri facias issued out of the Court of common pleas held 13th June 1845 at the suit of **Joseph Foster** against **William Floyd** of Spartanburg Dist, for $53.50 with

Interest, damages and costs. Wit: **John Bomar Jr., William Petty**. Signed, **R.C. Poole** S.S.D. Witness oath, 18 Sept 1849: Singed, **William Petty** to **J.B. Tolleson** Clk & Mag Ex iffo. Registered 18th Sept. 1849.

p. 326-327. 28 April 1849. Lease. **William Brashers** of Spartanburg Dist, to **William S. Mills** of Rutherford Co., N.C., leases all my **Elijah Pettit** place for the purpose of Gold mining for the Term of Ten years with all the privileges of Water and Every thing Else for mining purposes For which **Mills** agrees to give the 1/7 part of all the gold collected to **Brashers** or his legal representative monthly or oftener if Required. The mine alluded to lies directly above and adjoining **Mills** land purchased from **Meredith Brashers**. **Mills** is not to dig up the Cane Break at the lower end without further leave. Wit: **William A. Mooney**. Signed, **William (x) Brashers, Wm S. Mills**. Witness oath, 12 Aug 1849: **Wm A. Mooney** to **James Caldwell** Mag S.D. Registered 19th Sept. 1849.

p. 327-328. 15 Sept 1849. Sheriff's Titles. **R.C. Poole**, Sheriff of Spartanburg Dist, to **H.H. Thomson** of Spartanburg Dist, for $5 sold 5 acres on the waters of Fair Forest Creek & bounded by **J.C. Zimmerman** & others, a part of a tract formerly owned by **Alexander Fleming**, decd, and whereon he died. Sold by writ of Fieri Facias issued out of the Court of Common pleas 1st Feb 1849 at the suit of **Alexander Fleming** against **Gilbert Fleming** for thir four Dollars [$34?], damages and costs. Wit: **J.B. Tolleson, J. Belton Tolleson**. Signed, **R.C. Poole**, S.S.D. Witness oath, 24 Sept 1849: Personally came before me, **John Belton Tolleson** & made oath that he saw **R.C. Poole** sign seal & deliver the within Deed of conveyance & that **J.B. Tolleson** together with himself and in the presence of each other witnessed the Execution thereof. Signed, **J. Belton Tolleson** to **J.B. Tolleson** Clk & Mag Ex iffo. Registered 24 Sept 1849. Original delivered to ~~ **H.H. Thomson** 24th Jany 1851.

p. 328-329. 14 Sept 1849. Deed of Conveyance. **Joseph Foster** of Spartanburg Dist, to **John T. Kirby** of Spartanburg Dist, for $400 sold 320 acres on the waters of Island Creek bounded by **Jacob Price, Thomas Evans, Richard Scruggs & James H. Ezelle** & a survey called **Gists** land. Wit: **Geo. W.H. Legg, T.A. Lewis**. Signed, **Joseph Foster**. Witness oath, 27 Sept 1849: **G.W.H. Legg** to **J.B. Tolleson** Clk & Mag Ex iffo. Registered 27th Sept. 1849. Original delivered to ~~ **John T. Kirby** 20th Jany. 1855.

p. 329-331. 3 Sept 1849. Deed of Conveyance. **H.H. Thomson, J. Waddy Thomson & Junius W. Thomson**, Executors of **R. Thomson** Decd, by order of the Court of Equity for Spartanburg Dist, in the case of **G. & C. Mills** and their wives against the Executors of **R. Thomson** Decd, sold, at the risk of the former purchaser to the highest bidder, sold to **G.W.H. Legg** for $1,500, sold 258 acres called the **Lancaster** Tract on Chinquepin Creek, bounded by **Jesse Cleveland**. Wit: **J.B. Tolleson, Govan Mills**. Signed, **H.H. Thomson, J. Waddy Thomson, J.W. Thomson**, Executors. Witness oath, 27 Sept 1849: Signed, **Govan Mills** to **J.B. Tolleson** Clk & Mag Ex iffo. Registered 27th Sept 1849.

p. 331-332. 16 Jan 1833. Deed of Conveyance. **Richard Cottrell** of Spartanburg Dist, to **John Taylor** of Laurens Dist, S.C., (1) for $800 sold 118 acres on Enoree River, bounded by **Thomas Farrow** on E, **Robert Hannah** on W, **Mrs Rosy Woodruff** on N, Enoree River on S; (2) 84 acres, part of Tract formerly belonging to **Joseph Crook**, bounded W by **William Terry**, N by **John Terry**, E by **Thomas Faylow [Farrow?]** and others. Wit: **John N. Young, Starling Tucker.** Signed, **R. Cottrell.** Witness oath, Laurens Dist, 22 May 1849: Signed, **John N. Young** to **Seborn Park**, M.L.D. Registered 27th Sept. 1849.

p. 332-333. 20 Aug 1849. Deed of Conveyance. **Whitfield Brooks** of SC, to **James Moore** of Spartanburg Dist, for $$545 sold 149 acres by computation, adjoining **Whitmire**, said **James Moore & Doct WinSmith**, the southern part of the Pinckney Fork Tract lately purchased by the said **W. Brooks** from **Joel Dean**. Wit: **A. Wofford, Perry West.** Signed, **Whitfield Brooks.** Release of Dower, 20 Aug 1849: Signed, **Mary P. Brooks** to **Hiram White,** Mag. Witness oath, 11 May 1849: Signed, **Perry West** to **H. White,** Mag. Registered 2nd Oct. 1849.

p. 333-334. 22 July 1848. Deed of Conveyance. **Robert Stacy** to **William B. Smith,** for $125 sold 50 acres by computation, on Cherokee Creek of Broad River bordering **Northy** and the creek. Wit: **P. Quinn Camp, James Ellis.** Signed, **Robert (x) Stacy.** Witness oath, 2 Sept 1849: Signed, **P. Quinn Camp** to **J.B. Tolleson** Clk & Mag Ex iffo. Registered 2nd Oct. 1849. Original delivered to ~~ **William Smith.**

p. 334-335. 24 Sept 1849. Deed of Conveyance. **James Tucker** of Greenville Dist, S.C., to **Benjamin Prewit Jun.** of Spartanburg Dist, for $33.33⅓ sold 110 acres on the head branches of Spencer's Creek, waters of Middle Tyger River, bounded by **Benjamin Prewit Sen.** Wit: **J.M. Dickie, Presley Davis.** Signed, **James Tucker.** Witness oath, 29 Sept 1849: **Presley Davis** to **B.F. Montgomery**, Mag. Registered 2nd Oct 1849.

p. 335-336. 9 Sept 1845. Deed of Conveyance. **Mary Smith** of Spartanburg Dist, to **Berryman H. Bearden** for $400 sold 200 acres on branches of Dutchmans creek waters of Tyger River, being part of Tract conveyed to me by **Samuel Morrow.** Wit: **Joel Dean, John Bearden.** Signed, **Mary Smith.** Witness oath, 9 Sept 1845: **John Bearden** to **Joel Dean** Mag. Registered 2nd Oct. 1849.

p. 336-337. 9 Sept 1849. Deed of Gift. **Mary Smith,** (widow) of Spartanburg Dist, to **Berryman H. Bearden** for the natural love and affection I have for my Son in law give him the 111 acres, whereon I now live, on the waters of Dutchmans creek, bounded by **Robert R. Smith** and others. Wit: **Wm Smith, Levi Rees, Sanford Smith.** Signed, **Mary Smith.** Witness oath, 2 Oct 1849: Signed, **Sanford Smith** to **W.W. Wilbanks** Mag. Registered 2nd Oct. 1849.

p. 337-338. 3 Sept 1847. Deed of Conveyance. **William Smith** of Spartanburg Dist, to **John W. Hutchings** of Spartanburg Dist, for $375 sold 118 acres between the Saluda Gap Road and Middle Fork of Tyger River, on the South side of said road and North to the middle forks of the river, bounded by **Mathew S. Moore, Bowin? Griffin** and **William McMakin**, a plot made by **James K. Dickson, D.S.** August 14th 1847 will more fully represent. Wit: **Samuel B. Hutchings, Equilla Burns.** Signed, **William Smith.** Witness oath, 7 Dec 1847: **Samuel B. Hutchings** to **D.J. Barnett,** M.S.D. Release of Dower, 27 Sept 1849: Signed, **Lucinda (x) Smith** to **Isham Wood,** M.S.D. Registered 2nd Oct 1849. Original delivered to ~~ **Rev. Thomas Hutchings.**

p. 338-339. 14 Sept 1849. Mortgage. **Stephen Sprinkles** is indebted to **H.H. Thomson** by three sealed notes of this date, each for $96, first due two years from date, second in three years and the third in four years, being part of the price of 179 acres today bought by **Sprinkles** from **Thomson;** land on Shoaly creek. Wit: **Thomas Lockwood, J. Thomas Rowland.** Signed, **Stephen Sprinkle.** Witness oath, 2 Oct 1849: Signed, **Wm Lockwood** to **J.B. Tolleson** Clk & Mag Ex iffo. Registered 2nd Oct. 1849. Original delivered to ~~ **H.H. Thomson** 24th Jany 1851.

p. 340-341.   3 Sept 1849. Mortgage. **G.W.H. Legg** is indebted to **H.H. Thomson, J. Waddy Thomson, Junius W. Thomson** for $1,500 by three sealed notes of this date, due one, two and three years, being for the purchase money of the **Lancaster** tract containing 258 acres, description in the deed made to **G.W.H. Legg.** Wit: **Alfred Tolleson, J.W. Tucker.** Signed, **Geo. W.H. Legg.** Witness oath 2 Oct 1849. **J.W. Tucker** to **J.B. Tolleson** Clk & Mag Ex iffo. Registered 2nd Oct. 1840. Original delivered to ~~ **H.H. Thomson** 24th Jany 1851.

p. 341-342. 24 Sep 1849. Deed of Conveyance. **J. Waddy Thomson** of Spartanburg Dist, to **H.H. Thomson** of Spartanburg Dist, for $726.63 sold two tracts which I bought at sale of Commissioner of Equity on 16th Nov. 1847; (1) designated as Lot N° 32 in plat on Laurens Road, bounded by **Poole & Walker,** containing 41 acres. (2) designated as Lot N° 33 bounded by the street, **Petre's** Shop, Laurens Road and **Walker;** containing 38 acres 8/100. Both in Town of Spartanburg. Wit: **G. Cannon, Tho. O. P. Vernon.** Signed, **J. Waddy Thomson.** Witness oath, 2 Oct 1849: Signed, **Tho. O. P. Vernon** to **J.B. Tolleson** Clk & Mag Ex iffo. Registered 2nd Oct. 1849. Original delivered to ~~ **H.H. Thomson** 24th Jany 1851.

p. 342-343.   7 Jan 1845. Deed of Conveyance. **William B. Scott** of Spartanburg Dist, to **William Mason** of Spartanburg Dist, for $450 sold 94 acres on both sides of the Georgia Road and the south side of Fergusons creek, marks & forms as plat shows. Wit: **James Calvert, Posey Mason.** Signed, **William B. Scott.** Witness oath, 26 Dec 1848: Signed, **P. Mason** to **Z. Lanford,** Magt. Release of Dower, 16 June 1849: Signed, **Emily Scott** to **Z. Lanford,** Magt. Registered 15 Oct. 1849. Original delivered to ~~ **William Mason** 19th July 1850.

p. 344.   22 Oct 1849. Deed of Conveyance. **Robert G. Hunt** of Spartanburg Dist, to **James Nesbitt** of Spartanburg Dist, for $58 sold all my interest (being one half) in 116 acres on Beaver dam Creek, the tract Willed by **R. M. Daniel** to my brother **Wiles V. Hunt** and myself, bounded by **John Bomar,** said **James Nesbitt.** Wit: **P.M. Wallace, W. Hunt.** Signed, **R.G. Hunt.** Witness oath, 22 Oct 1849: Signed, **W. Hunt** to **H.J. Dean** Not. Pub & Magt Ex off. Registered 22nd Oct. 1849.

p. 345-346. 22 Oct 1849. Sheriff's Titles. **R.C. Poole**, Sheriff Spartanburg Dist, to **J.W. Ross** for $400 sold 250 acres, land of **Robert Stacy**, Decd, in this district on the waters of Broad River, bounded by **M.C. Stacy, George Bobett, William B. Smith, James Ellis, Northies [Norhty's?],** **Sarratt & Ross.** Sold by order of the Court of the Ordinary tested 3 Sept 1849. Wit: **Dr. F.L. Parham, J. Belton Tolleson.** Signed, **R.C. Poole,** S.S.D. Witness oath, 22 Oct 1849: **J. Belton Tolleson** to **R. Bowden** Ex off Mag. Registered 22nd Oct. 1849.

p. 346- 347. 10 Nov 1848. Deed of Conveyance. **William E. Ward** of Spartanburg Dist, to **Daniel**

E. Dolton of Spartanburg Dist, for $250 sold 104 acres on the waters of North Tyger, a part of the tract granted to **Daniel Walden**. Wit: **Charles Thompson, Davis Tinsley**. Signed, **William E. Ward**. Release of Dower, 24 Oct 1849: Signed, **Elizabeth (x) Ward** to **B.F. Montgomery**, Mag. Witness oath, 2 April 1849: Signed, **Charles Thompson** to **J.B. Tolleson** Clk & Mag Ex iffo. Registered 26th Oct. 1849.

p. 347-348.   25 Sept 1849. Deed of Conveyance. **J. Waddy Thomson** of Spartanburg Dist, to **Rev. J.D. McCulloch** of Spartanburg Dist, for $1795 sold 123 acres on Chinquepin creek partly in the incorporated limits of the Town of Spartanburg, North side of Road, **Dr. Golding, Dean & Walker, Cleveland** and near **Junius Thomson**. Wit: **Govan Mills, J.W. Tucker**. Signed, **J. Waddy Thomson**. Witness oath, **J.W. Tucker Esqr** to **J.B. Tolleson** Clk & Mag Ex iffo. Registered 30th Oct 1849. Original delivered to ~~ **Rev. J.D. McCulloch.**

p. 348-349.   26 Oct 1849. Deed of Conveyance. **Randolph W. Vaughn** in consideration that **Richard B. Smith** will pay all the Just Debts I now owe & in consideration of the love that I have to him (as my Son in law) I convey all my Title and Claim to 127 acres whereon I now live, which was conveyed to me by **James Meadows**, on waters of Dutchman's creek adjoining **Samuel McCravey, Turner Roundtree & Doct J. WinSmith**; also Negroes: **Cupid**, a very old man, **Nancy**, about 45 years old, **Sarah**, about 20 years old, **Ned** about 11 years old; my two horse mules, all my stock of cattle consisting of about 8 or 10 head, all my stock of hogs, all my household & kitchen furniture, all my farming tools, one Road waggon and a one horse carriage. Wit: **H.H. Thomson, Elihu P. Smith**. Signed, **R.W. Vaughn**. Witness oath, 5 Nov 1849: Signed, **Elihu P. Smith** to **J.B. Tolleson** Clk & Mag Ex iffo. Registered 5th Nov. 1849.

p. 349-350.   26 Dec 1848. Deed of Conveyance. **Joseph Smith** of Spartanburg Dist, to **Isaac Clayton** of Spartanburg Dist, for $142 sold 142 acres by estimation, on waters of Wolf Swamp creek waters of Middle Tyger River, joining **John Balinger, Joseph Smith, John Loftis** and others on the Gogeant[?] Road. Test: **John Odam, A.P. Turner**. Signed, **Joseph Smith**. Witness oath, 7 Feb 1849: Signed, **A.P. Turner** to **B.F. Montgomery**, Mag. Registered 5th Nov. 1849.

p. 350-352.   5 Sept 1849. Deed of Conveyance. **Henry J. Rowland** of Spartanburg Dist, to **James Robbs** of Spartanburg Dist, for $1,000 sold 346 acres, all that plantation (except 3 or 4 acres which I sold to **Z. Wall Esqr**) on both sides of Richland creek, waters of Packolet River, bordering **James Burnett, Z. Wall** and **H. Dodd**. Wit: **E.A. Brannon, M.O. Rowland**. Signed, **H.J. Rowland**. Witness oath, 15 Sept 1849: Signed, **M.O. Rowland** to **Elias Wall**, Mag. Release of Dower, 15 Sept 1849: Signed, **Lucy W. Rowland** to **Elias Wall** Magistrate. Registered 5th Nov. 1849. Original delivered to ~~ **James Robbs.**

p. 352-353.   24 July 1849. Deed of Conveyance. **Martha Hammett** of Spartanburg Dist, to **Calvin McDowell** of Spartanburg Dist, for $65 sold 9 acres on a branch of South Packolet River. Wit: **J.B. Davis, John McDowell, Pinckney Hammett**. Signed, **Martha (x) Hammett**. Witness oath, 5 Nov 1849: Signed, **John B. Davis** to **W.H. Willbanks**, Mag. Registered 5th Nov. 1849.

p. 353-354.   25 Sept 1849. Mortgage. **Revd J.D. McCulloch** today purchased from **J. Waddy**

Thomson 123 acres partly in the Town of Spartanburg on Chinquepin Creek, more particular description on the deed and a plat made by **Col. W.W. Harris,** attached to deed; for which **Rev McCulloch** gave **J. Waddy Thomson** his sealed note of this date for $1,795. Wit: **J. Tho. Rowland, Col. H.H. Thomson.** Signed, **Jno. D. McCulloch.** Witness oath, 2 Oct 1849: Signed, **H.H. Thomson** to **J.B. Tolleson** Clk & Mag Ex iffo. Registered 5th Nov. 1849. Original delivered to ~~ **H.H. Thomson** 12th April 1856 [or 1851].

p. 354-356.   20 Sept 1849. Deed of Conveyance. **James Kirby** of Spartanburg Dist, to **Reubin Bryant Jur** of Spartanburg Dist, for $1400 sold 230 acres in both Spartanburg and Union on waters of Packolet River, Mill Creek on both sides of Grindle Shoal Road, deeded to me by **Richard Kirby** and **Terry Kirby** and the Commissioner of Equity; bounded by **Reid, Bolin & Terry Kirby's** line, **Littlejohn & John Wood.** Wit: **John H.L. Wood, William L. Wood.** Signed, **James Kirby.** Release of Dower, 27 Sept 1849: Signed, **Lucinda Kirby** to **B.F. Bates,** N.P. Mag Ex Officio. Witness oath, 27 Sept 1849: Signed, **J.H.L. Wood** to **B.F. Bates,** N.P.& Mag. Registered 5th Nov. 1849.

p.356-357.   6 Nov 1849. Deed of Conveyance. **William Carver** of Spartanburg Dist, for $150 to me secured to be paid by **Henry Abbott,** sold **George Washington Abbott** and **Andrew Jackson Abbott,** the Sons of **Henry Abbott,** supposed to be 1¼ acre in the Village of Spartanburg beginning on the upper side of **Nolin's** lot & opposite **R.C. Poole's** Lot & runs with the street leading to Fair Forest, until it strikes the back line of a lot I bought of **H.H. Thomson** near the old road. Attest: **J. Belton Tolleson, Wm B. Bishop.** Signed, **Wm Carver.** Witness oath, 7 Nov 1849: Signed, **J. Belton Tolleson** to **John Linder** Mag. Registered 7th Nov. 1849.

p. 357-358.   4 March 184[8? Ink smear]. Deed of Conveyance. **James Wood** of Spartanburg Dist, to **Nancy Wood** of Spartanburg Dist, for $800 sold 139 acres on the North Side of Packolet River, on a Road near **Jesse Griffin.** Wit: **John H.L. Wood, George T. Wood.** Signed, **James Wood.** Witness oath, 5 Nov 1849: Signed, **John H.L. Wood** to **W.H. Willbanks** Mag. Registered 7 Nov. 1849.

p. 358-359.   27 Oct 1845. Deed of Conveyance. **John Raygan** of Spartanburg Dist, to **Nancy C. Golightly** [not stated], for $200 sold 170 acres on the South West prong of Holston Creek waters of South Pacolet River, the beginning corner on the line between me and my brother **Simpson Raygan,** a part of two tracts originally granted to **Thomas Monroe** and **Robert Harper.** Wit: **William H. Golightly, William Walker A.S.H.** Signed, **John Reagan.** Witness oath, 27 Oct 1845: Signed, **Wm H. Golightly** to **William Walker,** Mag. Release of Dower, 11 Nov 1845: Signed, **Rebecca M. Reagan** to **J.B. Tolleson,** Clerk. Registered 15th Nov 1849. Original delivered to ~~ **Hiram Mitchell** 15 Nov./49.

p. 359-360.   [Blank] __1810__. **Vincent Bennett** of Spartanburg Dist, to **John Tapp** of Spartanburg Dist, for $160 sold 170 acres where **John Tapp** lives, part of land originally granted to **Thomas Bennett,** on branches of South Packolet River; beginning on an original corner of **Thomas Bennet's** old survey, between **George Bennett's** old spring branch & the branch called the school house branch, the Waggon Road from **Cunningham's** to Spartanburg Court House, a stake where the Path leading from **Bennetts** old place to **Mr. Littlefieds**. Wit: **Lewis (x) Bennett, Saml (x) Kimmins**. Witness oath, 28 Sept. 1811: Signed, **Samuel (x) Kimmings** to **James Young** J.Q. Registered 15th Nov. 1849.

p. 360-361.   10 Nov 1849. Deed of Conveyance. **John Nolen** of Spartanburg Dist, to **Fieldin Cantrell** of Spartanburg Dist, for $615 sold 200 acres on the South East Side of **Thomson's** Creek waters of Pacolet River, east bank of the creek, bounded by **L. Clements** land and **J.C. Kimbrell**. Wit: **Wilson N. Cantrell, Abner Cantrell**. Signed, **John Nolin**. Witness oath, 10 Nov 1849: Signed, **W.N. Cantrell** to **Elias Wall**, Mag. Release of Dower, 10 Nov 1849: Signed, **Malissa Nolen** to **Elias Wall** Magistrate. Registered 15th Nov. 1849. Original delivered to ~~ **Fieldin Cantrell**.

p. 362.   3 March 1838. Deed of Gift. I, **John Wingo** of Spartanburg Dist, have given unto my son **Alberry J. Wingo** for love and attachment and other good causes 145 acres on Camp Branch waters of Lossons fork, bounded on NE & SE by **Dodd's** land and all other sides by **John Wingo;** plot annexed. Wit: **Moses Foster, Elijah McMillen**. Signed, **John Wingo**. Witness oath, 2 June 1838: Signed, **Moses Foster** to **John Chapman**, J.Q. Registered 15th March 1849.

p. 363.   2 Nov 1849. Deed of Gift. I, **John Wingo** of Spartanburg Dist, for the natural affection which I have for my son, **A.J. Wingo** have given him 136 acres on Camp Branch of Lossons Fork Creek waters of Pacolet River. Test: **R.G. Whitman, J.N. Chapman**. Signed, **John Wingo**. Witness oath, 5 Nov 1849: Signed, **Robt. G. Whitman** to **Elias Wall** Magt. Registered 15th Nov. 1849.

p. 364.   6 Nov 1849. Deed of Conveyance. **L.B. Hines** of S.C., to **Kinchen Hines** of Spartanburg Dist, for $275 sold 100 acres Lot N° 4 at the head of Little Branch, bound by **Wm Little**. Wit: **W.H. Willbanks, W.N. Cantrell, John Parris**. Signed, **L.B. (x) Hines**. Witness oath, 6 Nov 1849: Signed, **W.N. Cantrell** to **W.H. Wilbanks** Mag. Registered 15th Nov. 1849. Original delivered to ~~ **W.H. Willbanks** 19th Sept 1850.

p. 365.   17 Feby 1847. Deed of Conveyance. **Henry Cunningham** of Spartanburg Dist, to **John Rochester** of Spartanburg Dist, for $20 sold about 1 acres near Glenn Springs bounded by **J.C. Zimmerman** on S, **M.A. Moore** on W, **Henry Cunningham** on the N, and **John Rochester** on the E. Wit: **Moris A. Moore, James Tinsley**. Signed, **Henry Cunningham**. Witness oath, 26 May 1849: Signed, **M.A. Moore** to **H. White**, Mag. Registered 19th Nov. 1849. Original delivered to ~~ **Joseph Foster.**

p. 365-367.   9 May 1849. **Henry Cunningham** of Spartanburg Dist, to **John Rochester** of Spartanburg Dist, for $515 sold 51½ acres near the Glenn Springs and Fair Forest Road, bounded by the Glenn Springs land. Wit: **J.C. Zimmerman, Elias Bearden**. Signed, **Henry Cunningham**. Release of Dower, 24 Sept 1849: Signed, **Jane (x) Cunningham** to **Hiram White**, Mag. Witness oath, 24 Sept 1849: Signed, **Elias Bearden** to **H. White**, Mag. Registered 19th Nov. 1849. Original delivered to ~~ **Joseph Foster.**

p. 367-368.   10 Nov 1849. **Benjamin Wofford** of Spartanburg Village, to **John A. Lee** of Spartanburg Village, for $1,100, 5 acres in all, in the Town of Spartanburg on the west side of

Church Street; bordered by **R. Owens.** A cross street within the measurements is at this time conveyed but not warranted. Also another lot purchased by **G.W.H. Legg** from **Jesse Cleveland** & sold to me by **R.W. Folger** on Church Street. Wit: **Hiram Mitchell, J.W. Tucker.** Signed, **Benj. Wofford.** Witness oath, 19 Nov 1849: Signed, **J.W. Tucker** to **J.B. Tolleson,** Clk & Mag Ex iffo. Registered 19 Nov 1849. Original delivered to ~~ **J.A. Lee** 24th Jany 1851.

p. 368-369. 10 Nov 1849. Mortgage. **John A. Lee** is indebted to **Benj. Wofford** for ten hundred dollars ($1,000) by three sealed notes each for $333.33⅓, due 1 Jany each year 1851, 1852, 1853, each with interest from 1 Jan 1850. As security for the notes, **John A. Lee** mortgages a Lot in Spartanburg Village on the west side of Church Street containing 5 acres, adjoining lots now owned by **R. Owen, L. Huet, Dr. A.W. Bivings & Jesse Cleveland,** which lot I have this day purchased from **Benj. Wofford.** Wit: **Hiram Mitchell, J.W. Tucker.** Signed, **John A. Lee.** Witness oath, 19 Nov 1849: Signed, **J.W. Tucker** to **J.B. Tolleson,** Clk & Mag Ex iffo. Registered 19th Nov. 1849.

p. 369-371. 1 Nov 1849. Mortgage. **James A. Fowler** is indebted to **Benj. Wofford** for $250 by two Sealed notes bearing date 13th day of Nov 1849, first due 12 months from date, with interest; the purchase money for 2 acres, a town Lot lying between **Mrs. R. Mullinax** on the South and **Mrs. Trimmier** on the North, by Rutherford Street on the East & by street running by the Baptist Church on the West the boundaries of which will more fully appear by reference to my Deed this day made by **Benjamin Wofford.** Wit: **H.H. Thomson, J.W. Tucker.** Signed, **James A. Fowler.** Witness oath, 13 Nov 1849: Signed, **J.W. Tucker** to **J.B. Tolleson,** Clk & Mag Ex iffo. Registered 19th Nov. 1849.

p. 371-372. 25 Jan 1847. Deed of Conveyance. **Joshua Richards** to **Lewis Clary** for $395 sold 240 acres on the SW of **Quinn's** Creek and **John Byars,** a part of land granted to **A.C. Markley** & deeded to **Mary Richards** by **B.A. Markley** Exor and by her to **John Linder** and by **Linder** to me. Wit: **J. Quinn Camp, James Quinn.** Signed, **Joshua Richards.** Witness oath, 25 Jan 1847: Signed, **P. Quinn Camp** to **J.R. Ellis,** Mag. Release of Dower, 5 Feb 1847: Signed, **Liley Richards** to **J.R. Ellis,** Mag. Registered 22nd Nov 1849.

p. 372-373. 19 Nov 1847. Deed of Conveyance. **Samuel Sharbutt** of Union Dist, S.C., to **Capt. James F. Sloan** of Spartanburg Dist, for $170 sold 90 acres on a branch of Richland Creek waters of Pacolet River, beginning twenty paces due North of **Capt. J.F. Sloan's** rock corner on my line near old **Mr. Sherbutt's,** then **F. Brown, James Brown** and **John Lee;** formerly part of land owned by **Thomas Brown,** deceased. Wit: **Thompson Gault, David Sloan.** Signed, **Samuel Sharbutt.** Witness oath, 19 Nov 1847: Signed, **David Sloan** to **John Wright,** Magt. Registered 22nd Nov. 1849. Original delivered to ~~ **Jas. F. Sloan.**

p. 373-374. 10 Oct 1849. **Abraham Fiendly** to **Mary Linder** for [$400] in four notes of $100, each due 25th Decr. each year 1850, 1851, 1852 and 1853, last three with interest from date; notes were for purchase money for [acres not given] in the Dist of Spartanburg near the Rolling mill or So. Ca. Ma. Co., bounded by **Henry Turner** and others, shape and marks represented by the Deed which was this day made to me by **Mary Linder** & a plat in the office of the Commissioner of Equity; [Lot] N° 4 & as the land is near the Iron Works I agree that I will only cut coal wood out of my clearings and will fence the land I cut down (before it is paid for). Wit: **J. M. Bowden, John Linder.** Signed, **Abraham (x) Fiendly.** Witness oath, 10 Oct 1849: Signed, **J.M. Bowden** to **Wᵐ Guthrie** Mag. Registered 22ⁿᵈ Nov. 1849.

p. 374-375. 3 Sept 1849. Mortgage. **Simpson Bobo** is indebted to **H.H. Thomson, J. Waddy Thomson & Junius W. Thomson,** Exors of **Richard Thomson,** Decd, by nine sealed notes in the sum of $7,097, it being for purchase money of the **Yates** tract, the **Grey** tract and the Cane Brake tract [amount omitted]; for boundaries reference the Deeds made this day to **Simpson Bobo.** Wit: **Benj. Wofford, James. F.V. Legg.** Signed, **Simpson Bobo.** Witness oath, 24 Nov 1849: **James F.V. Legg** to **J.B. Tolleson,** Clk & Mag Ex iffo. Registered 22ⁿᵈ Nov. 1849. Original delivered to ~~ **H.H. Thomson** 24ᵗʰ Jany 1850.

p. 376-377. Deed of Conveyance. **H.H. Thomson** of Spartanburg Dist, to **Jacob Zimmerman** for $4250 sold two lots, both lots supposed to contain near 2½ acres, in the Town of Spartanburg. (1) The lot on the public square on S side of the street leading to the Jail. Beginning on a stone on main street near the corner of the Piazza of the Store Houses and runs with the public square to the lower end of the **Murray** Grocery to a corner on the Grocery now owned by **Junius W. Thomson.** Thence with the line of the **Junius Thomson** Lot to back street. Thence with back street to corner of the **Greener [or Greiner]** House on Jail Street. Thence with Jail Street to the beginning. (2) Other Lot lying on street leading out back of Jail on S side of said street. Beginning on a stone on said street nearly opposite the big gate on Jail Lot and runs S 65 W to the back line of the Lot I bought of **Richard Thomson** Joining **Linder's** Lot. Thence Southward with said line to a corner of a Lot I sold to **Wᵐ Carver.** Thence N 83 E 58 Links to a stone **Wᵐ Carver's** corner. Thence N 50 West crossing branch to a stone on said street near the Bridge. Thence with said street to the beginning corner. Wit: **Benj. Wofford, J.B. Tolleson.** Signed, **H.H. Thomson.** Witness oath, 20 Nov 1849: Signed, **Benj. Wofford** to **J.W. Tucker,** Magt. Release of Dower, 24 Nov 1849: Signed, **Mildred E. Thomson** to **J.W. Tucker,** Magst. Registered 24ᵗʰ Nov. 1849.

p. 377-379. 26 Nov 1849. Deed of Conveyance. **Benj. Wofford** of the Town of Spartanburg, to **Joseph Foster & D.C. Judd** of the Town of Spartanburg, sold for $1,300 sold a fraction of an acre, a lot in the Town of Spartanburg fronting on the public square and adjoining a Lot now occupied by **Campbell & Seay** being known as Lot Nº 2. Beginning on the NE corner of the Lot now occupied by **Messrs Campbell & Seay** which last named lot is here designated as Lot Nº 2 being Lot Nº 3 running with the line of Lot Nº 2 S 25 E Sixty and a half Feet to a stone. Same course 83 Links to a stone. Thence N 69 E along back of street Twenty Two Feet to a stone. Thence N 23 W 87 L to a Stone. Thence N 25 W Sixty and a half Feet to the public Square. Thence along the line of said Square S 62 W Twenty Four Feet to the beginning corner. Said Lot bounds on the S on a street Twelve Feet in [width] running nearly at right angles with the Jail Street from said street to **Mr. Jesse Cleveland's** Lot which I give for the benefit of the purchasers. Wit: **J.B. Archer, Wᵐ Petty.** Signed, **Benj. Wofford.** Witness oath, 24 Nov 1849: Signed, **J.B. Archer** to **J.B. Tolleson** Clk & Mag Exiffo. Release of Dower, 24 Nov 1849: (**Mrs. Maria Scott Wofford**) Signed, **Miria S. Wofford** to **J.B. Tolleson** Clk. Registered 24ᵗʰ Nov. 1849.

p. 379-380. 9 Oct 1849. Deed of Conveyance. **Josiah Sparks Senr.** Of Union Dist, S.C., to **Jesse**

Griffin of Spartanburg Dist, for $500 sold 100 acres in Union Dist. Bounded on S by Wm T. **Nuckolls**, W by **Littlejohn**, N by **Jesse Griffin**, and E by **James Littlejohn**. Wit: Wm **Littlejohn Jun, Thomas H. Littlejohn**. Signed, **Josiah (x) Sparks**. Witness oath, Union Dist, 22 Oct 1849: Signed, **Thomas H. Littlejohn** to **Reubin Coleman**, Magt. Release of Dower, Union Dist, 15 Oct 1849: Signed, **Lydia (x) Sparks** to **Reubin Coleman**, magistrate. Registered 3rd Dec. 1849. Original delivered to ～ **Jesse Griffin**.

p. 380. 12 Jan **1847*** [or 1841 or 1846?]. Deed of Conveyance. **Thomas R. Tucker** of Spartanburg Dist, to **John Wheeler** of Spartanburg Dist, for $25 sold all my interest in two Lots being parts of a tract originally granted to **John Tucker**. One on the E end containing 100 acres and bounded on the S by **Sirpatin Tinsley**, on the W by **John Wheeler**, E and N of line. The other on the W containing 82 acres bounded S by **Sirpatin Tinsley**, W old line, N by **Vernon**, E by **John Wheeler**. Test: **William E. Ward, Presley Davis**. Signed, **Thomas R. Tucker**. Witness oath, 16 Jan **1846***: Signed, **William E. Ward** to **Thomas Ballenger**, M.S.D. Registered 3 Dec 1849. Original delivered to ～ **John Wheeler** 6th May 1850.

p. 381. 12 Jan **1847***.[or 1841? or 1846?]. **Thomas R. Tucker** of Spartanburg Dist, to **John Wheeler** of Spartanburg Dist, for $175 sold 327 acres, part of a tract originally granted to **John Tucker** bearing date 1805, part of which conveyed to me by said **John Tucker** in 1814, balance I claim for part payment for the maintenance of **Mary Tucker** the widow of sd. **John Tucker** and my mother, it being on both sides of Shoaly Fork Creek of North Tyger River, bordered by **Vernon**. Wit: **Presley Davis, William E. Ward**. Signed, **Thomas R. Tucker**. Witness oath, 16 Jan **1846***: **William E. Ward** to **Thomas Ballenger**, M.S.D. Registered 3rd Dec. 1849. Original delivered to ～ **John Wheeler** 6th May 1850.

p. 382. 30 Oct 1846. Deed of Conveyance. **Joseph Walden** of Spartanburg Dist, to **John Wheeler** of Spartanburg Dist, for $237.87 sold 100 acres on Wolf creek waters of Middle Tyger River. Bordered by **James McMakin**, the Georgia Road. Wit: **Thomas R. Tucker, Thomas Ballenger**. Signed, **Joseph (x) Walden**. Witness oath, 31 Oct 1846: Signed, **Thomas R. Tucker** to **Thomas Ballenger** Mag. Registered 3rd Dec. 1849. Original deliver to ～ **John Wheeler** 6th May 1850.

p. 383. 5 Sept 1848. Deed of Conveyance. **Ephraim Potter** of Spartanburg Dist, to **Thomas Potter & Emily Potter** the son and daughter of **Joseph Potter** of Spartanburg Dist, for $200 paid by **Thomas & Emily** for 75 acres on Island Creek joining lands of **Benjamin Cash** what is called the old meeting house tract, running with **Abner Potter's** line up the road to the cross road to **James Potter's** line. Wit: **William (x) Potter, Abner Potter**. Signed, **Ephraim (x) Potter**. I, **Ephraim Potter** appoint my son, **John Potter**, Guardian for **Joseph Potter's** two children **Thomas Potter** and **Emily Potter** in the land that I deeded to them, 5th September 1848. Signed, **William (x) Potter, Abner Potter**. Witness oath, 3 Dec 1849: **William (x) Potter** to Wm **Guthrie**, Mag. Registered 3rd Dec. 1849.

p. 384-385. 17 Sept 1846. Deed of Conveyance. **John Barnes** of Spartanburg Dist, to **William Crocker Jr.** of Spartanburg Dist, for $150 sold 80 acres on N side of Pacolet River, just above **William Crocker's** old mill place, NE not far from the spring and **Crocker's** line near the house.

N a straight line over to the Gold Branch, formerly **Crocker's** Corner near **Spencer's**. The tract purchased by **John Barnes** from **E. Patterson**. Gold and Mineral rights excepted for **William Neghe [or Meghe]** to work a small branch and search for Gold. Attest: **B.F. Bates, Adison T. Crocker.** Signed, **John (x) Barns**. Release of Dower, 22 Sept 1846: Signed, **Polly (x) Barnes** to **B.F. Bates**, Mag. Witness oath, 3 Dec 1849: **A.T. Crocker** to **Geo. W.H. Legg**. Registered 3 Dec/ 1849. Original delivered to ~ **William Crocker.**

p. 385-386.   26 Nov 1849. Deed of Conveyance. **Benjamin Wofford** of the Town of Spartanburg, to **John B. Archer** of the Town of Spartanburg, for $1,000 sold a Town Lot in Spartanburg Village on the Public Square & running back on Jail Street. Beginning at the NW corner of the Piazza fronting the court house on the Public Square being part of a Lot sold to me by **John T. Kirby** running thence S 25 E along cross street about one hundred twelve feet to a stone. Thence N 69 E nineteen feet and three inches along back street to a stone. Thence N 26 W 81 Links to a stone. Thence N 25 W sixty & a half feet to main street or Public Square. Thence with the line of said Square S 62 W twenty feet & eleven inches to the beginning corner, excepting and reserving within said boundaries at the Southern extremity of said Lot on Jail Street a portion of the same sixteen feet on Jail Street & eighteen feet along back street which I do not convey, being a square of 16 X 18 feet. Said lot bounds on a street twelve feet in width which [I] give for the benefit of the purchaser. Wit: **Alfred Tolleson, Wm Petty.** Signed, **Benj. Wofford.** Witness oath, 15 Dec 1849: **Alfred Tolleson** to **J.B. Tolleson** Clk & Mag Exiffo. Release of Dower, 14 Dec 1849: Signed, **Maria S. Wofford** to **J.B. Tolleson** Clk & Mag Exiffo. Registered 14th Dec. 1849.

p. 386-387.   7 Sept 1849. Deed of Conveyance. **Mahala Wood**, Executrix, and **Isham Wood & J.W. Wood**, Executors of the last will and testament of **William J. Wood** Decd, of Spartanburg Dist, to **Benjamin B. Wood** for $204 sold 95 acres on the waters of Rocky field creek waters of Enoree River, bordering **John McClimons, William Hughes,** and a walled in graveyard. Test: **D.M. Wood, B.J. Wood.** Signed, **Mahala Wood, Isham Wood, J.W. Wood.** Witness oath, 19 Dec 1849: Signed, **B.J. Wood** to **Isham Wood** Mag. S.D. Registered 21st Dec. 1849.

p. 388.   24 Oct 1849. Deed of Gift. I, **L.B. Hines** have this day given to my daughter, **Nancy Hines,** one negro Girl named **Sarah** about 15 years of age, and one negro Girl named **Hulda** about 8 years of age, which negroes I give to my daughter **Nancy** for the love and consideration I have for her and hereby Set as the value of said negroes at Eight hundred Dollars, which sum she is to account for in her distributive Shear of my Estate. Test: **Gabriel Cannon, W.H. Willbanks, John Watts.** Signed, his mark, **L.B. (x) Hines.** Witness oath, 20 Dec 1849: Signed, **W.H. Wilbanks** to **Elias Wall** Magistrate. Registered 21st Dec. 1849.

p. 388-389.   24 Oct 1849. Deed of Gift. **L.B. Hines** have this day given to my Son **G.F. Hines** a negro woman named **Louisa** about 38 years of age and a negro boy named **London** about 3 years of age which said negroes I give to my Son **G.F. Hines** for the love and consideration I have for him & I hereby Set the value of said negroes at $500, which sum he is to account for in his distributive shear of my Estate. Wit: **Gabriel Cannon, W.H. Wilbanks, John Watts.** Signed, his mark, **L.B. (x) Hines.** Witness oath, 20 Dec 1849: Signed, **W.H. Wilbanks** to **Elias Wall** Magistrate. Registered 21st Dec. 1849.

p. 389.   24 Oct 1849. Deed of Gift. **L.B. Hines** have this day given to my Son **Isham Hines** a negro Girl named **Nicy** about 14 years of age and a boy named **Jim** about 3 years of age which said negroes I give to my Son **Isham** for the love and consideration I have for him & I hereby Set the value of said negroes at $600, which sum he is to account for in his distributive share of my Estate. Wit: **Gabriel Cannon, W.H. Wilbanks, John Watts.** Signed, his mark, **L.B. (x) Hines.** Witness oath, 20 Dec 1849: Signed, **W.H. Wilbanks** to **Elias Wall** Magistrate. Registered 21st Dec. 1849. Original delivered to ~~ 18th Feby 1850. **Isham Hines.**

p. 389-390.   24 Oct 1849. Deed of Gift. **L.B. Hines** have this day given to my Son **John Hines** one negro named **Bob** about 20 years of age and one negro Girl named **Adaline** about 6 years of age which said negroes I give to my Son **John** for the love and consideration I have for him & I hereby Set the value of said negroes at $800, which sum he is to account for in his distributive shear of my Estate. Wit: **Gabriel Cannon, W.H. Wilbanks, John Watts.** Signed, his mark, **L.B. (x) Hines.** Witness oath, 20 Dec 1849: Signed, **William H. Wilbanks** to **Elias Wall** Magistrate. Registered 21st Dec. 1849.

p. 390.   24 Oct 1849. Deed of Gift. **L.B. Hines** have this day given to my Son **Kindred N. Hines** a negro man named **Cambridge** about 50 years of age and a negro Girl named **Avonilla** about 10 years of age which said negroes I give to my Son **Kindred N.** for the love and consideration I have for him & I hereby Set the value of said negroes at $600, which sum he is to account for in his distributive share of my Estate. Wit: **Gabriel Cannon, W.H. Wilbanks, John Watts.** Signed, his mark, **L.B. (x) Hines.** Witness oath, 20 Dec 1849: Signed, **William H. Wilbanks** to **Elias Wall** Magistrate. Registered 21st Dec. 1849.

p. 391.   24 Oct 1849. Deed of Gift. **L.B. Hines** have this day given to my daughter **Mary Elizabeth Hines** a negro Girl named **Arissa [or Arispa]** about 10 years of age also another negro Girl named **Amanda** about 8 years of age which said negroes I give to my daughter **Mary Elizabeth** for the love and consideration I have for him & I hereby Set the value of said negroes at $800, which sum he is to account for in his distributive share of my Estate. Wit: **Gabriel Cannon, W.H. Wilbanks, John Watts.** Signed, his mark, **L.B. (x) Hines.** Witness oath, 20 Dec 1849: Signed, **W.H. Wilbanks** to **Elias Wall** Magistrate. Registered 21st Dec. 1849.

p. 391-392.   24 Oct 1849. Deed of Gift. **L.B. Hines** have this day given to my Son **Kinchen Hines** a negro woman named **Juliet** about 20 years of age and her child a boy named **Archy** about 1 year old which said negroes I give to my Son **Kinchen Hines** for the love and consideration I have for him & I hereby Set the value of said negroes at $550, which sum he is to account for in his distributive shear of my Estate. Wit: **Gabriel Cannon, W.H. Wilbanks, John Watts.** Signed, his mark, **L.B. (x) Hines.** Witness oath, 20 Dec 1849: Signed, **William H. Wilbanks** to **Elias Wall** Magistrate. Registered 21st Dec. 1849. Original deliver to ~~ **W.H. Wilbanks** 19th Sept 1850.

p. 392-393.   24 Nov 1849. Deed of Conveyance. **James Alexander** of Spartanburg Dist, to **Wilson Alexander** of Spartanburg Dist, for $2,500 sold 360 acres, the tract where **Thomas F. Murphy** lived and a tract he purchased of **T.W. Waters**; bounded N by **Moses Casey** hatter and **Mary Ann Mongomery**, E by **Z.D. Bragg**, S by **Jane Waters & Archibald Lynch**, W by **Hiram**

Yarborough, Curtis Hughes & Fieldin Clayton. Wit: **Alexander Alexander, William Alexander.** Signed, **James Alexander.** Witness oath, 27 Nov 1849: Signed, **Alexander Alexander** to **Z. Lanford** Magt. Release of Dower, 4 Dec 1849: Signed, **Mary Alexander** to **Z. Lanford** Magt. Registered 29th Dec. 1849. Original delivered to ~~ **Wilson Alexander.**

p. 393-394. 24 Sept 1849. Deed of Conveyance. **James Tucker** of Greenville Dist, to **Roderick Prewitt** of Spartanburg Dist, for $33.33⅓ sold 100 acres on the head waters of Spencer's creek waters of Middle Tyger River; bounded by **Benjamin Prewett.** Wit: **J.M. Dickie, Presley Davis.** Signed, **James Tucker.** Witness oath, 29 Sept 1849: Signed, **Presley Davis** to **B.F. Montgomery** Mag. Registered 29th Dec. 1849.

p. 294-396. 19 Dec 1849. Deed of Conveyance. **Z.L. Holmes** of Spartanburg Dist, to **T.B. Collins** of Spartanburg Dist, for $1,500 sold 175 acres on Fair Forest Creek and its waters; bordering **McDaniel, Wells** and **Hurt.** Wit: **D.C. Judd, Joseph Foster, R.W. Folger.** Signed, **Z.L. Holmes.** Witness oath, 22 Dec 1849: Signed, **D.C. Judd** to **J.B. Tolleson** Clk & Mag Exiffo. Release of Dower, 22 Dec 1849: Signed, **Catherine N. Holmes** to **J.B. Tolleson** Clk & Mag Exiffo. (Clerk of the Court of Common Pleas & General Sessions and Ex Officio Magistrate). Registered 29th Dec. 1849.

p. 396-397. 21 Dec 1849. Sheriffs Titles. **R.C. Poole** Sheriff of Spartanburg Dist, to **William Dodd** of Spartanburg Dist, for $500, sold 51½ acres, land of **Pleasant Ballenger** Decd, by order of the Court of Ordinary, tested 8 June 1848. Land on the waters of Lossons Fork Creek and bounded by **Lovina Cothrine, Gabriel Cothrine [Cothran] & William Dodd.** Wit: **J. Belton Tolleson, Ja' F. Sloan.** Signed, **R.C. Poole,** S.S.D. Witness oath, 29 Dec 1849: Signed, **John Belton Tolleson** to **J.B. Tolleson** Clk & Mag Exiffo. Registered 29th Dec. 1849.

p. 397-398. 22 Dec 1849. Mortgage. **John Watts** of Spartanburg Dist, is indebted to **William A. McSwain** by promissory Note for $500 due by 1 Jan 1851 with Interest. Mortgage on about 426 acres on Buck Creek & Back Branch & bounded in the N by **C. Parris & John Steadman,** E by **D. Cantrell & W. Wilson,** S by **P.W. Heand & Jefferson Cooley,** W by **John Heatherington & L.B. Hinds.** Wit: **H.H. Durant, Martin Eady.** Signed, **John Watts, W.A. McSwain.** Witness oath, 3 Jan 1850: **H.H. Durant** to **J.W. Tucker** Magst. Registered 3rd Jan 1850. The above mortgage was cancelled this day by the payment of the note for which it was given. Feb 9th 1853. Signed, **William A. McSwain.**

p. 399. 5 Nov 1842. Deed of Conveyance. **Joshua Swanson** to **Benjamin Price** for $100 sold 50 acres, by computation, on Horse Creek where **James Byars** now lives adjoining **James T. Wiley, John Coventon** and others. Wit: **P. Quin Camp, Wm Webber.** Signed, **Joshua Swanson.** Witness oath, 7 Jan 1850: Singed, **P. Quin Camp** to **J.B. Tolleson** Clk & Mag Exiffo. Registered 7th Jany. 1850.

p. 399-400. 17 Dec 1844. **Wiley Sanders** to **Benjamin Price** for $225 sold 319 acres, by computation, on both sides of the Old Green River Road & on the head branches of Rocky Fork of Thickoty and heads of some branches that empties into main Thickoty waters of Broad River, beginning on the old line where the dividing line of **William Guthrie** strikes near the creek, E to **Jacob Pughes** corner, **Wm Williams & Vincent Sprouce** lines. Wit: **P. Quin Camp, J.R. Richards.** Signed, **Wiley (x) Sanders.** Witness oath, 7 Jan 1850: Signed, **P. Quin Camp** to **J.B. Tolleson** Clk & Mag Exiffo. Registered 7th Jany. 1840.

p. 400- 401. 12 Jan 1847. Deed of Conveyance. **Joshua Richard** to **Alison Clary** for $10 sold the part of real Estate of **Joseph Richards** Decd, which I purchased of **Simpson Richards** [amount not mentioned]. Wit: **J.R. Ellis, Lewis (x) Clary.** Signed, **Joshua Richards.** Witness oath, 19 Dec 1849: Signed, **J.R. Ellis** to **A. Bonner** Mag. Registered 7th Jany. 1850.

p. 401.   27 Nov 1847. Deed of Conveyance. **Smith Richards** of Rutherford Co., N.C., to **John Allison Clary** for $10 sold all my interest or child's part, [amount not mentioned] on both sides of Quins Creek, Fork of Thicoty where **Joshua Richards** lived when he died. Wit: **P. Quin Camp, Aaron P. (x) George.** Signed, **Smith Richards.** Witness oath, 19 Dec 1849: Signed, **P. Quin Camp** to **A. Bonner**, Mag. Registered 7th Jany 1850.

p. 402.   9 April 1836. Deed of Conveyance. **John Sarratt** of Spartanburg Dist, to **John R. Ellis** of Spartanburg Dist, for $150 sold 200 acres on both sides of the Cowpens Road. Wit: **Benjamin Ellis, William G. Clark.** Signed, **John Sarratt.** Witness oath, 17 Feb 1839: Signed, **William G. Clark** to **A. Bonner**, J.Q. Registered 7th Jany. 1850.

p. 402-404. 1 Dec 1849. Deed of Conveyance. **James B. Deshields** of Spartanburg Dist, to **William A. Young** of Spartanburg Dist, for $400 sold 82 acres on the waters of Cedar Shoal Creek. Bounded on the N by **Ambrose Watson**, E by **Jesse Waldrip**, S by **James Waldrip**, W by **William A. Young**. Wit: **R.J. Young, John H. Walker.** Signed, **J.B. Deshields.** Witness oath, 1 Dec 1849: Signed, **R.J. Young** to **John H. Walker**, Magistrate. Release of Dower, 1 Dec 1849: Signed, **Sally (x) Deshields** to **John H. Walker**, Magistrate. Registered 8th Jany. 1850.

p.404-405. 4 Jan 1850. Sheriffs Titles. By order of the Court of Ordinary on 9 Nov 1843 to sell lands of **Jesse Stone** Decd, **R.C. Poole** Sheriff of Spartanburg Dist, sold to **Pricilla Stone** of Spartanburg Dist, for $36.50 paid to **Wm Trimmier**, former Ordinary, the 200 acres on waters of Lossons Fork bounded by **Edward Ballenger, William Gowan & Z.M. Pollard**, formerly lands of **Bishop** [no comma] **Grambling & others**. Wit: **J.V. Trimmier, R. Bowden.** Signed, **R.C. Poole**, S.S.D. Witness oath, 4 Jan 1850: Signed, **R. Bowden** to **J.B. Tolleson** Clk & Mag Exiffo. Registered 8th Jany 1850.

p. 405-406. 9 Jan 1850. Deed of Conveyance. **Wilson Alexander** of Spartanburg Dist, to **John D. Montgomery** of Spartanburg Dist, for $1850 sold 185 acres on both side of Cedar Shoal Creek waters of Enoree River and W side of Union Road. Bounded by **Archibald Lynch, Jane Waters, Z.D. Bragg, Mary Ann Montgomery, Moses Casey H.T.**, said **Alexander** and **H. Yarborough**. Wit: **John Gibbs, Hiram Yarburgh** Signed, **Wilson Alexander.** Witness oath, 9 Jan 1850: Signed, **John Gibbs** to **P.R. Bobo** Magt. Release of dower, 9 Jan1850: Signed, **Mary Alexander.** [Magistrates statement says **J.**, or **I, Mary Alexander**]. Registered 14th Jany 1850.

p. 407-408.   13 Oct 1834. Deed of Conveyance. **John Cooper** of Spartanburg Dist, to **John Rickmon Ellis** of Rutherford Co., N.C, for $400 sold 300 acres, by computation, on Cherokee Creek, bounded by **William Fondren**. Wit: **Arthur Dillingham, Wiley Arrendall**. Signed, **John Cooper**. Witness oath, 13 Oct 1844: Signed, **Wiley Arrendall** to **Joseph Camp**, J.Q. Release of Dower, 17 Oct 1834: Signed, **Sarah (x) Cooper** to **Joseph Camp**, J.Q. Registered 14th Jany 1850.

p. 408-409.   16 Jan 1850. Mortgage. **J.W. Quinn** is indebted to **Doct. A.W. Bivings** for $56.66 by two sealed Notes both dated 16 Jan 1850, due 16 Jan 1851 & 1852 with interest in, in part to be paid for a Lot today conveyed to **J.W. Quinn**. Lot beginning on Church Street on **B. Wofford's** corner running southwardly with the street half the distance of the line of the Lot which **R.D. Owens** bought of **S. Bobo**, thence westwardly to **S. Bobo's** line so as to be equidistant on the back line of the lot **Owens** bought, then with **Bobo's** line to **Wofford's** Lot, being the one half of the Lot **Owens** bought of **S. Bobo**. Test: **Hiram McAbee, J. Belton Tolleson**. Signed, **J.W. Quinn**. Witness oath, 16 Jan 1840: Signed, **J. Belton Tolleson**. Registered 21st Jany 1850.

p. 409-410.   15 Dec 1849. Deed of Conveyance. **Adam T.P. Hempley** of Spartanburg Dist, to **Richard Moss** & others Trustees, for the erection of a School House in the neighborhood by the contribution of the Neighbors on the old field lying near the Fair Forest immediately on that is turned the Upper Greenville Road and generally known by the name of the Mulberry Tree old field, and do bargain and agree with **Richard Moss, John Martin, William Smith & Hiram Bullman** Trustees of the school to be kept there, that school house shall be built on the old field above mentioned and as above specified and that having been built it shall be left and kept open and for the use and occupation of the neighborhood as and for a school house for the term of 10 years from the time of the completion. Said building to be erected according to and under the directions of those who undertake to build the same, free from any control and interference and it is further agreed that the said School shall have free access to the Spring and all other like conveniences essential to its Ease and well being, and further for the purposes of Fire Wood &c. the school shall be permitted to gather and trim the dead wood around or near the School House from my land if desired. Wit: **Jas. Bivings, John Keast**. Signed, **Adam T.P. Hempley**. Witness oath, 23 Jany 1850: Signed, **John Keast** to **J.B. Tolleson** Clk & Mag Exiffo. Registered 21st Jany 1850. Original delivered to ~~ **Richard Moss**.

p. 410-411.   21 Jan 1850. Dower. **Charles Shaw**, wife **Susan**, to **Simpson Bobo**. Signed, **Susan (x) Shaw** to **O.E. Edwards**, Not. Pub & mag. Exoff. Registered 21st Jany 1850.

p. 411-412.   11 Jan 1850. **Josiah Kilgore** of Greenville Dist, in consideration of the love and affection I have and bear for my daughter **Harriet Isabella Hunter** and for divers other causes and in consideration of the Sum of one cent to me paid by my Son **Dr Benjamin F. Kilgore** have conveyed unto **Benjamin F. Kilgore** the following 19 slaves Viz. **Jack** about 49 years old, **Tener** 46, **Cato** 34, **Jane** 36, **Pinckney** 10, **Andrew** 8, **Joe** 6, **Rosa** 4, **Sarah** 2, **Sally** 24, **Margaret** 6, **Eliza** 4, **Polly** 2, **Caroline** 23, **Berry** 3, **Jane Adeline** 1½, **George** 18, **Cupid** 13, & **Martha** 11, with all their Increase In trust nevertheless that the said Slaves and their Increase are to be kept and employed for the Sole use and benefit of my said Daughter **Harriet I. Hunter** & her family free from any charge or debts of her husband during her natural life, and at her death to be Equally divided among her children that may Survive her, and the children of those that may die before her representing their parents, and if my daughter **Harriet I. Hunter** should die leaving neither child or children or their descendants who shall live until they are 21 years of age or marry then and in that case the said Slaves and their Increase are to revert back to my Estate. It is further expressly understood and provided by these presents that Should any of the aforesaid Slaves not suit my daughter **Harriet I. Hunter** the said **B.F. Kilgore** shall have power and his is hereby authorized by and with her advice and consent to exchange them or Either of them for another Slave or Slaves who shall be substituted. Should the said **B.F. Kilgore** die or the parties remove to an Inconvenient distance from Each other or anything should happen to make it inconvenient for her to act as trustee my daughter **Harriet I. Hunter** shall have full power to Subject another Trustee in his place. It is expressly understood that the Slaves or their Increase are not to be removed over 30 miles from my residence without the consent of the Trustee and my daughter **Harriet I. Hunter**. Test: **J.J. Wood.** Signed, **Josiah Kilgore.**

I, **Benjamin F. Kilgore** do hereby consent to act as Trustee under the within Deed of Trust, 11th Jany 1850. Test: **J.J. Wood.** Signed, **B.F. Kilgore.**

Witness oath, 12 Jan 1850: Signed, **Joseph Jackson Wood** to **Z. Lanford**, Mag. Registered 23rd Jany 1850.

p. 412-414.   25 Jan 1850. Deed of Conveyance. **John Davis** of Spartanburg Dist, to **Wilson Alexander** of Spartanburg Dist, for $3500 sold parcels of land in different tracts all joining, the papers call for 380 acres. Bounded by **Floyd's** land on the branch, **D. Miles, L. Waters, A.C. Shands, S. Taylor**, on west side of Hackee Creek Road to the road leading from X Anchor to **A.C. Shands** line. Wit: **A.C. Shands, John Snead.** Signed **John Davis.** Witness oath, 26 Jan 1850: Signed, **John Snead** to **P.R. Bobo** Magst. Release of Dower, 26 Jan 1850: Signed, **Harriet Davis** to **P.R. Bobo** Magst. Registered 28th Jany 1850. Original delivered to ~ **Aaron Hughes.**

p. 414-416.   [day & month omitted] 1850. Sheriffs Titles. **R.C. Poole,** Sheriff of Spartanburg County, by order of Court of Ordinary, sold 102 acres to **S. Bobo** and transferred to **Aquilla Jones** for $95. On [blank] of [blank] 1848, **Frances Green** petitioned the Court setting forth that **Edward Green** departed this life intestate on [blank] of [blank] 1847, in possession of 102 acres on S side of Cherokee Creek, the waters of Broad River bounded by lands formerly **John Vinsets** [also,**Vinsent**] & others and now bounded by **John Sarratt, Ervin Sarratt, George Lavinder & James Lemons.** Division of the land remained to be made and on 19 May 1848, **R. Bowden Esq,** Ordinary, ordered that the land be sold. Wit: **J.V. Trimmier, J. Belton Tolleson.** Signed, **R.C. Poole** S.S.D. Witness oath, 28 Jan 1850: Signed, **J. Belton Tolleson** to **R. Bowden** Ex off mag. Registered 28th Jany 1850. Original delivered to ~ **Aquilla Jones.**

p. 416-417.   28 Aug 1847. Deed of Conveyance. **A. Brock** of Spartanburg Dist, to **J.W. Westmoreland & L.D. Westmoreland** of Spartanburg Dist, for $150 sold [acreage not mentioned] land beginning on the wagon Road leading to the Widow **Jacksons,** bounded by **J. Davis, C.C. Lancaster** and **Alverson.** Attest: **J.G. Harris, James Loftis.** Signed, **A. Brock.** Witness oath, 28 Jan 1850: Signed, **J.G. Harris** to **James Caldwell** Magt. Registered 31st Jany 1850.

p. 417-418.   10 Sept 1849. Mortgage. **Catharine Bragg** of Spartanburg Dist, in consideration of **John Pearson** of Spartanburg Dist, having bound himself in a Bond to the Ordinary of Spartanburg

District as my security as Guardian for the minor heirs of **Curtis Bragg** Decd, **Jefferson** and **Jonas Bragg**, and for the purpose of saving **John Pearson** unharmed on account of being my security, sells [mortgages] 106 acres on James's Creek, waters of Tyger River, bounded by **E. Drummond** and **John Pearson. Catherine Bragg** must on or before 23 March 1865 cause a clear and absolute discharge of **John Pearson.** Wit: **S.S. Roebuck, David Pearson.** Signed, **Catharine Bragg.** Witness oath, 26 Jan 1850: Signed, **David Pearson** to **Z. Lanford** Magt. Registered 31ˢᵗ Jany. 1850.

p. 418-420. 20 Dec 1849. Deed of Conveyance [Mortgage?]. **Isaac Johnson** to **Samuel N. Evans** of Spartanburg Dist, for $1,000 sold (1) 100 acres on waters of Wards Creek, land I bought of **Jesse Pinson** and on which I now live, having such boundary as set forth in **Pinsons** Deed to me; (2) 100 acres adjoining the **Pinson** tract that was conveyed to me by **T.A. Rogers** 5 Dec 1846, having such boundaries as represented in his deed; (3) 244 acres on Wards branch conveyed to me by **Henry Steadings** on 30 March 1839 as represented by his deed to me, and adjoining the other two tracts. Signed, **Isaac Johnson.** The condition of the above obligation is **S.N. Evans** today loaned **Isaac Johnson** $1,000. If the Note is paid the above obligation is void. Test: **A.C. Jackson, Alexander (x) Biter.** Signed, **Isaac Johnson.** Witness oath, 4 Feb 1850:, Signed, **A.C. Jackson** to **J.B. Tolleson** Clk & Mag Exiffo. Registered 4ᵗʰ Feby 1850.

p. 420-421. 2 Nov 1849. Deed of Conveyance. **Thomas J. Durham** of Spartanburg Dist, to **Luke M. Demcey** of Spartanburg Dist, for $100 sold 150 acres on branches of Alexander's Creek, waters of South Packolet River. A road mentioned, no name. Wit: **C.C. Lancaster, Maj. J.B. Davis.** Signed, **Thomas J. Durham.** Witness oath, 4 Feb 1950: Signed, **J.B. Davis** to **J.B. Tolleson** Clk & Mag Exiffo. Registered 4ᵗʰ Feby 1850. Original delivered to ~~ **Col. S.N. Evans.**

p. 421. 10 Nov 1849. Deed of Conveyance. **Joseph Lawrence** of Spartanburg Dist, to **Samuel Burns** of Spartanburg Dist, for $210 sold 106 acres on both sides of Holston creek the waters of South Packolet River. Test: **Reubin Gramling, James Lawrence.** Signed, **Joseph Lawrence.** Witness oath, 4 Feb 1850: Signed, **Reubin Gramling** to **J.B. Tolleson** Clk & Mag Exiffo. Registered 4ᵗʰ Feby1850. Original delivered to ~~ **Samuel Burns**, 1850.

p. 422-423. 4 Feb 1850. **William Cartee** of Spartanburg Dist, is indebted to **Calvin Wall** of Spartanburg Dist, for $250 in 5 different Notes of $50 each, due 15 Mar 1851, 1852, 1853, 1854, and 27 Dec 1854 and mortgages a tract [acreage not mentioned] on the waters of Lawsons Fork and on the W side of Barton's branch, a part of two tracts. Bounded by **Thompson** East line, a conditional corner between **Emond** and **S. Bishop** and **A. Bishop, John Burnetts** East line. Deed void when notes of $250 plus interest and cost are paid. Wit: **Zachariah Wall, L.P. Wolf.** Signed, **William (x) Cartee.** Witness oath, 4 Feb 1850: Signed, **L.P. Wolf** to **J.B. Tolleson** Clk & Mag Exiffo. Registered 4ᵗʰ Feby 1850.

p. 423-424. 19 Jan 1850. Mortgage. **Margaret Sarratt** of Spartanburg Dist, to **John Sarratt & Ira Phillips** for $766.82¼ sell one negro woman **Milly** and child **Willis,** one sideboard, one cupboard and clock, two beds, bedsteads and Furniture, also my interest in the land where I now live that may hereafter be laid off to me for Dower. Note of hand (for the above amount) given to **J.R. Bowden** administrator of **Samuel Sarratt** deceased. If the debt is paid on or before 18 Jan 1851, bill of sale is void. Wit: **J.R. Ellis, Irvine Sarratt**. Signed, **Margaret (x) Sarratt**. Witness oath, 26 Jan 1850: **Irvine Sarratt** to **A. Bonner** Mag. Registered 4th Feby 1850.

p. 424-425.   19 Dec 1849. Deed of Gift. **R. Bowden** of Spartanburg Dist, for the Love and affection I have for my daughter **Polly Ann & R.J. Foster** her husband and for $70 paid by **R.J. Foster** have sold and given 140 acres on Holson branch waters of Fair Forest Creek, which is to be accounted for as advancement out of my daughter **Polly Ann Foster's** portion of my estate at my death. If I should die intestate [valued] at $420. Bounds beginning on an ash in **Bowden's** old Mill Pond, near **Wingo's** Road. Wit: **A.B. Foster, J.J. Foster**. Signed, **R. Bowden**. Witness oath, 4 Feb 1850: Signed, **J.J. Foster** to **J.B. Tolleson** Clk & Mag Exiffo. Registered 4th Feby 1850.

p. 425-426.   1 April 1841. Deed of Conveyance. **Elijah Holtsclaw** to **Josiah Kilgore** for $150 sold 102 acres being part of (396) acres granted to **John Dempsey** 5 June 1797 & part of 500 acres granted to **Robert Philp** 23 June 1794, on branches of Abners Creek Including the plantation where **John Greer** now lives. Wit: **William Hoy, Thomas Wood**. Signed, **Elijah Holtsclaw**. Witness oath, 1 Jan 1850: Signed, **W[m] Hoy** to **Mark Bennett** Magst. Registered 4th Feby. 1850.

p. 426-428.   2 Sept 1849. Deed of Conveyance. **John S. Brown & Joseph Brown** of Spartanburg Dist, to **Josiah Kilgore** for $330 sold 135 acres, part of a tract of 1000 acres granted to **Daniel Heyward** 2 April 1773, on waters of South Tyger River. Wit: **E.A. Brown, John T. Brown**. Signed, **John S. Brown, Joseph Brown**. Releases of Dower, 1 Jan 1850: to **Mark Bennett**, Signed, **Mary (x) Brown** (Wife of **Joseph Brown**). [The name of the wife of **John S. Brown** was blank and there was no signature.] Witness oath, 1 Jan 1850: Signed, **John T. Brown** to **Mark Bennett** Magst. Registered 4th Feby. 1850.

p. 428-429.   25 Jan 1850. Mortgage. **William Smith** is indebted to **Robert Jackson** for $267.91 by a note dated 14 Jan 1850 for loaned money and **Robert Jackson** has endorsed a promissory note for $375 dated 15 Jan 1850 payable to **Benjamin Wofford** or bearer; for better securing of the debt **William Smith** gives deed to 426 acres on both sides of Beaver Dam Creek a branch of South Packolet River, a part of which includes where **W. Smith** now lives originally granted to **Abigail Terrel** by patent 5 Nov 1771 for 150 acres; the other part joining that survey. Wit: **J.G. Harris, W.W. Harris**. Signed, **William Smith**. Witness oath, 26 Jan 1850: Signed, **J.G. Harris** to **James Caldwell** Mag. S.D. Registered 4 Feb 1850. Original delivered to ~~ **Robert Jackson** 1 April 1850.

p. 430-431.   1 Feb 1850. Mortgage. **E.L. Huggins** is indebted to **H.H. Thomson** for $100 by four sealed Note of $25 due in one, two, three & four years with interest from date being the price of a lot bought this day from **H.H. Thomson**. Lot, 2 acres in the Town of Spartanburg, bounded by a street leading from Spartanburg Court House to Fair Forest Creek beyond the Stone Bridge and **M.B. McCree's** back line. Wit: **R.E. Cleveland, A.J. McMakin**. Signed, **E.L. Huggins**. Witness oath, 6 Feb 1850: Signed, **R.E. Cleveland** to **J.W. Tucker**, Not. Pub. Registered 6th Feby. 1850. Original delivered to ~~ **H.H. Thomson** 24th Jany 1851.

p. 431-432.   1 Nov 1849. Deed of Conveyance. **W.G. Briant** of Spartanburg Dist, to **Alfred Tolleson** of Spartanburg Dist, for $110 sold 61 acres on the waters of Mill Creek, bounded by **Reid**.

Wit: **J.H. Wilson, J.S. Finch.** Signed, **W.G. Briant.** Witness oath, 1 Nov 1849: Signed, **J.H. Wilson** to **G.W.H. Legg** Magt. Release of Dower, 6 Feb 1850: Signed, **Lovina (x) Briant.** Registered 6th Feby. 1850.

p. 432-434. 1 Jan 1850. Mortgage. **Machan B. McCree** indebted to **H.H. Thomson** for four sealed notes for $25 each ($100) with interest due in one, two, three & four years as the price of a 2 acre Lot in the Town of Spartanburg on the street leading to Fair Forest & beyond the Stone Bridge, beginning at **Norman Abbott's** NW corner on street. Wit: **John Linder, J.B. Archer.** Signed, **M.B. McRee.** Witness oath, 8 Feb 1850: Signed, **J.B. Archer** to **J.B. Tolleson** Clk & Mag Exiffo. Registered 8th Feby. 1850. Original deliver to ~~ **H.H. Thomson** 24th Jany 1851.

p. 434-435. 17 Sept 1849. Deed of Conveyance. **H.J. Dean** of Spartanburg Dist, to **James Lee** of Spartanburg Dist, for $775 sold 283 acres on Lawsons Fork of Packolet bounded by **Eli Briant, John Weathers** and said **J. Lee,** represented by a plat made by **W.W. Harris.** Wit: **Capt. A.J. Daniel, James Edward Henry.** Signed, **H.J. Dean.** Witness oath, 16 Jan 1850: **A.J. Daniel** to **J.B. Tolleson** Clk & Mag Exiffio. Release of Dower, 24 Dec 1849: Signed, **Mary Owen Dean** to **J.B. Tolleson** Clk & Mag Exiffo. Registered 8th Feby. 1850.

p. 435-437. 8 Feb 1850. Sheriffs Titles. **R.C. Poole** Sheriff of Spartanburg Dist, to **John Snoddy** of Spartanburg Dist, for $500 sold 300 acres. Sold by order of Court of Common Pleas held 3 June 1845 at suit of **Jesse Cleveland** against **Enoch Brannon** for $475 with interest, damages and costs. The land, 300 acres, bounded by **Edward Bomar, Simpson Finch, John Bomar, Sam & John Snoddy** on Cobb Branch the waters of North Tyger River was purchased by **Albert Cunningham** and transferred to **John Snoddy.** Wit: **J.B. Cleveland, A.W. Bivings.** Signed, **R.C. Poole,** S.S.D. Witness oath, 8 Feb 1850: Signed, **J.B. Cleveland** to **J.B. Tolleson** Clk & Mag Exiffo. Registered 8th Feby. 1850.

p. 437-438. 30 Oct 1849. Mortgage. **William Carver** bought from **H.H. Thomson** two lots in the Town of Spartanburg; (1) on the street which leads from the Public Square by the Jail and contains about 1¼ acres; (2) on the streeet which leads from the Public Square on by the Stone Bridge; for the lots **Carver** gave to **Thomson** four sealed notes all of this date: one for $125 which may be discharged in Bricks, the other three notes are each for $33.33 with interest due in one, two & three years. Wit: **Hiram Mitchell, Oklav Greiner.** Signed, **William Carver.** Witness oath, 8 Feb 1850: Signed, **Oklav Greiner** to **J.B. Tolleson** Clk & Mag Exiffo. Registered 8th Feby. 1850. Original delivered to ~~ **H.H. Thomson** 24th Jany. 1851.

p. 438-440. 3 Feb 1850. Sheriffs Titles. **R.C. Poole** Sheriff of Spartanburg Dist, sold <u>43 acres</u> to **G.W.H. Legg** for $30. The land sold by order of the Court of the Ordinary at the petition of **S. Bobo Esqr.** attorney for **William Hill, James Hill, Polly Barns, Mouring [Mourning?] Hill, Thomas Hill, William Hill Jr., Jerry Lee** and **Mahala** his wife, on [blank] of [blank] 1848, setting forth that **Lovina Hill** departed this life Intestate & possessed of <u>50 acres</u> on Packolet River bounded by **John Canon, Turner** and others and division had not been made; **R. Bowden Esq.** Ordinary, on 9 July 1848, ordered the land to be sold, and sold to **A.J. McMakin** & transferred to **G.W.H. Legg,** 43 acres as shown by a Plat made by **Col. W.W. Harris** Surveyor. Wit: **R.D. Owen, James F.V. Legg.**

Signed, **R.C. Poole**, S.S.D. Witness oath, 12 Feb 1850: Signed, **James F.V. Legg** to **J.B. Tolleson** Clk & Mag Exiffo. Registered 12th Feby. 1850.

p. 440-441. 9 Feb 1850. Executor's Titles. **Simpson Ginnings & Ransom Ginnings** Exec rs, of the last will and testament of **William Ginnings** deceased, in obedience of the will did sell at Public Outcry, for $409 sold to **Hiram McAbee** 182 acres called the **McCarley** tract on Ford's Creek waters of Fair Forest, bordered by **Drury McAbee, Foster's** OR **Pettit's, Capt. Ralph Smith** and **William Bullington**. Executors warrant and forever defend the premises unto **Hiram McAbee**, Except the Dower of **Elijah Jinnings** wife, the Tract of Land being sold subject to her children. Wit: **William Petty, J.V. Trimmier**. Signed, **Simpson Ginnings, Ransom Ginnings** Executors of the last will and testament of **William Ginnings**. Witness oath, 12 Feb 1850: Signed, **J.V. Trimmier** to **J.B. Tolleson** Clk & Mag Exiffo. Registered 12th Feby. 1850. Original deliver to ∼ **Hiram McAbee** 10th Feby 1851.

p. 441- 443. 9 Jan 1850. Commissioner Titles. **T.O.P. Vernon Esqr,** Commissioner of Court of Equity for Spartanburg Dist, sold 289 acres to **J.W. Tucker** for $507. **Edwin White** on or about 18 April 1849 Exhibited his Bill of complaint against **Owen White & James White &** others praying for a division of the Real Estate of **Daniel White** Decsd, and cause was heard at June Term 1849. The Court decreed that the Plantations designated as Lots 1, 2 ,3, 4, 5 & 6 be sold at Public auction. On the first Monday in August 1849 sold to **J.W. Tucker** for $507 (subject to a claim of 3 acres of **W. & M. Seay** as will appear by dotted lines on Plat), on furnace road, bounded by **Mathew Seay, I. Clements &** others. Wit: **J. Belton Tolleson, Wm B. Bishop.** Signed, **Thos. O.P. Vernon,** C.E.S.D. Witness oath, 12 Feb 1850: Signed, **J. Belton Tolleson** to **J.B. Tolleson** Clk & Mag Exiffo. Registered 12th Feby. 1850.

p. 443-444. 11 Feb 1849. Deed of Conveyance. **James Couch** to **Jesse Campbell** of Spartanburg Dist, for $400 sold 76 acres on Enoree River, having such shape marks and bounds as represented by Plat. Wit: **James Waldrip, Eli Campbell.** Signed, **James Campbell.** Witness oath, 11 Feb 1849: Signed, **Eli Campbell** to **W.H. Wilbanks** Mag. Release of Dower, 11 Feb 1850: Signed, **Rebecca Couch** to **W.H. Wilbanks** Mag. Registered 12th Feby. 1850.

p. 444-446. 1 Jan 1850. Mortgage. **Norman Abbott** is indebted to **H.H. Thomson** for $60 by three Single Bills of this date each for $20 due in one, two & three years from date with interest, it being the price of a Lot purchased this day of the said **Thomson;** the lot, 2 acres, in the Town of Spartanburg lying on the Street beyond the Stone Bridge on both sides of Street, bounded by **Carver.** Wit: **J.B. Archer, W.S. Archer.** Signed, **Norman Abbott.** Witness oath, 12 Feb 1850: Signed, **J.B. Archer** to **J.B. Tolleson** Clk & Mag Exiffo. Registered 12th Feby. 1850. Original delivered to ∼ **H.H. Thomson** 24th Jany. 1851.

p. 446. 4 Feb 1850. Lease. **Willis Lee** is indebted to the estate of **James Ed Henry** the balance of a judgment and to **H.J. Dean** the balance of a note or Single Bill and to **Henry & Dean** a note or Single Bill. For better securing the payment of the above debts & Interest due, I convey my all my interest & Estate of every kind & description in the real & personal Estate of my father, **John Lee** Decd. Wit: **C.W. Styles.** Signed, **Willis (x) Lee.** Witness oath, 7 Feb 1850: Signed, **C.W. Styles** to

J.B. Tolleson Clk & Mag Exiffo. Registered 12th Feby. 1850.

p. 447-448. 31 Dec 1849. Deed of Conveyance. **William Cowan & John C. Cowan** Executors of the last Will and Testament of **James Cowan** Decd, by Virtue of the authority vested in us by said Will and by permission of **R. Bowden** Ordinary, on 24 October 1849 at the late residence of **James Cowan,** offered at public outcry to the highest Bidder the Tract of land hereinafter described and sold to **Harvy Vandike** for $700; land is 320 acres on North and Middle Tyger Rivers, bounded by the said **John C. Cowan, Caldwell** and lands belonging to the Estate of **John Crawford** Decd. and is more fully represented by a resurvey made by **James Leonard** on 29 Sept 1849. Wit: **W.H. Caldwell, J.Z. Coan.** Signed, **Wᵐ Coan, J.C. Coan.** Witness oath, 7 Jan 1850: Signed, **W.H. Caldwell** to **J.C. Caldwell** Magistrate. Registered 15 Feby. 1850.

p. 448-450. 12 Feb 1850. Deed of Conveyance. **Mary Linder, John Linder, John Turner, Reubin Bowden,** and **Abner E. Smith** of Spartanburg Dist, for $1200 paid to us by **Jefferson Choice** of Greenville Dist, S.C., sold 2 and near ¼ acres in the Town of Spartanburg, on Main Street, being Lot № 2 of **Lee Linder's** Estate and conveyed to us by **T.O.P. Vernon,** Commissioner in Equity as will be seen by reference to the Plat on file in the commissioners office. Wit: **J.M. Bowden, Eliphus L. Linder.** Signed, **Mary Linder, John Linder, John Turner, R. Bowden, Abner E. Smith.** Witness oath, 12 Feb 1850: Signed, **Elifus Linder** to **Joel Cannon** Mag. Wives of **John Linder (Louisa Linder), John Turner, Reubin Bowden, Abner E. Smith** Release of Dower, 12 Feb 1850: Signed, **Louiza Linder, Sinthy Turner, Nancy (x) Bowden, Charity (x) Smith.** Registered 16th Feby. 1850.

p. 450-451. 17 Nov 1849. Deed of Conveyance. **Alfred L. Moore** of Spartanburg Dist, for $1200 paid by **John Bazwell** of Spartanburg Dist, sold 298 acres on N side of South Tyger River adjoining **John S. Collins, Hiram Wakefield** and others conveyed to me by division among the heirs of my father, **Michael Moore,** Decd, and designated by Plat № 6. Wit: **James Leonard, J.A. Miller.** Signed, **Alfred L. Moore.** Witness oath, 12 Jan 1850: Signed, **J.A. Miller** to **J.C. Caldwell** Magistrate. Registered 25th Feby. 1850.

p. 451-452. 16 Feb 1850. Deed of Conveyance. **George Gilland** of Spartanburg Dist, for $735 sold to **W.M. Grisham** of Spartanburg Dist, by computation, 207 acres , part of lands purchased by **William Clark** from **Wilson Nesbitt,** on the N side of the South Fork of Tyger River, bounded by **Joseph Nesbitt** and others, on the big road. Wit: **Joseph Nesbitt, Jo Ja Howe** [Jo Ja Howe in two places]. Signed, **George Gilland.** Witness oath, 28 Feb 1850: Signed, **Joseph Nesbitt** to **J.B. Tolleson** Clk & Mag Exiffo. Registered 28th Feby. 1850.

p. 452-453. 19 Jan 1850. Deed of Conveyance. **Davis Newman** of Spartanburg Dist, for $175 paid by **William Newman,** sold 65 acres where **Newman** lives, on Cedar Shoal Creek near Enoree River, on heads ford road, bounded by **Davis Newman, Benjamin Newman, Johnson Newman, Alex Glenn** and **William Starnes.** Wit: **Ja' J. Newman** [written once as **Jonathan Newman**] , **Zechariah Strowd.** Signed, **Davis Newman.** Witness oath, 19 Jan 1850: Signed **Jas. J. Newman.** Release of Dower, 26 Jan 1850: Signed, **Nancy (x) Newman** to **P.R. Bobo** Magt. Registered 4th March 1850.

p. 453-454.   19 Jan 1850. Deed of Conveyance. **Davis Newman** of Spartanburg Dist, for $125 paid by **Johnson Newman** sold 69 acres, a part of the tract where he lives, on Cedar Shoal Creek, on heads ford road, bounded by **Benjamin Newman, William Newman, Alex Glen** and **John D. Montgomery.** Wit: **David T. McCrackin, Zechariah Strowed.** Signed, **Davis Newman.** Witness oath, 19 Jan 1850: Signed, **Zachariah Stroud** to **P.R. Bobo** Magt. Release of Dower, 26 Jan 1850: Signed, **Nancy (x) Newman** to **P.R. Bobo** Mag. Registered 4 Mar 1850.

p. 454-455.   5 Sept 1832. Deed of Conveyance. **Nimrod Horton** for $100 paid by **George Horton** sold 160 acres on Ashworth Creek & joining **Thomas Wyatt,** being a part 555 acres granted to **Grashaw Camp.** Wit: **James Templeman, Carter Burnett.** Signed, **Nimrod Horton.** Witness oath, 26 Sep 1848: Signed, **Carter Burnett** to **Wᵐ Guthrie** Mag. Registered 4 March 1850.

p. 455-457.   19 Sept 1849. Deed of Conveyance. **John T. Wood** of Spartanburg Dist, for $500 paid by **Isham Wood** of Spartanburg Dist, sold 140½ acres on South Tyger River bounded by **Abram Mayfield, Elizabeth Mason & Sarah Wood** and on the road running to **D.W. Moore's** factory. Test: **J.W. Wood, J.P. Wood.** Signed, **John T. Wood.** Witness oath, 2 Feb 1850: Signed, **J.P. Wood** to **Mark Bennett** Mgt. Release of Dower, [day & month not entered] 1850: Signed, **Martha D. Wood.** Registered 4 March 1850.

p. 457- 458.   19 Sept 1849. Deed of Conveyance. **Isham Wood** of Spartanburg Dist., for $400 sold to **John T. Wood** of Spartanburg Dist, 106 acres on the N side of the Buncomb Road and bounded by **John Johnson.** Test: **John P. Wood, J.W. Wood.** Signed, **Isham Wood.** Witness oath, 2 Feb 1850: Signed, **J.P. Wood** to **Mark Bennett** Magt. Release of Dower, 2 Feb 1850: Signed, **Thuriza Wood** (in magistrate's statement, spelled **Theriza**). Registered 4 March 1850. Original delivered to **John T. Wood** 30ᵗʰ Sept. 1850.

p. 458-459.   [no day] Feb 1850. Deed of gift. I, **Samuel Seay** of Spartanburg Dist, in for the Love and affection which I bear to my daughter **Christehany B. Seay** and divers other good and Valid considerations do hereby convey to **Catherine Pettit** the wife of **Benjamin Petit** with myself in trust for **Christehany B. Seay** all that tract of land containing 63 acres more or less, on the head waters of Shoaly Creek and Cherokee Creek water of Lawsons Fork and Pacolet River; beginning on a corner of **Col. H.H. Thomson's Spratt** tract, now **Reubin Brannon's,** and to Little Cherokee Creek on **Col. H.H. Thomson's** line now **James Norton.** Conveyed to **Catherine Petit** with myself in trust for **Christehany B. Seay,** who is the daughter of **Catherine Petit** born previous to her marriage to **Benjamin Petit,** which is at this time a minor and when she that is **Christehany** becomes 21 years of age the right to be hers forever. Wit: **John Epting, Wᵐ F. Green.** Signed, **Samuel Seay.** Witness oath, 4 Feb 1850: Signed, **Wᵐ F. Green** to **J.W. Martin,** Not. Pub. Registered 4ᵗʰ March 1850. Original delivered to ~ **Catharine Petit.**

p. 459-460.   10 March 1845. Deed of Conveyance. **T.F. Murphy** of Spartanburg Dist, for $117.81 paid by **Wᵐ S. Stone & Leander Stone** of Spartanburg Dist, sold 105 acres on the N side of Enoree River, bounded on S by Enoree River, W by land where **Col. T.F. Farrow** now lives, N & E by **John Murphy** where **L. Stone** formerly lived & died. To them forever reserving at the same time a Life Estate or right which shall rest in their Mother **Jane Stone,** widow of the late **L. Stone.** Wit:

John Murphy, Jesse Campbell. Signed **T.F. Murphy.** Witness oath, 14 Jan 1850: Signed, **Jesse Campbell** to **P.R. Bobo,** Magst. Registered 4th March 1850.

p. 460-461.   23 Jan 1850.   Mortgage. **Green B. Sarratt** of Spartanburg Dist, for $161.56 paid by **Elias Morgan** sold all my interest in the following property, all my Interest in the estate of **Samuel Sarratt** Decd. A note for the above amount was given to **J.R. Bowden,** administrator of **Samuel Sarratt** Decd, to be paid on or before 18 Jan 1851 to **Elias Morgan,** then deed is void. Wit: **J.R. Bowden, Tillman Sarratt.** Signed, **Green B. Sarratt.** Witness oath, 7 Mar 1850: Signed, **J.R. Bowden** to **John Linder** Magt. Registered 8th March 1850.

p. 461-462.   17 Sept 1849.   Deed of Conveyance. **Williamson Kelly** of Spartanburg Dist, for $500 paid by **Anders Floyd** of Spartanburg Dist, sold 160 acres where **Sealy Kelly** now lives, the tract of land given to **Thos. Kelly Jun.** by the last will of **Thos. Kelly** decd, bounded by **Edward Kelly, Thos. P. Miles** and others. **Floyd** to have **W. Kelly's** share of the present crop of oats, corn, fodder & cotton. Wit: **John H. Walker, Thomas W. Fowler.** Signed, **Williamson Kelly.** Witness oath, 17 Sept 1849: Signed, **Thomas W. Fowler** to **John H. Walker,** Mag. Release of Dower, 21 Sept 1849: Signed, **Elvira Jane Kelly** to **John H. Walker** Magistrate. Registered 8th March 1850.

p. 462-464.   27 Oct 1848. Deed of Conveyance. **Thomas D. Wofford** of Spartanburg Dist, for $725 paid by **Nimrod Arnold** of Spartanburg Dist, sold 180 acres on N side of Furgesons Creek waters of Tyger River, bounded by **Nimrod Arnold** and **Peden.** Wit: **O.G.B. Smith, Aaron Arnold.** Signed, **Thomas Wofford.** Release of Dower, 10 Feb 1849: **Nancy E. Wofford** to **Jonas Brewton,** J.Q. Witness oath, 15 Sept 1849: Signed, **Aaron Arnold** to **Mark Bennett** Magst. Registered 8th March 1850. Original delivered to ~~ **N. Arndol,** 1 April 1850. [An additional measurement was added beneath "delivered to" and signed, **L. Rodgers.**]

p. 464-465.   17 March 1847. Deed of Conveyance. **Rachel McBee** of Spartanburg Dist, sold for $100 paid by **Jeremiah McBee** of Spartanburg Dist, 100 acres on Waters of Horse creek, bounded by a conditional line between said parties. Attest: **W.F. Covington, James Davidson.** Signed, **Rachel (x) McBee.** Witness oath, 23 Oct 1847: Signed, **W.F. Covington** to **W.B. Turner** Mag. Registered 8th March 1850.

p. 465-466.   8 Oct 1849. Deed of Conveyance. **Reubin Vise** of Spartanburg Dist, for $109.66 paid by **Robert N. Morrow** of Spartanburg Dist, sold 32 & 28/100 acres on both side of Blackstock Road on branch waters of Dutchmans creek, bordered by **G. Smith, R.R. Williams, Tho' Peak, R. Morrow** and **A. Prewit.** Wit: **T.M. Vise, John Vise.** Signed, **Reubin Vise.** Witness oath, 27 Oct 1849: **J. John Vise** to **Harvey Wofford** Mag. Release of Dower, 7 Dec 1849: Signed, **Sarah (x) Vise** to **Harvey Wofford** Mag. Registered 8th March 1850.

p. 466-468.   11 Dec 1846. Deed of Conveyance. **Jaret McHam** of Spartanburg Dist, for $215 paid by **John Davis** of Spartanburg Dist, 55 acres where I now live commencing at Dutchmans creek at **Mr. Bogan's** corner on **Davis** land, to a rock at the edge of the Road at **Henry Fergurson's** corner then to the fork of the branch and with **Fergurson's** line to Dutchmans creek and the beginning to **Mr. Bogan's** corner. Wit: **Anders Floyd, W.M.G. Ross.** Signed, **Jaret McHam.** Witness oath, 17

Dec 1846: Signed, **W.M.G. Ross** to **D. Cooper**, M.S.D. Release of Dower, 17 Dec 1846: Signed **Selea (x) McHam** to **D. Cooper**, M.S.D. Registered 8ᵗʰ March 1850.

p. 468-469.   16 Jan 1850.   Deed of Conveyance. **Thomas Peake** of Spartanburg Dist, for $300 paid by **Robert N. Morrow** sold 100 acres, a part of the land where **James Bearden** formerly lived and owned, on the waters of Dutchmans Creek, a part of a tract of land originally granted to **Ephraim Hill** being a part of a tract willed by **Isaac Bearden** to his heirs; bounded on the N by **Wᵐ Bearden**, W by **Peake & Williams**, on the S and E by **R.N. Morrow**. Wit: **H.W. Ducker, Thomas P. Ham**. Signed, **Thomas Peake**. Witness oath, 16 Jan 1850: Signed, **Thomas P. Ham** to **H. Wofford** Mag. Registered 8ᵗʰ March 1850.

p. 469-471.   10 Dec 1849.   Deed of Trust. I, **Jonas Brewton Snr.** of Spartanburg Dist, in consideration of the natural Love and affection which I have for **Jonas Brewton Jr.** of Spartanburg Dist, and in consideration of $1,200 to me paid by **Jonas Brewton Jr.** and of $5 to me paid by **David Brewton** of Spartanburg Dist, have sold 500 acres on Furgersons creek, bounded by **Phillip Brewton, John Brewton**, said **Jonas Brewton Jr., Joel Maddox** and others, the Plantation where I now reside which is composed of sundry Tracts and parts of Tracts which I have from time to time purchased, all adjoining; unto the said **David Brewton** in trust always for the following uses and purposes in trust first the said **Jonas Brewton Jr** is at liberty to build upon, occupy, use and enjoy and appropriate to his own use any portion of the cleared and uncleared land which is not in use and occupation of the said **Jonas Brewton Sr.** and **Jonas Brewton Jr** is to have the right and privilege of using any timber, stone, earth for building fencing, roads and ways which is not now in use; and in trust secondly, that **Jonas Brewton Sr.** shall have the privilege of using and occupying any portion of the Plantation which is now open and under cultivation and the right to open and put into cultivation any part of the uninclosed land he may choose so that he does not interfere with that part which **Jonas Brewton Jr.** may have previously occupied and appropriated to his own use by building or otherwise. At the death of **Jonas Brewton Sr.** the within tract shall rest absolutely and in fee in the said **Jonas Brewton Jr.** or if he be dead then to his heirs and assigns forever unto the said **David Brewton** Trustee for the uses & purposes above set forth. Wit: **Philip Bruton, John M. Crook**. Signed, **Jonas Brewton**. I do consent to act as Trustee in the within Deed, 10ᵗʰ December 1849. Wit: **Philip Brewton, John M. Crook**. Ssigned, **David Brewton**. Witness oath, 11 March 1850: Signed, **John M. Crook** to **Geo. W.H. Legg** Mag. Registered 11ᵗʰ March1850. Original delivered to ~~ **Jonas Brewton** [may be S] 8ᵗʰ April 1850.

p. 471-472.   8 March 1850.   Mortgage. **Eli Johnson** of Spartanburg Dist, for $517 which I am in debt to **Sandford G. Seay** for land together with interest by reference to six notes I have given said **Seay** and have sold to **Seay** the following articles of personal property, one bay mare, three head of cattle, two cows and one yearling, 23 head of hogs, one Still and Stands and all the house hold and kitchen furniture that I am now in possession of. If **Eli Johnson** discharges the debt the bill of sale becomes void and of no effect. **Eli Johnson** is to retain possession of the articles. Wit: **Lefford French, Benjamin D. Strickland**. Signed, **Eli Johnson**. Witness oath, 9 March 1850: Signed, **Lefford French** to **J.B. Tolleson** Clk & mag Ex. Registered 11ᵗʰ March 1850.

p. 472-473.   4 March 1850. An Assignment. **William H. Thomson** of Union Dist, S.C. for $1538 paid by **James Farr** of Union Dist, S.C., have granted bargained assigned transferred and let over to **James Farr** all the right I have or may have in the real Estate belonging to the Estate of my late Father **Richard Thomson** of Spartanburg Dist, S.C., or any and all funds that may now be due me as the proceeds of the real Estate of the decd. and I hereby authorize and direct **H.H. Thomson, Junious Thomson, J. Waddy Thomson** Executors of said Estate to pay over to **James Farr** all such monies as may due me on account of the real estate aforesaid. Wit: **Wᵐ J. Keenan, David Gallman.** Signed, **W.H. Thomson.** Witness oath, 4 March 1850: Signed **David Gallman** to **Jaᵗ D. Keenan** Deputy Clerk. Registered 11ᵗʰ March 1850. Original delivered to ~~ **James Farr.** 10ᵗʰ July 1850.

p. 473-474. 1 Jan 1850. Deed of Conveyance. **E.C. Leitner** for $483 paid by **A.W. Bivings** of Spartanburg Dist, sold 575 acres on **Polly Wood** branch waters of Lawsons Fork, bounded by **Henry Bishop, Barney Bishop** and **Benson & Little's** lands, represented by the annexed plat made by **Jno. N. Barrillon** D.S., it being the same that was sold by **John N. Barrillon** Atty. [of] **Dr. E. & Eliza C. Brailsford** heirs at law of **Wᵐ Moultrie** to **D.W. Moore** and by **Moore** to **E.C. Lietner.** Wit: **Wasington Poole. J.M. Bagwell.** Signed, **E.C. Leitner.** Witness oath, 1 Jan 1850: Singed, **W. Poole** to **J.W. Cooper** Mag. Release of Dower, [no day] Jan 1850: Signed, **E.B. Leitner [Elizabeth B.]** to **J.W. Cooper** Mag. Registered 11ᵗʰ March 1850.

p. 374-375. 16 Feb 1850. Mortgage Deed. **John Nolen** of Spartanburg Dist, promises to pay $54.19 on or before the 25ᵗʰ day of December next to **Daniel F. Maberry** of Spartanburg Dist. Test: **J.V. Trimmier.** Signed, **John Nolen. John Nolen** sells [mortgages] 49¾ acres on a branch of Lawsons Fork creek and on the Road leading to Boiling Springs. Wit: **J.V. Trimmier, F.L. Parham.** Signed, **John Nolen.** Witness oath, 25 March 1850: Signed, **J.V. Trimmier** to **J.B. Tolleson** Clk & mag Exoffi. Registered 25 March 1850.

p. 376-477. 26 March 1850. Mortgage. **A. Brawley** is indebted to **H.H. Thomson** for $75 by three sealed notes of $25 each due 1ˢᵗ Jany. 1851, 1852 & 1853, the purchase money of a 2 acre Lot in the Town of Spartanburg which **A. Brawley** bought this day of **H.H. Thomson;** beginning on SE back corner of the Parsonage lot and adjoining **Jesse Cleveland.** Wit: **J.W. Tucker, Govan Mills.** Signed, **A. Brawley.** Witness oath, 26 March 1850: Signed, **Govan Mills** to **J.B. Tolleson** Clk & mag Exoffi. Registered 26ᵗʰ March1850. Original delivered to ~~ **H.H. Thomson.** 24ᵗʰ Jany 1851.

p. 477-478. 13 Nov 1848. An Agreement. **John Brown** of Hall Co., GA, being now in State and District above named (Spartanburg), and whereas I am about to Join in Wedlock with **Milly Duncan** widow of Spartanburg Dist, and whereas **Milly** has several children and is also possessed of sundry property the title of which is now fully Vested in her and she has consented to become my Lawful wife, Lawfully wedded, I have consented to agree and by this Instrument do agree and bind myself to allow her to retain in her own right & title Such Negro or other property as she may deem proper for her own use & benefit & finally to dispose of in Such way as she may desire. I further agree that She may take with her to my House Such negroes as she has selected Viz. **Mariah, Evaline, Ben, Berry** & child **Tennessee** & they are to be kept at my house at my Expense Subject to her will & should **Milly** not Sell or transfer said negroes during her natural Life & Should die Intestate then & in that case they Shall be considered as belonging to her Estate & be subject to division amongst her heirs agreeably to the stature of distribution & the Law, as though she had continued to Live a Widow until her death. Wit: **W.A. Hawkins, G. Cannon** Not Pub. Signed, **John E. Brown.** Witness oath, 7 March 1850: Signed, **Gabriel Cannon** to **J.M. Elford** Mag. Registered 26th March 1850.

p. 478-479. 26 Nov 1849. Deed of Conveyance. **Benjamin Wofford** of the Town of Spartanburg, for $1,000 paid by **Alfred Tolleson** of Town of Spartanburg, sold a lot of a fraction of an acre, in Town of Spartanburg fronting on the public Square and adjoining on the W a Lot known as Lot Nº 4 now occupied by **G.W.H. Legg Esq.** The lot bounds on the S upon a street twelve feet in width which I do hereby give for the benefit of those purchasing Lots fronting on the Public Square which street runs nearly at right angles with the Jail Street Extending to **Jesse Cleveland's** Lot. Wit: **J.B. Archer, W[m] Petty.** Signed, **Benj. Wofford.** Witness oath, 12 Feb 1850: Signed, **John B. Archer** to **J.B. Tolleson** Clk & mag Exoffi. Release of Dower, 25 March 1850: Signed, **Maria S. Wofford** [**Maria Scott Wofford**]. to **J.B. Tolleson** Clk & mag Exoffi. Registered 26th March 1850.

p. 480. 1 April 1850. Mortgage. **Enoch Pinson** of Spartanburg Dist, for $6.95 paid by **Anderson Rogers** sold one bay colt & 11 Spotted hogs to be his Property until the above Sum of $6.95 is paid to **A. Rogers.** Test: **F. Ward.** Signed, **Enoch (x) Pinson.** Witness oath, 1 April 1850: Signed, **F. Ward** to **J.B. Tolleson** Clk & mag Exoffi. Registered 3rd April 1850.

p. 480-481. 3 Sept 1843. Deed of Conveyance. **Samuel Floyd** of Spartanburg Dist for $312 paid by **Toney Thomas** of Spartanburg Dist sold 78 acres on the S side of Tyger River, beginning at the mouth of my spring branch, adjoining **Richard Willis.** Wit: **Spencer M. Scott, John Thomas.** Signed, **Samuel Floyd.** Witness oath, 1 Nov 1843: Signed, **Spencer M. Scott** to **Jonas Brewton** Mag. Registered 3rd April 1850. Original delivered to **Tomy Thomas** 6th May 1850.

p. 481-482.   30 Dec 1841. Deed of Conveyance. **Cornelius Caster & Ann Wilmot** both of Spartanburg Dist, for $6 per acre to us paid by **Thos. Thomas** of Spartanburg Dist, sold 100 acres on the S side of Fergasons creek. Beginning at the mouth of said **Thomas** line and with **Scott's** line. Wit: **G. Nichols, George E. DBard** . Signed, **Cornelioud Castor, Ann (x) Wilmot.** Witness oath, 30 Dec 1841: Signed, **George E. Dbard.** Registered 3rd April 1850. Original delivered to ~~ **Tomy Thomas** 6th May 1850.

p. 482-484. 10 April 1848. Mortgage. **Alfred Austell** of Campbell Co., GA, administrator of the Estate of **William W. Austell** late of Campbell Co., GA, Deceased, for $35 paid by **Gabriel Cannon, Joseph Finger & Henry Kestler** of Spartanburg Dist, sold a Quit claim to any right or claim that the said **William W. Austell** had in his lifetime to 140 acres on waters of Little Buck Creek bounded by **Elizabeth Harris** and **John Heatherington.** Wit: **Robert O. Beavers, Eli R. Goodrich,** J.P. Signed, **Alfred Austell** adm of **W.W. Austell** Decd. 16 Oct 1848, **Reubin C. Beavers** clerk of the Inferior court of Campbell Co., GA, certifies that **Eli R. Goodrich** is an acting Justice of the Peace. 16 Oct 1848, **William M. Butt,** one of the Justices of the Inferior court of Campbell Co., GA certifies that **Reubin C. Beavers** is the legal acting clerk of the Inferior court of said county. Registered 3rd April 1850. Original delivered to ~~ **G. Cannon.**

p. 484-485. 15 March 1848. Deed of Conveyance. **Joseph Finger** of Spartanburg Dist, for $1200 paid by **Gabriel Cannon, Joseph Finger & Henry Kestler** (otherwise the Packolet Manufacturing Co) of Spartanburg Dist, sold 55 acres on both sides of North Packolet River and on **Ezell**'s branch, bounded by **D. McMakin, J. Finger's** Mill. Excepting such privileges as I have reserved to myself, one half of the water for the use & benefit of my Grist Mill with the free privilege Ingress & Egress, also the privilege of keeping my present Mill dam in good repair and the above named persons the other half with the privilege of keeping up a dam or dams as they may desire; also the privilege of opening out and using the water from my mill race to the full extent of one half the same. It is hereby agreed that neither myself or the above named three persons or Co. shall at any time obstruct the other.Wit: **J.M. Jackson, A.W. Bullington.** Signed, **Joseph Finger.** Witness oath, 16 March 1849: Signed, **A.W. Bullington** to **Elias Wall** Magistrate. Registered 3rd April 1850. Original delivered to ~~ **G. Cannon.**

p. 485-486. 6 Nov 1848 [or 8 Jan 1850?]. Sheriffs Titles. **R.C. Poole** Sheriff of Spartanburg Dist, by order of the Court if Ordinary, sold 126 acres to **James L. Pearson** for $170. On 19 Aug 1848, **Jane Davis** petitioned the Court for part and division of the estate of **William Davis** who departed this life intestate [no date] possessed in fee 126 acres on the waters of Little Buck Creek bounded by **Wm J. Hynes** & others. On 13 Oct 1848, **R. Bowden Esq**, Ordinary of Spartanburg Dist, ordered that the land be sold by the sheriff. Wit: **J.S. Collins, J.B. Tolleson.** Signed, **R.C. Poole**, S.S.D. Witness oath, 8 April 1850: Signed, **J.B. Tolleson** to **O.E. Edwards**, Not. Pub. Registered 8th April 1850. Original delivered to ~~ **James L. Pearson** 8th April 1850.

p. 487-488. 9 Feb 1850. Deed of Conveyance. **William Copeland Senr.** of Spartanburg Dist, for $91.50 paid by **Anderson Calvart** of Spartanburg Dist, sold 122 acres on both sides of Bear Creek waters of North Pacolett river (a tract which was granted to **William & James Gilmore** in 1809); bounded by the NC line, **James Seay, W. Chapman** and **William Blackwood.** Wit: **Jackson Robbins, Elias Johnson.** Signed, **William Copeland.** Witness oath, 2 April 1850: Signed, **Elias Johnson** to **Gabriel Cannon** Not. Public. Registered 9th April 1850. Original delivered to ~~ **Anderson Calvart.**

p. 488-489. 5 April 1850. Deed of Conveyance. **Robert D. Owens** of Spartanburg Dist, for $300 paid by **John B. Archer** sold ½ acre [Town of Spartanburg?] on the W side of church street bounded by a cross street, **J.W. Quinn** and **L. Hewitt.** Wit: **Wm Walker, J. Guinn Harris.** Signed, **R.D. Owens.** Witness oath, 5 April 1850: Signed, **J. Gwinn Harris** to **J.W. Tucker** Not. Pub. Release of Dower, 9 April 1850: Signed, **F.R. Owen** to **J.B. Tolleson** Clk & mag Exoffi. Registered 7th April 1850.

p. 489-490. 21 Jan 1850. Deed of Conveyance. **Benj. Wofford** of Spartanburg Dist, for $800 paid by **William B. Seay & Anthony G. Campbell** of Spartanburg Dist, sold a lot of a fraction of an acre, in the Town of Spartanburg adjoining a Lot on the E now owned by **Joseph Foster & D.C. Judd** and on the W by a Lot now owned by **J.B. Archer**, on S by the Public Square & on the S by a street running from Jail Street to a Lot now owned by **Jesse Cleveland.** Wit: **J. Zimmerman, J. Gwinn Harris.** Signed, **Benj. Wofford.** Release of Dower, 25 March 1850: Signed, **Maria S. Wofford [Mrs. Maria Scott Wofford** in clerk's statement] to **J.B. Tolleson** Clk & mag Exoffi. Witness oath, 29 March 1850: Signed, **J. Zimmerman** to **J.B. Tolleson** Clk & mag Exoffi. Original delivered to ∼ **A.G. Campbell** 7th June 1850.

p. 490-491. 9 April 1850. Deed of Conveyance. **John T. Kirby** of Spartanburg Dist, for $300 paid by **William Walker, a.s.h.** of Spartanburg Dist, sold 6 acres in Spartanburg Village on the Greenville Road, adjoining **W. Lows, Walker & Wyatt** and **Widow Bomar**. Wit: **J. Gwinn Harris, J. Belton Tolleson**. Signed, **Jno. Kirby**. Witness oath, 9 April 1850: Signed, **J. Gwinn Harris** to **William Walker**, N.P.S.D. Registered 9th April 1850. [Added: Note given this day by me for purchase money. Land Stands good for Said note. $220 due twelve months after date, this 9th April 1850. Attest: **J. Belton Tolleson**. Signed, **William Walker**]

p. 492-493. 9 April 1850. Deed of Conveyance. **John T. Kirby** of Spartanburg Dist, for $219.93 paid by **John Wyatt Jun.** of Spartanburg Dist, sold a parcel of land [amount not given] in Spartanburg Village on the Greenville Road, adjoining **W. Walker, Kirby** and **Widow Bomar**. Wit: **J. Gwinn Harris, J. Belton Tolleson**. Signed, **Jno. Kirby**. Witness oath, 9 April 1850: Signed **J. Belton Tolleson** to **William Walker**, N.P.S.D. [Added: Note given this day by me for purchase money. Land Stands good for Said Note $139.93 due twelve months after date this 9th April 1850. Attest: **J. Belton Tolleson**. Signed, **John Wyatt**. Registered 9th April 1850.

p. 493-494. [no day] Oct 1849. Deed of Conveyance. **Catharine M. Nicholls** Executrix of the last Will and testament of **George Nicholls** deceased, of Spartanburg Dist, for $50 paid by **Elizabeth C. Trail, David W. Trail, Mary Ann Trail, George P. Trail, Olive C. Trail & John F. Trail** all of Spartanburg Dist, sold 215 acres on which **John Trail** now lives, bounded by lands formerly owned by **Jonathan Floyd** but now owned by **Wiley Johnson**, by **R. Lanford, John Gentry, Jesse Pinson, Thomas Thomas** & others. Wit: **Lecil Beardin, James Crook**. Signed, **C.M. Nicholls** Executrix. Witness oath, 4 March 1850: Signed, **Lecil Beardin** to **H. White** Mag. Registered 9th April 1850.

p. 494-495. 4 Jan 1841. Deed of Conveyance. **Fielding Turner** agt To **James Robbins**. **Fielding Turner** agent and attorney in fact for **William Cantrell** of Alabama, for $280 paid by **James Roberts** of Spartanburg Dist, sold 391 acres to **James Robins**, land on waters of Buck creek adjoining **Robbins** line, NC line. Wit: **W[m] Trimmier, Thomas Shields**. Signed, **W[m] Cantrell** by atty **Fielding Turner**. Witness oath, 26 June 1841: Signed, **Thomas Shields** to **Samuel Ezell** J.Q. Registered 10th April 1850. Original delivered to ∼ **Jackson Robbins**.

p. 495-496. 28 March 1850. Deed of Conveyance. **H.H. Thomson** of Spartanburg Dist, for $246.33 sold to **J.B. Morgan** 3 acres & 4/10 in the Town of Spartanburg; adjoining SE corner of **Carver's** Lot, a new street and a contemplated street, the branch of **Linder's** line. Wit: **W.W. Harris, J.W. Tucker**. Signed, **H.H. Thomson**. Witness oath, 10 April 1850: Signed, **W.W. Harris** to **J.B. Tolleson** Clk & mag Exoffi. Registered 15th April 1850. Original delivered to ∼ **J.B. Morgan**.

p. 496-497. 28 March 1850. Deed of Conveyance. **H.H. Thomson** of Spartanburg Dist, for $120 paid by **J.W. Wood** of Spartanburg Dist, sold 2 acres and 4/10 in the Town of Spartanburg bounded by a cross street leading from **Col. R.C. Poole's** which intersects a street which runs by **A. Tolleson's** Lot, **Poole's** line. Wit: **W.W. Harris, John Linder**. Signed, **H.H. Thomson**. Witness oath, 10 April 1850: Signed, **W.W. Harris** to **J.B. Tolleson** Clk & mag Exoffi. Registered 15th April 1850.

p. 497-498. 28 March 1850. Mortgage. **J.W. Wood** is indebted to **H.H. Thomson** by three sealed notes in the sum of $100 for the price of a Lot which **Wood** bought this day from **H.H. Thomson**. The lot, 2 acres & 4/10 in the Town of Spartanburg bounded by the street that runs from **R.C. Poole's** at new street, **Poole's** corner. Wit: **John Linder, W.W. Harris**. Signed, **J.W. Wood**. Witness oath, 10 April 1850: Signed, **W.W. Harris** to **J.B. Tolleson** Clk & mag Exoffi. Registered 15th April 1850. Original delivered to ~ **H.H. Thomson** 24th Jany 1851. [Written in margin]: This mortgage is satisfied. **H.H. Thomson.**

p.498-500. 28 March 1850. Mortgage. **J.B. Morgan** is indebted to **H.H. Thomson** in the sum of $246.33 by three sealed notes for a Lot in the Town of Spartanburg which **J.B. Morgan** purchases from **H.H. Thomson**; the lot, 3 acres & 4/10 bounded by **Wm Carver's** SE corner, a street and new street, **Linder's** line. Wit: **Col. W.W. Harris, J.W. Tucker**. Signed, **J.B. Morgan**. Witness oath, 10 April 1850: Signed, **W.W. Harris** to **J.B. Tolleson** Clk & mag Exoffi. Registered 15th April 1850. Original delivered to ~ **H.H. Thomson** 24th Jany 1851.

p. 500-501. 25 Jan 1850. Mortgage. **Wilson Alexander** of Spartanburg Dist, for $3,500 paid by **John Davis** of Spartanburg Dist, sold 383 acres where **John Davis** now lives on the waters of Tyger River bounded by **A.C. Shands, Floyd** and others, more fully explained in a Deed from **John Davis** to **Wilson Alexander**. Provided **Wilson Alexander** pays to **John Davis** the Just Sum of $3,500 in three annual installments of $1166.66 on 25 Dec 1850, 1851, 1852. Wit: **A.C. Shands, John Snead**. Signed, **Wilson Alexander**. Witness oath, 1 March 1850: Signed, **A.C. Shands** to **P.R. Bobo** Magst. Registered 18th April 1850.

p. 501-502. 10 April 1849. Deed of Conveyance. **P.M. Wallace** of Spartanburg Dist, for $1,600 paid by **John Davis** of Spartanburg Dist, sold (1) 230 acres on a Branch called Hackies creek waters of Tyger River and S of said creek, the plantation I purchased from **Charles H. Dillard** which **Dillard** Purchased from **Jesse Lamb** and **Lamb** from **Golding Tinsley**, and such bounds as the plat represents in **Golding Tinsley's** Deed to **Jesse Lamb**; (2) also 3/8 of an acres in three small pieces of Land which I purchased from **Thomas Kelly** and **Lelia Kelly** as described in their Deed to me; (3) 35 acres known as the **Blackstock** Place which I purchased at a Sale by the commissioner of Laurens Dist, designated by Plat Nº 6 in his office. The whole of these several tracts being bounded by **L. Waters** on the E, on the S by **Isaac Tinsley** and **James Lambright**, on the W by **W.J. Whitmore, Samuel Gentry** and **Jefferson Dodd**, on the N by **Williamson Kelly** and **Thomas Miles**. Wit: **Francis A. Miles, Jerry Harrison**. Signed, **P.M. Wallace**. Witness oath, 18 Oct 1849: Signed, **F.A. Miles** to **John H. Walker** Mag. Registered 18th April 1850.

p. 502-503. 12 May 1848. Deed of Conveyance. **G. Nicholls** of Spartanburg Dist, for $400 paid by **James N. Nolly** of Spartanburg Dist, sold (1) Lot in the Town of Spartanburg on the E side of Church Street known as the **Harley** Lot, Including 1 acre & 3/10, bounded by the Methodist Church Lot on the S. on the E by the estate of **R. Thomson** decd, N by **W.B. Seay**, W by Church Street; (2) another lot of 1 acre in the Town of Spartanburg near the Baptist Church on S side of the Greenville

Road known as the **Rollings** Lot. Wit: **Wm B. Seay, D.C. Judd.** Signed, **G. Nicholls.** Witness oath, 13 April 1850: Signed, **D.C. Judd** to Geo. **W.H. Legg** Mag. Registered 18th April 1850. Original delivered to ⁓ **J.N. Nolly.** 14th Sept. 1850.

p. 503-504.   2 March 1850. Mortgage. **James Ellis** of Spartanburg Dist, for $19.76 paid by **J.R. Bowden** and **L.H. Sarratt** sold a bay horse, and 1 horse wagon, two cows and one yearling, one red one and three other yearlings. If **James Ellis** pays off two notes before 1 April next, one for $8.76 to **J.R. Bowden**, the other to **Samuel Sarratt** now in the hands of **J.R. Bowden**, administrator of **Samuel Sarratt**, this bill of sale to be void. Wit: **Robert Byars, Hamilton (x) Morgan.** Signed, **James Ellis.** Witness oath, 13 Apr 1850: Signed, **Robt. Byars** to **A. Bonner,** Mag. Registered 18th April 1850.

p. 504-505.   4 March 1850. Deed of Gift. I, **A.G.W. Gordan** for the natural love and affection I bear to **Francis Marion Gordan** of Spartanburg Dist, give 100 acres bounded by **Yarborough** and a road, also a Small bay Horse. Test: **Wm Huff, Davis Newman, H.A. Vaughn.** Signed, **A.G.W. Gordan.** Witness oath, 4 March 1850: Signed, **Wm Huff** to **P.R. Bobo** Magst. Registered 22nd April 1850. Original delivered to ⁓ **A.G.W. Gordan.**

P. 505-506.   4 March 1850. Deed of Conveyance. **A.G.W. Gordan** of Spartanburg Dist, for $1,000 paid by **Davis Newman** sold 205 acres on waters of Enoree bounded by **Phillimon Waters, Nancy Hill, John Hollis [or Hillis], Thomas Lamb, Hiram Yarborough** & others. Test: **Wm Huff, H.A. Vaughn.** Signed, **A.G.W. Gordan.** Witness oath, 4 March 1850: Signed, **Wm Huff** to **P.R. Bobo** Magst. Registered 22nd April 1850.

p. 506-507.   13 April 1850. **J.B. Morgan** is indebted to **J.N. Nolly** for $400 by three sealed notes of $133.33⅓ due on the 8th of April 1851, 1852, 1853. To better secure the payments **J.B. Morgan** conveys to **J.N. Nolly** a lot in the Town of Spartanburg, 1 and 3/10 acres on Church street adjoining the Methodist Church Lot and bounded by **J.B. Cleveland** and **W.B. Seay**, which was purchased this day from **J.N. Nolly.** Wit: **Jas. F.V. Legg, J.N. Murray.** Signed, **J.B. Morgan.** Witness oath, 13 April 1850: Signed, **Jas. F.V. Legg** to **G.W.H. Legg** Magst. Registered 22nd April 1850. Original delivered to ⁓ **J.N. Nolly** 14th Sept. 1850.

p. 507-508.   20 Aug 1839. Deed of Conveyance. **Jacob Hedden** of Spartanburg Dist, for $1,050 paid by **Samuel N. Evans** of Spartanburg Dist, sold 197 acres in Spartanburg Dist. Wit: **Hugh Caldwell, A.W. Drummond.** Signed, **Jacob Hedden.** Release of Dower, 9 Nov 1839: Signed, **Nancy (x) Hedden** to **Thomas Leonard** J.Q. Witness oath, 4 Feb 1850: Signed, **Hugh Caldwell** to **J.B. Tolleson** Clk & mag Exoffi. Registered 22nd April 1850.

p. 509.   15 Feb 1850. Deed of Conveyance. **T.B. Collins** of Spartanburg Dist, for $238 paid by **Andrew Holshouser** of Spartanburg, sold 57 acres on the waters of Fair Forest creek. Beginning at a stake on the road leading from Spartanburg to Poolsville, bounded by lands on the S of said **Holshouser**, W by **Ransom White**, N by **H.H. Thomson** and E by **Thomson.** Wit: **D.C. Judd, J.N. Murray.** Signed, **T.B. Collins.** Witness oath, 22 April 1850: **D.C. Judd** to **J.B. Tolleson** Clk & mag Exoffi. Registered 22nd April 1850.

p. 510-513. 1 Jan 1848. Agreement. **Gabriel Cannon, Joseph Finger & Henry Kestler** have this day entered into partnership for the purpose of Manufacturing cotton & wool, the firm to be known by the name of Paco<u>lett</u> Manufacturing Company; Said co having purchased a parcel of **Joseph Finger** on North Paco<u>lett</u> River near where **Finger's** mill now stands, with such privileges as their Deed of Conveyance will show; have agreed as Joint Partners to erect & build at the Expense of said co. on the premises above named, a building with the necessary appurtenances & machinery for the manufacturing cotton yarn, building to be constructed agreeable to a plan agreed to Subject however to Such alterations as shall be unanimously agreed to. The mill at the head of the Race formerly owned by **Jos. Finger**, also the Wool Carder below **Finger's** Mill with the buildings and all their appurtenances together with the Store house now used by **G. Cannon** are hereby acknowledged to belong to the firm of the Pacolet Man co. Each of the Partners shall pay over to the agent of said Co. such sums of money as shall be jointly agreed upon from time to time to be used for the purchase of machinery, the hire of labour & the purchase of such other materials as may be necessary for the use of said Co. not to Exceed in the whole of $10,000.

The parties agree that **Henry Kestler** shall be employed as principal workman in Erecting & fitting up said work and while engaged and actually employed at the same time shall receive the sum of $1.50 per day and boarded at the expense of said Co. It is further agreed that when the work is completed and the Spinning commenced **Kestler** is to be employed as machinist also to overlook the business in and about the factory to do and attend to the business faithfully to the Interest and benefit of the Co, to board himself and receive as a compensation for his services the sum of $400 per annum. **Joseph Finger** is also to be employed as a workman such time as he can leave his other business wherever the Co. may require his services for which he is to be paid a reasonable compensation. It is also agreed that **Gabriel Cannon** is to be appointed agent and Superintendent of the Co. to keep books, make purchases and sales, to receive and pay out monies in behalf & for the use of the Co. and he shall whenever called upon by the other Stock holders within a reasonable time make a full and fair exhibit of the Books together with such notes or other evidence of Debt as may be due the Co, also the amount of their indebtedness as near as may be ascertained. **Cannon** shall board himself & furnish his own Horse (traveling Expenses Excepted) and receive a compensation of $300 per annum.

It is also agreed by the parties that no distillery of or retailing or otherwise trading & trafficking in Spiritous liquors shall at any time be allowed on the premises and the parties further agree that the same shall not be allowed on either of their private possessions. It is further agreed that if either **Gabriel Cannon** or **Henry Kestler** shall be at liberty to discontinue their services provided they shall first give Six months notice to the other stock holders but doing so would have no effect as to the partnership.

It is further understood that the Co. shall commence their work as may be convenient, say some time during the present winter or the Ensuing Spring. Attest: **W.P. Compton, T.J. Caldwell.** Signed, **Gabriel Cannon, Jo' Finger, Henry Kestler.** Witness oath, 26 April 1850: Signed, **T.J. Caldwell** to **J.B. Tolleson** Clk & mag Exoffi. Registered 26th April 1850. Original delivered to ~~ **Gabriel Cannon** 10th May 1850.

p. 513-515. 15 Nov 1849. Deed of Conveyance. **Anders Floyd** of Spartanburg Dist, for $960 paid by **Samuel McCravey** of Spartanburg Dist, sold 176 acres on the N side of Tyger River on both sides of Cane Creek and bound on the S by Tyger River, on the E by **A. Pruet,** on the N by **Sum**

Sumner and on the W by **Samuel McCravy**. Test: **Stephen Taylor, A.C. Shands**. Signed, **Anders Floyd**. Witness oath, 25 Feb 1850: Signed, **A.C. Shands** to **H. Wofford** Mag. Release of Dower, 22 Feb 1850: Signed, **Lucinda Floyd** to **Henry Wofford**, J.P. & Mag. Registered 26th April 1850.

p. 515-516. 3 Dec 1849. Deed of Conveyance. **Ephraim Woodward** of Spartanburg Dist, for $700 paid by **Samuel McCravy** of Spartanburg Dist, sold 193 acres beginning on **McCravy's** corner, formerly **O'Shields** corner, bounded on SE by **Mrs. Frances Shands** and **George Cathcart** and all other sides by **Samuel McCravy**. Wit: **Eliphas C. Smith, Jas. Smith**. Signed, **E. Woodward**. Witness oath, 3 Dec 1849: Signed, **Jas. Smith** to **Sum Sumner** Mag. Release of Dower, 5 Dec 1849: Signed, **Elizabeth (x) Woodward**. Registered 26th April 1850.

p. 516-518. 11 Oct 1845. Deed of Conveyance. **John T. Kirby** of Spartanburg Dist, for $150 paid by **David Miller** of Spartanburg Dist, sold ½ acre on the SE side of the Village of Spartanburg, bounded by **Richard Thomson, James Daniel,** and the street leading from **James Hunt's** old house, within forty feet of a well on said lot then to prescribe an area of a circle so as to include one half of the well. The well to be jointly owned by **J.T. Kirby** and **David Miller**. Wit: **Jno. C.C. Legg, Geo. W.H. Legg**. Signed, **Jno. Kirby**. Witness oath, 11 Oct 1845: Signed, **J.C.C. Legg** to **G.W.H. Legg**. Release of Dower, 2 May1850: Signed, **P. Kirby [Patsy Kirby** in Clerks statement] to **J.B. Tolleson** Clk & mag Exoffi. Registered 2nd May 1850.

p. 518-520. 1 May 1850. Deed of Conveyance. **Z.J. Bates** of Spartanburg Dist, for $500 paid by **Majr. John T. Kirby** of Spartanburg Dist, sold 124 acres on the main road leading to Columbia from Spartanburg Court House on the waters of Fair Forest, the tract of land which I bought of **Richard Thomson** except 71 acres which I heretofore sold to my Sister **Clarissa Bates** and which is included in the above boundaries, after the exception contains 124 acres. Wit: **H.H. Thomson, Dr. J.B. Morgan**. Signed, **Z.J. Bates**. Release of Dower, 2 May 1850: Signed **Ibbeline (x) Bates [Ibeline** in clerk's statement]. Witness oath, 2 May 1850: **J.B. Morgan** to **J.B. Tolleson** Clk & mag Exoffi. Registered 3rd May 1850.

p. 520-521. 27 April 1850. Mortgage. **J. Ramsey Bowden** is indebted to **H.H. Thomson** by three sealed notes for $275 being for the purchase of a lot of 4 acres which **Bowden** this day bought of **H.H. Thomson**; the lot in the Village of Spartanburg beginning on a stone at cross street beyond Stone Bridge running with main street. Wit: **Dr. J.B. Morgan, J.B. Archer**. Signed, **J.R. Bowden**. Witness oath, 2 May 1850: Signed, **J.B. Morgan** to **J.B. Tolleson** Clk & mag Exoffi. Registered 3rd May 1850. Original delivered to ∼ **H.H. Thomson** 24th Jany 1851.

p. 521-522. 7 Aug 1849. Deed of Conveyance. **Josiah Kilgore** for $345 paid by **Joseph Brown** sold 99 acres on Wards creek of Tyger River, a part of a grant of 1250 acres to **Thomas Heyward** the 20th July 1772. Wit: **Philip C. Lester, Philip (x) Donagan**. Signed, **Josiah Kilgore**. Witness oath, 28 Aug 1849: Signed, **Phil C. Lester** to **Isham Wood** Mag S.D. Registered 6th May 1850. Original delivered to ∼ **Joseph Brown** 24th Jany 1851.

p. 522-523. 14 Aug 1848. Deed of Conveyance. **Thomas Hutchings** for $60 paid by **Joseph Brown** sold 11 acres, part of a tract of 1,250 acres granted to **Thos. Heyward Jun.** in 1772, on

Wards creek of Tyger River. Wit: **Joel Farmer, Samuel B. Hutchings.** Signed, **Thos. Hutchings Jun.** Witness oath, 20 Nov 1849: Signed, **Joel Farmer** to **Isham Wood** Mag S.D. Registered 6th May 1850. Original delivered to ~ **Joseph Brown**27th Jany 1851.

p. 523-525.   6 May 1850. Sheriffs Titles. **R.C. Poole** Sheriff of Spartanburg Dist, for $1350 paid by **John Wheeler,** sold 300 acres on Middle Tyger River adjoining lands of **Mary McMakin, Alexander Wheeler** & others. The land was sold by order of the Court of the Ordinary by the petition of 15 Aug 1849 by **Alexander Wheeler** for division of the land of **David Wheeler** who departed this life intestate [no date]. Wit: **William Dodd, J. Rufus Poole.** Signed, **R.C. Poole** S.S.D. Witness oath, 6 May 1850: Signed, **J.R. Poole** to **R. Bowden** Exoffo Mag. Registered 6th May 1850.

p. 525.   6 May 1850. Mortgage. **Muse Gossett** promises one day after date to pay **James Wood** $362.29 for value recd. He pledges and makes chargeable unto **James Wood** for the above debt: three negroes, one woman named **Ginnetta** about 25 years old, a boy named **William Henry** about 2 years old, a Girl named **Fanny** about 3 years old. Wit: **B.F. Bates, J. Belton Tolleson.** Signed, **Muse Gossett.** Witness oath, 6 May 1850: Signed, **B.F. Bates** to **J.B. Tolleson** Clk & Mag Exiffo. Registered 6th May 1850.

p. 525-526.   13 March 1850. Deed of Conveyance. **Adam Keitt** of Orangeburg Dist, for $1,800 paid by **T.W. Waters** of Spartanburg Dist, sold 324 acres on Waters of Fair Forest creek bounded by the Cedar Springs land, estate of **John Black, Mrs. Kennedy, Simpson Bobo** and the estate of **E. Foster.** Wit: **J.V. Trimmier, J. Belton Tolleson.** Signed, **Wade A. Shuler.** Witness oath, 10 May 1850: Signed, **J. Belton Tolleson** to **J.B. Tolleson** Clk & Mag Exiffo.   Registered 10th May 1850.

p. 526-527.   1 Dec 1849. Deed of Conveyance. **James D. Wood** of Spartanburg Dist, for $25.85 paid by **Leroy Burns** of Spartanburg Dist, sold ten head of Hogs, one bed and furniture, one cupboard and contents, one chest, three head of sheep, to have and to hold - unless **Wood** repays the $28.85 before 25 Dec 1850. Test: **William W. Hendricks, Thomas (x) Evans.** Signed, **James D. Wood.** Witness oath, 18 May 1850: Signed, **William W. Hendricks.** Registered 18th May 1850. Original delivered to ~ **L.W. Flemming** 10th Nov 1850.

p. 527-528.   26 Jan 1850. Deed of Conveyance. **James J. Tucker** for $50 paid by **John Waldin** sold 100 acres on the waters of Spencers creek of Middle Tyger River, part of a tract originally granted to **C.M. Lankford** & by him conveyed to **John C. Hoyt** & by him to me; bounded by **Rhoderick Prewitt** and **B. Prewitt.** Wit: **J.M. Dickey, M.K. Dickey.** Signed, **James Tucker.** Witness oath, 11 April 1850: Signed, **J.M. Dickey** to **R.P. Goodlett** M.S.D. Registered 18th May 1850.
p. 528-529.   25 April 1850. Deed of Trust. **Labella K. Shelton** for an equivalent stipulation reinafter mentioned, conveys to **D. Thompson Sims** of Spartanburg Dist, the following negroes to wit, **Caroline, Sarah, Jo, Cornelia, Minerva** and **Loucinda** and all their increase in trust for the use and benefit of **James Shelton Sims** and **Charles Blanton Sims** infant children of **D. Thompson Sims,** to become the absolute property of **J.S. Sims & C.B. Sims** upon their attaining the age of 21 and the survivor share and share alike, with the stipulation that **D. Thompson Sims** as the legal owner of the above property, secures me a comfortable support and maintenance during my natural

life out of the process of the above property. Attest: **J.F. Clark, James M. Clark**. Signed, **Labella K. Shelton**. Witness oath, 25 May 1850: Signed, **James M. Clark** to **J.W. Tucker** Not. Pub. Registered 24th May 1850.

p. 529-530.   9 Nov 1849. Deed of Conveyance. **John Yarborough** Executor of the Estate of **Reubin Newman** Decd, of Spartanburg Dist, for $2,000.55 paid by **Aaron M. Smith** of Spartanburg Dist, sold 439 & 1/5 acres belonging to the Estate of **R. Newman,** marks & boundaries represented by the attached Plat lately made by **H.W. Ducker;** bounded by **James Cathcart, William Young, John F. Fowler** on the W; by **C.C. Layton, D.F. Hughston & Emanuel Allen** on the S; by **Martha Powell** and **Elisha Stations** on the E; and by Tyger River on the N; said land being sold by me according to the last Will and Testament of **Reubin Newman,** decd. Wit: **A.C. Shands, G.A. Smith.** Signed, **John Yarborough** Exr of **Reubin Newman** Deceased. Witness oath, 9 Nov 1849: Signed, **G.A. Smith** to **John H. Walker** Mag. Registered 28th May 1850.

p. 530-533.   16 Feb 1850. Mortgage. **Thomas Taylor** is indebted to **H.J. Dean** for $23.76 by Single Bill due with Interest from 27 Oct 1847, and to **H.J. Dean** survivor of **Henry & Dean** for $50 by Single Bill with Interest from 27 Oct 1847; and whereas **H.J. Dean** has this day become surety for **Thomas Taylor** to **John Davis** for $340 to be paid to **John Davis** before 1 Dec 1850; now this Indenture is that **Thomas Taylor** for the said sums of money and $623 to **Thomas Taylor** paid by **H.J. Dean** conveys to **H.J. Dean** 215 acres on the waters of Dutchmans creek, the tract where I now live, adjoining **J. Winsmith, Samuel McCravey, W. West, Elizabeth Dukes, & Revᵈ Mr. Owens.** If **Taylor** pays **H.J. Dean** all the above amounts by the various due dates, the deed shall be utterly null and void. Wit: **Calvin Foster, C.W. Styles.** Signed, **Thomas (x) Taylor, H.J. Dean.** Witness oath, 30 May 1850: Signed, **Calvin Foster** to **O.E. Edwards**, Not. Pub and Mag Exoff. Registered 31st May 1850.

p. 533-534.   9 March 1849. Deed of Conveyance. **James L. Pearson** for $800 paid by **George Bobbitt** sold 200 acres, by computation, on N side of Cherokee creek, beginning on the bank of the creek on the beginning of the **Nesbitt** Iron Manufacturing Company lands, adjoining **Gaffney.** Wit: **W.B. Smith, W.W. Howerton.** Signed, **Jas. L. Pearson.** Witness oath, 12 March 1850: Signed, **W.B. Smith** to **D.B.P. Moorman** Mag. Registered 5th June 1850.

p. 534-535.   17 July 1831. Deed of Conveyance. **William Clark** of Spartanburg Dist, for $50 paid by **John P. Evins** sold 17 acres between the South & Middle forks of Tyger Rivers, bounded on the SW by **John P. Evins,** on the SE by **William Clark** and on the Ne by **Thomas Lathrop** and on the Gap Creek Road. Wit: **Thos. Lathrop, Abner McCay.** Signed, **Wᵐ Clark.** Witness oath, 4 May 1850: Signed, **Abner McCay** to **Isham Wood** Mag S.D. Registered 5th June 1850.

p. 535-536.   3 June 1850. Deed of Conveyance. **Dr. J. Winsmith** by order of the Court of Chancery in the case of **Thomas Taylor** against me, convey to **Thomas Taylor** 215 acres adjoining lands of **J. Winsmith, Samuel McCravy, William West** & others, the same tract of land conveyed to me by **Thomas Taylor** 12 Oct 1846. Wit: **S. Bobo, Tho. O.P. Vernon.** Signed **J. Winsmith.** Witness oath, 4 June 1850: Signed, **Tho. O.P. Vernon** to **J.B. Tolleson** Clk & Mag Exiffo. Registered 5th June 1850.

p. 536-537. 13 Feb 1849. Deed of Conveyance. **William Terry** of Spartanburg Dist, for $383.50 paid by **Benjamin F. Kilgore** sold 59 acres near Coxes Creek, part of the tract formerly known as the **Berry** Tract, bounded by **B.F. Kilgore, Mrs. Sims** and **William Fowler**. Wit: **John W. Harris Jr., J.N. Wood.** Signed, **William Terry.** Witness oath, 29 Oct 1849: Signed, **J.W. Terry Jr.** to **Josiah Kilgore**, M.G.D. Registered 15th June 1850.

p. 537-538. 10 Dec 1849. Deed of Conveyance. **John Bazwell** of Spartanburg Dist, for $1,200 paid by **Alfred L. Moore** of Spartanburg Dist, sold 206 acres on the S side of James creek adjoining **Henry Howe, A.L. Moore, Dr. J.J. Vernon, Bryce** and others, including all that part on N side of Nazareth Road conveyed to me by **James Anderson Senr.** Wit: **J.A. Miller, W.J. McElrath.** Signed, **John Bazwell.** Witness oath, 6 May 1850: Signed, **J.A. Miller** to **J.B. Tolleson** Clk & Mag Exiffo. Release of Dower, 28 Dec 1849: Signed **Matilda H. Baswell** to **J.C. Caldwell** Magistrate. Registered 15 June 1850.

p. 539-541. 10 June 1850. Deed of Trust. This Indenture made between **Samuel Sweitzer, Mrs. Sarah Miller & David A. Chamblin.** Whereas a marriage is intended shortly to be Solemnized between **Samuel Sweitzer** of the first part and **Mrs. Sarah Miller** of the second part, **Sarah Miller** for $5 doth convey to **David A. Chamblin** of the third part, in fee simple all the property & Estate described in schedule hereunto attached; In trust for the use of **Sarah Miller** until the solemnization of the marriage, then in trust for use of **Samuel Sweitzer** who is to have possession and management of said property & to have and Enjoy the Rents and profits of the same, during the Joint Lives of **Samuel Sweitzer** and **Sarah Miller;** and if **Sarah** should be the Survivor then **D.A. Chamblin** is to hold the property for her use discharged of all trusts conditions & liabilities; & if **Samuel Sweitzer** should be the Survivor, then **David** shall hold the property in trust for the use the children of **Sarah** now living in fee. Equally divided among them, the children of any deceased child or children of **Sarah** to represent their parent. Further agreed that **Samuel Sweitzer** have no title whatever in the corpus of the Estate, if he is the Survivor. It is further covenanted between the parties that in consideration of the Premise, **Sarah** is bound of all claim of dower in the Lands of **Samuel,** & of all distributive share in his Estate in the event of **Sarah's** Survivorship. Further, if **Samuel** is the survivor, **Sarah** shall have the power of making provisions by Will or Deed for any of her children out of the corpus of the Settled Estate. Wit: **John J. Miller, William D. Chamblin.** Signed, **Samuel Sweitzer, Sarah J. Miller.** Schedule of Settled Estate referred to: One tract of land adjoining lands of **Fred Sweitzer, Thomas Miller, Joel W. Miller, Andrew Barry & William Miller** Supposed to contain between 200 & 300 acres, the following Negroes: **Martin, Anthony, Mahala, Chloe, Mary, Philes, Mose, Cato, Andrew, Harriet, Sealy, Ann, Louisa,** four mules & two Horses, Household and Kitchen furniture, one carriage, one four horse wagaon. Signed, **Samuel Sweitzer, Sarah J. Miller.** Witness oath, 15 June 1850: Signed, **William D. Chamblin** to **J.W. Tucker** Not. Pub. Registered 25th June 1850.

p. 541.   26 Feb 1850. Mortgage. This Indenture between **John W. Hunt** and the heirs (**Nancy Sutherland** Et Al) of **James Sutherland** Deceased, whose names are mentioned in a Deed which they have made to him of the partition, for $400 sold and mortgaged the tract of Land where **William H. Morgan's** residence now is originally belonging to **James Sutherland** Decd, and for the better securing the payment due the Legatees, I, **John W. Hunt** have conveyed by mortgage Deed the said tract of land to the Legatees till the purchase money be paid and if the purchase money should be paid this Instrument shall be void, Else this Instrument shall remain in full force. Test: **William Sutherland, Esqr., J.B. Sutherland.** Signed, **John W. Hunt.** Witness oath, 1 June 1850: Signed, **Wm Sutherland.** Registered 27th June 1850.

p. 542-543.   8 May 1850. Deed of Conveyance. **William B. Quinn Sr.** of Spartanburg Dist, for $100 paid by **Robert C. Quinn** of Spartanburg Dist, sold 50 acres on the waters of Pacolet River, part of a Tract I Purchased of **Henry White** known as part of the Lot N⁰ 1 assigned by **John Tolleson** Decd. to **J.B. Tolleson** in division of **John Tolleson's** land amongst his heirs; bounded by **A. Tolleson, R. Bryant** and **Kinnett's** old line. Wit: **B.F. Bates, G.J.S. Wood.** Signed, **Wm B. Quinn.** Witness oath, 1 July 1850: Signed, **B.F. Bates** to **J.B. Tolleson** Clk & Mag Exiffo. [Clerk's statement states "**B.B. Quinn Senr**" instead of **William B. Quinn Senr**]. Registered 2nd July 1850.

p. 543-544.   30 May 1850. Deed of Gift. **David McDowell** of Spartanburg Dist, for the natural love which I have for my son, **John H. McDowell** of Spartanburg Dist, and for divers other good causes, have conveyed 131 acres on Bee Tree branches, waters of South Pacolet River. Wit: **John B. Davis, James N. McDowell.** Signed, **David McDowell.** Witness oath, 1 July 1850: Signed, **John B. Davis** to **J.B. Tolleson** Clk & Mag Exiffo.   Registered 2nd July 1850. Original delivered to ~ J.H. McDowell 3 April 1851.

p. 544-545.   15 March 1850. Mortgage Deed. I, **J.V. Trimmier** of Spartanburg Dist, have this day purchased from **Benjamin Wofford** of Spartanburg Dist, a lot in the Town of Spartanburg lying between lots owned by **Margaret Trimmier** on the N and **Jas. Fowler** on the S, on the E by the public street or the road commonly known as the Rutherfordton Road, and on the W by a public street or an old Road or lands now owned or formerly owned by **Benj. Wofford.** My three obligations in writing or Single Bills dated this day, payable at one, two and three years, each for $25 bearing interest from date. For better securing payment, the above lot is conveyed to **Benj. Wofford.** If debt is paid, deed is null and void. Wit: **T.W. Wingo, J.W. Tucker.** Signed, **J.V. Trimmier.** Witness oath, 6 July 1850: Signed, **T.W. Wingo** to **J.B. Tolleson** Clk & Mag Exiffo.   Registered 8th July 1850.

p. 546-547.   21 Jan 1850. Mortgage. **William B. Seay & A.G. Campbell** stand indebted to **Benjamin Wofford** for $800 by Sealed Note coming due five years after today's date, Interest paid annually. For better securing the debt, **Wm B. Seay & A.G. Campbell** convey to **B. Wofford** a lot in Spartanburg adjoining a lot now owned by **Foster & Judd** on the E, by a lot now owned by **J.B. Archer** on the W, by the public Square on the N & by a street running from the Jail street to a lot now owned by **Jesse Cleveland.** Deed null & void if debt paid. Wit: **Jacob Zimmerman, J. Guinn Harris.** Signed, **A.G. Campbell, W.B. Seay.** Witness oath, 6 July 1850: Signed, **J. Zimmerman** to **J.B. Tolleson** Clk & Mag Exiffo.   Registered 8th July 1850.

p. 547-549.   26 Nov 1849. Mortgage. **Alfred Tolleson** is indebted to **Benjamin Wofford** for $1,000 by three sealed notes for $333.33 each, falling due on the 1st day of January 1850, 1852, 1853, interest on all three paid annually from today's date. In consideration of the premises and for better securing the debt, **Tolleson** conveys to **Wofford**, a lot of a fraction of an acre, purchased this day from **Wofford,** in Spartanburg Village fronting on the public square, known as Lot № 5, adjoining Lot № 4 on the W now occupied by **G.W.H. Legg.** Wit: **J.B. Archer, William Petty.** Signed, **Alfred Tolleson.** Witness oath, 6 July1850: Signed, **Wᵐ Petty** to **J.B. Tolleson** Clk & Mag Exiffo. Registered 8ᵗʰ July 1850.

p. 549-551. 26 Nov 1849. Mortgage. **John B. Archer** is indebted to **Benjamin Wofford** for $1,000 by three sealed notes each $333.33⅓ due on the 1ˢᵗ Jan 1851, 1852, 1853, interest payable annually. In consideration of the premises and for better securing the debt **Archer** conveys to **Wofford** a lot of a fraction of an acre, purchased this day from **Wofford,** in Town of Spartanburg known as Lot № 1. Wit: **Alfred Tolleson, William Petty.** Signed, **J.B. Archer.** Witness oath, 6 July 1850: Signed, **Wᵐ Petty** to **J.B. Tolleson** Clk & Mag Exiffo. Registered 8ᵗʰ July 1850.

p. 551-552. 10 Oct 1848. Deed of Conveyance. Whereas my father **William W. Cannon** Decd, by his last will & testament, among other things devised his lands and other property to his widow **Lucy Cannon** during her life or widowhood and at her death he devised that $65 should be paid to the undersigned & the same amount to some other of the family, and that the remainder should be equally divided among all his children. Now, I, **Wilson Cannon** for $120 paid by the South Carolina Manuf Company all the interest which I have under the will of **William Cannon,** both in real and personal Estate, and I do authorize the Executor of the last will and testament of **William Cannon** to pay over & account to said Company. Wit: **J.H. Garrison, J.W. Moore.** Signed, **W.W. Cannon.** Witness oath, 10 Oct 1848: Signed, **J.H. Garrison** to **John Linder** Mag. Release of Dower, 31 Oct 1848: Signed, **R.J. Cannon** to **John Linder** Mag. I, **Holeman Cannon** administrator with the will annexed of **William Cannon** Decd, do hereby assent to the legacies in the will of **W.W. Cannon** & agree to account to So Ca M Company for the portion of the Estate assigned to them provided so much is due on the final division of the estate agreeable to the will. Registered 22ⁿᵈ July 1850.

p. 552-555. 22 Dec 1849. Agreement entered into by and between **John Damron** on the one part and **John T. Kirby, G.W.H. Legg, Wᵐ B. Seay & A.G. Campbell** known as **Campbell & Seay,** and **Junius W. Thomson** on the other part. **John Damron** agrees and obligates himself to make & furnish and lay of good, well burnt and Substantial brick, the walls of 5 buildings; the brick are to be moulded 9 inches long 4½ wide and 3 inches thick, to be laid in lime mortar and pencilled and the work in every respect to be complete and done in a workman like manner. **Kirby, Legg, Campbell & Seay** and **Thomson** obligate themselves to furnish **Damron** by the 1ˢᵗ day of April next a full and complete plans and specifications of the 5 buildings and point out the place where they are to be put (which shall be within corporate limits of the Town of Spartanburg) and **Damron** binds and obligates himself to have the walls of the 5 building completed & finished by the 1ˢᵗ day of Novʳ next, unless he is delayed and hindered with the brick work on account of the carpenters work not being completed & ready (which carpenters work **Kirby, Legg, Campbell & Seay** and **Thomson** are to have done) and it is agreed that the time which **Damron** may be delayed for want of the carpenters work or the digging of cellars, after the 1ˢᵗ day of April next shall be added to the 1ˢᵗ of Nov and in that way the time allowed for completing the brick work may be Extended. **Damron** is also to have put on three coats of plastering in a workmanlike manner on the walls of the first story of each of the 5 buildings, the plastering done as soon as soon as the carpenters work has progressed sufficiently. **Kirby, Legg, Campbell & Seay** and **Thomson** agree Separately and individually (not

Jointly) to pay **Damron** $8 per 1000 brick measuring 18 brick to the Square foot, one half only to be paid for the doors and windows and to pay **Damron** for each of the 5 buildings $20 for the plastering, one half of the cost of the buildings to be paid on the 1ˢᵗ day of Novʳ or when the brick work is completed and the other half twelve months after with Interest from the 1ˢᵗ day of Novʳ or when the brick work is completed, unless **Damron** is delayed by the fault of **Kirby, Legg, Campbell & Seay** and **Thomson** & in that case the payment shall be made on 1ˢᵗ Novʳ. Further agreed that if **Damron** fails to complete the brick work by 1ˢᵗ Novʳ, unless hindered by above, he shall pay to for each building $100 and he fails to have it done by 1ˢᵗ day of Decr. thereafter he shall pay for each building $100 to each of the owners. To be paid for ½ the plastering when done and the other ½ twelve months thereafter with Interest. It is expressly understood that this contract is Several and not Joint, that each of the owners is to be liable for the amount their building may cost, that is to say, **John T. Kirby** is to pay for 2 of the buildings, **G.W.H. Legg** for 1, **Campbell & Seay** for 1, and **Junius W. Thomson** for 1. [The name of **Simpson Bobo** was struck out and that of **Junius W. Thomson** Inserted in its place before Signed by the consent of all the parties to this agreement]. Wit: **Maj. H.J. Dean, P.M. Wallace.** Signed, **John Damron, Jno. T. Kirby, Geo. W.H. Legg, J.W. Thomson, William B. Seay, A.G. Campbell.** Witness oath, 22 Jul 1850: Signed, **H.J. Dean** to **J.B. Tolleson** Clk & Mag Exiffo.   Registered 22ⁿᵈ July 1850.

p. 555.   1 June 1850. Deed of Gift. I, **George Story** of Spartanburg Dist, for consideration of the love and affection I have for my Grand Daughter, **Margaret Amanda Story**, of Lincoln Co., Tennessee, (and daughter of my son **Samuel Story** Decd, give and deliver to **Margaret A. Story** a Negro girl named **Cornelia,** to have and to hold the said **Cornelia** and her issue as long as she lives and at the death of **Margaret A. Story** the above **Cornelia** and her issue are to go to and belong to the children of **Margaret Amanda Story.** Wit: **Dr. M.A. Moore, Alfred Moore.** Signed, **George Story.** Witness oath, 23 July 1850: Signed, **M.A. Moore** to **J.B. Tolleson** Clk & Mag Exiffo. Registered 23ʳᵈ July 1850. Original delivered to ~~ **Dr. M.A. Moore** 23 July 1850.

p. 555-556.   4 Sept 1847. Deed of Conveyance. **John Wheeler** of Spartanburg Dist, for $200 paid by **Dillingham Ballenger** of Spartanburg Dist, sold 307 acres, part of a Tract originally granted to **John Tucker** in 1805; on both sides of Shoaly Creek, waters of North Tyger River bounded by **Vernon.** Wit: **John Odam,** John Ballenger. Signed, **John Wheeler.** Witness oath, 5 Jan 1848: Signed, **John Odam** to **Thomas Ballenger.** Registered 23ʳᵈ July 1850. Original delivered to ~~ **D. Ballenger** 8ᵗʰ May 1851.

p. 557-558.   2 Feb 1850. Deed of Conveyance. **Z.L. Holmes** for $200 paid by **A.G. Campbell** of Spartanburg Dist, sold 94 acres on or near the waters of Beaver Dam branch of the Fair Forest creek bounded by **Jackson, Hiram McEarly,** the old **Rainwater** land, the old grant with plat is in the hands of **Esq. Bowden,** the present District Ordinary. Wit: **William B. Seay, D.C. Judd.** Signed, **Z.L. Holmes.** Witness oath, 30 April 1850: Signed, **Wᵐ B. Seay** to **Geo. W.H. Legg** Magst. Release of Dower, 14 June 1850, Laurens Dist: Signed, **Catharine N. Holmes** to **B.R. Campbell,** M.L.D. Registered 23ʳᵈ July 1850. Original delivered to **Dr. A.G. Campbell.**

p. 558-559.   22 Aug 1848. Deed of Conveyance Spartanburg Dist. **Joseph A. Lovett** of St. Frances Co., Arkansas, agent for **Elizabeth Lovett, Richard Austell & Francis A. Mistill,** all of the said

State & county , for $285 to me paid by **Michael Gaffney** of the State and District aforesaid sold 140 acres on the N side of Beaverdam creek Waters of Thickoty creek, a part of a Tract originally granted to **William Hart** in 1773. Beginning on originally **William Bostick's** line, to the mouth of a branch that divides said tract and **Thos. Littlejohns** land, **Hart's** old line. Wit: **J. Eams, Joseph Austell.** Signed, **Jas. A. Lovett** agent. Witness oath, 8 June 1849: Signed, **Joseph Austell** to **D.B.P. Moorman** Mag. Registered 25th July 1850.

p. 559-561. 14 June 1850. Deed of Conveyance. **Robert R. Smith** of Spartanburg Dist, for $47.28 paid by **Thomas Peak** [Peake in Witness oath] of Spartanburg Dist, sold 6 acres, one road [rod?] and Twenty nine poles, a part of the tract originally granted to **Robert Cowden** now known as part of the **Samuel Morrow** land Dest. [deceased?], a part of which was deeded to **Mary Smith** and from her to **Robert R. Smith;** on W side of Dutchmans creek, more fully shown in a Plot of said land. Lying on the S side of the **Maj. Morrow** branch and bounded on the S by **Thomas Peak,** on the E by Dutchmans Creek and **Thomas Peak,** on the N by **William W. West** and **Thomas West,** on the W by **Robert R. Smith.** Wit: **William Beardin, H. Wofford.** Signed, **Robert R. Smith.** Witness oath, 14 June 1850: Signed, **William Beardin** to **H. Wofford** Mag. Release of Dower, 14 June 1850: Signed, **Mary Smith** to **Harvey Wofford** Mag. Registered 29th July 1850.

p. 561-563. 11 Feb 1850. Deed of Conveyance. **Robert N. Morrow** of Spartanburg Dist, for $310.35 paid by **Thomas Peake** of Spartanburg Dist, sold 109 acres, part of a tract originally granted to **Robert Cowden** now known as the **Samuel Morrow** land part of which was deeded to **Robert N. Morrow** from **Samuel Morrow,** Decd; on Dutchmans Creek branch Waters Tyger River, bounded on the N by **Robert R. Smith,** E by **Thos. Peake,** S by **Robert N. Morrow** and **William Beardin,** W by **Robert R. Williams** and **R.R. Smith.** Wit: **H.W. Ducker, Thomas P. Peak** [Magistrate's statement says witness was **T.P. Hamm**]. Witness oath, 27th April 1850: Signed, **Thomas P. Hamm** to **H. Wofford** Magst. Release of Dower, 14 June 1850: Signed, **Sarah (x) Morrow** to **Harvy Wofford** Mag. S.D. Registered 29th July 1850.

p. 563-564. 29 Jan 1848. **Richard Lanford** of Spartanburg Dist, $825 paid by **Washington Lanford** of Spartanburg Dist, sold 101¼ acres on Dildine creek, waters of Enoree River bounded by **J. Page.** Wit: **James Carnel, Chany Lanford.** Signed, **Richard Lanford.** Witness oath, 29 Jan 1848: Signed, **Chany Lanford** to **Z. Lanford** Magt. Release of Dower, 29 Jan 1848: Signed, **Pamelia Lanford** to **Z. Lanford** Magst. Registered 2nd Augst. 1850.

p. 565-566. 8 July 1847. Deed of Conveyance. **William S. Page** of Spartanburg Dist, for $140 paid by **Chany Lanford** of Spartanburg Dist, sold 70 acres on the branches of Buffalo creek, waters of Enoree River; bounded by **Styles, Jones** Spring branch. Wit: **Washington Lanford, James Carnel.** Signed, **William S. Page.** Witness oath, 8 July 1847: Signed, **James Carnel** to **Z. Lanford** Magt. Release of Dower, 2 Aug 1847: Signed, **Cinthia R. (x) Page** to **Z. Lanford** Magt. Registered 2nd Augst. 1850.

p. 566-567. 1 June 1850. Deed of Conveyance. **H.H. Thomson** of Spartanburg Dist, for $157.50 paid by **Anthony G. Campbell** of Spartanburg Dist, sold 6 acres & 3/10 in the town of Spartanburg on **Wyatt's** Street, bounded by **Jesse Cleveland** and **Alfred Brown.** Wit: **William Walker**

(A.S.H.), **John Linder.** Signed, **H.H. Thomson.** Release of Dower, 11 June 1850: Signed, **Mildred E. Thomson** to **J.B. Tolleson** Clk & Mag Exiffo. Witness oath, 6 Aug 1850: Signed, **William Walker (A.S.H.)** to **J.B. Tolleson** Clk & Mag Exiffo. Registered 9ᵗʰ Augst 1850. Original delivered to ~~ **A.G. Campbell** 16ᵗʰ Augst. 1850.

p. 568-569. 30 Oct 1849. Deed of Conveyance. **Col. H.H. Thomson** of Spartanburg Dist, for $225 paid by **William Carver** sold two lots [4 acres] of land in the corporate limits of the town of Spartanburg; (1) Supposed to contain something over one acre, beginning at the Bridge or the street that leads out from the public square by the Jail; (2) also a lot on street leading by Stone Bridge to Fair Forest creek Supposed to contain 3 acres, beginning on a P.O. stump on S side of said street nearly opposite the street which leads into the Greenville Road, to the line formerly **Hall's** but now **Carver,** back line of **Nolen's** Lot and **P. Turner.** Wit: **Hiram Mitchell, Oklav Greiner.** Signed, **H.H. Thomson.** Release of Dower, 11 June 1850: Signed, **Mildred E. Thomson** to **J.B. Tolleson** Clk & Mag Exiffo. Witness oath, 8 Aug 1850: Signed, **Hiram Mitchell** to **J.B. Tolleson** Clk & Mag Exiffo. Registered 9ᵗʰ August. 1850.

p. 569-571. 25 Oct 1848. Deed of Conveyance. **H.H. Thomson** of Spartanburg Dist, for $50 paid by **Doct. William C. Bennett** of Spartanburg Dist, sold (1) a 1 acre lot in the Town of Spartanburg known as Lot Nº 16, in the Plat called the **Poole** Lots, W of the Tanyard branch; (2) Lot Nº 17 in the **Poole** Lots, except what lies N of the Greenville Road, containing a fraction less than 1 acre. Warrants unto **Dr. Bennett** against all persons, Except the claim which **Jane Poole** has of Wood, Interest from **William Poole.** Wit: **Hiram Mitchell, J.W. Tucker.** Signed, **H.H. Thomson.** Witness oath, 8 Aug 1850: Signed, **Hiram Mitchell** to **J.B. Tolleson** Clk & Mag Exiffo. Release of Dower, 11 June 1850: Signed, **Mildred E. Thomson** to **J.B. Tolleson** Clk & Mag Exiffo. Registered 9ᵗʰ August. 1850. Original delivered to ~~ **Dr. W.C. Bennett** 8ᵗʰ April 1850.

p. 571-573. 31 May 1850. Deed of Conveyance. **Col. H.H. Thomson** of Spartanburg Dist, for $230 paid by **Z.J. Bates** of Spartanburg Dist, sold 9 acres & 1/5 in the town of Spartanburg, lying back of the lot of **Z.J. Bates** and **Jas. Wilson,** on a new street and a cross street leading out from **Stafford's** Work Shop, adjoining **William B. Seay, Wilson & Bates.** Wit: **W.W. Boyd, J.A. Lee.** Signed, **H.H. Thomson.** Witness oath, 8 Aug 1850: Signed, **W.W. Boyd** to **J.B. Tolleson** Clk & Mag Exiffo. Release of Dower, 11 June 1850: Signed, **Mildred E. Thomson** to **J.B. Tolleson** Clk & Mag Exiffo. Registered 9ᵗʰ August. 1850.

p. 573-574. 19 Jan 1850. Deed of Conveyance. **H.H. Thomson** of Spartanburg Dist, for $226.50 paid by **Patrick Oshanesey** of York Dist, SC, sold 151 acres in what is known as the flat woods, a part of the **Prattof**[?] Land commencing on a stake on old line of the **Spratt** tract Joining **Hines** or **Berry's** land. Wit: **Joseph W. Black, D. Hilliard Smith.** Signed, **H.H. Thomson.** Release of Dower, 11 June 1850: Signed, **Mildred E. Thomson** to **J.B. Tolleson** Clk & Mag Exiffo. Witness oath, 8 Aug 1850: Signed, **D.H. Smith** to **J.B. Tolleson** Clk & Mag Exiffo. Registered 9ᵗʰ August. 1850. Original delivered to ~~ **Patrick Oshanesey** 9 Augst. 1850.

p. 574-576. 22 July 1844. Deed of Conveyance. **Jesse Cleveland** of Spartanburg Dist, for $130 paid by **James Lawrence Jr.,** sold 150 acres where **Tho' Brannon** now lives, on Fawns branch, waters of Lawsons Fork creek bounded by **Daniel White** on the S and W, by **Isham Clement** on the E, **Nathan Seay** on the N.   Wit: **John B. Cleveland, W.B. Cleveland.** Signed, **Jesse Cleveland.** Witness oath, 6 Aug 1844: Signed, **J.B. Cleveland** to **H. White** Mag. Release of Dower, **Polly (x) Brannon** to **Henry White** Mag. **Polly Brannon** the wife of **Thomas Brannon** who sold to **Jesse Cleveland** and **Cleveland** to **James Lawrence.** Registered 9th Augst. 1850.

End of Book AA

Book BB

p. 1-2. 28 Sept 1842. Deed of Conveyance. **John Wheeler** of Spartanburg Dist, for $741.75 paid by **Perry Smith** of Spartanburg Dist, sold 247¼ acres on branch waters of Tyger River. Wit: **Joel Ballenger, Wilson Wingo.** Signed, **John Wheeler.** Witness oath, 8 Feb 1843: Signed, **Wilson Wingo** to **Thomas Ballenger** J.P. Release of Dower, 1 Aug 1843: Signed, **Jincy Wheeler** to **Thomas Ballenger** J.Q. Registered Examined and certified 10ᵗʰ Augst 1850. Original delivered to ~ **Perry Smith** 14ᵗʰ Decr. 1850

p. 2-3. 14 Aug 1850. Deed of Conveyance. **David Miller** of Spartanburg Dist, for $1,000 paid by **David M. Crawford** of Spartanburg Dist, sold two lots (1) of 1 acre in the Village of Spartanburg on the E side of the main St. leading from **Mills** Hotel to **John T. Kirby's**, bordering **Kirby** and **Lewis.** (2) Also back lot, beginning at the back corner of **Lewis & Miller's** acre lot running E to **Thomsons & Lewis** new corner, then S to **Thomsons & Miller's** line. Wit: **R.E. Cleveland, Jas. F.V. Legg.** Signed, **David Miller.** Witness oath, 14 Aug 1850: Signed, **Jaˢ. F.V. Legg** to **G.W.H. Legg** Magt. Registered 10ᵗʰ Augst. 1850.

p. 4-5. 25 Nov 1844. Deed of Conveyance. **Coleman Wood** of Spartanburg Dist, for $600 paid by **Davis Whitman** of Spartanburg Dist, sold 300 acres on Wilson's Mill Creek waters of North Tyger River, bordering **H. Hawkins, Prince's** old road, to the road that leads from **H. Hawkins** to **John Wingo's**, then running with a deed made by **John Wingo** to **John Wood, William Laurence,** Wilsons Creek; parts of tracts originally granted to **J. & H. Prince, Gabriel Benson** and **Wadsworth** and deeded by **H. Prince, Gabriel Benson & John Wingo** to **John Wood.** Wit: **Herbert Hawkins, Hezekiah Pollard.** Signed, **Coleman Wood.** Witness oath, 5 Aug 1850: Signed, **Hezekiah Pollard** to **J.B. Tolleson** clk & mag Exiffo. Registered 10ᵗʰ August 1850.

p. 5-7. 1 May 1850. Mortgage. **Z.J. Bates** is indebted to **H.H. Thomson** by three sealed notes for $230 with interest from date due one, two, & three years from date 31ˢᵗ May 1850, being the purchase money for a lot in the Town of Spartanburg purchased this day of **H.H. Thomson;** 9 and one fifth acres on back of **Wilson's** and said **Bate's** lot on a new street, and on the street leading from **Stafford's** shop and with **William B. Seay's** line. Wit: **W.W. Boyd, J.A. Lee.** Signed, **Z.J. Bates.** Witness oath, 8 Aug 1850: Signed, **W.W. Boyd** to **J.B. Tolleson** clk & mag Exiffo. Registered 10ᵗʰ August 1850.

p. 7-9. 7 Aug 1849. Commissioner's Titles. **Tho' O.P. Vernon**, Esq. Commissioner of the Court of Equity for Spartanburg Dist, sold to **Rial B. Seay** at the complaint of **Edwin White,** on or about the 18ᵗʰ April 1849, in the Court of Equity against **Owen White, James White** and others praying for division of the lands of **Daniel White** Deceased. At June Term 1849 the court ordered the land as platted and numbered be sold at public auction by the commissioner; plat Nº 5, 172 acres sold to **Rial B. Seay** for$157; on furnace Road, and across Fawn branch, down Brannon Road bounded by **Mathew Seay** on the E, on the S by **William Dodd,** on the W by Lot Nº 6, and on the N by Lot Nº 7. Wit: **Hiram Mitchell, Wᵐ Petty.** Signed, **Tho' O.P. Vernon,** C.E.S.D. Witness oath, 8 Aug 1850: Signed, **Hiram Mitchell** to **J.B. Tolleson** clk & mag Exiffo. Registered 10ᵗʰ August 1850.

p. 9-11.   1 Aug 1850. Deed of Conveyance. **John Keast** of Spartanburg Dist, for $500 paid by **Richard Moss** of Spartanburg Dist, sold 150 acres on Fairforest Creek beginning on **Richard Moss'es** corner on the creek a little above the road leading from the Court House to Mount Zion Church to a fork in the Boiling Springs Road, along road to a willow oak on what is called Ready Branch known formerly as **James McCarley's** corner now **R. Bowden's**, the line described thus far being the line of land owned by **Richard Moss** previous to this time, thence down said Ready branch to its junction with Fairforest Creek and up said creek to the beginning. Wit: **Tho' O.P. Vernon, J.R. Poole**. Signed, **John Keast**. Release of Dower, 13 Aug 1850: (**Margaret Keast** in clerk's statement) Signed, **Marget Keast** to **J.B. Tolleson** clk & mag Exiffo. Witness oath, 13 Aug 1850: Signed, **J.R. Poole** to **J.B. Tolleson** clk & mag Exiffo. Registered 13 Augst 1850.

p. 11-13.   11 Feb 1850. Deed of Conveyance. **Major D. Beshears** who is lawful attorney for **Meredith Beshears** for $60 paid by **James McMakin** of Greenville Dist SC, sold 50 acres in Spartanburg Dist, on both sides of Motley's Creek, adjoining lands of **James McMakin, William Beason** & others. One measurement is on the North hill of Easeley's Creek to **James Berchfield's** line being on the old **Goodgrant's** line. It being a part of grant to **Robert Goodgiant**. Wit: **Adam R. Smith, Jefferson Burton**. Signed, **Major D. Beshears**, Lawful attorney for **Merida Beshears**. Witness oath, 11 Feb 1850: Signed, **Jefferson Burton** to **James Caldwell**, Mag. S.D.   Power of Attorney, Greenville Dist, 4 April 1849: **Merida Beshears** of Spartanburg Dist, appoints my son **Major D. Beshears** her lawful agent. Wit: **Solomon Clayton, John (x) Prewit, R.P. Goodlett**. Signed, **Merida (x) Beshears** to **R.P. Goodlett**, M.G.D. Registered 13 Augst. 1850.

p. 13-14.   7 Jan 1816. Deed of Conveyance. **John Keenum** of Spartanburg Dist, for £50 sterling paid by **Thomas Brannon** sold 50 acres on Fawn branch, bounded by **John Burnett**. Wit: **William Brannon, Josiah Seay**. Signed, **John Keenum**. Witness oath, 20 Jan 1818: Signed, **Josiah Seay** to **Elsh. Lewis** J.P. Registered 13th Augst. 1850.

p. 14-16.   17 Jan 1850. Deed of Conveyance. **Joseph Thomson** [and **Thompson**] **& Samuel M. Snoddy** Executors of the last will and Testament of **John Snoddy** Dec[d], on 17th Nov 1849 at the late residence of **John Snoddy** Dec[d], for $500 sold to **Mrs. Margaret Caldwell** of Spartanburg Dist, 154 acres on waters of Tyger River; on Nazereth Church Road bordered by **Mrs. Nesbitt** and **Andrew F. Collins**. Wit: **John T. Howell, Hamilton Pollard**. Signed, **S.M. Snoddy, Joseph Thomson**, Executors. Witness oath, 17 Aug 1850: Signed, **John T. Howell** to **J.C. Caldwell** Magistrate. Release of Dower, 25 May 1850: Signed, **E.P. Snoddy** to **J.C. Caldwell** Magistrate. Registered 19th Augst. 1850.

p. 16-18.   23 Aug 1850. Deed of Conveyance. **N.H. Waldrop** for $1482 paid **William A. Young** of Spartanburg Dist, sold 161¾ acres of Heads ford Road and on several small branches; bounded by **Thomas Rhodes Sen[r], T.B. Poole, John Rhodes, T.B. Deshields & W[m] Waldrop**. Wit: **James S. Jackson, P.R. Bobo**. Signed, **N.H. Waldrop**. Witness oath, 23 Aug 1850: Signed, **James S. Jackson** to **P.R. Bobo** Magst. Release of Dower, 23 Aug 1850: Signed, **Sarah Ann Waldrop** to **P.R. Bobo** Magst. Registered 24th Augst. 1850.

p. 18-21.   27 July 1850. Deed of Trust. **Margaret Caldwell** of Spartanburg Dist, for $5 paid by

Samuel C. Miller and for the natural love which I have for my daughter **Elizabeth Hadden** and her husband **Robert Hadden** of Spartanburg Dist, sold to **Samuel C. Miller** 154 acres on waters of Tyger River and Nazareth Church Road; bounded by **Mrs. Nesbitt** and **A.F. Collins;** it being the land where **Elizabeth** and **Robert Hadden** reside; to **Samuel C. Miller** in trust always, **Elizabeth and Robert Hadden** to live on and have the profits for the support of **Elizabeth** and her minor children, free from debts of **Robert** during their joint lives and life of the survivor as long as **Robert** remains the widower of **Elizabeth.** If both **Elizabeth & Robert** die or if **Elizabeth** dies and **Robert** remarries, the land to be held in trust for the maintenance, Support and education of their children, and a home for them until the youngest arrives at age 21, then to be sold and divided equally between the children. Wit: **Daniel Hawkins, J.H. Vandike.** Signed, **Margaret (x) Caldwell.** Trustee Consent, 27 July 1850: Signed, **Samuel C. Miller.** Witness to consent: **Daniel Hawkins, J.H. Vandike.** Witness oath, 23 Aug 1850: **J.H. Vandike** to **J.C. Caldwell** Magistrate. Registered 24th Aug 1850.

p. 21-22. 21 Aug 1850. Deed of Conveyance. **Robert M. McDowell** of Spartanburg Dist, for $102 paid by **John J. McDowell** of Spartanburg Dist, sold 128 acres on the branch waters of the South fork of the Pacolet River; bounded by **David McDowell, Branson Hall, Elmore McDowell** and **Elijah Alverson.** Wit: **William G. McDowell, A.C. McDowell.** Signed, **Robert M. McDowell.** Witness oath, 22 Aug 1850: Signed, **William G. McDowell** to **J.B. Tolleson** clk & Mag Exoffo. Registered 24th Augst. 1850.

p. 22-23. 26 Feb 1850. Deed of Conveyance. **Hiram Mitchell** and **Harriet M. Mitchell** his wife, and **Cornelia F. Camp** for a Deed of Conveyance made to us today conveying to us certain lands, sell to **W.W. Harris** all our interest, since Jan 1844, in 500 acres known as the plantation of **W.W. Harris;** bounded on the W by **James R.** [blank], on the N by the estate of **Amos Liles,** and on the E and S by the Estate of **David Golightly** Deceased. Wit: **Ramon Owens, Ja' Gwinn Harris.** Signed, **Hiram Mitchell, Harriett M. Mitchell, C.F. Camp.** Witness oath, 22 Feb 1850 [date of oath before date of deed]: Signed, **Ramon Owens** to **Geo. W.H. Legg** Magst. Release of Dower, [no date]: Signed, **Harriet M. Mitchell.** Registered 28th Augst. 1850. Original delivered to ~~ **W.W. Harris,** 6th March 1851.

p. 23-24. 4 June 1850. Deed of Conveyance. **H.H. Thomson** of Spartanburg Dist, for $80 secured to be paid by **Abner E. Smith** of Spartanburg Dist, sold all the interest I have in 78 acres **Abner E. Smith** & myself bought at Sheriff sale at Spartanburg court house as the property of **Henry Emborson,** including that part only of which we recovered in a suit against **Haney Emberson.** The land sold lies on Packolet River and adjoins **Haney Emberson** and others. Plat which was made in the suit is in the clerk;s office. Wit: **W.W. Harris, J.W. Tucker.** Signed, **H.H. Thomson.** Witness oath, 2 Sept 1850: Signed, **J.W. Tucker** to **J.B. Tolleson** clk & Mag Exoffo. Registered 2nd Sept. 1850.

25-27. 5 July 1847. Commissioner's Titles. **Tho' O.P. Vernon,** Esq. Commissioner of the Court of Equity, for Spartanburg Dist, and **Elias J. Wingo** of the other part. Whereas **Sarah Criswell &** others on or about 19th April 1845 Exhibited their bill of complaint in the Court of Equity against **James Smith &** others for a partition of 211 acres on Kelsy Creek known as Cedar Spring tract;

court of June Term 1847 ordered it sold and on 5th July 1847 was sold to **Elias J. Wingo** for $975; bounded by **John Black's** store house lot, **J. Zimmerman, Calvin Foster,** the road leading from Spartanburg to Glenn Springs and **Absolem Walker;** described by the red lines in a Plat filed in the records in the case, Excepting Lots N° 9 & 10 reserved to **J. Zimmerman** (and excepting) the use of the Grove which is supposed to be about 2 acres between the Springs & dwellings and the use of the spring which were reserved by the consent of the Parties for the benefit of the church and the individuals owning private Lots. Wit: **G. Nicholls, J.W. Tucker.** Signed, **Tho' O.P. Vernon** C.E.S.D.Witness oath, 2 Sept 1850: Signed, **J.W. Tucker** to **J.B. Tolleson** clk & Mag Exoffo. Registered 2nd Sept. 1850. Original delivered to ~~ **Elias J. Wingo** 28th April 1851.

p. 27- 28. 3 Jan 1850. Deed of Conveyance. **M.V.R. Shields** of Hardin Co., TN, for $190 paid by **W.W. Harris** of Spartanburg Dist, sold 129 acres bounded by **Bird Low** on the S, by lands claimed by **John Golightly** on the E being a part of a tract originally granted to **John Golightly**. Wit: **J. Gwinn Harris, Bird Low.** Signed, **M.V.R. Shields.** Witness oath, 3 Jan 1850: Signed, **Bird Low** to **Geo. W.H. Legg** Magistrate. Release of Dower, 3 Jan 1850: [clerk's statement, **Winiford C. Shields**] Signed, **Winneyfield C. Shields** to **Geo. W.H. Legg** Magistrate. Registered 2nd Sept. 1850.

p. 28-30. 26 Aug 1850. Deed of Conveyance. **Davis Newman** of Spartanburg Dist, for $400 paid by **Thomas Newman**, my son, sold 48½ acres where he now lives, beginning on a branch by the River [?], bounded by lands of my own, **William Newman & Benjamin Newman.** Wit: **Ja' J. Newman, P.R. Bobo.** Signed, **Davis Newman.** Witness oath, 26 Aug 1850: Signed, **Ja' J. Newman** to **P.R. Bobo.** Release of Dower, 26 Aug 1850: Signed, **Nancy (x) Newman** to **P.R. Bobo** Magst. Registered 2nd Sept. 1850.

p. 30-31. 6 May 1850. Deed of Conveyance. **John Brannon Sen'** of Spartanburg Dist, for $34 paid by **John Branon Jun'** of Spartanburg Dist, sold 23 acres adjoining **John Willis, John Branon Jun',** **Jeferson Branon** and **John Branon Sen'.** Wit: **John Epting, J. Belton Tolleson.** Signed, **John Brannon Senr.** Witness oath, 2 Sept 1850: Signed, **John Epting** to **J.B. Tolleson** clk & Mag Exoffo. Registered 2nd Sept. 1850.

p. 31-32. 2 Sept 1850. Deed of Gift. **Edmond Cooly Sen.** of Spartanburg Dist, for the love and affection I bear for my Daughter **Elizabeth Cantrel** and her husband **James Cantrel Sen',** of Spartanburg Dist, I give a tract of land on both sides of the Furnace Road and on branch waters of Cases Creek, bounded by lands of the Cherokee Springs Company, **Henry Hines, John Cooley** and others, such as a Plat annexed Laid out by **John Epting** D.S. the 8th August 1850 will represent, it being part of a tract originally granted to **Amos Spice.** Wit: **John Epting, A.J. Henderson.** Signed, **Edmond (x) Cooly.** Witness oath, 2 Sept 1850: Signed, **John Epting** to **Elias Wall** Mag. Registered 2nd Sept. 1850.

p. 32-34. 30 April 1850. Deed of Conveyance. **John Cannon** of Spartanburg Dist, for the love and regard I have for my Son **Ibra Cannon** release 627 acres, a part of the land where I now live and on the N side of Pacolet River; bounded by **David Thompson**, mouth of Meadow branch, **Turner,** down a hollow to the Doctor's branch to the mouth of Parks branch, **A.E. Smith,** S.C. M. Co.'s land; (which land chargeable to him at $3 per acre in final settlement of my Estate as part of his distributive share); Subject to certain conditions expressed in a will which I have made for the settlement of my estate but should said will be lost or in anywise destroyed or invalidated, the above Deed Shall not thereby become Void, but Shall be ample and full as though no condition had been expressed in said will. Wit: **John Turner, A.E. Smith.** Signed, **John Cannon.** Witness oath, 2 Sept 1850: Signed, **John Turner** to **J.B. Tolleson** clk & Mag Exoffo. Registered 2nd Sept. 1850,

p. 34-36.   17 Jan 1850. Mortgage. On 7 Jan 1850, **Daniel F. Mayberry** sold 20 acres located on Wolf's branch waters of L<u>osso</u>ns fork creek to **William Cantrell** who agrees to pay $80 for the above described premises. Wit: **Dr. A.W. Bivings, C.H. Maberry.** Signed, **William Cantrell.** Witness oath, 8 Aug 1850: Signed, **A.W. Bivings** to **J.B. Tolleson** clk & Mag Exoffo. Registered 2nd Sept. 1850.

p. 36-37.   30 May 1850. Mortgage. **F. Greiner** is indebted to **H.H. Thomson & J. Waddy Thomson** $521.16 with interest from this date in three sealed notes due one, two & three years from date, the purchase money for a lot in the Town of Spartanburg sold today to **F. Greiner**; the lot, 1 acre on Church street. Wit: **J.M. Elford, Esq., Oktav Greiner.** Signed, **F. Greiner.** Witness oath, 2 Sept 1850: Signed, **J.M. Elford** to **J.B. Tolleson** clk & Mag Exoffo. Registered 2nd Sept. 1850. Original delivered to **H.H. Thomson** 24th Jany 1851.

p. 38.   22 June 1850. Deed of Gift. **Sampson Bobo** of Spartanburg Dist, for the love and affection which I bear unto my daughter, **Mary Ann Todd** late **Mary Ann Bobo** the wife of **William Todd** of Laurens Dist, SC, gives a Negro woman named **Cinda** and her increase to **Mary Ann's** Sole and Separate use during her Natural life, not subject to liabilities of her husband, and at **Mary Ann's** death to be equally divided among her children or in case she has no children to be returned to my Estate. Wit: **B.G. Kilgore, Jonas Brewton.** Signed, **Sampson Bobo.** Witness oath, 4 Sept 1850: Signed, **Jonas Brewton** to **Z. Lanford** Magst. Registered 9th Sept. 1850.

p. 39.   1 April 1850. Deed of Conveyance. **John Brannon Senr** of Spartanburg Dist, for $69 paid by **Jefferson Brannon** of Spartanburg Dist, sold 46 acres on Meadow branch waters of Lawson's Fork, bounded by **James Edging, John Brannon Jun., John Brannon Sen., & John Golightly**, as on a plat made by **John Epting** D.S. Wit: **John Baber, John Epting.** Signed, **John Brannon Senr.** Witness oath, 16 Sept 1850: Signed, **John Epting** to **J.B. Tolleson** clk & Mag Exoffo. Registered 9th Sept. 1850.

p. 40-41.   6 Jan 1848. Deed of Conveyance. **Joseph Whitmire, Henry Whitmire** and **Thomas Whitmire** of Newberry Dist, SC, for $4,000 to be paid by **W.J. Whitmire** of Spartanburg Dist, sold 604 acres bounded by **Thomas R<u>ead</u>, James Lambright, Daniel Sheloam** and others. Wit: **William McE<u>lreath</u>, John Hogan.** Signed, **Joseph Whitmire, Henry Whitmire, Thomas Whitmire.** Witness oath, 31 Aug 1850: Signed, **William McE<u>lrath</u>** to **J. Hamilton** Magst. Release of Dower, 31 Aug 1850: Signed, **Frances A. Elizabeth Whitmire** to **Jeremiah Hamilton**, Magt. Registered 11th Sept. 1850.

p. 41-42.   15 March 1850. Deed of Conveyance. **William Beshears** of Spartanburg Dist, for $162.50 paid by **James McMakin** of Greenville Dist, SC, sold 50 acres on both sides of Motleys

creek in Spartanburg Dist, bounded by **Ithra Beshears**, S bank of Easleys Creek, W bank of Fall branch and **Adam McElrath**. Wit: **Ithra Beshears, Solomon Clayton**. Signed, **William (x) Beshears Sen'.** Witness oath, 10th Sept 1850: Signed, **Ithra Beshears** to **James Caldwell** Magt S.D. Registered 12 Sept. 1850.
bazel
p. 42-43.   23 Oct 1848. Deed of Gift. Greenville Dist, SC. **William Tucker** of Greenville Dist, for the Love I have for my child have given unto **Ph. Deliam Howard** (and her bodily heirs) wife of **George Howard** of Greenville Dist, 123½ acres in Spartanburg Dist on North Tyger River, head waters. Beginning on a stake on the line between **Thomas R. Tucker** and myself. Wit: **William J. Howard, Vashty (her mark) Howard**. Signed, **William Tucker**. Witness oath, 17 Jan 1850: Signed, **William J. Howard** to **R.P. Goodlett**, M.G.D. Registered 17th Sept. 1850.

p. 43-45.   22 Sept 1849. Deed of Conveyance. **Henry Abbot** of Spartanburg Dist, for $215 paid by **Isaac Epting** of Spartanburg Dist, sold 39 acres on Pacolet River adjoining **James Bivings, Carter Burnett, George A. Fike** & Pacolet River. Test: **J. Rufus Poole, John Epting**. Signed, **Henry Abbott**. Witness oath, 17 Sept 1850: Signed, **J.R. Poole** to **J.B. Tolleson** clk & Mag Exoffo. Release of Dower, 17 Sept 1850: Signed, **Elizabeth (x) Abbott**. Registered 17th Sept. 1850.

p. 45-46.   19 Jan 1842. Deed of Conveyance. **Johnson J. Hembree** of Spartanburg Dist, for $190 paid by **Alexander Bennett** sold 40 acres, a part of 115 acres conveyed by **Jethro Osheals** to **Thomas Taylor** originally granted to **Samuel Lancaster**. Wit: **John F. Donor, Eber Cathcart**. Signed, **J.J. Hembre**. Witness oath, 19 Jan 1843: Subscribing Justice, **John F. Donor** to **H. Osheals** Mag. Release of Dower, 2 May 1843: Signed, **Catharine (x) Hembree** to **Henry Osheals**. Registered 17th Sept. 1850.

p. 46-48.   27 Nov 1849. Deed of Conveyance. **Nathaniel Vise Senior** of Spartanburg Dist, for $745 paid by **Joseph Wofford** of Spartanburg Dist, sold 149 acres on the N side of Tyger River; a part of a tract formally belonged **Nathaniel Heraldson**. Wit: **John S. Vise, William Edwards**. Signed, **Nathaniel Vise**. Witness oath, 21st Dec 1849: Signed, **William Edwards** to **H. Wofford** Mag. (In **William Edwards'** witness of oath, he saw **John J. Vise** sign as a witness). Release of Dower, 21 Dec 1849: Signed, **Dorcas (x) Vise** to **H. Wofford** Mag. Registered 18th Sept. 1850.

p. 48-49.   28 Jan 1848. Deed of Conveyance. Greenville Dist, SC. **William E. Wickliff** of Spartanburg Dist, for $118.57 paid by **John Butler Peace** of Spartanburg Dist, sold 100 acres in Spartanburg Dist, on both sides of Spivys creek, bounded by **John Cothran**, Rutherford Road and **Earle**. Wit: **W.D. Threlkeld, Isaac Wickliffe**. Signed, **W.E. Wickliffe**. Witness oath, 29 Jan 1848: Signed, **W.D. Threlkeld** to **C.J. Elford** M.G.D. Registered 18th Sept. 1850.

p. 49-50.   1 Dec 1849. Deed of Conveyance. **John Cothram** and **Elizabeth Cothram** of Spartanburg Dist, for $180 paid by **John B. Peace** of Spartanburg Dist, sold 91 acres on both sides of Spiveys creek waters of South Pacolet River bounded by **Earle's**. Test: **W.B. Durham, E.T. (x) Jackson**. Signed, **John Cothram, Elizabeth Cothram, John C. (x) Cothram**. Witness oath, 11 June 1850: Signed, **W.B. Durham** to **James Caldwell** Mag. Registered 18th Sept. 1850.

p. 50-52. 3 Sept. 1844. Deed of Conveyance. **William Clayton** of Spartanburg Dist, for $700 paid by **Bazel Calvert** of Spartanburg Dist, sold 240 acres on James Creek, beginning on James Creek just above the ford, adjoining **Harris** old line. Wit: **S.S. Robuck, D.B. Clayton.** Signed, **Wm Clayton.** Witness oath, 5 Sept 1844: Signed, **D.B. Clayton** to **Jonas Brewton** Mag. Release of Dower, 5 Sept 1844: Signed, **Elizabeth Clayton** to **Jonas Brewton** Mag. Registered 19th Sept. 1850.

p. 52-53. 19 Jan 1850. Deed of Conveyance. **C.P. Woodruff** of Spartanburg Dist, for $115.37½ paid by **Bazil Calvert** sold 35½ acres on Jimmys Creek and Georgia Road, bounded on the N by **B. Calvert,** on the E by **Mary White,** on the S by **A.B. Woodruff,** on the W by **C.P. Woodruff.** Wit: **Samuel Pilgrim, J. Pinckney Hannah.** Signed, **C.P. Woodruff.** Witness oath, 21 Feb 1850: Signed, **J. Pinckney Hannah** to **Jonas Brewton** Mag. Registered 19 Sept. 1850.

p. 54-56. 12 Sept 1845. Deed of Conveyance. **G. Nichols,** Sheriff of Spartanburg Dist, by writ fieri facias issued by the Court of Common Pleas, 22 March 1838, the suit of **Joseph Michael & Co,** directed to my predecessor **A.C. Bomar,** commanding him that of the goods, lands and tenements of **Thos Kimbrell** to levy $153.60, damages and costs.The sheriff seized and sold for $70 paid to **A.C. Bomar** by **J.T. Kirby; J.T. Kirby** admitted the deed to **Wm G. Gramling** for 160 acres on Fairforest Creek and on both sides of the Mount Zion Road, bounded by **Richard Moss** on the N & E, on the S by **James McCarly** and Fairforest Creek. Wit: **W.H. Wilbanks, William Walker.** Signed, **G. Nicholls,** S.S.D. Security or Bond of $300, to warrant legal title, so far as the claim **Thomas Kimbrel** is concerned or any other person before him, 15 Sept 1845: Signed, **Simpson Bobo, Jno. Kirby,** wit: **O.E. Edwards. Genl. Bomar,** Please to make the rights of the **Kimbrel** land purchased by me to **Mr. S. Bobo** and oblige yours &c. Feb the 13th 1843, Signed, **Jno. Kirby.** Wit oath, 26 Sept 1850: **Mr. O.E. Edwards** made oath that he Signed the above Instrument & that he saw **John T. Kirby** sign the above. **O.E. Edwards** to **J.B. Tolleson** clk & Mag Exoffo. Wit oath and delivery of deed, 26 Sept 1850: Signed, **William Walker A.S.H.** to **J.B. Tolleson** clk & Mag Exoffo. Registered 29th Sept. 1850.

p. 56-57.   1 Oct 1850. Deed of Conveyance. Cleveland Co., NC. **Elizabeth Furgerson** of Spartanburg Dist, for $15 paid by **Robert McMullin** of Spartanburg Dist, sold 200 acres on the waters of North Pacolet river bounded by **S.G. Seay, J. [or I.] Stricklin, Wm Wilky** and others; the tract laid out to me as my dower in the land of my late husband, **Wm Furgerson.** Wit: **David McMillin, Jno. T. Beam.** Signed, **Elizabeth (x) Furgerson.** Witness oath, 2 Oct 1850: Signed, **David McMillin** to **A. Bonner** Mag. Registered 3 day of October 1850.

Handwriting changed and "Spartanburgh" reappears as the name of the District.

p. 57-58.   9 Oct 1847. Deed of Conveyance. **Noah Wolf** of Spartanburgh Dist, for $150 paid by **Lem^l P. Wolf** of Spartanburgh Dist, sold all of my interest in to all which belongs to **George Wolf** late of Spartanburgh Dist, deceased; Contained in two distinct tracts on one of which **Elizabeth Wolf** widow of **George Wolf,** deceased, now resides, 250 acres bounded by **James Burnett, Zachariah Wall, Hugh McDowell & Wilson Cantrell**; the other about 150 acres bounded by **Henry White, Wilson N. Cantrell** making in the whole about 402 acres, my interest being that to which I am entitled as one of the children or heirs at law of **George Wolf** deceased. Wit: **W.N.**

Cantrell, Wesly Wall. Signed, **Noah Wolf.** Witness oath, 9 Oct 1847: Signed, **W.N. Cantrell** to **Elias Wall** Magst. Release of Dower, 29 Oct 1847: Signed, **Jane Wolf** to **Elias Wall** Magistrate. Registered 4 day of Oct 1850.

p. 59. 9 Sept 1845. Deed of Conveyance. **Mary Smith** of Spartanburgh Dist, for $300 paid by **Robert R. Smith,** sold 150 acres on the West side of Dutchmans Creek conveyed to me by **Samuel Morrow.** Wit: **Joel Dean, John Bearden.** Signed, **Mary Smith.** Witness oath, 9 Sept 1845: Signed, **John Bearden** to **Joel Dean.** Registered the 4 Oct 1850. Original delivered to ~ **R.R. Smith** 22nd April 1851.

p. 60-61. 28 Jan 1850. Deed of Conveyance. **James Philips** Rutherford Co., NC, for $400 paid by **Pinckney Young** of Cobb Co., GA, sold 200 acres by computation, on Pacolet River adjoining **Wesley Hammett & Jesse Humphies** (also **Hunphers**) & **Wm Turner.** Wit: **Capt. Isaac Young, Tilman Philips.** Signed, **James Philips.** Release of Dower, 16 May 1850: Signed, **Emily (x) Philips** to **Andrew Bonner** J.Q. Witness oath, 4 Oct 1850: Signed, **Isaac Young** to **J.B. Tolleson** clk & Mag Exoffo. Registered 4 Oct 1850.

p. 61-62. 2 Jan 1849. Deed of Conveyance. Union Dist, SC. **Thomas Lamb** of Union Dist, for $433.50 paid by **P.M. Waters** of Spartanburgh Dist, sold [acres not given] in Spartanburgh and Union Districts, on a branch of Elishas Creek Waters of Enoree River; bounded by **A.G.W. Gorden, Mrs. Nancy Hill, Green Hill, Aaron Starns** and said **P.M. Waters.** Wit: **James Jeans, John Sneed.** Signed, **Thomas Lamb.** Witness oath, 28 March 1849: Signed, **James Janes** to **John H. Walker,** Mag. S.D. Release of Dower, [no day & month] 1849: Signed, **Amy (x) Lamb** to **Mathew Myers,** Magst. Registered the 4 day of October 1850.

p. 62-63. 6 April 1850. Deed of Gift. **J.W. Farrow** of Spartanburgh Dist, for the natural love and affection which I have for my son **Madison Farrow** of Laurence Dist, SC, give him all my Library of Books of every description, **Francis A. Farrow & Mariae** Antoinetts books excepted, one Shot Gun, two sets of Silver bullet Buttons, also one horse colt, named Redjacket, Second colt of Sety. Wit: **Frederick Harley.** Signed, **J.W. Farrow.** Witness oath, 4 Oct 1850: Signed, **Frederick Harley** to **Z. Lanford** Magt. Registered 7 Oct 1850.

p. 63-64. 2 Oct 1850. Deed of Conveyance. **Jorial Barnett** and my wife **Cassa Barnett** of Spartanburgh Dist, for $300 paid or secured to be paid by **James M. Nesbete** of Spartanburgh Dist, sold 75 acres, 50 acres of which was conveyed to my wife **Cassa Barnett** by **Benjamin Nicholls** decd, and 25 acres bought of **George Nicholls,** bounded on the N by **Moore,** W & SW by **Moore,** S by **George Nicholls** and on the E by **A. Pettit.** Wit: **John M. Crook, Azariah Vice.** Signed, **Jorial Barnett, Cassey Barnett.** Witness oath, 8 Oct 1850: Signed, **John M. Crook** to **John H. Walker** Mags. Registered the 8th October 1850.

p. 64-65. 7 Oct 1850. Mortgage. **John C. Zimmerman** is indebted to **Thos. O.P. Vernon,** Commissioner of the Court of Equity for Spartanburgh Dist, by four Bonds for money, each for $1,500 , due 7th Oct 1851, 1852, 1853, 1854, bearing interest from date; for securing the payment of $6,000 for 700 acres on the waters of Fairforest known as the place whereon **John Oland Senr**

deceased resided and whereon his widow **Mrs. Oland** now resides. All which will more fully appear by reference to the pleadings & to the order of Court made at June Term 1850, by his Honor **Chancellor Geo. W. Dargan**. Wit: **R.C. Poole, J.B. Tolleson**. Signed, **Tho. O.P. Vernon**, **C.E.S.D., John C. Zimmerman**. Witness oath, 10 Oct 1850: Signed, **R.C. Poole** to **G.W.H. Legg**, Magt. Registered 10 Oct 1850.

p. 66.   29 April 1850. Deed of Conveyance. **Isham Wood** of Spartanburgh Dist, for $500 paid by **Oliver P. Wood** of Spartanburg Dist, sold 144¼ acres on South Tyger River on S side, bounded by lots Nº 1 & 3, **Abraham Mayfield** and **Elizabeth Mason**. Test: **John T. Wood, Daniel M. Wood**. Signed, **Isham Wood**. Witness oath, 15 Oct 1850: Signed, **John T. Wood** to **J.B. Tolleson** Clk & Mag Exoffo. Registered 15 Oct 1850.

p. 67.   24 Sept 1850. Deed of Conveyance. **Mary Wyatt** of Spartanburgh Dist, for $1 paid by **Tillotson Brookshear** of Spartanburgh Dist, sold all my right and interest in the 75 acres whereon my husband **Aaron Templeman** lived at the time of his death, that is to say all my right and interest to the part of the tract which said **Brookshear** bought of **J.M. Linder** bounded by **John Linder, Zech Cannon, Lewis Cannon & James Templeman** on Pacolet river. Wit: **Absolem McAbee, Aaron Templeman**. Signed, **Mary (x) Wyatt**. Witness oath, 4 Oct 1850: Signed, **Absolem McAbee** to **Joel Cannon** Mag. Registered 14 October 1850.

p. 67-68.   23 March 1850. Award. Spartanburgh District. In a matter of controversy between **John S. Finch, Susan Neighbors** and **Catharrie Neighbors** relative to a small tract of land lying on Meadow Creek and on which the **Miss Neighbors** recently resided, it being the same tract which **George McFearson** attempted to convey to their mother & we whose names appear below were chosen as arbitrators by the parties to determine on the true title to the aforesaid Land and after hearing the evidence which was adduced by both parties do say on our oaths that the **Miss Neighbors** cannot legally hold said Land. Therefore we award the said Land to the said **Finch** and through a Sympathetic feeling towards the unfortunate young Ladies do Say that the said **Finch** shall pay them the sum of Fifty dollars upon their executing to him a Deed of Conveyance for the said Land from themselves and their heirs Only. Given under our hands and seals this 23rd of March 1850. Signed, **F.H. Legg, Larkin Ballenger, Reuben Gramling, William West, Tel. Stone, M. Seay, Sam¹ M. Snoddy**. Registered 14 Oct 1850.

p. 68-69.   28 Feb 1843. Deed of Conveyance. **William Pearson** of Spartanburgh Dist, for $225 paid by **Miles H. Scott** of Spartanburgh Dist, sold [acres not given] tract of land bounded by **John Pearson**. Wit: **Wᵐ Lanford, John (x) Pearson**. Signed, **William (x) Pearson**. Witness oath, 28 Feby 1843: Signed, **John (x) Pearson** to **Z. Lanford** Mag. Release of Dower, 16 Dec 1843: Signed, **Nancy (x) Pearson** to **Z. Lanford**, J.Q. Registered 18 Oct 1850.

p. 69-70.   15 Feb 1849. Deed of Conveyance. **John Letherwood, James Letherwood, Jesse Leatherwood & Bazel Calvert** of Spartanburgh Dist, and **Zechariah Leatherwood** of Benton Co., Alabama, for $376 paid by **Epharim Calvert** of Spartanburgh Dist, sold 53 acres on the N bank of Jimies Creek the waters of Tyger River, it being the land owned by **George Letherwood** decd. Wit: **Jonas Brewton, J.P. Hannah**. Signed, **John Leatherwood, Jesse Leatherwood, Bazil Calvert**,

Spartanburg District Conveyances

James **Leatherwood**, Zechariah **Leatherwood**, Agness **Leatherwood** per John **Leatherwood** Atty. Witness oath, 20 Oct 1850: Signed, **J.P. Hannah** to **Jonas Brewton**, and **J.P. Hannah** stated he saw all the signers sign their names including **Agness Letherwood** wife of **Zechariah Letherwood**. Registered 20 Oct 1850.

p. 71-72.   9 Oct 1850. Deed of Conveyance. **Wᵐ J. Whitmire** of Spartanburgh Dist, for $10 paid by **P.R. Bobo, Z.D. Bragg, Benjamin Dehay, G.H. Sheldon, D.H. Sheldon, Jesse Lamb & W.S. Gregory** Trustees of **Bragg** Division Nº 46, Sons of Temperance in Spartanburgh Dist, sold to **P.R. Bobo** & others Trustees, and to their successors in office, a lot containing ½ acre on the S side of the main road from Cross Keys to Cross Anchor fronting the residence of **Zechariah Allen**; Fifty yards on the road adjoining **Wᵐ J. Whitmire**. Wit: **J. Wᵐ Bobo, B.H. Lancaster**. Signed, **W.J. Whitmire**. Witness oath, 15 Oct 1850: Signed, **J. Wᵐ Bobo** to **P.R. Bobo**, Mag. Registered 21 day of October 1850.

p. 72-73.   3 April 1850. Sheriff Titles. **R.C. Poole** Sheriff of Spartanbugh Dist, by order of the Court of Common Pleas on 29 January 1849, at the suit of **J.T. Kirby**, to levy the sum of $1,130.85 with Interest, damages & costs, against **Z.D. Cottrell**; sold 8 acres in the Village of Spartanburgh & beginning in the Center of the road at the fork of the road leading from **Junius W. Thomson's** to Spartanburgh Village, NE down the center of Thompson's road; a lot which **R.W. Folger** purchased of **E.C. Leitner, Z.D. Cottrell** purchased from **R.W. Folger**; bought for $1,000 by **J.D. McCullough** of Spartanburgh Dist. Wit: **Jno. Kirby, Jno. Earle Bomar**. Signed, **R.C. Poole**, S.S.D. Witness oath, 24 Oct 1850: Signed, **Jno. Earle Bomar** to **G.W.H. Legg** Magst. Registered 25 Oct 1850. Original delivered to ∼ **Rev. J.D. McColloch** 24ᵗʰ Feby 1851.

p. 73-74.   26 Oct 1850. Deed of Conveyance. **Richard Turner** of Spartanburgh Dist, $1,075 paid by **William Barnett** of Greenville Dist, SC, sold 337 acres in Spartanburgh Dist, on S side of Peters Creek, bordered by **Joab Briant** and **Gasaway Briant**, being where I now live and which I purchased from **Thos. Rees** on the 7ᵗʰ day of September 1821. Wit: **James A. Wooton, Huey[?] Abbott**. Signed, **Richard Turner**. Witness oath, 6 Oct 1850: Signed, **Henry[?] Abbott** to **H.J. Dean** Not. Pub. & mag Exoff. Release of Dower, 26 Oct 1850: Signed, **Tennesse (x) Turner** to **H.J. Dean**. Registered the 26 October 1850.

p. 74-75.   26 Oct 1850. Mortgage. **William Barnett** of Greenville Dist, SC, for $1,000 paid by **Richard Turner** of Spartanburgh Dist, mortgages the same 337 acres mentioned above. Deed void if **William Barnett** pays **Richard Turner** $1,000 with Interest on or before 25ᵗʰ day of Dec. next. Wit: **James A. Wooton, Heuy[?] Abbott**. Signed, **William Barnett**. Witness oath, 26 Oct 1850: Signed, **Henry Abbott** to **H.J. Dean** Not Pub & Magst Ex Off. Registered 30 Oct 1850.

p. 76.   25 Dec 1849. Deed of Conveyance. **John Bullington** of Spartanburgh Dist, for $52 paid by **Charles Thompson** of Spartanburgh Dist, sold 40 acres on branches of Lossons Fork creek waters of Pacolet River. Wit: **T.W. Wingo, William E. Ward**. Signed, **John J. Bullington**. Witness oath, 4 Nov 1850: Signed, **T.W. Wingo** to **J.B. Tolleson** Clk & mg Ex off. Registered the 4 Nov 1850.

p. 77-78.   3 Aug 1848. Deed of Conveyance. **William Robbs** of Spartanburg Dist, for $150 paid by **Frederick Williams** of Spartanburgh Dist, sold 142 acres where **Peter Pack** now lives; on the waters of South Pacolet River originally granted to **William Ramsey;** bounded by **Dalton, West, Bullington** and **Dickson.** Wit: **Elias Wall, Edmond (x) Cooley.** Signed, **William Robbs.** Witness oath, 7 Aug 1848: Signed, **Elias Wall** to **Z. Lanford** Magst. Release of Dower, 20 Dec 1848: Signed, **Malinda (x) Robbs** to **Elias Wall** Magistrate. Registered the 4 Nov 1850. Original delivered to ~~ **Fred Williams** 30 Nov 1850.

p. 78.   28 April 1839. Deed of Conveyance. **John Sarter** of Spartanburgh Dist, for $100 paid by **Robert I. [or J.] Wall** of Spartanburgh Dist, sold 30 acres on the S side of Jacobs Creek, bounded by **Daniel White.** Wit: **William Foster, Frances Foster.** Signed, **John Sarter.** Witness oath, 11 Jan 1841: Signed, **William Foster** to **H. Dodd** J.P. Registered 8th Nov 1850.

p. 79.   5 April 1839. Release. **Abey Liles** of Rutherford Co, NC, holds a mortgage of **John Sarter's** land and hereby renounces a claim to 30 acres which **Sarter** has sold to **Robert Wall.** Wit: **Joshua Richards, Liley Richards.** Signed, **Abey (x) Liles.** Registered 8 Nov 1850.

p. 79-80.   7 Nov 1819. Deed of Conveyance. **James Young** of Spartanburgh Dist, $120 paid by **Robert Wall** of Spartanburgh Dist, sold 31 acres, part of the land conveyed to me from **George McWilliams & James Younger;** on a small branch of Obeds Creek bounded on the NE by said **Wall,** on the NW by **James Younger,** and on S said **Young's** land. Wit: **Benjamin C. Wall, W**[m] **Young.** Signed, **James Young.** Witness oath, 7 Jan 1823: Signed, **William Young** to **James Young** J.Q. Registered 8 Nov 1850.

p. 80-81.   28 Feb 1815. Deed of Conveyance. **Jonathan Wall** of Spartanburgh Dist, $100 paid by **Robert J. [or F.] Wall** of Spartanburg Dist, sold 60 acres in the fork of Jacobs creek & Richland creek; bounded by **George Rowland** and **John Clark,** up Jacobs Creek to a butlerwood (buttonwood ?) tree that leans over said creek with a hole in the side. Wit: **Zech. Wall, Polly Wall.** Signed, **Jonathan Wall.** Witness oath, 11 April 1815: Signed, **Zechariah Wall** to **James Young** J.Q. Registered the 8. Nov. 1850.

p. 81-82.   13 Jan 1840. Deed of Conveyance. **Henry Turner Ju**[r] of Spartanburgh Dist, for $50 paid by **John Cash Ju**[r] of Spartanburg Dist, sold 20 acres on the ridge between Island Creek & Pacolet River; bounded by said **Henry Turner's** conditional line, the old road and the said **Cash.** Wit: **A.B. Thomason, Shadrick Cash.** Signed, **Henry Turner.** Witness oath, 22 Feb 1840: Signed, **Shadrick Cash** to **J.W. Martin,** J.Q. Registered the 20 Nov 1850.

p. 82-83.   16 Sept 1834. Deed of Conveyance. **Peyton Turner** of Spartanburgh Dist, for $225 paid by **John Cash** of Spartanburgh Dist, sold 150 acres on Island Creek; bounded by the creek on the far edge of the waters up just above the ford at the saw mill, the road and **Henry Turner's** conditional line. Wit: **Henderson Cash, Henry Turner Ju**[r]. Signed, **Peyton Turner.** Witness oath, 20 Sept 1834: Signed, **Henry Turner Ju**[r] to **Henry Turner** J.Q. Release of Dower, 25 Sept 1834: Signed, **Lucinda Turner** to **Henry Turner** J.Q. Registered 20 Nov 1850.

p. 83-84.   16 Jan 1829. Deed of Conveyance. **Hiram Procter** of Spartanburgh Dist, for $250 paid by **Shadrick Cash** of Spartanburg Dist, sold 160 acres on Island Creek ; bounded by **Burch, Eda Edwards** and **Aaron Cash**. Wit: **Mathew Guthrie, John (x) Dunaway**. Signed, **Hirum (x) Procter**. Witness oath, 16 Jan 1829: Signed, **Mathew Guthrie** to **Henry Turner** J.Q. Release of Dower, 25 Dec 1829: Signed, **Betty (x) Procter** to **Henry Turner** J.Q. Registered the 20 Nov 1850.

p. 84-85.   13 Jan 1840. Deed of Conveyance. **Abner B. Thomason** of Spartanburgh Dist, for $350 paid by **Shadrick Cash** of Spartanburgh Dist, sold 341 acres on both sides of waters of Island Creek; bounded by **Potter** and **C.W. Cannon**. Wit: **Fielden Turner, Henry Turner Ju^r** Signed, **Abner B. Thomason**. Witness oath, 22 Feb 1840: Signed, **Fielden Turner** to **J.W. Martin** J.Q. Release of Dower, 6 Aug 1842: Signed, **Nancy (x) Thomason** to **A. Dewberry** Mag. Registered the 20 Nov 1850.

p. 85-87.   4 Nov 1850. Deed of Conveyance. **Austin (Augustin) Shands** of Spartanburgh Dist, for $4,000 paid and secured to be paid by **James L. Williams** of Spartanburgh Dist, sold 530 acres on on both sides of Storys Creek a branch of Fairforest; beginning on a post oak near a School house, bounded by **White, Dr. S. Means, Capt. Cunningham, Story, Montgomery** and **Cates**. Wit: **W.W. Harris, W.C. Camp**. Signed, **A. Shands**. Witness oath, 5 Nov 1850: Signed, **W.W. Harris** to **J.B. Tolleson** Clk & mg Exiffo. Release of Dower, 4 Nov 1850: Signed, **Sarah C. Shands** to **J.W. Tucker** Not. Pub. Registered the 20 November 1850.

p. 87-90.   1 July 1850. Memorandum of Agreement. Between the President & Directors of the Bank of the State of South Carolina and the Swedish Iron Manufacturing Company of South Carolina in conformity with the Resolutions of the Board adopted on the 21st June 1850 acceeding to the proposition of **Col. Hampton** in relation to said premises.
First.
The Bank agrees to sell to the company all the real estate & mining privileges of taking oars lately belonging to the **Nesbett** Manufacturing Company and now the property of the Bank in Union, Spartanburg & York district, about 9,682 acres, 80 negroes Viz 48 men, 9 women, 23 children to be selected from the gang of Negroes on the premises by **C.W. Hammarskold** in families (the sale to include all the horses, mules, waggons, farming & other implements and Manufactured Iron & ore on hand at and for the price of one hundred and fifty thousand dollars [$150,000], to be paid as follows: $5000 in cash [Totals $115,000, instead of $150,000]

$5000 on 1 Jany 1851	$5000 on 1 July 1851	$5000 on 1 Jany 1852	$5000 on 1 July 1852
$5000 on 1 Jany 1853	$5000 on 1 July 1853	$5000 on 1 Jany 1854	$5000 on 1 July 1854
$5000 on 1 Jany 1855	$5000 on 1 July 1855	$6000 on 1 Jany 1856	$6000 on 1 July 1856
$6000 on 1 Jany 1857	$6000 on 1 July 1857	$6000 on 1 Jany 1858	$6000 on 1 July 1858
$6000 on 1 Jany 1859	$6000 on 1 July 1859	$6000 on 1 Jany 1860	$6000 on 1 July 1860

or sooner at option of the purchasers and interest on the whole at the rate of six pr. cent pr. annum to be paid half yearly on the first days of January and July in each and every year.
Second.
It is further agreed that the above payments shall be secured by the obligations of the several members of the company in a manner satisfactory to the Bank.
Third.
The purchasers are to place improvements on the property within 12 months to the value of $10,000.

Fourth.

That none of the negroes agreed to be sold shall be removed from the property without the previous assent of the Bank being obtained in writing to that effect setting forth particularyly what property it is agreed may be removed.

Fifth.

The Title of the property shall remain in the Bank until such payments shall have been made as to satisfy them fully of the whole debt being punctually paid as it becomes due.

Sixth.

The Bank shall have authority from time to time by is officers or agents to enter upon the premises for the purpose of inspection & examination to see that the improvements are made and the property kept in repair and that the negroes are forthcoming.

Seventh.

In case the works should be abandoned before the debt is fully paid the Bank shall have the power to sell the property at their discretion and apply the proceeds to the extinguishment of the debt as far as they will go.

Eighth.

In case of failure to pay any of the installments after 60 days notice the Bank shall be at liberty to consider the condition of trial as forfeited and to enter into & take possession of the premises and sell the whole property for payment of the debt.

Ninth.

In making titles to the property the purchasers shall receive a guit claim from the Bank and mortgage the property for the purchase money in arrear.

Charleston, S.C. 1st July 1850. Witness: **E.W. Pettit, C. Decemus Barbot** } [the following]:
C.W. Hammerskold, Klinck & Wickenberg, H.P. Cameron, J.H. Kalb, H. Schroder, P.H. Hammarskold, Jacob Small, Carl Epping Atty.

Wit: **Benj. F. Hunt Ju**r	} — **C.F. Kohuke**
Wit: **J.H. Furgerson**	} — **Geo. S. Cameron**
Wit: **M.R.E. Becker**	} — **W. Tepen**
Wit: **P.J. Fink**	} — **C.H. Paukorin**
W.M. Benckit	}

Witness oaths, 12 Nov 1850, Dist of Charleston: all the individual witnesses for the signatures of the members of the Company for which he was a witness sworn to **Thos. S. Jones**, N.P. & Ex off Magistrate.   Except 29 Aug 1850: **E.W. Pettit** as witness with **C. Decemus Borbot**, to **Jon. D. Alexander**, Not. Pub. Approval, 3 July 1850: I approve of the within as containing the true interest & meaning of the contract between the Bank & **Mr. Hammarskold** and his friends. Signed, **J.L. Pengersh(?).** Secretary's of State Office, Charleston, So. Car. Nov 12, 1850: The within agreement is recorded in Miscellaneous Record Book 6 D's pages 517, 518 & 519. Examined and certified by **Thos. S. Jones** deputy Secretary of State. Registered, examined and certified the 20 November 1850. Original Sent to Charleston to **Thos. R. Waring** 2 Decr 1850.

p.90-91.   13 Nov 1850. Mortgage. **Henry Rollins** has this day bought a Lot in the Town of Spartanburgh from **H.H. Thomson** for which **Rollins** gave three sealed notes for $75 each, due one, two and three years from this date with interest from date [total $225 plus interest]. If **Henry Rollins** pays the debt, this deed to **H.H. Thomson** is void. The lot is 3 acres on Greenville Street and on street by **Bowden's** lot. Wit: **J.B. Archer, W.T. Archer.** Signed, **Henry (x) Rollins.** Witness oath, 4 Dec 1850: Signed, **J.B. Archer** to **J.B. Tolleson** Clk & Mag Exiffo. Registered 4 December 1850. Original delivered to ~~ **H.H. Thomson** 24th Jany 1851.

p. 91-93.   13 Nov 1850. Mortgage. **William Dye** has this day bought a Lot in the Town of Spartanburg from **H.H. Thomson** for $225, for which **Dye** has gave three sealed notes for $75 each payable one, two & three years from date with interest from date. If **William Dye** pays the debt, the deed for the lot to **Thomson** is void. The lot is nearly 3 acres on Greenville Street beginning on NE corner of **H. Rollins'** lot. Wit: **J.B. Archer, W.T. Archer.** Signed, **William Dye.** Witness oath, 4 Dec 1850: Signed, **J.B. Archer** to **J.B. Tolleson** Clk & Mag Exiffo. Registered the 4 Dec. 1850. Original delivered to ~~ **H.H. Thomson** 24th Jany 1851.

p. 93-95. 1 July 1850. Commissioner's Mortgage. **Junius W. Thomson** is indebted to **Thos. O.P. Vernon** commissioner of the Court of Equity, by thee single bills or Bonds each money each for the sum of $925 due on 1st Monday in July in 1851, 1852 and 1853. The Bonds for better securing the payment of $2,775.06 for (1) 339 acres, the **David Thomson** tract, bounded by **Cleveland, Roberson & Neber(?),** to where the cane brake crosses Lawson Fork, **Bagwell, Bomar** and **J.W. Thomson.** (2) The **Gray** tract № 1 which is bounded by the **David Thomson** tract, the cane brake tract, containing 24 acres. Wit: **John Bomar Jun, W.W. Harris.** Signed, **J.W. Thomson.** Witness oath, 4 Dec 1850: Signed, **W.W. Harris** to **J.B. Tolleson** Clk & Mag Exiffo. Registered the 4 Decr 1850.

p. 95-96. 30 Nov 1850. Sheriff's Deed. On 5 March 1850, **Anthony Pearson** exhibited his petition in the Court of the Ordinary at Spartanburgh Court House to partition or divide 72 acres on Abners Creek of **Thomas Pearson Senr** who died intestate [no date].; bordered by **Eli Hughs, Hezekiah Hughs** and others. On 12 July 1850, **R. Bowden Esqr,** Ordinary of Spartanburgh Dist, ordered the land be sold. On 5 August 1850 it was sold by **J.R. Poole,** Sheriff of Spartanburg Dist, to **John D. Pearson** for $105. Wit: **Thomas Wood, John A. Monk.** Signed, **J.R. Poole,** Sheriff. Witness oath, 30 Nov 1859: Signed, **John A. Monk** to **J.B. Tolleson** Clk & mag Exoffo. Registered 4 December 1850.

p. 96-97.   29 June 1850. Deed of Conveyance. **Jesse Cleveland** of the town of Spartanburgh for $565 to be accounted for by **Jefferson Choice** or his legal representatives in the final settlement of my future Estate, sell to **Jefferson Choice** 113 acres in the Dist of Spartanburgh, beginning on the old line, mentioned "the mile stone marked 1 M.S.C.H". and up Howard Gap Road; bounded on the N by **Jesse Cleveland,** on the E by the Estate of **T. Earle,** on the S by **Maj. J.G. Kirby** and on the W by **Mrs. Mullinax.** Wit: **J.W. Weber, G.W.H. Legg.** Signed, **Jesse Cleveland.** Witness oath, 29 June 1850: Signed, **J.W. Weber** to **Geo. W.H. Legg** Magt. Registered 4th Decr. 1850.

p. 98-99.   9 Jan 1850. Deed of Conveyance. **Benjamin Wofford** of the town of Spartanburgh, in consideration of Sufficient inducements & $1 paid by **J.W. Tucker** of the same place, sold a lot in the Town of Spartanburgh on the street leading from the public square to the Jail on the E side of said street adjoining a Lot which I sold to **J.B. Archer,** on the N & adjoining another on the S now owned by me fronting on said Street Sixteen by Eighteen feet containing a fraction of an acre. Wit:

W.W. Boyd, E.L. Patterson. Signed, **Benj. Wofford.** Witness oath, 8 Aug 1850: Signed, **W.W. Boyd** to **J.B. Tolleson** Clk & mag Exoffo. Registered 4th Decr. 1850.

p. 99-100.   7 Dec 1849. Deed of Conveyance. **Riol B.   Seay** of Spartanburg Dist for $356 paid by **J.W. Tucker** of Spartanburg Dist, sold 172 acres purchased at Commissioners Sale as the property of **Daniel White** decsd, lying on Fawn Branch immediately above the furnace Road; known as the **Kiah Seay** tract Lot Nº 5, on a plat of record in office of Commissioners. Wit: **Daniel Johnson, Dr. A.W. Bivings.** Signed, **Riol B. Seay.** Witness oath, 8 Aug 1850: Signed, **A.W. Bivings** to **J.B. Tolleson** Clk & mag Exoffo. Release of Dower, 19 July 1850: Signed, **Emily (x) Seay** to **J.B. Tolleson** Clk & mag Exoffo. Registered 4th Decr. 1850.

p. 100-102.   7 Dec 1849. Deed of Conveyance. **Daniel Johnson** of Spartanburg Dist for $300 paid by **J.W. Tucker** of Spartanburg Dist, sold 150 acres where I now live, on waters of Fawn Branch adjoining lands of **Mat Seay, Isham Clemens, Riol B. Seay & J.W. Tucker**, on the Furnace Road; which I purchased from **James Lawrens.** Wit: **Riol B. Seay, Dr. A.W. Bivings.** Signed, **Daniel Johnson.** Witness oath, 8 Aug 1850: Signed, **A.W. Bivings** to **J.B. Tolleson** Clk & mag Exoffo. Release of Dower, [Magistrate's statement says "**Nancy Johnson** wife of the within named **J.M. Johnson**"], 19 July 1850: Signed, **Nancy (x) Johnson** to **J.B. Tolleson** Clk & mag Exoffo. Registered 4th Decr. 1850.

p. 102-103.   8 Nov 1850. Deed of Conveyance. **J.W. Quinn** of Spartanburg Dist, for $160 paid by **Z.J. Bates** of Spartanburg Dist, sold ½ acre in the Village of Spartanburg, bounded by church street, **Benj. Wofford,** half the distance of the line of the lot which **R.D. Owen** bought of **S. Bobo Esqr.** and **S. Bobo.** Wit: **A.W. Bivings, Dr. J.B. Morgan.** Signed, **J.W. Quinn.** Witness oath, 11 Nov 1850: Signed, **J.B. Morgan** to **J.B. Tolleson** Clk & mag Exoffo. Release of Dower, 11 Nov 1850: Signed, **R.A. Quinn** [Magistrate's statement says **Rhodah Ann Quinn**]. Registered 4th Decr. 1850.

p. 103-105.   19 Sept 1845. Deed of Conveyance. **David Bettis** of Spartanburg Dist, for $6 per acre paid by **Phillip Bettis** of Spartanburg Dist, sold 12 acres bounded by **Samuel Nesbitt** on the S, **James A. Miller** on the W and on other sides by **Anthony Pearson & Sarah Bettis** being the NE part of the land by me owned before I sold a part of it to **Nancy Robbins** alias **Jesse Arthur** in trust for her. Wit: **E.C. Leitner, S.C. Miller.** Signed, **David Bettis.** Witness oath, 4 Nov 1850: Signed, **E.C. Leitner** to **J.B. Tolleson** Clk & mag Exoffo. Registered 4th Decr. 1850.

p. 105-106.   19 Jan 1849. Deed of Conveyance. **Joseph Finger** of Spartanburg Dist, for $54 paid by **Elijah Robbins** of Spartanburg Dist, sold 54 acres on the waters of Buck Creek, a part of the survey granted to **Ann Barton** in 1842; bordering **Elijah Robbins** and **Johnson.** Wit: **C.S.W. Scruggs, Thomas Shields.** Signed, **Joseph Finger.** Witness oath, 6 June 1849: Signed, **C.S.W. Scruggs** to **G. Cannon** Not. Public. Registered 4th Decr. 1850. Original delivered to ~~ **Jackson Robbins** (admist?).

p. 106-107.   21 April 1836. Deed of Conveyance. **Thomas Coggins** of Spartanburg Dist, for $271 paid by **Elijah Robbins** of Spartanburg Dist, sold 180 acres on the South side of Buck Creek, bordering **John Johnson, Bradford,** the head of the race paths, **James's** line and **Thomas Shield's** line. Wit: **Joseph P. Peeple, Thomas A. Shields**. Signed, **Thomas Coggins**. Witness oath, 25 June 1836: Signed, **Thomas A. Shields** to **Tho' Cantrell** J.P. Registered 4th Decr. 1850.

p. 107-109. 26 Nov 1850. Mortgage. **M.C. Stacy** [or **Chester M. Stacy**] is indebted to **Tho' O.P. Vernon** Commissioner in Equity of Spartanburg Dist, by one Single Bill or monied bond of $267.50, payable 5 August 1851 with interest, for one Negro man **Prince** whom I bought at a sale made by him as Com. on the 5th August 1850. If the bill is not paid, **Prince** is to be taken into custody of **T.O.P. Vernon** and detained to his own use and behoof as his own proper goods and chattels. Wit: **James V. Trimmier, R.C. Poole**. Signed, **M.C. Stacy**. Witness oath, 4 Dec 1850: Signed, **J.V. Trimmier** to **J.B. Tolleson** Clk & mag Exoffo. Registered 4th Decr: 1850.

p. 109-111. 26 Nov 1850. Mortgage. **William Lockhart** is indebted to **T.O.P. Vernon** Commissioner in Equity for Spartanburg Dist, by one monied Bond or Single Bill for $690 with interest, payable the 5th August 1851, for a Negro man named **Henry**. If the bill is not paid, **Henry** is to be taken into custody of **T.O.P. Vernon** and detained to his own use and behoof as his own proper goods and chattels. Wit: **James V. Trimmier, R.C. Poole**. Signed, **William Lockhart**. Witness oath, 4 Dec 1850: Signed, **J.V. Trimmier** to **J.B. Tolleson** Clk & mag Exoffo. Registered 4th Decr. 1850.

p. 111-112. 28 April 1849. Deed of Conveyance. **Barney Bishop** of Spartanburg Dist, for $100 paid by **Hamilton Bishop** of Spartanburg Dist, sold 87½ acres on the East side of Boiling Springs Road, bordered by **R. Moss & D. Dantzler** and West side of Howard Gap Road. Wit: **C.H. Mayberry, Lemuel Bullington**. Signed, **Barney Bishop**. Witness oath, 14 Oct 1850: Signed, **Lemuel Bullington** to **J.B. Tolleson** Clk & mag Exoffo. Registered 4th Decr 1850.

p. 112-113. 15 Aug 1850. Deed of Conveyance. **Lewis Bishop** for $50 paid by **James P. Miller**, sold 30 acres on the waters of Shoaly Creek adjoining **Samuel Seay**, head of **Belcher's** Still branch on the old line between **Aaron Bishop** and **Seay**. Test: **Solomon Bishop, John Belton Tolleson**. Signed, **Lewis Bishop**. Witness oath, 4 Dec 1850: Signed, **J. Belton Tolleson** to **J.B. Tolleson** Clk & mag Exoffo. Registered 4th Decr. 1850.

p. 113-114. 23 Oct 1850. Power of Attorney. State of Arkansas, County of Montgomery. **Felix Green** and **Maiden Green** of Montgomery Co., Arkansas, heirs at law of **David Tanner** Deceased of Spartanburg Dist, appoint **Aldrige Green** of Greenville Dist, SC, our lawful agent to collect the amount coming to us as heirs of **David Tanner** Deceased. Signed, **Felix Green, Maiden Green**. 23 Oct 1850: **John Cook**, J.P., Montgomery Co., AL, personally knows **Felix Green** and **Maiden Green**, she acknowledges the within letter of attorney to be her act and deed free from coercion. 23 Oct 1850. Signed, **James S. Fleming**, Clerk of Circuit Court, State if Ark, Montgomery Co., certifies that **Cook** is an acting and qualified J.P. of Montgomery Co., Ark. Registered 4th Decr 1850.

p. 114-116. 30 Oct 1850. Deed of Conveyance. **James Austell** of Spartanburg Dist, for $465 paid by **Lansford Hopper,** sold 155 acres in the fork of Thickoty creek and Beaver Dam in Spartanburg Dist, bounded **G.B. Humphries**. Wit: **Peter Quinn Camp, Green B. Humphries**. Signed, **James**

Austell. Witness oath, 30 Oct 1850: Signed, **P. Quinn Camp** to **A. Bonner** Mag. Release of Dower, 30 Oct 1850: [**Mary** in **A. Bonner's** statement] Signed, **Polly Austell.** Registered 4th Dec 1850.

p. 116-118.   16 Nov 1847. Commissioner's Titles. Indenture between **Thomas O.P. Vernon**, Commissioner of Court of Equity for Spartanburg Dist, and **John B. Cleveland. Junius W. Thomson** on about 1 Oct 1845 exhibited his complaint in the Court of Equity against **H.H. Thomson, J.M. Thomson & J.W. Thomson,** heirs at law of **Richard Thomson**, deceased, for partition of certain lands, and the issue heard at June Term 1847. The court ordered the lands to be sold at public auction by the commissioner who sold Lot Nº 9 for $100 to **John B. Cleveland;** commencing on **J.B. Cleveland**'s corner on church street, to **Nichol's** corner to the church lot, to a corner at **Miss Betsy Wright's** house on church street; Lot in town of Spartanburg bounded on S by **J.B. Cleveland,** E by Lot Nº 11 same estate, N by **G. Nicols's** lot, W by the Methodist Church lot and Church street. Wit: **R.C. Poole, J.V. Trimmier.** Signed, **Tho' O.P. Vernon** C.E.S.D. Witness oath, 18 Dec 1850: Signed, **J.V. Trimmier** to **J.B. Tolleson** Clk & mag Exoffo. Registered 18th Dec. 1850.

p. 118-119.   [no day] April 1850. Deed of Gift. **Edmond Cooley Senior** of Spartanburg Dist, for the love and affection I bear to my son **Joseph Cooley,** give him 194 acres on Packolet River; beginning on the river at the mouth of Barton's Creek, up Barton's creek. Wit: **John Epting, J.W. Martin.** Signed, **Edmond (x) Cooley.** Witness oath, 4 Feb 1850: Signed, **John Epting** to **J.W. Marin,** Not. Pub. Registered 18th Dec 1850. Original delivered to ~~ **Joseph Cooley** 18th Dec 1850.

p. 119-121.   6 Dec 1850. Mortgage. **Zera Alverson** has this day bought of **Charles Thomson**, two tracts, one known as the **Bullington** tract & the other as the **Foster** tract [acres not mentioned] for which he has this day given four Single Bills amounting to $338; one for $60 due next Apr 1st, $78 due 25th Dec 1851, $100 due 25th Dec 1852, $100 due 25th Dec 1853. Wit: **R. Bowden, J.V. Trimmier.** Signed, **Zera Alverson.** Witness oath, 6 Dec 1850: Signed, **J.V. Trimmier** to **J.B. Tolleson** Clk & mag Exoffo. Registered 18th Dec. 1850. Original delivered to ~~ **Charles Thomson** 23rd Dec.

p. 121-123.   29 Nov 1850. Deed of Conveyance. **Richard Moss** of Spartanburg Dist, for $100 paid by **R. Bowden** of Spartanburg Dist, sold about 2 acres on the waters of Fairforest Creek, a small part of a tract which I purchased from **John Keast,** designed to be used by **R. Bowden** for a mill pond; Beginning at a corner mark on the lower edge of the Shoal on Fair forest creek known as the still house shoal and on the NE side of the main channel about 20 feet therefrom and near a crevice in rock or Shoal running up and down and resembling a wagon track which crevice has a hole in the lower extremity opposite and about one foot from said corner mark. The deed is for the area of land that will be covered by the pond when the water level is raised to intersect with Reedy branch. **R. Bowden & Richard Moss** agree to keep up between them at equal expense and equal labor by them and their heirs a division fence to be built and run along the water's edge as close as can be built. Wit: **A. Wingo, J.V. Trimmier.** Signed, **Richard Moss.** Witness oath, 4 Dec 1850: Signed, **J.V. Trimmier** to **J.B. Tolleson** Clk & mag Exoffo. Registered 18th Dec. 1850.

p. 123-124.   11 June 1850. Sheriff's Titles. By a writ of fieri facias issues by the Court of Common

Pleas, Dist of Spartanburg, tested 23 March 1843, at the suit of **James Nesbitt** against **Patience Elder** and **Abagail Smith** to levy $115.59 with Interest, damages and costs, **R.C. Poole** Sheriff of Spartanburg Dist, had taken 100 acres of **Patience Elder**; bounded by **James Nesbitt, Elizabeth Rogers, James Rogers** and others; purchased by **James Nesbitt** for $25. Wit: **J.R. Poole, W.J. Poole.** Signed, **R.C. Poole,** S.S.D. Witness oath, 4 Dec 1850: Signed, **[Col.] R.C. Poole,** to **J.B. Tolleson** Clk & mag Exoffo. Registered 18th Dec. 1850.

p. 125-126. 28 Feb 1846. Deed of Conveyance. **John C. Hoyt** of Spartanburg Dist, for $200 paid by **Rodolphus Long** of Spartanburg Dist, several parcels in the Districts of Greenville and Spartanburg: (1) 2,268 acres on Holston Creek in Spartanburg; (2) adjoining the above, 4,872 acres granted to **C.M. Lankford;** (3) 300 acres on Birds Creek on Howard Gap Road; (4) 445 acres in Dist of Spartanburg near Bird's Mountain; (5) 91 acres in Greenville and Spartanburg District on Jimisons Mill creek; and (6) all my right and title to 200 acres in Greenville Dist on the head waters of the North fork Saluda River; that is to say, I convey unto **Rodolphus Long** one sixth part of all the three first mentioned, it being an undivided said tracts, the other parts belonging to **John Gault, Guilford Eaves, David Parten** and **C.M. Lankford;** to **Rodolphus Long,** the whole of the 441 acres and the whole of the 91 acres described above and one third part of the last mentioned 200 acres; for a full description reference may be had to Deeds and Plats now in possession of **John C. Hoyt.** Wit: **C.N. Dayton, R.D. Long.** Signed, **John C. Hoyt.** Witness oath, 31 Jan 1850: Signed, [Rodolphus] **R.D. Long** to **Jno. Watson,** O.G.D. Registered 17th Dec. 1850.

p. 126-127. 4 July 1850. Deed of Conveyance, Greenville Dist. **Rodolphus Long** of Greenville Dist, for $20 paid by **James Tucker** of Greenville Dist, sold 547 acres in Spartanburg Dist, the tract of land sold by **John C. Hoyt** to **James Tucker.** Wit: **John C. Hoyt, Wm Hubbard.** Signed, **Rodolphus Long.** Witness oath, 20 July 1850: Signed, **John C. Holt** to **R.P. Goodlett.** Registered 27th Dec 1850.

p. 128. 30 Dec 1850. Mortgage. For a note due by **Joseph Turner** to **Lawson Bolin** for $75, for better securing the payment, **Turner** mortgages to **Bolin:** 5 head of hogs, 5 head of cattle & one bay mare, and all of my household furniture. Condition of mortgage is that if I do not pay the note & Interest, **Bolin** has the right to advertise the property four years from date by giving 10 days legal notice of sale. Wit: **G.W.H. Legg.** Signed, **Joseph Turner.** Witness oath, 30 Dec 1850: Signed, **G.W.H. Legg** to **J.B. Tolleson** Clk & mag Exoffo. Registered 30th Dec. 1850.

p. 128-129. 1 Dec 1850. Deed of Gift. **Elisha Poole** of Spartanburg Dist, for the love, good will and affection which I have and do bear towards my loving Son, **Luther Poole,** of Spartanburg Dist, give 104 acres on Richland Creek, a part of a tract deeded to **Elisha Poole** by **James Poole;** bounded by N side of Richland Creek, **Isaac Neighbors,** corner known as the **Dickson** Corner, **E.P. Brown** and **Thompson Coggin.** Wit: **E.H. Coggin, S.E. Coggin.** Signed, **Elisha Poole.** Witness oath, 21 Dec 1850: Signed, **E.H. Cooper** to **J.W. Cooper** Mag. Registered 6th Jany 1851.

p. 129-131. [no day] Oct 1850. Deed of Conveyance. **Wiley D. Wood** of Spartanburg Dist, for $460.87 paid by **J.W. Smith** of Spartanburg Dist, sold 152½ on the waters of Frohock creek waters of South Tyger River; bounded by **P. Mason,** Greenville line, a road and a branch. Wit: **James**

Leonard, R.B. Wood. Signed, **W.D. Wood.** Witness oath, 21 Dec 1850: Signed, **R.B. Wood** to **Isham Wood** Mag. Registered 6th Jany 1851. Original delivered to ~~ **Dr. J.B. Powell** 21st Jany 1851.

p. 131-133. 25 Oct 1850. Deed of Conveyance. **Perry D. Gilbert** & wife **Emaline Gilbert** of Spartanburg Dist, for $150 paid by **Lemuel Pinckney Wolf** of Spartanburg Dist, sold all of our interest and title of, in or to all the lands of which belonged to **George Wolf** late of Spartanburg Dist, decd; contained in two distinct tracts, (1) 250 on which **Elizabeth Wolf**, widow of **George Wolf**, now resides, bounded by **James Burnett, Zachariah Wall, Hugh McDowell & Wilson N. Cantrell;** (2) about 152 acres, bounded by **Henry White & Wilson N. Cantrell,** making in the whole about 402 acres; Interest being that which we are entitled as one of the children of **George Wolf,** to wit, **Emeline Gilbert** formerly **Emaline Wolf,** being one of the eight children of **George Wolf.** Wit: **John F. Wolf, Leland Wolf.** Signed, **Perry D. Gilbert, Emaline Gilbert.** Witness oath, 23 Dec 1850: Signed, **John F. Wolf** to **Elias Wall** Magst. Release of Dower, 23 Dec 1850: Signed, **Emaline Gilbert** to **Elias Wall** Magt Registered 6th Jany 1851.

p. 133-135. 5 Dec 1850. Mortgage. **Alfred Brown** is indebted to **H.H. Thomson** for $600 with interest by four sealed notes, one for $200 due one day after date, the other three for $133⅓ due 1st August 1852, 1853 & 1854; all for the purchase money for 91 acres sold this day to **Alfred Brown** by **H.H. Thomson;** bounded by a branch and Well's Road. Wit: **William Walker (a.s.h.), J.B. Archer.** Signed, **Alfred Brown.** Witness oath, 6 Jany 1851: Signed, **J.B. Archer** to **J.B. Tolleson** Clk & mag Exoffo. Registered 6th Jany 1851. Original delivered to ~~ **H.H. Thomson** 24 Jany 1851.

p. 135-137. 20 Dec 1850. Mortgage. **Aaron G.W. Land** is indebted to **H.H. Thomson** for $225 by three sealed notes of $75 each with interest due one, two and three years from date being the purchase money for a lot this day bought from **Thomson;** the lot something less than 3 acres in the Town of Spartanburg on a cross street leading towards Greenville, bounded by **Dye,** Greenville Street; fifteen feet inside of the line is reserved & declared as a street & twenty feet outside of it is also given as a street. Wit: **J.B. Archer, A. Brawley.** Signed, **A.G.W. Land.** Witness oath, 6 Jany 1851: Signed, **J.B. Archer** to **J.B. Tolleson** Clk & mag Exoffo. Registered 6th Jany 1851. Original delivered to ~~ **H.H. Thomson** 24th Jany 1851.

p. 137-138. 19 Nov 1850. Mortgage. **Abial Foster** is indebted to **B. Wofford** for $1,200 by three sealed notes due on the 1st day of Jany 1852, 1853 & 1854; mortgages a house and lot in the Town of Spartanburg on the Public Square, where **J.B. Morgan** now occupies, which **Abial Foster** had this day purchased from **B. Wofford.** Wit: **D.C. Judd, J.W. Tucker.** Signed, **Abial Foster.** Witness oath, 6 Jany 1851: Signed, **J.W. Tucker** to **J.B. Tolleson** Clk & mag Exoffo. Registered 6th Jany 1851.

p. 139-140. 30 Oct 1850. Deed of Conveyance. **Wiley Johnson** of Spartanburg Dist, for $770 paid by **George F. Steading** of Spartanburg Dist, sold 101 acres, bounded by **Scott, J.B. Page** (now **Thomas Thomas**), line of the **Trail** land to a branch, near a road not far from the house where **J.F. Floyd** formerly lived (now where **Wiley Johnson** lives). The above boundary includes 79 acres which **J.F. Floyd** bought of **Enoch Floyd**, 8 acres which **J.F. Floyd** bought of **Edward Floyd**, 11 acres which **Henry Steading** bought of **R. Lanford** and 3 acres which **J.F. Floyd** bought of **J.B. Page.** Wit: **Thomas Thomas, James Crook.** Signed, **Wiley Johnson.** Release of Dower, 15 Nov 1850: Signed, [**Orilla** in Magistrate's statement] **Orrilla Johnson** to **Harvey Wofford** Mag. Witness oath, 15 Nov 1850: Signed, **James Crook** to **H. Wofford** Mag. Registered 6th Jany 1851.

p.140-143.   7 Jany 1850. Mortgage. **Hiram Wakefield** at the special instance & request of **John F. Brown** both of Spartanburg Dist, did become jointly bound for unto **Tho' O.P. Vernon** Commissioner in Equity for Spartanburg Dist, as surety to two Guardian bonds made by **J.S. Brown** to **T.O.P. Vernon** for $1,000 total, one for $600 for the faithful discharge by **J.S. Brown** of his duties as Guardian for his minor children, **E.A. Brown, J.T. Brown & E.E. Brown;** the other for $400 for the honest execution of his trust as Guardian for **Mary E. Brown & Martha J. Brown.** **John S. Brown** to the end that **Hiram Wakefield** be kept safe and harmless on account of the bonds, mortgages 185 acres known as the forge tract on the S side of the South Tyger River; **John S. Brown** as a cultivator of the land is to have the NW corner of the tract on **N. McLewrath's** line, W side of the forge branch. Wit: **J.V. Trimmier, Judge Edwards.** Signed, **John S. Brown.** Witness oath, 11 Jany 1851: Signed, **J.V. Trimmier** to **J.B. Tolleson** Clk & mag Exoffo. Registered 13th Jany 1851.

p. 143-144.   16 Dec 1850. Deed of Conveyance. **William W. Crow** of Spartanburg Dist, for $705 paid by **Silas G. Lanford** of Spartanburg Dist, sold 81¼ acres on the E side of the road running from **Rhode's** store to the Mountain Shoals; bounded on the N by **James Rhodes,** on the E by **George Hanna,** along the road to the Widow **Crow** and W by the road. Wit: **David Brewton, Willis Allen.** Signed, **Wm W. Crow.** Witness oath, 16 Dec 1850: Signed, **Willis Allen** to **Z. Lanford** Magt. Release of Dower, 21 Dec 1850: Signed, **Elizabeth Crow** to **Z. Lanford** Magt. Registered 13th Jany. 1851.

p. 144-146.   9 Jan 1850. Sheriff's Titles. **J.R. Poole** Sheriff of Spartanburg Dist, by order of the Court of Common Pleas on 28 Feb 1849, at the suit of **McLure & Wilson** to levy $365.53, damages and costs against **Mrs. Ann C. Sims,** have seized 800 acres on Meadow Creek above the rock ford, bordered by Lockhart's Branch and **D. Clark;** purchased by **McClure & Wilson** of Union Dist, SC, for $1,115, the highest bid. Wit: **John Stroble Jr., David W. Moore.** Signed, **J.R. Poole,** S.S.D. Witness oath, 9 Jany 1851: Signed, **David W. Moore** to **J.B. Tolleson** Clk & mag Exoffo. Registered 13th Jany 1851.

p. 146-148.   20 Sept 1847. Sheriff's Titles. **R.C. Poole,** Sheriff of Spartanburg Dist, by order of the Court of Common Pleas on 11 March 1846, at the suit of **S.S. Farrar** to levy $137.14 with Interest, damages and costs against **Henry Alley,** have seized 149 acres on Packolet River; bordered by **Nesbitt's** road, a path, a dividing fence, Coulter's Ford or **J.W. Martin's** formerly but now **James Turner, Edward Turner** formerly but now **James D. Bivings;** the tract conveyed by **James Turner** to **William Turner** on the 29th Oct 1825 except one acre sold to **J.W. Martin;** highest bid of $120 by **John Linder** & the bid transferred and land sold to **G.W. Spencer.** Wit: **Javan Barnett, R. Bowden.** Signed, **R.C. Poole,** S.S.D. Witness oath, 16 Jan 1851: Signed, **Reubin Bowden** to **J.B. Tolleson** Clk & mag Exoffo. Registered 17th Jany 1851.

p. 148-150.   17 Jan 1851. Mortgage. **James N. Nolly** of Spartanburg Village, is indebted to **William Choice** of Greenville Dist, $350 payable twelve months after date; for better securing the debt, **Nolly** mortgages a Negro Man Slave named **James**. Wit: **Jefferson Choice, John W. Webber.** Signed, **Ja' N. Nolley, William Choice.** Witness oath, 18 Jan 1851: Signed, **J.W. Webber** to **Jefferson Choice** Not. Pub & Exoffo Magistrate. Registered 18th Jany 1851.

p. 151-152.   13 Jan 1851. Deed of Conveyance. **Sam¹ N. Evins** of Spartanburg Dist, $745 paid by **John Thomson** of Spartanburg Dist, sold 149 acres on the waters of North Tyger River; bounded by the river and a branch; Wit: **James K. Dickson, T.E. Montgomery.** Signed, **Saml. N. Evins.** Witness oath, 13 Jan 1851: Signed, **James K. Dickson** to **B.F. Montgomery** Mag. Registered 18th Jany 1851.

p. 152-153.   19 Nov 1850. Deed of Conveyance. **Benjamin Wofford** of the town of Spartanburg, for $1,200 paid by **Abial Foster** of Spartanburg Dist, sold Lot in the town of Spartanburg on the Public Square fronting the Court House, now occupied by **J.B. Morgan** adjoining lands of **Jesse Cleveland** on the E, the lot now occupied by **Alfred Tolleson** on the W, Public Square on the N, & by Street running East & West on the S, containing a fraction of an acre according to a survey made by **Col. W.W. Harris** of which he may have the notes of survey showing the boundaries, the lot here deeded known as Lot N⁰ 6 in that survey. Wit: **D.C. Judd, J.W. Tucker.** Signed, **Benj. Wofford.** Witness oath, 16 Jan 1851: Signed, **D.C. Judd** to **J.B. Tolleson** Clk & mag Exoffo. Registered 18th Jany 1851.

p. 153-155.   27 Jan 1851. Mortgage. **Simpson S. Gilbert** is indebted to **John C. Kimbrell** for $100 in one Single Bill due 1 Nov next (1851); **Gilbert** also paid $100 in hand paid to **Kimbrell;** mortgages [acres not mentioned] on the waters of Sophia branch, on the N of the old ridge road, running northward to the head of **Mathew Gore's** spring branch till it intersects with Old spring branch, then E up to the head of said branch to **Isaac Gilbert's** land, then N on **Isaac Gilbert's** line. Wit: **Capt. J.W. Kimbrell, J.B. Tolleson.** Signed, **Simp. S. Gilbert.** Witness oath, 27 Jan 1851: Signed, **J.W. Kimbrell** to **J.B. Tolleson** Clk & mag Exoffo. Registered 28th Jany 1851.

p. 155-158.   16 Jan 1851. **Margaret Sarratt** of Spartanburg Dist, for $100 paid by **Tillman Sarratt** and also the natural love and affection I have for my son **Tillman Sarratt** give, subject to the uses and trusts hereinafter expressed, 101 acres on the waters of Cherokee Creek; bounded by **John Sarratt, Nancy Phillips** and others, land formerly owned by **Saml. Sarratt,** deceased; being the land set apart and awarded to me by the Commissioners appointed in the Court of Ordinary to partition and divide the real estate of my late husband **Saml. Sarratt** Decd, as my third part; that is to say, in trust by **Tillman** for me to my own separate use and benefit during my natural life, subject to my enjoyment and control, excepting the selling or conveying away to any other person, and after the termination of my natural life to **Tillman** forever. Also, under the same terms: 2 Negro slaves, one known and named as **Milly,** a Negro woman aged about 51, and her son named and known as **Willis,** aged about 2 years; a sideboard, a walnut cupboard, 2 bedsteads and furniture; a large chest, one spinning wheel, a Lot of Chains, a clock, a cow & calf, all of which articles and items of property which I purchased at the sale of the Personal Estate of my late husband **Saml. Sarratt,** decd. Test: **Jas. M. Sarratt, Elias Morgan, D. Lipscomb.** Signed, **Margaret (x) Sarratt.** Witness oath, 20 Jan

1851: Signed, **Jas. M. Sarratt** to **J.V. Trimmier** Notary Pub. Trust agreement, 17 Jan 1851: Signed, **Tillman Sarratt**. Registered 1st Feby 1851. Original delivered to **James V. Trimmier** 3rd Feby 1851.

p. 158-159. 28 Dec 1850. Deed of Conveyance. **Benj. Newman** of Spartanburg Dist, for $750 paid by **Tho' D. Newman** of Spartanburg Dist, sold 64 acres on Enoree River adjoining lands of **Davise Newman, J.D. Montgomery, Johnson Newman** & Enoree River. Wit: **John Stewart, William Stewart**. Signed, **B.J. Newman**. Witness oath, 10 Jan 1851: Signed, **William Stewart** to **M.P. Evins** M.S.D. Release of Dower, 11 Jan 1851: Signed, **Rachel R. Newman** to **M.P. Evins** M.S.D. Registered 1st Feby 1851.

p. 160-161. [no day & month] 1847. Deed of Conveyance. **Benjamin M. Gramling & Mary Gramling** wife of **B.M. Gramling** for $150 paid by **William Bush**, all of Spartanburg Dist, sold 69½ acres Lawsons Fork waters of Packolet River; bounded by the creek, on N & E by **Col. Wm Harris**, S by **Folger**, E by **Henderson**, and W by **Story Bush**. Wit: **John Ray, Wm Johnson**. Signed, **B.M. Gramling, Mary (x) Gramling**. Release of Dower, 18 Jan 1851: Signed, **Mary (x) Gramling** to **Davis Moore**, Mag. Witness oath, 6 Jan 1851: Signed, **John Ray** to **J.B. Tolleson** Clk & mag Exoffo. Registered 1st Feby 1851.

p. 161-163. 25 July 1850. Deed of Conveyance. **Jesse Cleveland** of the Town of Spartanburg, for $80 paid by **John Keast** of Spartanburg Dist, sold 1 acre near the Town of Spartanburg beginning on a stake on church street near the NW of the Parsonage lot; bounded by church street and the Parsonage lot. Wit: **W.W. Harris, Capt. J.W. Weber**. Signed, **Jesse Cleveland**. Release of Dower, 8 Aug 1850: Signed, **Mary Cleveland** to **J.B. Tolleson** Clk & mag Exoffo. Witness oath, 8 Aug 1850: Signed, **J.W. Weber** to **J.B. Tolleson** Clk & mag Exoffo. Registered 1st Feby 1851. Original delivered to ~ **J. Keast** 10th Feby 1851.

p. 163-165. 23 Dec 1850. Deed of Conveyance. **James Robbs** of Spartanburg Dist, for $1,200 paid by **Daniel P. White** of Spartanburg Dist, sold all that tract of land (except 3 or 4 acres which I sold to **Z. Wall** Esqr) containing 346 acres on both sides of Richland Creek waters of Packolet River; bounded by **James Burnett, Z. Wall** and **H. Dodd**. Wit: **Oliver Clark, M.G. Clark**. Signed, **James Robbs**. Release of Dower, 31 Dec 1850: Signed, **S.C. Robbs** to **Elias Wall** Magistrate. Witness oath, 31 Dec 1850: Signed, **Oliver Clark** to **Elias Wall** magistrate. Registered 3rd Feby 1851.

p. 165-166. 28 Jan 1851. Deed of Conveyance. **John Martin** of Spartanburg Dist, for $270 paid by **John Ruppe Jur.** of Spartanburg Dist, sold 207 acres by computation, on Ashworth & Sarratt's creek, bounded by the North Carolina line, **Henry Ruppe**, the edge of the coaling ground and **Wm Harris**. Wit: **Peter Quinn Camp, Pinckney Bonner**. Signed, **John Martin**. Witness oath, 28 Jan 1851: Signed, **P. Quinn Camp** to **A. Bonner** Mag. Registered 3rd Feby '51.

p. 166-168. 1 Jan 1850. Deed of Conveyance. [**Leevi** or] **Levi Rees** of Spartanburg Dist, for $540 paid by **William Smith** of Spartanburg Dist, sold 90 acres where **Levi Rees** lives; bounded by **Robert James, Daniel White, Thomas Aiken** and others. Wit: **B.H. Beardin, John S. Rees**. Signed, **Levi Rees**. Release of Dower, 1 Feb 1851: Signed, **Lettice Rees** to **Sum Sumner** Mag. Witness oath, 1 Feb 1851: Signed, **John S. Rees** to **Sum Sumner** Mag. Registered 3 Feby 1851.

p. 168-169. 7 Nov 1848. Deed of Conveyance. **William Lee** of Spartanburg Dist, for $450 paid by **John W. Lee** 100 acres where **William** now lives; on the N side of Richland Creek, beginning on **Wood's** corner on the Soapstone Hill, bounded by **John Crocker,** to mouth of **Jeremiah Lee's** spring branch, on a road leading from **Crocker's** ford to Spartanburg Court House, along within three feet on the S side of a cross fence between **William Lee** and **Richard Lee** and **W.L. Wood;** bounded by **James T. Sloan** and others. Wit: **James Hermon, John B. Briant.** Signed, **William (x) Lee.** Witness oath, 8 Jan 1849: [**Harmon** in N.P.'s statement] Signed, **James Herman** to **B.F. Bates** Not Repub. Registered 3rd Feby 1851.

p.169-171. 20 April 1850. Deed of Conveyance. **Wilson Alexander,** for $705 paid by **Anders Floyd,** sold 70½ acres bounded by lands of my own, **Anders Floyd, Doct. A.C. Shands** and the road. Wit: **John Gibbs, John H. Walker.** Signed, **Wilson Alexander.** Witness oath 20 Apr 1850: Signed, **John Gibbs** to **John H. Walker** Mag. Release of Dower, 28 Sept 1850: Signed, **Mary Alexander** to **John H. Walker** Mag. Registered 3rd Feby 1851.

p. 171-173. 30 Nov 1850. Deed of Conveyance. **William W. Crow** of Spartanburg Dist, for $495 paid by **Sampson Bobo** of Spartanburg Dist, sold 45 acres bounded by **Sampson Bobo, James Rhodes,** the Mountain Shoals road and **A.C. Crow.** Wit: **Isaac S. Hanna, John H. Walker.** Signed, **Wm W. Crow.** Witness oath, 30 Nov 1850: Signed, **Isaac S. Hanna** to **John H. Walker** Mag. Release of Dower, 30 Nov 1850: Signed, **Elizabeth (x) Crow** to **John H. Walker** Magistrate. Registered 7th Feby 1851.

p. 173-174. 30 Nov 1850. Deed of Conveyance. **James Crow** of Spartanburg Dist, for $600 paid by **Sampson Bobo** of Spartanburg Dist, sold 100 acres bounded by **Sampson Bobo, Widow Brown,** the Mountain Shoals road, **A.C. Crow** and **W.W. Crow.** Wit: **John H. Walker, Isaac S. Hanna.** Signed, **James (x) Crow.** Witness oath, 30 Nov 1850: Signed, **Isaac S. Hanna** to **John H. Walker** Mag. Registered 7 Feby 1851.

p. 174-176. 3 Feb 1849. Deed of Conveyance. **William W. Crow** of Spartanburg Dist, for $243 paid by **Sampson Bobo** of Spartanburg Dist, sold 54 acres on a branch of Two Mile Creek waters of Enoree River. Wit: **James (x) Crow.** Signed, **Wm W. Crow.** Nov 30th 1850: The above named **W.W. Crow** acknowledges before me that he signed Sealed and delivered the above conveyance to **Sampson Bobo.** Signed, **John H. Walker,** Mag. Witness oath, 30 Nov 1850: Signed, **Jas. (x) Crow** to **John H. Walker** Mag. Release of Dower, 30 Nov 1850: Signed, **Elizabeth (x) Crow** to **John H. Walker** Magistrate. Registered 7th Feby 1851.

p. 176-177. 14 Feb 1849. Mortgage. **Lowry Burnett** of Spartanburg Dist, is indebted to **Edmond Cooley** of Spartanburg Dist, for $1,086 due **Cooley** on two separate notes, one for $800 and one for $286, both given on 25th April 1848 and due one day after date, which notes were given for a tract of land sold to **Burnett** by **Cooley.** I gave him the notes as payment and he gave me a Bond for Titles. To better secure the payment of the notes, I hereby mortgage to **E. Cooley** all my Interest in the estate of my father **John Burnett** Decd, or so much thereof as necessary for the payment of the notes. A condition of this obligation is that **Cooley** is to wait until the death of my mother **Sarah Burnett** at which time and not until than will my Interest in said estate be full and complete. Wit:

C.S.W. Scruggs, Gabriel Cannon. Signed, **Lowry Burnett.** Witness oath, 10 Feb 1851: Signed, **G. Cannon** to **Elias Wall** magis. Registered 10th Feby 1851.

p. 178-179.   14 Jan 1851.   Deed of Conveyance. **L.D. Westmoreland** of Spartanburg Dist, for $50 paid by **Joseph W. Westmoreland** of Spartanburg Dist, sold all his right, title and interest in 75 acres on a branch of the South Packolet river; bounded by Sillhouse branch and a road. Wit: **Noah (x) Gasperson, J. Bankston Davis.** Signed, **L.D. Westmoreland.** Witness oath, 3rd Feb 1851: Signed, **J. Bankston Davis** to **J.B. Tolleson** Clk & mag Exoffo. Registered 10th Feby 1851.

p. 179-180.   25 Jan 1851.   Deed of Conveyance. **A. Brock** of Spartanburg Dist, for $100 paid by **L.D. Westmoreland,** of Spartanburg Dist, sold 20 acres including the house where **Martha McMillen** now lives; on branches of South Packolet River, and the Public Road, bounded by **H.J. Dean** and Still House branch. Wit: **J.W. Westmoreland, J. Bankston Davis.** Signed, **A. Brock.** Witness oath, 3 Feb 1851: Signed, **J. Bankston Davis** to **J.B. Tolleson** Clk & mag Exoffo. Registered 10 Feby 1851.

p. 180-182.   13 April 1850. Deed of Conveyance. **J.N. Nolley** of Spartanburg Dist, for $400 paid by **J.B. Morgan** of Spartanburg Dist, sold a lot of 1 & 3/10 acres in the Town of Spartanburg, on church street, bounded by the Methodist Church Lot and **J.B. Cleveland** and **W.B. Seay.** Wit: **J.N. Murray, Ja' F.V. Legg.** Signed, **Jas. N. Nolly.** Witness oath, 13 April 1850: Signed, **Jas. F.V. Legg** to **Geo. W.H. Legg** Magt. Release of Dower, 2 May 1850: Signed, **Sarah M. Nolly** to **J.B. Tolleson** Clk & mag Exoffo. Registered 10th Feby 1851. Original delivered to ~ **J.B. Morgan** 9th June 1851.

p. 182-184.   14 Sept 1850. Deed of Conveyance. **David W. Moore** of Spartanburg, for $150 paid by **J.N. Nolly** of Spartanburg, sold a lot in the Town of Spartanburg, the west portion of Lot № 20 in the division of **Richard Thomson's** Estate and sold for division on the 16th Novr. 1847. Beginning at the persimmon stump on Greenville Street & running S until it reaches the boundary of said Lot on that side and all of said Lot W of that line. Wit: **Charles Thomson, Younger Neal.** Signed, **David W. Moore.** Witness oath, 1 Feb 1851: **Charles Thomson** to **J.B. Tolleson** Clk & mag Exoffo. Release of Dower, 1 Feb 1851: Signed, **Mary C. Moore** to **J.B. Tolleson** Clk & mag Exoffo. Registered 10th Feby 1851.

p. 184-185.   1 Feb 1851.   Deed of Conveyance. **Ephraim Jackson** of Spartanburg Dist, for $350 paid by **R.C. Poole** of Spartanburg Dist, sold 250 [or 258] acres on both sides of Holston Creek of Fairforest Creek; known as Lot № 2 in the division of estate of **John Rainwaters** deceased. Wit: **William Thomas, Jo Thomas.** Signed, **Ephraim (x) Jackson.** Witness oath, 10 Feb 1851: Signed, **William Thomas** to **J.B. Tolleson** Clk & mag Exoffo. Registered 10th Feby 1851. Original deliver to ~ **R.C. Poole** 31st March 1851.

p. 185-188.   11 Feb 1851. Mortgage. **J.B. Morgan** has made promissory notes obligating himself to pay **Jacob Zimmerman** $512.96, to be paid in two equal installments of $256.48, plus interest, on 1 January, 1853 and 1854. To better secure payment of the notes **Morgan** Mortgages to **Zimmerman** a lot in the Town of Spartanburg on the S side of main street, a part of the lot formerly owned by **H.H. Thomson** & sold to **Jacob Zimmerman;** NE of **D.W. Moore's** lot, line running with wall of **Moore's** house being the house now occupied by **H. Mitchell;** the lot is on the Public Square, facing the buildings, and includes the larger portion of the room now occupied by **R.C. Poole & Company.** Wit: **J.V. Trimmier, J.E. Henry.** Signed, **J.B. Morgan.** Witness oath, 11 Feb 1851: Signed, **J.V. Trimmier** to **O.E. Edwards** N.P. Registered 13th Feby 1851. Original delivered to ~~ **J. Zimmerman** 21st Feby 1851.

[Written vertically in left hand margin and could be for either the above or below mortgages : "This mortgage is fully satisfied to **J. Zimmerman.** See his certificate on the mortgage dated the 1st August 1859. **J.B. Tolleson** R.M.C."]

p. 188-190. 3 Jan 1851. Mortgage. **Giles J. Patterson** is indebted to **Jacob Zimmerman** for $3100 for the purchase money for a tract of land **Giles** today purchased from **Zimmerman;** payment in four sealed notes of $775, due in one, two, three and four years on this date; mortgage is on 140 acres partly in the corporate limits of the Town of Spartanburg; bounded by Union Road, **J.T. Kirby** and **Mrs. Patterson.** Wit: **Col. H.H. Thomson, Z.J. Bates.** Signed, **Giles J. Patterson.** Witness oath, 10 Feb 1851: Signed, **H.H. Thomson** to **J.B. Tolleson** Clk & mag Exoffo. Registered 13th Feby 1851. Original delivered to ~~ **J. Zimmerman** 21st Feby 1851.

p. 190-192. 31 Jan 1851. Mortgage. **James W. Rogers** is indebted to **H.H. Thomson** for $225 by three sealed notes for $75, due one, two and three years from this date with interest. For better securing payment **Rogers** mortgages 2½ acres in the Town of Spartanburg, beginning on Greenville street at **Elias Low's** yard fence; 15 feet on all sides are dedicated for streets. Wit: **J.R. Poole, James Low.** Signed, **Jas. W. Rogers.** Witness oath, 10 Feb 1851: Signed, **J.R. Poole** to **J.B. Tolleson** Clk & mag Exoffo. Registered 13th Feby 1851.

p. 192-194. 2 Jan 1850. Commissioner's Titles. **Tho' O.P Vernon** Esqr, Commissioner of the Court of Equity for Spartanburg Dist, to **H.H. Durant. Junius W. Thomson** on or about 1 Oct 1845, exhibited his complaint against **H.H. Thomson, J.M. Thomson & J. Waddy Thomson** to partition certain lands and was heard in Court in 1847. The Court adjudged the land should be sold at public auction by the commissioner and the ½ acre lot was sold to **Junius W. Thomson** who assigned it to **H.H. Durant** for $500; Lot № 8 on the Sale Book of Commissioners; boundaries: church street, **John Poole's** corner, **J.W. Thomson's** corner, **Junius W. Thomson** and **Benjamin Wofford.** Wit: **R.C. Poole, J.R. Poole.** Signed, **Tho' O.P. Vernon** C.E.S.D. Witness oath, 10 Feb 1851: Signed, **J.R. Poole** to **J.B. Tolleson** Clk & mag Exoffo. Registered 13th Feby 1851.

p. 195-196. 10 Dec 1850. Deed of Conveyance. **William B. Smith** of Spartanburg Dist, for $120 paid by **Jasper Ballenger** [or **Balinger**] of Spartanburg Dist, sold 60 acres by estimation, on waters of Wolfswamp creek waters of Middle Tyger River joining land of **John Balinger, Eber Tinsley, W.B. Smith** and others. Wit: **A.C. Hardin, John Ballenger.** Signed, **W.B. Smith.** Witness oath, 17 Feb 1851: Signed, **John Ballenger** to **B.F. Montgomery** M.S.D. Registered 17th Feby 1851.

p.196-197. 8 Feb 1851. Revocation of Dower. **Sabra Hammett** of Spartanburg Dist, for reasons satisfactory to myself do execute this Deed of revocation, to wit, I signed a paper at the earnest request of others & under the instruction that in doing so I was but protecting my property from sale due for a debt of less than $10, then due on **John Bomar Jr.** but which I afterward paid & was ready & willing to pay without suit; which paper I never heard read, nor did I ever know the legal effect or consequence I refer to was a paper purporting to be a Deed of Gift of my Negro girl **Violet** to **Nancy Turner** wife of **Henry Turner** with remainder of his children, reserving the use & control of said **Violet** to myself during my natural life bearing date 4th September A.D. 1846; witnessed by **Simpson Bobo** proved before **G.W.H. Legg** Esqr. & now left in the Clerks Office of this District for the purpose of being recorded; the consideration of said Deed being natural love and affection & for $5 paid as expressed in said Deed. I am instructed that I may according to law, revoke the said Deed at any time during my life. Now therefore I do hereby revoke, countermand & vacate the said Deed to all interests & purposes & I do reassume and reassert my right to the property. Wit: **J.W. Tucker**. Signed, **Sarbra (x) Hammett.** Witness oath, 15 Feb 1851: Signed, **J.W. Tucker** to **J.B. Tolleson** Clk & mag Exoffo. Registered 17th Feby 1851. Original delivered to ∼ **J.W. Tucker** 8th May 1851.

p. 197-198. 21 Dec 1850. Deed of Conveyance. **Calvin Stephens** of Spartanburg Dist, for $100 paid by **William Stephens** of Spartanburg Dist, sold 70 acres on the waters of Tyger River, the land purchased by **Calvin Stephens** from **Ralph Smith.** Beginning on a branch that divides my land and **Benj. Finch's** land, to **Rowland's** path at the branch, then down the meanders of the branch to the beginnning. Wit: **J.V. Trimmier, J.B. Tolleson.** Signed, **Calvin Stephens.** Witness oath, 17 Feb 1851: Signed, **J.V. Trimmier** to **J.B. Tolleson** Clk & mag Exoffo. Registered 17th Feby 1851. Original delivered to ∼ **W. Stephens** 6th March 1851.

p. 199-200. 16 Feb 1849. Mortgage. **Woodson Burnett** of Spartanburg Dist, is in debt to **Edmond Cooley** for $200 due on a Note of hand given the 29th of May 1845 and due in 1845; note was given as payment for land sold to **Burnett** by **Cooley** and **Cooley** gave **Burnett** Bond for Titles; to better secure payment of the note, **Burnett** mortgages to **Cooley** "all my interest in the Estate of my Father **John Burnett** Decd, or so much may be necessary for the payment of above note"; condition of the obligation is **Cooley** is to wait for the principal of the note "until the death of my mother **Sarah Burnett**, at which time and not until will my interest in said estate be complete." Wit: **A. McCallister.** Signed, **W. Burnett.** Witness oath, 12 Feb 1852: Signed, **A. McCallister** to **Elias Wall** magt. Registered 20th Feby 1851.

p. 200-202. 9 Jan 1851. Deed of Conveyance. **Macajah R. Guthrie** of Spartanburg Dist, for $550 paid by **Franklin Barton** of Greenville Dist, SC, sold "all my interest in the land where my mother **Rebeccah Guthrie** now resides, containing 200 acres on South Packolet River adjoining lands of **John Rudicil, H. Parris, Wm Smith** and others; my interest being one Eighth part, by reference to the will of my Father, **Absolem Guthrie**, will fully appear; also I transfer to **Barton** all my interest in the following Negro Slaves: **Rachel, Judy, Lurind, Agga, Jefferson** or **Frank, Jake, Tone, Amy, George & Jane** with the future increase of the females"; slaves now in the care & possession of my mother **Rebecca Guthrie.** Wit: **John W. Hunt, David Patton.** Signed, **Micajah R. (x) Guthrie.** Witness oath, 19 Feb 1851: Signed, **David Patton** to **H.J. Dean,** Not. Pub. & Mag Exoff. Registered 20th Feby 1851.

p. 202-203. 21 Dec 1846. Deed of Conveyance. **J.N. Covington** of Spartanburg Dist, for $200 paid by **J.H. Cudd** of Spartanburg Dist, sold 100 acres on the Camp fork of Horse Creek of main Broad River and on the Spartanburg Road. Attest: **Wm F. Covington, Washington Keyes.** Signed, **J.N. Covington.** Witness oath, 19 Feb 1848: Signed, **Wm F. Covington** to **W.B. Turner** Mag. Registered 20th Feby 1851.

p. 203-205. 1 Jan 1850. Deed of Conveyance. **H.H. Thomson** of Spartanburg Dist, for $100 paid by [**M.B. McKee** or] **Meachan B. McCree** of Spartanburg Dist, sold 2 acres in the Town of Spartanburg on the street leading to Fairforest beyond the Stone Bridge and on S side of said street; bounded by **Norman Abbott.** Wit: **John Linder, J.B. Archer.** Signed, **H.H. Thomson.** Witness oath, 25 Feb 1851: Signed, **J.B. Archer** to **J.B. Tolleson** Clk & mag Exoffo. Release of Dower, 29 Jan 1851: Signed, **Mildred E. Thomson** to **J.B. Tolleson** Clk & mag Exoffo. Registered 25th Feby 1851.

p. 205-207. 3 Feb 1851. Deed of Conveyance. **Harvey Wofford** and **Benj. Wofford,** Executors of **B. Wofford** Decd of Spartanburg Dist, $1,000 for one parcel of land & $750 for an other, to us or secured to be paid by **Alfred Tolleson & A.J. McMakin** of the Town of Spartanburg, sold a Lot in the Town of Spartanburg on the Public Square, the premises now occupied by **G.W.H. Legg** and running back to the cross street running from **Jesse Cleveland's** Lot to Jail Street containing a fraction of an acre; the other parcel fronting Jail Street adjoining **Jesse Cleveland's** Lot and bounded on the S and W by the two streets running by the Jail, on the N by a cross street running from **Jesse Cleveland's** Lot to Jail Street, containing a fraction of an acre. Wit: **R.R. Williams, J.W. Tucker Esq.** Signed, **Harvey Wofford, Benj. Wofford.** Witness oath, 25 Feb 1851: **J.W. Tucker** to **J.B. Tolleson** Clk & mag Exoffo. Registered 25th Feby 1851.

p. 207-209. 26 Sept 1850. Deed of Conveyance. **Norman Abbott** of Spartanburg Dist, for $130 secured to be paid by **William Carver** of Spartanburg Dist, sold 2 acres in the Town of Spartanburg, lying beyond the Stone Bridge on the street leading to Fairforest Creek; on the S side of the street adjoining said **Carver.** Wit: **H.H. Thomson, Wm P. Duggins.** Signed, **Norman Abbot.** Witness oath, 25 Feb 1851: Signed, **H.H. Thomson** to **J.B. Tolleson** Clk & mag Exoffo. Release of Dower, 4 Feb 1851: Signed, **Eliza (x) Abbot** to **J.B. Tolleson** Clk & mag Exoffo. Registered 25th Feby 1851.

p. 209-211. 3 Jan 1851. Deed of Conveyance. **Jacob Zimmerman** of Spartanburg Dis,. for $3,500 secured to be paid by **Giles J. Patterson** of Spartanburg Dist, sold 140 acres partly within the corporate limits of the Town of Spartanburg; beginning on the right hand side of Union Road below the Brick Academy, near a branch on **J.L. Kirby's** line and adjoining **Mrs. Patterson.** Wit: **H.H. Thomson, Z.J. Bates.** Signed, **Jacob Zimmerman.** Witness oath, 25 Feb 1851: Signed, **H.H. Thomson** to **J.B. Tolleson** Clk & mag Exoffo. Release of Dower, 1 Feb 1851: Signed, **Mary Ann Zimmerman** to **J.B. Tolleson** Clk & mag Exoffo. Registered 25th Feby 1851.

p. 211-213. 27 Feb 1851. Deed of Trust. **Alfred Dean** of Spartanburg Dist, for $5 and the love and affection I have for my daughter **Francis C. Hoy,** wife of **Major William Hoy,** sold to **Joel W. Miller** the following Negro Slaves: **Caroline,** about 27 years old, and her children, a boy **Preston,** about 5 years old, girl **Louiza** about 3 years old, and boy **Charles** about 1 year old; unto **Joel W. Miller** In Trust for the purposes here expressed, that is to say, for the Sale and separate use of

Francis C. Hoy for and during her natural life, free from the control and management or in any form or shape being libel for the debts and contracts of her present or any future husband. At the death of **Francis C. Hoy**, the slaves, proceeds, etc, to be equally divided between her children, but if **Francis** should die leaving no child or children, the slaves, proceeds, etc., to descend to her brothers and their children. Wit: **M.O. Dean, H.J. Dean**. Signed, **Alfred Dean**. Agreement, 27 Feb 1851: Signed, **Joel W. Miller**. Witness oath, 27 Feb 1851: Signed, **H.J. Dean** to **J.B. Tolleson** Clk & mag Exoffo. Registered 27 Feb 1851. Original delivered to ~~ **H.D. Dean** 8th March 1851.

p. 214-216. 22 Jan 1851. Deed of Conveyance. **John T. Kirby** of Spartanburg Dist, for $178.50 paid by the South Carolina Manufacturing Company of Spartanburg Dist, sold 119 acres, adjoining **Wells**. Wit: **J.B. Tolleson, J. Belton Tolleson**. Signed, **Jno. Kirby**. Witness oath, 25 Feb 1851: Signed, **J. Belton Tolleson** to **J.B. Tolleson** Clk & mag Exoffo. Release of Dower, 1 Feb 1851: [**Patsy Kirby** in Magistrate's statement] Signed, **P. Kirby** to **J.B. Tolleson** Clk & mag Exoffo. Registered 27th Feby. 1851.

p. 216-218. 28 Jan 1851. Deed of Conveyance. **John T. Kirby** of Spartanburg Dist, for $457.50 paid by South Carolina Manufacturing Company of Spartanburg Dist, sold 300 acres "I bought of **Genl. Joseph Collins** on the waters of Thickoty Creek; also the land lying in the bounds of the Pine, Poplar and with the creek to the Gum which latter I do not warrant the title of. Wit: **John Epting, John Belton Tolleson**. Signed, **Jno. Kirby**. Witness oath, 25 Feb 1851: Signed, **J. Belton Tolleson** to **J.B. Tolleson** Clk & mag Exoffo. Release of Dower, 1 Feb 1851: Signed, **P. Kirby** to **J.B. Tolleson** Clk & mag Exoffo. Registered 27th Feby. 1851.

p. 218-220. 22 Jan 1851. Deed of Conveyance. **John T. Kirby** of Spartanburg Dist, $400 paid by the South Carolina Manufacturing Company of Spartanburg Dist, sold 320 acres, known as **Floyd** tract adjoining **Jacob Price, Thomas Evans, Richard Scruggs, James H. Ezell** and a survey called the **Gist** land on the waters of Island Creek. Wit: **J.B. Tolleson, John Belton Tolleson**. Signed, **Jno. Kirby**. Witness oath, 25 Feb 1851: Signed, **J. Belton Tolleson** to **J.B. Tolleson** Clk & mag Exoffo. Release of Dower, 1 Feb 1851: Signed, **P. Kirby** to **J.B. Tolleson** Clk & mag Exoffo. Registered 27 Feby 1851.

p. 220-221. 22 March <u>1830</u>. Deed of Trust. **Michael Dickson** of Spartanburg Dist, for and in consideration of divers good and sufficient causes me thereunto moving and for $75 paid by **Andrew B. Moore, James Chamblin** and **John Crawford**, a committee from the Trustees of the Poplar Springs Academy. — do grant, bargain and release with the said committee, in trust, and for the use of the academy, 7 and 6/10 acres on the waters of Tyger River; bounded by the road, **Drummond, James Chamblin** and myself; unto the said Trustees and their Successors forever, in trust and for the use of the said Academy; they are hereby authorized to build or permit the members of the Presbyterian congregation of Nazareth to build a church on the premises when and in what manner they may deem expedient and for the said uses and purposes. Wit: **A. Vernon, W**[m] **Trimmier**. Signed, **M. Dickson**. Witness oath, 28 Feb 1851: Signed, <u>**J.V. Trimmier**</u> to **J.B. Tolleson** Clk & mag Exoffo. Registered 28th Feby 1851.

p. 222-224. 28 Feb 1851. Sheriff's Titles. <u>**J.R.** Poole</u> to **Nancy A. Crow. Nancy McCarely** on about 23 Jan 1849 exhibited her petition in the Court of Ordinary at Spartanburg Court House, setting forth that **Hiram McCarely** departed this life intestate about in Jany 1849, seized in fee of 100 acres of land bounded by lands of **Z.L. Holmes, John S. Finch** and others on the waters of Fairforest Creek, that partition yet remained to be made. On 25 Jan 1849, **R. Bowden** Esq., Ordinary of Spartanburg Dist, ordered that the land be sold. **R.C. Poole**, Sheriff of Spartanburg Dist, sold the land to **D. Bettis** & transferred to **Nancy Ann Crow** for $162. Wit: **R.C. Poole, J.J. McMakin.** Signed, **J.R. Poole**, S.S.D. Witness oath, 28 Feb 1851: Signed, **J.J. McMakin** to **G.W.H. Legg** Mag. Registered 1st March 1851.

p. 224-226. 28 Feb 1851. Mortgage. **Nancy Ann Crow** is indebted to **G.W.H. Legg** for $198.53 to be paid to **G.W.H. Legg** on order on or before 25 Dec next, with interest; **Nancy Ann** mortgages 100 acres on the waters of Fairforest Creek bounded by **Z.L. Holmes, John S. Finch** and others, the same this day conveyed to **Nancy Ann Crow** by **J.R. Poole** Sheriff. Wit: **H.J. Dean, J.J. McMakin.** Signed, **N.A. Crow.** Witness oath, 28 Feb 1851: Signed, **H.J. Dean** to **O.E. Edwards** Not Pub. Registered 1st March 1851.

p. 226-228. 30 Dec 1850. Deed of Conveyance. **Samuel Bell** of Spartanburg Dist, for $900 paid by **Alfred P. Bobo** of Spartanburg Dist, sold 144 acres "where I now live," bounded by **George Chumly & S.W. Tucker** on the N, on the E by **N.H. Waldrip & John Chumly**, on the S by **S.B. Woodruff** and on the W by **Z. Knighton & Thomas Bell.** Wit: **N.H. Waldrip, Z. Knighton.** Signed, **Samuel Bell.** Witness oath, 30 Dec 1850: Signed, **N.H. Waldrip** to **John H. Walker** Mag. Release of Dower, 30 Dec 1850: Signed, **Lackey Bell** to **John H. Walker** Magistrate. Registered 3rd March 1851.

p. 228-229. 11 Jan 1851. Deed of Conveyance. **John C. Abernathy** of Spartanburg Dist, for $320 paid by **David Holcombe** of Spartanburg Dist, sold 312 acres "where I now live;" bounded by **C.R. Bobo, W. Hill** and others. Test: **Asail Littlefields, John H. Walker.** Signed, **John C. Abernathy.** Witness oath, 11 Jan 1851: Signed, **A. Littlefields** to **John H. Walker** Mag. Registered 3 March 1851.

p.229- 231. [no day] March 1851. Deed of Conveyance. **Martha L. Golightly** widow of **William Golightly** deceased, of Spartanburg Dist, for $400 paid by **Gabriel Cannon & Joseph Finger** of Spartanburg Dist, sold 448 acres, all that tract of land described in a plat of Survey made by **Elisha Poole** on the 19th of Feb 1849; afterwards changed on the lines between said land and **Benjamin Gilbert** & also on the line between said land and **John Heathering** on the W side by **Elias Johnson** as said plat fully represents; said land a part of a tract originally granted to **William Wells & James Smith** on the 4th of January 1802; on the waters of Packolet River & Buck Creek, Bartons Creek, McNight Road and Rutherford Road. Attest: **Johnson Coggins, Hiram M. Neighbours.** Signed, **Martha L. Golightly.** Witness oath, 3 March 1851: Signed, **Johnson Coggins** to **Thos. OP. Vernon** J.Q. Exoff. Registered 3d March 1851.

p. 231-233. 26 April 1851. Renunciation of Dower & Arbitration. **Elizabeth Margaret Kestler**, widow of **Henry Kestler** deceased, for $135.35 paid **Gabriel Cannon** and **Joseph Finger** of Spartanburg Dist, relinquished and sold her claim to Dower in two separate tracts purchased in copartnership by **Gabriel Cannon, Joseph Finger** and **Henry Kestler;** (1) 140 acres purchased from **A. Austell,** Admr of **W.W. Austell** decd, on Little Buck Creek; (2) 55 acres purchased form **Joseph Finger** on both sides on North Packolet River upon which **Cannon, Finger** and **Kestler** had erected a cotton factory and other buildings. Wit: **C.O. Green, John Heatherington, P.C. Rudisail.** Signed, **E.M. Kestler.** Witness oath, 4 March 1851: Signed, **C.O. Green** to **Elias Wall** Mag. Arbitration: We the undersigned arbitrators find that **Gabriel Cannon, Joseph Finger** and **Henry Kestler** bought in copartnership the following tracts of land: The **Austell** tract containing about 140 acres of poor ridge land and 55 acres on North Packolet River, upon which they had built and were building for the purpose of manufacturing cotton and wool, &c.We also find that under an agreement between **Cannon, Finger & Kestler, Kestler** had paid in his money and labour the sum of $1,052.14. We therefore award and decide that **Cannon & Finger** pay **Elizabeth Margaret Kestler** $175.35 for her dower in the land and premises and **Elizabeth** release all her right and claim to the premises. 26 April 1851: Signed, **C.O. Green, John Heatherington, P.C. Rudisail.** Registered 4th Mar 1851.

p. 233-235. 30 July 1850. Deed of Conveyance. **Joseph C. Lancaster** of Spartanburg Dist, for $220 paid by **L.M. Glenn** of Spartanburg Dist, sold 125 acres, by estimation on Beaver Dam Creek; bounded by **Williams** and **Gowan's** old road. Wit: **G.W.H. Legg, Ja' F.V. Legg.** Signed, **J.C. Lancaster.** Witness oath, 30 July 1850: Signed, **G.W.H. Legg** to **J.B. Tolleson** clk & mag Exoff. Release of Dower, 4 Dec 1850: Signed, **E.C. Lancaster** to **James Caldwell** Mag. Registered 4th March 1851.

p. 235-237. 21 Sept 1850. Deed of Conveyance. **T.J. Dodd** for $875 paid by **John Davis,** sold 94½ acres in two tracts (1) 44½ acres on Hacker Creek waters of Tyger River, South side of the river; bounded on the E by **Mrs. Kelly's** land, on the W by **Samuel Gentry,** and on the N by a tract known by the name of the Red land, known by the **Williamson Kelly** tract. (2) 50 acres, what is called the **Layton** tract, on branches of Hacker Creek, waters of Tyger River, on the west side of (1). Test: **J.H. Stevens, Dixon R.E. Davis.** Signed, **T.J. Dodd.** Release of Dower, 13 Nov 1851: Signed, **Eleander (x) Dodd** to **P.R. Bobo** Magst. Witness oath, 4 Dec 1850: Signed, **J.H. Stevens** to **P.R. Bobo** Magst. Registered 4th March 1851.

p. 237-239. 12 Nov 1850. Deed of Conveyance. **Wilson Alexander** of Spartanburg Dist, for $1,172 paid by **John Davis** of Spartanburg Dist, sold 175 acres on the E side of Hacker Creek Road leading from **Floyd's** Mill and part of the W side of the road, a part of a tract that **Wilson Alexander** purchased from **John Davis;** bounded by **Dr. A.C. Shands,** on the West side of the road near a large mud hole, **Daniel Miles** to what is known as **Landon Waters** old corner, **John Yarborough** and **Stephen Taylor.** Attest: **H. Fergerson Esq, George W. Beardin.** Signed, **Wilson Alexander.** Witness oath, 4 March 1851: Signed, **Henry Fergerson.** Registered 4th March 1851.

p. 239-241. 29 Nov 1850. Deed of Conveyance. **James M. Anderson** of Spartanburg Dist, for $700 paid by **Moses B. Crow** of Spartanburg Dist, sold 220 acres on a branch of Brushy fork creek a branch of Bens creek, waters of South Tyger River; bounded by **Perry Leonard,** Lightwood Knot Road and on Green Pond line. Wit: **Dny Anderson, David Anderson.** Signed, **James M. Anderson.** Release of Dower, 25 Feb 1851: Signed, **Mary Anderson** to **Mark Bennett** Magistrate.

Witness oath, 25 Feb 1851: Signed, **Dny Anderson** to **Mark Bennett** Mag. Registered 4th March 1851.

p. 241-243. 19 Nov 1850. Deed of Conveyance. **James M. Ponder** of Spartanburg Dist, for $1,100 paid by **George W. Walker** and **Stanhope W. Walker** of Rutherford Co, NC, sold (1) 100 acres on the N side of South Packolet River; beginning on the N side of a ditch which is **Thomas Prince's** line and on the river, the land conveyed to "us" by **James M. Ponder**. (2) 100 acres adjoining (1), **L.H. Edwards**, the clear branch and on **Batholomew Grogan's** old corner, near Blackstocks Road. Wit: **H.F. Parrish, Walker Parrish.** Signed, **J.M. Ponder.** Release of Dower, 31 Dec 1850: Signed, **Elvira Ponder** to **James Caldwell** Mag. S.D. [Magistrate's statement says **Elvine Ponder**]. Witness oath, 4 March 1851: Signed, **H.F. Parrish** to **James Caldwell** Mag. Registered 4th March 1851.

p. 243-245. 18 Feb 1851. Deed of Conveyance. **James Morningstar** of Spartanburg Dist, for $70 paid by **Lewis Clearly** of Spartanburg Dist, sold 6¾ acres in all, on Cherokee Creek waters of the Broad River, known as part of the **Richard Arrendale** old tract, including a part of 4½ acres sold by **Wm Gillum** to **Richard Arrendale**; bounded by **J. Pennington** and **Lewis Clearly**. Wit: **John E. Henry, Mary (x) Vineset.** Signed, **James (x) Morningstar.** Witness oath, 18 Feb 1851: Signed, **John E. Henry** to **A. Bonner** Mag. Release of Dower, 18 Feb 1851: Signed, **Rhody (x) Morningstar** to **A. Bonner** Mag. Registered 4th March 1851.

p. 245-247. 22 Nov 1842. Deed of Conveyance. **Charles Hill** of Spartanburg Dist, for $700 paid by **Jas. M. Ponder** of Greenville Dist, SC, sold (1) 100 acres on the N side of South Packolet River, on the N side of a ditch which is **Tho' Prince's** line, the tract conveyed to me by **John Dilback**. (2) 100 acres beginning on **Earle's** corner, near Blackstocks Road, a mark on or near clear branch and **Batholuolmew Grogan's** old corner. Wit: **L.P. Carruth, John Campbell.** Signed, **Charles Hill.** Release of Dower, 4 Dec 1843: Signed, **Temperance (x) Hill** to **James Caldwell**, J.Q. Witness oath, 7 Dec 1843: Signed, **L.P. Carruth** to **James Caldwell**, J.Q. Registered 4th March 1851.

p. 247-248. 27 Dec 1849. Deed of Conveyance. **J.M. Woodruff** of Spartanburg Dist, for $1,180 paid by **Chaney Lanford** of Spartanburg Dist, sold 147½ acres on Dildine Creek, on Georgia Road and bounded at this time by **Col. James Parks, Richard Woodruff, Chaney Lanford & J.M. Woodruff** and **J. [or S.] Willis.** Wit: **Washington Lanford, Stephen Griffith.** Signed, **J.M. Woodruff.** Witness oath, 4 March 1851: Signed, **Washington Lanford** to **J.B. Tolleson** clk & mag Exoff. Registered 4th March 1851.

p. 249-250. 15 Aug 1849. Deed of Conveyance. **John Clement** of Spartanburg Dist, for $102 paid by **Isham Clement** of Spartanburg Dist, sold 205 acres on Furnace Road. Wit: **Lemuel Clement, James P. Clement.** Signed, **John Clement.** Witness oath, 4 March 1851: Signed, **Lemuel Clement** to **Elias Wall** Mag. Registered 4th March 1851.

p. 250-251.   18 Dec 1850. Renunciation of Dower. **Lucinda Newman** the widow of **Gabriel Newman** Decd, for $150 paid by **John Yarborough** Executor of the Estate of **Reubin Newman**, did in accordance with an award of **Stephen Taylor, Tho' Young, John Davis, E. Allen** and **John**

H. Walker, arbitrators chosen by her and **Yarbrough** to settle her claim of Dower in the said estate, that she does voluntarily relinquish to **A.M. Smith** (who purchased the lands) her claim of Dower in the real estate of **Reubin Newman** deceased. Signed, **Lucinda (x) Newman** to **John H. Walker** Magistrate. Registered 4ᵗʰ March 1851.

p. 251-252.   8 May 1848. Deed of Conveyance. **Elizabeth T. Crawford** of Spartanburg Dist, $34.32 paid by **James Bivings** of Spartanburg Dist, sold on River of Middle Tyger, (1) 4 acres on the bank of the river and the Factory tract on **Bivings** line; (2) 10 acres and twenty one rods, on the **Bivings** line and factory corner, on N bank of the river adjoining said **E.T. Crawford**. Wit: **M.A. Dickson, W.F. Pearson.** Signed, **Elizabeth T. Crawford.** Witness oath, 3 March 1851: Signed, **M.A. Dickson** to **G.W.H. Legg** Magt. Registered 4ᵗʰ March 1851.

p. 252-254.   20 Dec 1850. Deed of Gift. **William Beshears** of Spartanburg Dist, for the love and affection which I have for my Grand Children, the lawful heirs of my daughter, **Mary S. Clayton,** give unto the Grand Children: **William A. Clayton, James E. Clayton, Josiah Clayton, Sampson Clayton,** 100 acres on branches of Mollows Creek [no 't' crossed], waters of South Packolet; bounded by **Clayton, McElrath,** the S line of **Beshears** grant. Wit: **A.C. Hardin, Alexander Beshears, John (x) Prewit.** Signed, **William (x) Beshears.** Witness oath, 23 Dec 1850: Signed, **John (x) Prewit** to **James Caldwell** Mag. S.D.   Registered 4ᵗʰ March 1851.

p. 254-255.   20 Dec 1850. Deed of Conveyance. **William Beshears** of Spartanburg Dist, for $160 paid by **Jethra Beshers** of Spartanburg Dist, sold 80 acres on Mollows [no 't' crossed] and Eslies Creek waters of South Packolet; beginning on bank of Eslies creek. Wit: **A.C. Hardin, Alexander Beshers, John (x) Prewitt.** Signed, **William (x) Beshers.** Witness oath, 23 Dec 1850: **John (x) Prewit** to **James Caldwell** Mag. Registered 4ᵗʰ March 1851.

p. 255-257.   20 Dec 1850.   Deed of Gift. **William Beshers** of Spartanburg Dist, for love and affection which I have for my son **Solomon Beshers** give 100 acres on branches of Motlows ['t' appears to be crossed] Creek branches of South Packolet River; bounded by **Mills, Prewit** and the road. Wit: **A.C. Hardin, Alexander Beshers, John (x) Prewit.** Signed, **William (x) Beshers.** Witness oath, 23 Dec 1850: Signed, **John (x) Prewit** to **James Caldwell** Mag. Registered 4ᵗʰ Mar 1851.

p. 257-258.   20 Dec 1850. Deed of Gift. **William Beshers** of Spartanburg Dist, for the love and affection I have for my son **William G. Beshers** of some of the Western States, give **William G. Boshers** 92 acres on branches of Mollows creek [no 't' crossed], waters of South Packolet River; bounded by **Prewit** and the S line of the **Boshers** part. Wit: **A.C. Hardin, Alexander Beshers, John (x) Prewit.** Signed, **William (x) Boshers.** Witness oath, 23 Dec 1850: Signed, **John (x) Prewit** ti **James Caldwell** Mag. Registered 4ᵗʰ March 1851.

p. 258-260.   29 Nov 1850. Deed of Conveyance. **James M. Anderson, Sr.** of Spartanburg Dist, for $800 paid by **Denny Anderson** [once mentions **Denny Anders**] of Spartanburg Dist, sold 200 acres on the head branches of Brushy Fork creek, a branch of Bens Creek, waters of South Tyger River. Wit: **David Anderson, Moses B. Crow.** Signed, **James M. Anderson.** Witness oath, 25 Feb

1851: Signed, **Moses B. Crow** to **Mark Bennett** Magistrate. Release of Dower, 25 Feb 1851: Signed, **Mary Anderson** to **Mark Bennett** Magistrate. Registered 5th March 1851.

p. 261-262. 15 Feb 1849. Deed of Conveyance. **Elisha Stations,** for $481 paid by **Emanuel Allen,** sold 72¼ acres, a part of a tract of land on S side of Tyger River; bounded by the river, lands of **Elisha Stations** and **Emanuel Allen.** Test: **Mary Allen, Williamson Kelly.** Signed, **Elisha (x) Stations.** Witness oath, 15 Feb 1849: Signed, **Mary Allen** to **P.R. Bobo** Magst [? & **D.H. Shelton**]. Release of Dower, 16 April 1849: Signed, **Martha (x) Stations** to **John H. Walker** Mag. Registered 8th March 1851. Original delivered to ⁓ **Emanuel Allen** 2 April 1851.

p. 262-264. 29 June 1848. Deed of Conveyance. **C.C. Layton** of Spartanburg Dist, for $240 paid by **Emanuel Allen** of Spartanburg Dist, sold 50¾ acres adjoining **Anders Floyd** & others and a road. Wit: **Mary Allen, James Layton.** Signed, **C.C. Layton.** Witness oath, 15 Bef 1851: Signed, **Mary Alexander** (formerly **Mary Allen**) to **John H. Walker** Mag. Release of Dower, 23 Dec 1848: Signed, **Rebecca Layton** to **John H. Walker** mag. Registered 8th March 1851. Original delivered to ⁓ **E. Allen** 2nd April 1851.

p. 264-265. 24 Jan 1851. Mortgage. **Jesse R. Blanton** for better securing the payment of two notes which I owe **John Linder** for the purchase money of the land I herein mortgage; one for $45 due in twelve months and one for $46 due in two years; land bought this day, 97 acres bounded by Widow **Sarah Jarrett, Jesse Hammett** & others. Attest: **Tilmon Mathis, Jas. Smith.** Signed, **Jesse R. Blanton.** Witness oath, 4 March 1851: Signed, **Jas. Smith** to **A. Bonner** Mag. Registered 8th March 1851.

p. 266-267. 8 March 1851. Deed of Conveyance. **Jesse Cleveland** of Spartanburg Dist, for $150 paid by **John B. Oneal** of Newberry Dist, SC, sold a 1 acre lot in the Town of Spartanburg commencing on a stake on **Turner's** Street running to a stake on the Howard Gap Road; adjoining **Quinn's** line. Wit: **J.B. Cleveland, J.W. Weber.** Signed, **Jesse Cleveland.** Witness oath, 8 March 1851: Signed, **J.B. Cleveland** to **Jefferson Choice** N.P. & Ex off mag. Release of Dower, 8 March 1851: Signed, **Mary Cleveland** to **Jefferson Choice** N.P. & mag. Registered 10 March 1851. Original delivered to ⁓ **J. Choice** 2nd April /51.

p. 268-269. 25 May 1847. Deed of Conveyance. Union Dist, SC. **Nathˡ Gist Sen,** of Union Dist, SC, for $160 paid by **Thomas Gist** of Union Dist, sold 2,690 acres in Spartanburg Dist on branches of Broad and Packolet Rivers; a part of the tract originally granted to **James Steadman**; the tract represented a Plat A by a survey made by **Richard Thomson** on 13 Oct 1839. Wit: **John C. Gist, J.L. Gibson.** Signed, **Nathˡ Gist Sen.** Witness oath, 15 May 1847: Signed, **John C. Gist** to **J.M. Gadberry** Mag. Registered 14th March 1851.

p. 269-271. 13 March 1851. Deed of Conveyance. **William Bishop** of Spartanburg Dist, for love and affection and services heretofore rendered and $5, make over to my beloved son **Anderson Bishop,** 179 acres on Standing Stone, a branch of Lawsons Fork; bounded by **Daniel Mayberry,** along the road to the ford on Standing Stone, along the branch, **Abel Bishop** and **Laban Bishop;** including the improvements where I now live, reserving to myself the use of the premises during my natural lifetime and also the natural lifetime of my wife, as we intend to occupy, use and enjoy the property during our lives and then it is then intended to vest in my son **Anders Bishop**. Wit: **W.W. Harris, Barney Bishop, Pinckney Bishop**. Signed, **William (x) Bishop**. Witness oath, 19 March 1851: Signed, **Barney Bishop** to **J.B. Tolleson** clk & mag Exoff. Registered 19th March 1851. Original delivered to **Anderson Bishop** 2nd May 1851.

p. 271-273. 15 Oct 1849. Deed of Conveyance. **William Copeland Sen'** of Spartanburg Dist, for $1,570 paid by **John M. Jackson** of Spartanburg Dist, sold 205 acres on the S side of North Packolet River, where **Copeland** now lives; bounded by the river, **John Liles**, the branch that is now the line betwixt me and **Thos. Brian** down the branch to a corner that was made between me and **Thos. Brian** by John C. Hoyt in the presence of **William P. Dickson & Robert Jackson**, the brink of the swamp. Wit: **Elias Johnson, Capt. Robert Jackson, Wm Giles**. Witness oath, 6 Jan 1851: Signed, **Robt. Jackson** to **J.B. Tolleson** clk & mag Exoff. Release of Dower, 28 Jan 1850: Signed, **Mary Copeland** to James Caldwell, J.Q, Registered 19th March 1851.

p. 273-275. 24 Feb 1851. Mortgage. **Simpson Ginnings** is indebted to **Ransom Ginnings** for $557.25 by one Single Bill on Note dated 21st Feb 1851. For better securing the sum of money also for $100 paid to **Simpson Ginnings** by **Ransom Ginnings, Simpson** conveys to **Ransom** 378 acres where **Simpson Ginnings** now lives, that he bought from **Hugh Bishop**; also a stallion colt **Simpson** bought from **Hiram McAbee**; also a bay mare, four "hed" of cattle, six head of Hogs, nine head of Sheep. Wit: **J.V. Trimmier, J. Belton Tolleson**. Signed, **Simpson Ginnings, Ransom Ginnings**. Witness oath, 24 March 1851: Signed, **J. Belton Tolleson** to **J.B. Tolleson** clk & mag Exoff. Registered 24th March 1851. Registered 24th March 1851. [Written vertically on the deed record on pages 273 & 274: "Satisfied"].

p. 275-277. 26 March 1851. Deed of Conveyance. **H.H. Thomson** of Spartanburg Dist, for $225 secured to be paid by **James W. Rogers** of Spartanburg Dist, sold about 2½   acres, a lot in the Town of Spartanburg; beginning on the W side of Greenville Street at the corner of **Elias Low**'s yard fence, along **Low's** line, (on two sides, 15 feet are reserved for streets with 20 feet outside the line given by **Thomson** for 30 foot wide streets). Wit: **J.R. Poole, James Low**. Signed, **H.H. Thomson**. Witness oath, 26 March 1851: Signed, **J.R. Poole** to **J.B. Tolleson** clk & mag Exoff. Release of Dower, 1 Feb 1851: Signed, **Mildred E. Thomson** to **J.B. Tolleson** clk & mag Exoff. Registered 27th March 1851.

p. 277-280. 26 June 1850. Deed of Conveyance. **Wm B. Archer** formerly of Spartanburg Dist, for $148 paid to **H.J. Dean** by **Elias Low** of Spartanburg Dist, sold to **Elias Low** 2 acres near the Village of Spartanburg; beginning on **Thomson's** corner immediately on the S side of Greenville Road, a part of the tract I bargained to **Wm Walker a.s.h.** Wit: **Joseph Foster, A.J. Fowler**. Signed, **Wm B. Archer** by his attorney in fact, **H.J. Dean**. Witness oath, 26 March 1851: Signed, **Joseph Foster** to **J.B. Tolleson** clk & mag Exoff. $250 note: On or before the 25th Decr, 1842, with interest from 25th Decr 1841, I promise to pay **Wm B. Archer** $250 for value Recd. For land. Test: **H. J. Dean**. Signed, **William Walker**. Assignment of note: I assign the within Note to **H.J. Dean** and authorize him in my name & for me to execute Titles to **Wm Walker** when the purchase money is paid (of which the within is a part) to the lot I now live on and for which this Note is given. 7th Nov'

1840. Wit: **W.E. Rector**. Signed, **Wᵐ B. Archer**.

    Wᵐ Walker bargained a part of the land (the within described lot) to **Wᵐ Petre & Wᵐ Petre** bargained it to the within named **Elias Low** as appears by his written agreement hereunto attached & which forms a part of this Deed. Witness, 26 June 1850: **Joseph Foster, A.J. Fowler**. Signed, **H.J. Dean**. — — **Wᵐ Walker** acknowledged the above statement is true and authorized & approved the making of the within Deed, 26ᵗʰ June 1850: Signed **William Walker a.s.h.** — — Statement: Having this day sold to **Elias Low** my interest in the lot I live on & which I purchased from **William Walker** on 23ʳᵈ Decr, 1843, I authorize **William Archer** or his Atty, **H.J. Dean** to execute Titles to the lot whenever **Elias Low** pays $148.04 with Int, from the 14ᵗʰ Oct 1847, to **H.J. Dean**. Wit, 23 Oct 1847: Signed, **William Petre** to **Wᵐ Walker A.S.H**. Registered 27ᵗʰ March 1851.

p. 280-281. 26 Nov 1840. Deed of Conveyance. **William White** of Spartanburg Dist, for $400 paid by **George W. Wetherford** and **Presley Brannon** of Spartanburg Dist, sold 478 acres on the N side of Lawson's fork and joining lands of **John Cunningham, David Golightly, Mathew Seay, William Dodd**'s Mill tract and **Richard Gramblin**. Wit: **John Cunningham, David Walker**. Signed, **William White**. Witness oath, 19 Dec 1840: Signed, **John Cunningham** to **Saml. Bullington** J.P. Registered 27ᵗʰ March 1851.

p. 281-282. 7 Sept 1846. **Sabra Hammett** of Spartanburg Dist, for the love and affection which I bear my daughter **Nancy Turner** and $5, give to my daughter, wife of **Henry Turner** of Spartanburg Dist, a Negro girl named **Violet,** aged about 45 years, for the term of her natural life, remainder to the children of **Nancy Turner** who may be living at **Nancy's** death; reserving to myself the use and control of **Violet** during my life; not to be liable either directly or indirectly for the debts of **Henry Turner** or for the debt of my future husband but benefit of **Nancy Turner** and her children. Wit: **Simpson Bobo**. Signed, **Sabra (x) Hammett**. Witness oath, 9 Sept 1846: Signed, **S. Bobo** to **G.W.H. Legg** Magt. Registered 27ᵗʰ March 1851.

p. 282-284. 15 March 1850. Deed of Conveyance. **Benjamin Wofford** of Spartanburg Dist, for $75 paid by **J.V. Trimmier** of Spartanburg Dist, sold a 1 acre lot in the Town of Spartanburg, between town Lots owned by **Mrs. Margaret Trimmier** on the N, and **James Fowler** on the S, on the E by the Public Street, and on the W by another public street, formerly an old road running through the Grave Yard. Wit: **T.W. Wingo, J.W. Tucker**. Signed, **Benj. Wofford**. Witness oath, 27 March 1851: Signed, **T.W. Wingo** to **G.W.H. Legg** Magts. Registered 27ᵗʰ March 1851.

p. 284-285. 6 Jan 1851. Deed of Conveyance. **James Templeman** of Spartanburg Dist, for $260 paid by **William Easler** of Spartanburg Dist, sold 99 acres on waters of Packolet River; bounded by **Joel Cannon, John Moore** and **Lewis Cannon**. Wit: **Col. H.H. Thomson, Aaron Templeman**. Signed, **James Templeman**. Witness oath, 18 Jan 1851: Signed, **H.H. Thomson** to **J.B. Tolleson** clk & mag Exoff. Registered 27ᵗʰ March 1851.

p. 285-287. 1 May 1850. Deed of Conveyance. **John T. Kirby** of Spartanburg Dist, for $600 to me paid by **Z.J. Bates** of Spartanburg Dist, sold a 1 acre lot in the Village of Spartanburg; beginning on Church street to **J.T. Kirby's** corner, then to the corner near the Parsonage Lot; bounded by Lots of **J.T. Kirby** and others. Wit: **Tho. O.P. Vernon, Wᵐ C. Camp**. Signed, **Jno. Kirby**. Witness oath,

27 March 1851: Signed, **Tho. O.P. Vernon** to **G.W.H. Legg** magt. Release of Dower, 2 May 1850: Signed, [**Patsey**] **P. Kirby** to **J.B. Tolleson** clk & mag Exoff. Registered 27th March 1851.

p. 287-289.   24 Feb 1851. Deed of Conveyance. **John Linder**, for $240 to me paid by **R. Bowden**, sold all my interest in a 2¼ acres Lot in the Village of Spartanburg where **Jestin Turner** now lives; plat in the Commissioner of Equity office in the Estate of **Lee Linder** Descd.; my interest consists of one undivided fifth part. The other four fifths as claimed by copartners in the purchase of said lot, viz: **John Turner, Mary Linder, A.E. Smith & R. Bowden** who are also entitled to one fifth each. Wit: **Tho' O.P. Vernon, J. Belton Tolleson**. Signed, **John Linder**. Witness oath, 27 March 1851: Signed, **J. Belton Tolleson** to **G.W.H. Legg** Magt. Release of Dower, 4 March 1851: Signed, **Louisa Linder** to **A. Bonner** Mag. Registered 27th March 1851.

p. 289-292.   8 Feb 1851. Mortgage. **John R. Bowden** became liable to pay $189 (by promissory notes) to **Jacob Zimmerman** by 1 Jan 1853 and $189 by 1 Jan 1854, with interest. **J.R. Bowden** mortgages a lot in the Town of Spartanburg joining **J.B. Morgan** and comprising a part or range or block of buildings formerly owned by the late **Richard Thomson**, on Main Street, now occupied by **Col. Green** and a part of the Room now occupied by **R.C. Poole** & Co. Wit: **Tho' O.P. Vernon, J.V. Trimmier**. Signed, **J.R. Bowden**. Witness oath, 27 March 1851: Signed, **Tho' O.P. Vernon** to **G.W.H. Legg** Magt. Registered 27th March 1851. Original delivered to ~~ **J. Zimmerman** 6th May 1851.

p. 292-294.   [no day, month] 1839. Deed of Conveyance. **Robert West** of Spartanburg Dist, for $1,000 to me paid by **Lowry Lanford** of Spartanburg Dist, sold 320 acres on the waters of Dutchmans creek; bounded by **Trail** and **Golightly;** a tract conveyed to me by the heirs of **Thomas Hanna** Decsd. Wit: **Enoch H. Smith, Noah H. Smith**. Signed, **Robert West**. Witness oath, 10 Jan 1842: Signed, **Enoch H. Smith** to **George Meadows** Mag S.D. Release of Dower, 9 March 1842: Signed, **Diannah (x) West** to **George Meadows** Mag. Registered 31st March 1851.

p. 294-295.   27 Aug 1844. Deed of Conveyance. **H.H. Thomson** for $20 secured to be paid by **Elizabeth Lands** of Spartanburg Dist, sold a 1 acre Lot in the Village of Spartanburg lying over the branch SW of the Village, Lot Nº 9 as laid off and sold by **Geo. Nicholls,** Sheriff of Spartanburg, sold as the property of **Wm Poole** at the suit of **H.H. Thomson**. The lot can be distinctly located by reference to the Plat as made out by **Geo. Nicholls** & lodged in the Clerk's office. Wit: **G.W.H. Legg, Stephen Kirby**. Signed, **H.H. Thomson**. Witness oath, 27 Aug 1844: Signed, **Stephen Kirby** to **J. Tapp** JQ Eoff. Registered 31st March 1851.

p. 295-297.   25 Jan 1851. Deed of Conveyance. **Ransom White** of Spartanburg Dist, for $159 to me paid by **H.H. Thomson** of Spartanburg Dist, sold 39¾ acres on N side of Poolsville Road. Wit: **John Epting, A. Holshouser**. Signed, **Ransom White**. Witness oath, 3 April 1851: **A. Holshouser** to **J.B. Tolleson** clk & mag Exoff. Release of Dower, 27 Jan 1851: Signed, **Parthenia (x) White** to **J.B. Tolleson** clk & mag Exoff.   Registered 3rd April 1851.

p. 297-298.   16 March 1850. Deed of Conveyance. **James Tapp** of Spartanburg Dist, for $30 to me paid by **James H. Vandike** of Spartanburg Dist, sold [acres not given, location not given] on the S side of the line formed by beginning on a stake. **James Tapp** binds himself and his heirs only to cease and quit all manner of claim to any lands lying SW of the aforesaid line. Wit: **F.H. Legg, Simpson Finch.** Signed, **James Tapp.** Witness oath, 22 Feb 1851: **F.H. Legg** to **J.C. Caldwell** Magt. Registered 7th April 1851.

p. 298-299.   9 Feb 1846. Deed of Conveyance. **John Stroble Jr.** of Spartanburg Dist, acknowledges that **George Nicholls** Sheriff of Spartanburg Dist, on 27 Oct 1843 made title to me for a 230 acres adjoining **Elizabeth Rogers** and others which was sold as the property of **John Stephens** at the suit of **Joel Hurt** for **James H. Hert**, that **Joel Dean** of Spartanburg Dist was a joint purchaser, paid one half of the purchase money and is the true owner of one half of the land described. Wit: **A.C. Jackson, J.W. Miller.** Signed, **John Stroble.** Witness oath, 7 April 1851: Signed, **J.W. Miller** to **J.B. Tolleson** clk & mag Exoff. Registered 7th April 1851.

p. 299-301.   31 Dec 1850. Deed of Conveyance. **Elijah Johnson** of Cass Co., GA, for $80 to me paid by **William Henson** of Spartanburg Dist, sold 50 acres on the E side of the Jordin Road and bounded by **Willis Johnson, Elias Ward, Fielding Ward** and others. Wit: **G.W. Rollins, Samuel Morgan.** Signed, **Elijah Johnson.** Witness oath, 28 Feb 1851: Signed, **Samuel Morgan** to **B.F. Montgomery** M.S.D. Release of Dower, 3 Jan 1851: Signed, **Casandra Johnson** to **Isham Wood** Mag S.D. Registered 7th April 1851.

p. 301-302.   3 April 1829. Deed of Conveyance. **James G. Harris** of Spartanburg Dist, sell and release [price not stated] to **Cintha Lancaster** of Spartanburg Dist, 44 acres on S side of Lossons Fork; bounded by said fork and **Francis Little.** Wit: **Allen Lancaster, D.F. Mabry.** Signed, **J.G. Harris.** Witness oath, 3 Oct 1829: Signed, **A. Lancaster** to **D. White** U.Q. Registered 7th April 1851.

p. 302-304.   7 April 1851. Sheriff's Titles. Whereas, **Losson Phillips** on or about the 6 Aug 1849 did exhibit his Petition in the Court of Ordinary at Spartanburg Court House setting forth that **Jacob Phillips** departed this life [no date], owning 347 acres on the waters of Suck Creek bounded by lands of **Drury Scruggs** and others, that division yet remained to be made; afterwards on 10th day of Sept 1849, **R. Bowden** Esqr, Ordinary of Spartanburg Dist, ordered that the land be sold by the Sheriff of Spartanburg Dist on the first Monday morning in October; **R.C. Poole**, Sheriff, publicly and according to the custom of auctions, sold the land to **Ira Phillips** for $600. Now, **J.R. Poole** Successor of **R.C. Poole** as sheriff releases the land to **Ira Phillips.** Wit: **T.W. Wingo, Wm Parris.** Signed, **J.R. Poole** S.S.D. Witness oath, 7 April 1851: Signed, **T.W. Wingo** to **J.B. Tolleson** clk & mag Exoff. Registered 7th April 1851.

p. 304-305.   15 Dec 1843. Mortgage. **Calvin C. Lancaster** of Spartanburg Dist, do mortgage, release and bargain unto **Abram Brock** of Spartanburg Dist, a tract of land (for particulars see **Brock Deed** to **Lancaster**) which **Abram Brock** has this day conveyed to me by deed; said tract contains 100 acres and is bounded by **Zera Alverson** & others, to have and hold under mortgage for $200. The condition of the above obligation is that if **C.C. Lancaster**, on or before the expiration of eight years and ten days from date pays **Brock** $200 the mortgage is null and void. Wit: **J.B. Davis, William Brock.** Signed, **C.C. Lancaster.** Witness oath, 16 April 1851: Signed, **J. Bankston**

Davis to **J.B. Tolleson** clk & mag Exoff. Registered 19th April 1851.

p. 305-306.   13 March 1851. Deed of Gift. **William Bishop** of Spartanburg Dist, for the Love, affection and divers good causes do make over and release unto my beloved Son, **Abel Bishop** of Spartanburg Dist, 96 acres, a part of the tract whereon I now live; bounded by the SE corner of a Lot laid out to my son **Labon Bishop**, a pond, **Law's & Seay's** lines. Wit: **Col. W.W. Harris, Barney Bishop, Pinckney Bishop.** Signed, **William (x) Bishop.** Witness oath, 7 April 1851: Signed, **W.W. Harris** to **J.B. Tolleson** clk & mag Exoff. Registered 19th April 1851.

p. 306-308.   16 April 1851. Mortgage. **Abiel Foster** this day did make unto **John T. Kirby** three promissory notes whereby **Foster** became liable to pay unto **Kirby**, $351.66 with interest on each 16th April in 1852, 1853 and 1854; the three notes being the purchase money ($1055) for 17½ acres near the Town of Spartanburg, this day sold by **Kirby** to **Foster;** on a street of 20 feet width between said lot and **A. Tolleson**, bounded by a small branch, **Kirby's** fence, a street between **H.H. Thomson** and **John T. Kirby.** Wit: **J.C. Caldwell Esqr, J.C. Zimmerman.** Signed, **Abial Foster.** Witness oath, 16th April 1851: Signed, **J.C. Caldwell** to **J.B. Tolleson** clk & mag Exoff. Registered 19th April 1851.

p. 308-309.   6 April <u>1839</u>. Deed of Conveyance. **John Sartin** if Spartanburg Dist, for $100 to me paid by **Robert Wall** of Spartanburg Dist, sold 30 acres on Jocb's [or Jack's] Creek waters of South Packolet River; bounded by said **Wall** and **Daniel White.** Wit: **William Foster, <u>Frances Foster</u>.** Signed, **John Sartin.** Witness oath, 26 April <u>1851</u>: Signed, <u>**Francis Wilkins**</u> to **Elias Wall** Magt. Registered 28th April 1851.

p. 309-311.   11 Nov 1850. Deed of Conveyance. **Amos Woodruff** of Spartanburg Dist, for $770.91 to me paid by **Isaac Woodruff** of Spartanburg Dist, sold 132½ acres on the waters of Dildine creek of Enoree River bounded by the creek, **Caleb Allen, James Parker** and **J. Castleberry.** Wit: **C.P. Woodruff, T.P. Woodruff.** Signed, **Amos Woodruff.** Witness oath, **T.P. Woodruff** to **Jonas Brewton** Mag. Release of Dower, 21 Jan 1851: Signed, **Levina Woodruff** to **Jonas Brewton**, J.Q. & Mag. Registered 28th April 1851. Original delivered to ~~ **Jonas Brewton** 7th May 1851.

p. 311-312.   15 Aug 1833. Deed of Conveyance. **Thomas Woodruff** of Spartanburg Dist, for $207 to me paid by **Isaac Woodruff** of Spartanburg Dist, sold 69 acres on the waters of Dildine creek, the waters of Enoree River; bounded by the branch, **Wm Philips, Isaac Woodruff** and **Simpson Drummond.** Wit: **John M. Crook, H.P. Woodruff, William Phillips.** Signed, **Thomas Woodruff.** Witness oath, 12 April 1851: Signed, **William Phillips** to **Jonas Brewton** Mag. Registered 28th April 1851. Original delivered to ~~ **Jonas Brewton** 7th May 1851.

p. 313-314.   18 Feb 1851. Power of Attorney. State of Georgia, Walker Co., **Martin Daffron** and **Polly Daffron** formerly **Polly Sarratt**, now wife of **Martin Daffron** both of Walker Co., GA, have appointed **Elias Morgan** of Spartanburg Dist, my true and lawful attorney for me and in my name to collect all monies due me from the estate of **Samuel Sarratt** Deceased, and take all lawful ways and means in my name that may be found necessary in the execution of the Power of attorney, in every respect as I myself might do were I personally present. Wit: **David Graham, Ausalem**

Graham J.P. Signed, **Martin Daffron, Polly (x) Daffron.** Clerk of Inferior Court, Walker Co., GA, statement, 20 Feb 1851: I certify that **Anselem Graham** is and was at the time of his assignment an acting Justice of the Peace for Walker Co., GA, his signature is genuine and that full faith and credit should be given to all his official acts. Signed, **Richard W. Ceysadey** Clk. I.C. Statement **David Stewart**, one of the Justices of the Inferior Court of Walker Co., GA, 20 Feb 1851: **Richard W. Caysadey** is clerk of said court duly commissioned and his signature is genuine and credit should be given to his acts as such. Signed, **D. Stewart** J.I.C.   Registered 28th April 1851. Original delivered to ~~ **Elias Morgan.**

p. 314-315. 4 Jan 1850. Deed of Conveyance. **Elijah Alverson** of Spartanburg Dist, for $47.70 to me paid by **William P. Dickson**, sold 70 acres, near the waters of South Packolet River bounded by **William P. Dickson, Margaret Jackson** and myself, beginning at a station on the original line between **Alverson** and **Dickson.** Wit: **A. Cannon, James K. Dickson.** Signed, **Elijah Alverson.** Witness oath, Greenville Dist, 5 May 1851: Signed, **James K. Dickson** to **John Weaver** M.G.D. Registered 6th May 1851.

p. 315-316. 4 Jan 1850. Deed of Conveyance. **Aaron Cannon** of Spartanburg Dist, for $135 to me paid by **William P. Dickson** of Spartanburg Dist, sold 9 acres, all the bends of land lying S side of the Ditch cut through my plantation for the purpose of draining the waters of South Packolet River, which formerly belonged to my tract by the old channel of the River, the said bends lying between **Margaret Jackson** and **Reubin Grambling's** corner, being Seven in number; bounded on the N by the new ditch and on the other sides by the old channel of the River. Wit: **James K. Dickson, William W. Harris.** Signed, **Aaron Cannon.** Witness oath, Greenville Dist, 5 May 1851: Signed, **James K. Dickson** to **John Weaver** M.G.D. Registered 6th May 1851.

p. 317-318. 5 May 1851. Deed of Conveyance. **Joseph W. Tucker** of the Town of Spartanburg, for $97.10 to me paid by **Albert W. Bivings** of the Town of Spartanburg, sold 2 acres in the Town of Spartanburg, bounded by the branch, **A. Smith** and **A. Land's** line. Wit: **J.L. Wofford, W**[m] **H. Young.** Signed, **J.W. Tucker.** Witness oath, 5 May 1851: Signed, **J.L. Wofford** to **Jefferson Choice** N.P & Ex Off Magistrate. Release of Dower, 5 May 1851: Signed, **Emily A. Tucker** to **Jefferson Choice** N.P & Ex Off Magistrate. Registered 6th May 1851. Original delivered to ~~ **A.W. Bivings** 17th May 1851.

p. 318-320. 31 Jan 1851. Deed of Conveyance. **Meachan B. McRee** of Spartanburg Dist, for $125 to me paid by **J.R. Poole** of Spartanburg Dist, sold 2 acres in the Town of Spartanburg on the S Side of the Street to Fairforest beyond the Stone Bridge; bounded by **Norman Abbott.** Wit: **J.M. Dean, J.B. Tolleson.** Signed, **M.B. McRee.** Witness oath, 8 May 1851: Signed, **J.B. Tolleson** to **J.W. Tucker** Not. Pub. Release of Dower, 31 Jan 1851: Signed, **Elizabeth (x) McRee** to **J.B. Tolleson** clk & mag Exoff. Registered 8th May 1851.

p. 320-321. 4 Feb 1850. Deed of Conveyance. **Catherine Stone** of Spartanburg Dist, for $410 to me paid by **Reubin Bryant** [or **Briant**] of Spartanburg Dist, sold 165 acres bounded by a branch of **Bryant's** line, **Easterwood,** the corner agreed on by said **Bryant** and **B.F. Bates** joint purchases from me, and **Quinn's** line. Wit: **Tho. O. P. Vernon, M.D. Bryant.** Signed, **Catherine Stone.**

Witness oath, 5 May 1851: Signeed, **Thoᵉ O. P. Vernon** to **J.B. Tolleson** clk & mag Exoff. Registered 8ᵗʰ May 1851.

p. 322-323.   11 March 1810. Deed of Conveyance. **Richard Kirby** of Spartanburg Dist, for $1 to me paid by **William Reed, Richard Lemaster,** and **Anthony Crocker,** Trustees for the Methodist Episcopal Church of Spartanburg Dist, sold 1 acre on the S side of Pacolet River, a part of a tract originally granted to **John Tolleson** on which the Methodist Meeting House now stands; bounded by Mill Creek and said **Kirby** on three sides and on the S by **Richard Lemaster.** Wit: **Nehemiah Norton, Richerson Whitby.** Signed, **Richard Kirby.** Witness signature, 3 March 1851: **James Quinn & Mathew Lemaster** say they have see **Richard Whitley** write and are acquainted with his handwriting and that they believe the Signature to the within Deed to be his. Signed, **Jaᵉ Quinn, Mathew Lemaster.** Registered 8ᵗʰ May 1851.

p. 323-324.   5 Oct 1829. Commissioner's Titles. **John Kirby** and other distributees of **Richard Kirby** Descd filed their Bill in the honorable Court of Equity against **James Kirby** on the 4ᵗʰ day of Mary 1829, praying partition & division of the real estate of **Richard Kirby** Descd, who died intestate; by order of the said Court, **William Trimmier,** commissioner of said Court, after legally advertising, sold at Spartanburg Court House on 5 Oct 1829, to **John Kirby** for $399; 120 acres on Mill Creek, waters of Packolet River, as represented by a Deed of the same made by **Adam Potter** to **Richard Kirby** Decsd, on 1ˢᵗ Dec 1794. Wit: **John W. Lewis, P. Moore.** Signed, **Wᵐ Trimmier** Com Eqty. Witness oath, 26 Nov 1849: Signed, **P. Moore** to **D.B.P. Moorman** Mag. Registered 8ᵗʰ May 1851.

p. 324-326.   12 June 1850. Sheriff's Titles. **John Thomas** and wife on or about 6 April 1849 petitioned the Court of Ordinary at Spartanburg Court House setting forth that **Frederick Guthrie** departed this life [no date] possessing 130 acres on the waters of Thickoty Creek bounded by **Westley Thomas, Esau Price, Joseph Thomas** and **William Pope;** that division yet remained to be made; 4 Sept 1849, **R. Bowden,** Esq, Ordinary of Spartanburg Dist, ordered the land to be sold by the Sheriff on the first Monday in October; **R.C. Poole,** Sheriff, advertised the land for sale by public outcry and according to the custom of auctions, sold to **A.J. McMakin** for **John Thomas** for $151. Wit: **J.R. Poole, W.J. Poole.** Signed, **R.C. Poole** S.S.D. Witness oath, 5 May 1851: Signed, **J.R. Poole** to **J.B. Tolleson** clk & mag Exoff. Registered 18ᵗʰ May 1851.

p. 326-328.   13 May 1850. Deed of Conveyance. **John T. Kirby** of Spartanburg Dist, for $1,400 to me paid by **James H. Wilson** of Spartanburg Dist, sold 1¼ acres, by estimation, in the Village of Spartanburg on Church Street, a lot **Kirby** purchased from **Revd. A.W. Walker** and a portion of a Lot he purchased from **J.W. Tucker;** adjoining **W.B. Seay, Z.J. Bates** and the **Tucker** lot. Wit: **J.B. Tolleson, J. Belton Tolleson.** Signed, **Jno. T. Kirby.** Witness oath, 14 May 1851: Signed, **J. Belton Tolleson** to **J.B. Tolleson** clk & mag Exoff.   Registered 14ᵗʰ May 1851.

p. 328-329.   21 April 1851. Deed of Conveyance. **James Bivings** of Spartanburg Dist, for $1,500 to me paid by **A.W. Bivings** of the Town of Spartanburg, sold (1) 118½ acres on the waters of Chinquepin Creek, beginning on a new corner known as **A.W. Bivings** corner on the **Bulou** [or **Bulow**] line, the Rutherford Road, to another corner of **A.W. Bivings.** (2) about 207 acres beginning on a new corner known as **Wingo's** corner, to old corner of the original grant, **Harris'** line and Rutherford Road. Wit: **J.W. Weber, R. Easley Cleveland,** Signed, **Ja' Bivings.** Witness oath, 14 May 1851: Signed, **J.W. Weber** to **J.B. Tolleson** clk & mag Exoff. Registered 14th May 1851. Original delivered to ~~ **A.W. Bivings** 17May 1851.

p. 329-331. 22 Feb 1851. Deed of Conveyance. **John L. Patterson** of Spartanburg Dist, for $280 paid to me by **H.H. Thomson** of Spartanburg Dist, sold 112 acres on Peters Creek, my father deeded to me; bounded on E & W sides of the creek adjoining **John D. Cannon.** Wit: **Hiram Mitchell, J.B. Archer.** Signed, **John L. Patterson.** Witness oath, 14 May 1851: Signed, **J.B. Archer** to **J.B. Tolleson** clk & mag Exoff. Registered 14th May 1851.

p. 331-333. 4 April 1851. Mortgage. **John Tewel** made to **H.H. Thomson** three promissory notes whereby **John Tewel** became liable to pay unto **Thomson** $55 with interest on each 4 April in 1852, 1853 & 1854; the notes the purchase money for a Lot sold by **H.H. Thomson** to and mortgaged by **John Tewel**; 1 acre & 65/100 in the Village of Spartanburg bounded by **J. Fletcher** on a new street, **Peyton Turner**, and on branch of a shoal. Wit: **A.J.W. Land, J.B. Archer.** Signed, **John Tewel.** Witness oath, 14 May 1851: Signed, **J.B. Archer** to **J.B. Tolleson** clk & mag Exoff. Registered 14th May 1851.

p. 333-335. 31 March 1851. Deed of Conveyance. **Alfred Brown** of Spartanburg Dist, for $1,000 to me paid by **A.W. Bivings** and **R.E. Cleveland** of the Village of Spartanburg, sold 91 acres on the waters of Lawsons Fork known as the **Crocker** tract which was sold as part of the Estate of **Richard Thomson** Decsd; bounded by a branch and S side of the road which runs from **Thomson's** Mills to **Tho' Wells**; conveyed to **Alfred Brown** by **H.H. Thomson** by deed dated 6 Dec 1850. Wit: **Jefferson Choice, E. Lawson Huggin.** Signed, **Alfred Brown.** Witness oath, 1 April 1851: Signed, **E.L. Huggin** to **Jefferson Choice** N.P. & Ex Off magistrate. Release of Dower, 1 April 1851: Signed, **Tamar (x) Brown** to **Jefferson Choice** N.P. & Mag. Registered 14th May 1851.

p. 335-336. 23 April 1851. Deed of Conveyance. **Fieldin Turner** of Spartanburg Dist, for $162.50 to me paid by **J.R. Poole** of Spartanburg Dist, sold all my interest in the ½ acre Lot that **G.W.H. Legg** bought of **Jesse Cleveland** and sold by him to **R.W. Folger** and from him to **Benjamin Wofford** and from him to **John A. Lee** & from him to **Fieldin Turner**; said interest being one half of said lot on Church Street; bounded by a Lot sold by **Fieldin Turner** to **O.E. Edwards.** Wit: **William Walker a.s.h., H.C. Poole.** Signed, **F. Turner.** Witness oath, 14 May 1851: Signed, **H.C. Poole** to **J.B. Tolleson** clk & mag Exoff. Release of Dower, 30 April 1851: Signed, **Martha J. Turner** to **J.B. Tolleson** clk & mag Exoff. Registered 14th May 1851.

p. 336-338. 22 April 1851. Deed of Conveyance. **Fieldin Turner & John A. Lee** of Spartanburg Dist, for $1,400 to us paid by **O.E. Edwards** of Spartanburg Dist, sold a 5 acre lot in the Town of Spartanburg where **F. Turner** now lives; bounded by **Z.J. Bates** formerly owned by **R.D. Owen**, the road near **L. Hewett's** Shop, a cross street now open and Church Street, **Hewett & Bates** on the S, on the E **Wilson** & the Parsonage Lot, **L. Durmit & Judge Oneal** on the N, and **Trimmier & Fowler** on the W, more fully described in a Deed from **Benj. Wofford** to **J.A. Lee.** Wit: **R.D. Owen, W.D.D. Poole.** Signed, **Fieldin Turner, J.A. Lee.** Witness oath, 14 May 1851: Signed, **R.D.**

Owen to **J.B. Tolleson** clk & mag Exoff. Release of Dower, 30 April 1851: Signed, **Martha J. Turner** to **J.B. Tolleson** clk & mag. Registered 14th May 1851.

p. 338-340. 1 March 1851. Deed of Conveyance. **R.C. Poole** of Spartanburg Dist, for $2,500 to me paid by **Fieldin Cantrell** of Spartanburg Dist, sold 2½ acres in Spartanburg Village whereon the mansion House is situated. Beginning on Main Street and running with the street between **Jefferson Choice** and said Hotel to a S side of the Branch and opposite **J.N. Murry's** new dwelling. Wit: **John Moore, H.C. Poole**. Signed, **R.C. Poole**. Witness oath, 14 May 1851: Signed, **H.C. Poole** to **J.B. Tolleson** clk & mag Exoff. Release of Dower, 25 March 1851: Signed, **Sibby Poole** to **J.B. Tolleson** clk & mag Exoff. Registered 14th May 1851.

p. 340- 342. 1 March 1851. Deed of Conveyance. **R.C. Poole** of Spartanburg Dist, for $500 to me paid by **J.R. Poole** of Spartanburg Village, sold two lots said to contain 1½ acres each, as Lots Nº 2 and 3; Lot Nº 2 beginning on Main Street at S or W corner of Hotel lot; Lot Nº 3 commencing on Main Street at corner of Lot Nº 2. Wit: **John Moore, H.C. Poole**. Signed, **R.C. Poole**. Witness oath, 14 May 1851: Signed, **H.C. Poole** to **J.B. Tolleson** clk & mag Exoff. Release of Dower, 30 April 1851: Signed, **Sibby Poole** to **J.B. Tolleson** clk & mag Exoff. Registered 14th May 1851.

p. 342-343. 22 Oct 1849. Deed of Conveyance. **Wm A. Young** of Spartanburg Dist, for $2,120 to me paid by **Jesse Casey Junior** of Spartanburg Dist, sold 212 acres on the Branch waters of Two Mile Creek formerly known by **Sam Crow** tract and including the **Mode Casey** Tract as Plat will show. The Plat calls for 216 acres but said **Young** will not permit they give him $2,120 for the boundary[.?] Commencing at **Crow's** corner and on **Wm Rhodes, Sabra Rhodes** and **Jesse's** lines, to **Young's** line and the beginning. Wit: **J.B. Deshields, Wofford Casey**. Signed, **Wm A. Young**. Witness oath, 26 Nov 1849: Signed, **J.B. Deshields**. Release of Dower, 24 Dec 1849: Signed, **Mary A. Young**. [Magistrates statement states **Mary W. Young**]. Registered 22nd May 1851.

p. 344-345. 30 Sept 1850. Deed of Conveyance. **Andrew M. Walker** of Spartanburg Dist, for $300 to me paid by **James McMakin** of Greenville Dist, SC, sold 646 acres on branch waters of South Pacolet River and where the Black Stock Road crosses the Road running from Greenville to Rutherford adjoining lands of **Wm Morgan, Walker**[,] **Parish, Felix Hill** and others; on the Greenville and Spartanburg line. Wit: **A.R. Smith, Wm Barnett**. Signed, **A.M. Walker**. Witness oath, 18 April 1851: Signed, **A.R. Smith** to **James Caldwell** Mag S.D. Release of Dower, 29 April 1851: Signed, **Jane E. Walker** to **James Caldwell** J.P. & Mag. Registered 22nd May 1851.

p. 345-347. [About 1 March 1835]. Deed of Conveyance. **Josiah C. Nott, Henry Juneris Nott** and **William B. Nott**, Executors of the late **A. Nott** and by decree of the Court of Equity, record in the Commissioner office of Union Dist, SC, for [amount not filled in] to us paid by **Dr. Maurice A. Moore** of York Dist, SC, have sold 1,150 acres in Union Dist, on N side of Fairforest Creek ; a part of the Real Estate of the late **Abram Nott** Decsd., plat attached; surveyed by **Richard Thomson** 8th January 1835. Wit: **Robert W. Gibbes, Ed. Wm Johnston**. Signed, **William B. Nott, Josiah C. Nott, Henry J. Nott**, Exrs. Witness oath, Richland Dist, SC, 24 Jan 1842: Signed, **Robert W. Gibbs** to **J. Fisher** N.P & Q.U. Exoff. Registered 22nd May 1851.

p. 347-350. 6 Dec 1805. Commissioner's Titles. **Dr. Maurice A. Moore** on about 24th May 1842 Petitioned the Court of Equity at Columbia, SC, setting forth among other things that **Abram Nott** departed this life [date not given] leaving a will and the following persons as his legatees: his widow, **Mrs. Angeline Nott** and the following sons and daughters, **W[m] B. Nott, Henry J. Nott, Josiah C. Nott, James E. Nott, Rufus A. Nott, G.A. Nott, Sophia Nott** who Intermarried with Petitioner and **Eliza & Selena Nott** which last two departed this life unmarried and intestate; and that **Henry J. Nott,** after the death of his sisters **Eliza & Selina,** departed this life Intestate leaving **Amelia A. Nott** his only child and heir at law. That upon a settlement made by the different members of the family under the will of **Abram Nott**, it was agreed upon by them that a tract of land of the testator lying in Union Dist on the W side of Fairforest Creek called the **Patton** Tract containing 902 acres should be assigned to **G.A. Nott** to equalize him with the other children, all members of the family being parties except **H.J. Nott** who had departed this life. That said **G.A. Nott** afterwards sold to **Maurice A. Moore** for the sum of $2,150, a tract, 802 acres, embracing the whole of it except 100 acres at the SW extremity of the land known as the Gold Mine, that the petitioner was advised that **G.A. Nott** cannot make perfect Titles for the same inasmuch as upon the death of **Eliza & Selina Nott**, their shares in the **Patton** tract as he was advised did not survive to **James, Rufus** and **Adolphus Nott,** but was distributable among all the brothers and Sisters and the mother of **Eliza & Selina**, the mother taking a brother or sister's part; and praying the court to deed what Interest the said **Amelia Nott** has in the 802 acres and enquiry be made whether it is proper (she being an infant) that the sale made by **G.A. Nott** to the petitioner as to his interest therein be confirmed and that Titles be made to him. Heard in chambers before the Honorable Court of Equity for Richland Dist at Columbia, SC, 1842, the court did adjudge and decree that **Amelia Nott** is entitled in right of her father to one eighth part of the said two fifths part of the real estate of devised to **Selina & Eliza Nott** and that **Edward J. Arthur,** Commissioner of the Court of Equity execute Titles to **Dr. Moore** for one Eighth part of two fifths of the 802 acres being the interest of **Amelia A. Nott,** then upon receiving from **Dr. Moore** a bond with security conditioned to pay said minor one eighth part of two fifths of the purchase money with interest from May 1834, and that the right of **Amelia A. Nott** in the 802 acres be extinguished and for $107.50 Payable as aforesaid, sold **Maurice A. Moore** one eighth part of two fifths of the land. Wit: **F.A. Tradewell, Jno. W. Bradley.** Signed, **Edward J. Arthur** C.E.R.D. Witness oath, 6th Decr. 1844: Signed, **John W. Bradley** to **James S. Guignard** clerk of court. Registered 22nd May 1851.

p. 350-352. 3 April 1851. Mortgage. **Joakin Fletcher**, became liable to **H.H. Thomson** by three promissory notes of $59.40 to be paid with interest on each 3 April, 1852, 1853 & 1854, the purchase money for a 1 & 1/10 acre Lot in Town of Spartanburg, sold this day by **Thomson** to **Joakin Fletcher.** Lot boundary on a new street, beginning on the SW corner of **Fielding Cantrell's** Lot and along his line to **Peyton Turner's** line and on a branch on a little shoal. Wit: **W[m] Reid Sen., John Linder.** Signed, **Joa. Fletcher.** Witness oath, 22 May 1851: Signed, **John Linder** to **J.B. Tolleson** clk & mag Exoff. Registered 22nd May 1851.

p. 352- 353.   21 Nov 1833. Deed of Conveyance. **Simpson Hester** Executor of the Estate of **Charles Hester** Descd, for $127 to me paid by **Lewis Blanton**, sold 298 acres by computation, on the waters of Beaver Dam. Bounded by **Sarratt** and **Hester.** Wit: **William G. Clark, Elijah Turner.** Signed, **Simpson Hester** Executor. Witness oath, 8 Dec 1835: Signed, **William G. Clark** to **J. Camp** J.P.   Recorded 2nd June 1851.

p. 353-354.   30 Sept 1819. Deed of Conveyance. **Charles Hester** for $400 to me paid by **Lewis Blanton**, sold 400 acres on Cales Creek of Thickoty; bounded by **Camp**. Wit: **Anthony Sarratt, Margaret Camp**. Signed, **Chs. Hester**. Witness oath, 30 Sept 1809: Signed, **Anthony Sarratt** to **J. Camp** J.P. Registered 2nd June 1851.

p. 354-356. 26 Dec 1850. Deed of Conveyance. **Laban Hannah** of Spartanburg Dist, for $1,446.50 to me paid by **William W. Crow** of Spartanburg Dist, sold 131½ acres on the N side of Enoree River, bounded at this time by **James Nesbitt, R.C. Hannah** and Enoree River. Wit: **Sampson Bobo, R.J. Cooper**. Signed, **Laban Hannah**. Witness oath, 26 Dec 1850: Signed, **Sampson Bobo** to **Z. Lanford** Magst. Release of Dower, [no day] Dec 1850: Signed, **Hepsey Hannah** to **Z. Lanford** Magt. Registered 2nd June 1851.

p. 356-357. [No date]. Deed of Trust. **Golden Tinsley** for $1 and the Love and affection I have for my daughter, **Parmelia Parham**, have conveyed to my friend, **Wm A. Young**, in trust for the following use and purposes, 80 acres I now live on for my own use and profit during my lifetime and to continue in my possession till my death. in trust Secondly for the Exclusive use and profit of my daughter **Permelia Parham** after my death during her natural life, the trustee to keep possession himself or deliver it to my daughter after my death at his discretion. At the death of my daughter **Parmelia**, I direct all the property that may be left to be sold by my Trustee and the proceeds therefore paid over to **Permelia's** surviving children, share and share alike, whether the children be legitimate or illegitimate. Test: **J.B. Deshields, Martin Deshields**. Signed, **Golding Tinsley**. Witness oath, 27 May 1851: Signed, **J.B. Deshields** to **John H. Walker** Mag. Registered 2nd June 1851.

p. 357-358. 29 July 1846. Deed of Trust. **Golding Tinsley** for $1 and the Love and Affection I have for my daughter, **Parmelia Parham**, have conveyed to my friend **William A. Young** in trust for the following uses and purposes; my Negro boys, **Sampson** now about 60 years of age and **John** now about 34; also one Sorrel Horse and one carryall in trust first for my own use and profit during my lifetime; Secondly for the exclusive use and profit of my daughter **Permelia Parham** after my death and during her natural life. Trustee to keep the possession himself or deliver to **Permelia** at his discretion. At the death of **Permelia** I direct all the property that may be left to be sold and the proceeds paid over, share and share alike, to the then surviving children of **Permelia**, whether they be legitimate or illegitimate. Wit: **Martin Deshields, Wm T. Farrow**. Signed, **Golden Tinsley**. Witness oath, 27 May 1851: Signed, **Martin Deshields** to **John H. Walker** Mag. Registered 2nd June 1851.

p. 358-359. 24 Sept 1840. Deed of Conveyance. **Joseph Smith** of Spartanburg Dist, for $513 to me paid by **James H. Hurt** of Spartanburg Dist, sold 171 acres, by estimation, on Wolfswamp creek branch waters of Middle Tyger River, adjoining land of **John Bomar, Eber Tinsley, Sirpatin Tinsley** and others. Wit: **A.C. Hardin, Eber Tinsley**. Signed, **Joseph Smith**. Witness oath, 2 June 1851: Signed, **Eber Tinsley** to **G.W.H. Legg** Magistrate. Registered 2nd June 1851.

p. 359-361. 8 May 1851. Deed of Conveyance. **Joseph Smith** of Spartanburg Dist, for $300 to me paid by **James H. Hurt** of Spartanburg Dist, sold 103 acres on the Gogiant Road, on Wolfswamp creek, branch of Tyger River, Middle; bounded by **James H. Hurt, Marrice Milton, Joseph Ballenger** and others. Wit: **Wilson Wingo, Eber Tinsley**. Signed, **Joseph Smith**. Witness oath, 2 June 1851: Signed, **Eber Tinsley** to **G.W.H. Legg** Magst. Registered 2nd June 1851.

p.361-362. 22 Dec 1849. Deed of Conveyance. **Thomas Peake** of Spartanburg Dist, for $200 to me paid by **J.B. Wofford** of Spartanburg Dist, sold 60 acres on the waters of Tyger River; bounded by Black Stock Road, **Alexander Prewitt**, a swamp and **Mark Bennett**. Wit: **Giles Beardin, Mary Peak**. Signed, **Thomas Peak**. Witness oath, 7 Sept 1850: Signed, **Giles Beardin** to **H. Wofford** Magt. Registered 2nd June 1851.

p. 362-363. 17 March 1851. Deed of Conveyance. **Francis Shands** of Spartanburg Dist, for the natural love I have for my daughter, **Juliet S. Wofford**, gives 50 acres where I now live; adjoining **Samuel McCravy** on the N and W; on the S and E by **George** and **Hamelton Cathcart**. Test: **Giles Beardin, Mark Bennett**. Signed, **Francis (her mark) Shands**. Witness oath, 29 May 1851: Signed, **Mark Bennett** to **H. Wofford** Magst. Registered 2nd June 1851.

p. 363-366. 9 April 1831. Deed of Conveyance. **Josiah Kilgore** of Greenville Dist, SC, for $236 to me paid by **Charles Pearson** 249½ acres on a branch of Snottey Creek; bounded by **Mrs. Ford, H.G. Earnest, Pearson** and **Moses Fowler**; part of **James Fords** land [sold?] by the Sheriff. Wit: **Tho' L. Gaston, Erasmus Vaughan**. Signed, **Josiah Kilgore**. Witness oath, 25 April 1831: Signed, **Tho' L. Gaston** to **Andrew McCravy** J.Q. Release of Dower, 25 April 1831: Signed, **Harriet M. Kilgore** to **Andrew McCravey** J.Q. Registered 2nd June 1851.

p. 366-367. 9 Dec 1850. Deed of Conveyance. **John P. McClemons** of Spartanburg Dist, for $1 to me paid, sold **William Mayfield, Jeremiah Glenn** and **Thomas Christopher,** Trustees for Liberty Hill Church and their successors, 3 acres near a Branch of Abners Creek, waters of Enoree River; for the sole use and purposes of the church beloning to the Protestant Methodist Denomination on condition that the church is to be free and open to all other orthodox denominations for preaching, except on the appointed meeting days of the said church; also for the further use and purposes of a house thereon to be erected for a School. Wit: **Wm A. Mayfield, Benjamin B. Wood**. Signed, **John P. McClemons**. Witness oath, 7 June 1851: Signed, **Wm A Mayfield** to **Isham Wood** Mag S.D. Registered 7th June 1851.

p. 367-368. 5 May 1851. Deed of Conveyance. **Patrick Oshanasy** of Spartanburg Dist, for $125 to me paid by **A.W. Bivings** and **Joseph W. Tucker** of the Town of Spartanburg, sold a ½ acres lot in the Town of Spartanburg; beginning on corner of **R. Thomson's** lot. Wit: **Jefferson Choice, W.H. Bagwell**. Signed, **Patrick Oshanasy**. Witness oath, 5 May 1851: Signed, **W.H. Bagwell** to **Jefferson Choice** N.P. Exoff Magistrate. Registered 7th June 1851.

p. 369-371. 16 Nov 1847. Commissioner's Titles. **Junius W. Thomson,** on or about 1 Oct 1845 exhibited his Bill of Complaint in Court of Equity at Spartanburg C.H. against **H.H. Thomson, J.M. Thomson & J.W. Thomson** praying for a Specific performance and partition of Lands, refer to the bill filed; the issue was heard by the court at June Term 1847, when the court decreed that the land described be sold by **Thomos O.P. Vernon**, Commissioner, and was sold by public outcry on the 16th & 17th days of Nov 1847 to **John T. Kirby** for $1,021; Lot N[o] 30, in the Town of Spartanburg, 101½ acres bounded by **Mrs. Bomar,** both sides of the old ford on the branch, S of the Village on Hobokin Street. Wit: **Alfred Tolleson, W.H. Wilbanks.** Signed, **Tho' O.P. Vernon,** C.E.S.D. Witness oath, 14 June 1851: Signed, **Alfred Tolleson** to **J.B. Tolleson** clk & mag Exoff. Registered 14th June 1851.

p. 371-373. 15 May 1851. Mortgage. **Alfred Brown** is indebted to **H.H. Thomson** by two notes each calling for $1,075, due each 1st Jan, 1852 & 1853; the purchase money for three tracts this day bought from **H.H. Thomson;** for better securing the payments, **Brown** mortgages the land to **Thomson.** (1) The **Carden** tract, 500 acres on Shoaly creek; for location reference a Deed made by **Jo' Tucker** to **H.H. Thomson;** (2) the **Landford Cantrell** tract, 200 acres adjoining the above on Shoaly Creek; for location reference **Henry Child's** Deed to **W[m] Turner;** (3) the **Aaron Bishop** tract, 107 acres, reference to a Deed of this land by **Aaron Bishop** to **H.H. Thomson.** Witness: **J.M. Wallace, Henry F. Evins.** Signed, **Alfred Brown.** Witness oath, 14 June 1851: Signed, **Henry F. Evins** to **J.B. Tolleson** clk & mag Exoff. Registered 14th June 1851.

p. 373-375. 5 June 1851. Deed of Conveyance. **William Hoy** of Spartanburg Dist, is indebted to **Josiah Kilgore** for $500 by note dated 30th May 1851; for better securing payment, delivers unto **Kilgore** the following slaves: **George** about 20 years old; **Jim** 15 years; **Mary** 18; **Virginia** 1; **Harriet** 17; **Little Mary** 15; **Grace** 12; **Simon** 10; **Savanna** 8; **Nancy** 10; **Quitman** 3; **Halo** 3; **Russel** 6 mo; **Victoria** 11 years; **Mathew** 10; **Robert** 6 yrs; **Tom** 3; **Yellow Henry** 2 years. Wit: **John M.C. Mayfield.** Signed, **W[m] Hoy.** Witness oath, 9 June 1851: Signed, **J.M.C. Mayfield** to **Mark Bennett** Magt. Registered 14th June 1851.

p. 375-377. 29 May 1851. Mortgage. **L.M. Glenn** of Union Dist, SC, by my Bond of $700 dated 9 May 1851, is indebted to **A.W. Bivings** for $350, to be paid in three installments, plus interest, $75 due on 29th Dec 1851; $137.50 due each 29th May, 1852 & 1853; for better securing the payment, **Glenn** releases a 2½ acre lot in the Town of Spartanburg, beginning on corner of **R. Thomson**'s lot, to **Andrew Smith's** inside corner, **W.A. Smith's** line to a small maple in the branch, **A. Land's** line near to his back corner, **P. Oshanessy's** line. Wit: **Jefferson Choice, E.L. Huggin.** Signed, **L.M. Glenn.** Witness oath, 14 June 1851: Signed, **E.L. Huggin** to **J.B. Tolleson** clk & mag Exoff. Registered 14th June 1851.

p. 377-379. 29 May 1851. Deed of Conveyance. **Albert W. Bivings** of Spartanburg Dist, for $350 to me paid by **L.M. Glenn** of Union Dist, SC, sold a 2½ acre lot in the Town of Spartanburg commencing on **R. Thomson's** corner, to **Andrew Smith's** inner corner, **A. Smith's** line to a small maple in the branch, **A. Land's** line and near to his back corner, **Patrick Oshanesey** line. Wit: **Jefferson Choice, E.L. Huggin.** Signed, **A.W. Bivings.** Witness oath, 11 June 1851: Signed, **E.L. Huggin** to **Jefferson Choice** N.P & Ex off Magistrate. Release of Dower, 11 June 1851: Signed, **Sarah E. Bivings** to **Jefferson Choice** N,P. & Ex off Magistrate. Registered 23rd June 1851.

p. 379-381. 27 Dec 1850. Deed of Conveyance. **Ralph Smith** of Spartanburg Dist, for $275 to me paid by **S.B. Foster** of Spartanburg Dist, sold 170 acres; bounded by **S.B. Foster, Richard Foster.** **Smith** warrants and defends title from all, except the claim of Dower which **Mrs. Rebecca Foster** holds until her death. Wit: **Littleton Bulman, J. Belton Tolleson**. Signed, **Ralph Smith**. Witness oath, 21 March 1851: Signed, **Littleton Bagwell** to **A.B. Foster** N.P. Release of Dower, 20 March 1851: Signed, **Susan Smith** to **A.B. Foster** Noty. Public. Registered 25th June 1851.

p. 381-382. 23 Dec 1843. Deed of Conveyance. **Branson Hall** of Spartanburg Dist, for $124.43 to me paid by **W.E. McDowell** of Spartanburg Dist, sold 84 acres on the S side of South Pacolet River; bounded by the river, **Ramsey, Robert McDowell** and **L. Ballenger.** Wit: **Noah Wolf, James N. McDowell**. Signed, **Branson Hall**. Witness oath, 6 Feb 1844: Signed, **J.N. McDowell** to **S. Bullington** Mag. Release of Dower, 6 Feb 1844: Signed, **Mary (x) Hall** to **S. Bullington** Mag. Registered 28th June 1851. Original delivered to ~ **W.E. McDowell** 28th June 1851.

p. 383-384. 20 Sept 1845. Deed of Conveyance. **W.B. Smith** of Spartanburg Dist, for $126.50 to me paid by **O.P. Williams** of Spartanburg Dist, sold 126½ acres, by competition; bounded by **Edward Williams** and a branch. Wit: **Robert Scruggs, A.H. Williams**. Signed, **W.B. Smith**. Witness oath, 10 Oct 1845: Signed, **Robert Scruggs** to **W.B. Smith** Mag. Registered 28th June 1851.

p. 384-385. 6 Feb 1841. Deed of Conveyance. **David W. Moore** of Spartanburg Dist, for $1,000 to me paid by **Elias C. Leitner** of Spartanburg Dist, sold 575 acres on **Polly Woods** branch, waters of Lawsons fork. Bounded by **Henry Bishop, Barney Bishop, Benson & Littles** land; plat annexed. Wit: **A.J. Vernon, A.J.W. Land**. Signed, **David W. Moore**. Witness oath, 9 July 1851: Signed, **A.J.W. Land** to **J.B. Tolleson** clk & mag Exoff. Release of Dower, 14 May 1851: Signed, **Mary C. Moore** to **J.B. Tolleson** clk & mag Exoff. Registered 9th July 1851.

p. 386-387. 4 April 1851. Deed of Conveyance. **James K. Means** of Spartanburg Dist, for $1,700 to me paid by **Govan Mills** of Spartanburg Dist, sold 3 acres in the Village of Spartanburg; beginning in the street corner of the lot originally belonging to **John Wilbanks** and conveyed by him to **William Walker** and bounded by **James E. Henry**. Wit: **G.W.H. Legg, John Kirby**. Signed, **J.K. Means**. Witness oath, 9 July 1851: Signed, **John Kirby** to **J.B. Tolleson** clk & mag Exoff. Release of Dower, [no day] July 1851: Signed, **Margaret Means** to **J.B. Tolleson** clk & mag Exoff. Registered 9 July 1851.

p. 387-388. 21 Nov 1850. Deed of Conveyance. **Aaron Cannon** and **Ibra Cannon**, Executors of **John Cannon** Deceased, of Spartanburg Dist, for $680 to paid by **Bryant** [or **Briant**] **Cash** of Spartanburg Dist, sold 340 acres known as the **Warren** land on the waters of Island Creek; bounded by **S. Cash, Procter,** S side of **Proctor's** branch, **Edwards** and **Widow Dewberry**. Wit: **Elisha Poole, Alberry Cash**. Signed, **A. Cannon, I. Cannon**. Witness oath, 17 July 1851: Signed, **Alberry Cash** to **J.B. Tolleson** clk & mag Exoff. Registered 17 July 1851.

p. 388-389. 25 Sept 1850. Deed of Trust. Catham Co., GA. **John W. Hutchings** of Catham [Chatham?] Co, GA, for $50 to me paid by **Edward W. Bucker** of Catham Co, GA, Trustee for **Lucretia R. Robbins** wife of **John W. Robbins,** sold 35½ acres in Spartanburg District between the Saluda Gap road and the Middle Tyger River; bounded by S bank of said river, **Boin Griffin, William McMakin** and others; reference Plat of the same made by **James K. Dickson** D.S. August 20th 1850. Wit: **Jno. T. Thomas, Dan¹ Remstart** N. Pub. Signed, **John W. Hutching.** Georgia, Witness oath, 5 May 1851: Signed, **John T. Thomas** to **Colomen Cohen** to Cas Com of Deeds for Georgia. Registered 21 July 1851.

p. 389-390.   14 Dec 1850. Deed of Trust. Catham Co. [Chatham?], GA. **John W. Hutchings** of Catham Co., GA, for $50 to me paid by **Edward W. Bucker** of Catham Co., GA, Trustee for **Eunice Hutchings** wife of **Thomas Hutchings**, sold 35¾ acres in Spartanburg District between the Saluda Gap road and the Middle Tyger River; bounded by S side of said road, **William McMakin, Lucretia Robbins, Lucy Flemming** and others; reference Plat of same made by **James K. Dickson** D.S. August 20, 1850. Wit: **Robert J. Christie, John T. Thomas.** Signed, **John W. Hutchings.** Georgia. Witness oath, 5 May 1851: Signed, **Jno. T. Thomas** to **Colomin Cohen** to Cas. Com. of deeds for Georgia. Registered 21 July 1851.

p. 391.   5 April 1851. A right to raise water called the telegraph carrier. Whereas **J.D. Willoughby** of Scotland, Franklin Co, Pennsylvania, has invented certain new and useful improvements in machinery for raising and conveying water called the Telegraph water carrier for which **Willoughby** obtained letters Patent of the United States bearing date Nov 6th 1849 and whereas **Stephen D. Boyd, J.W. Boyd, H.P. Boyd** and **J.H. Lewin** of the County of Warren, Virginia have purchased from **Willoughby** all his right title & interest for and to, in the State of North Carolina, certain counties in Virginia and the District of Spartanburg, SC. This indenture for $150 to me in hand paid, I have assigned unto **J.S. & T.N. Finch** all the right title and interest which was conveyed to **Boyd & Lewin** by **Willoughby** for the Dist of Spartanburg, SC, and in no other place except however two individual rights made unto **William Bagwell** and **Mr. Perry** which are not included in this instrument. The same to be held and enjoyed by **J.S. & T.N. Finch** for their own use and their legal representatives. Test: **James A. Finch.** Signed, **Stephen D. Boyd** for **Boyd & Lewin.** Witness oath, 18 July 1851: Signed, **J.A. Finch** to **J.B. Tolleson** clk & mag Exoff. Registered the 21 July 1851.

p. 392.   29 Sept 1849. Deed of Conveyance. **John Wheeler** and **Thomas Ballenger** of Spartanburg Dist, for $188 paid by **William Brown** of Spartanburg Dist, sold 94 acres on Wolfswamp branch waters of Middle Tyger River, a part of land originally granted to **Sarah Grey.** Test: **John Adam, James S. Wheeler.** Signed, **Thomas Ballenger, Jno. Wheeler.** Witness oath, 5 Oct 1849: Signed, **John Adam** to **B.F. Montgomery** Mag. Registered the 21 July 1851.

p. 393-394.   22 July 1851. Deed of Conveyance. **Benjamin Prewitt Sen'** of Spartanburg Dist, for $50 to me paid by **Riley Prewitt** of Spartanburg Dist, sold 100 acres, a part of the tract that I purchased from **Jesse Prewitt** that he purchased of **James Ridings** that was granted to **Ridings;** on the N side of Motlows Creek; bounded by the creek, **Wᵐ Beshears, Thomas,** head of a branch and down a swamp. Wit: **John (x) Prewitt, A.C. Hardin.** Signed, **Benjamin (x) Prewitt.** Witness oath, 28 July 1851: Signed, **John (x) Prewitt** to **James Caldwell** Mag. S.D. Registered the 4 August 1851. Original delivered to ～ **John Prewett,** Fees paid.

p. 394-395. 23 July 1851. Deed of Conveyance. **Riley Prewett** of Spartanburg Dist, for $150 to me paid by **Elias Prewett** of Spartanburg Dist, sold 100 acres, by estimate, on the N side of Easley Creek bounded by **S. Brown,** Easters Creek and **Sanford Brown;** it a part of a tract surveyed for **Robert Goodjion** the 16th day of June in the year 1785. Wit: **Benjamin (x) Prewitt, A.C. Hardin.** Signed, **Riley (x) Prewitt.** Witness oath, 28 July 1851: Signed, **Benjamin (x) Prewett** to **James Caldwell** Mag S.D. Registered the 4 Augst 1851.

p. 395-396. 4 Jan 1850. Deed of Conveyance. **William P. Dickson** of Spartanburg Dist, for $80 to me paid by **Aaron Cannon** of Spartanburg Dist, sold all the binds of land lying on the N side of the Ditch cut through my plantation for the purpose of draining the waters of South Pacolet River which formerly belonged to my tract by the old channel of the River, said binds lying between **Margaret Jackson's** corner on the river and **Reubin Gramling** corner and being eight in number [8 bends?] and containing 3¼ acres; bounded on the S by new ditch and on the other sides by the old channel of the river. Wit: **James K. Dickson, William W. Harris.** Signed, **William P. Dickson.** Witness oath, 27 July 1850: Signed, **William W. Harris** to **James Caldwell** Mag. S.D. Registered the 4 August 1851.

p. 396. 27 Sept 1850. Deed of Conveyance. **Reuben Gramling** of Spartanburg Dist, for $7.50 to me paid by **Aaron Cannon** of Spartanburg Dist, sold all that land lying on the N side of the ditch cut through my land for the purpose of draining the water of South Pacolet river which formerly belonged to my tract by the old channel of the river, lands lying below **Joseph R. Gramling** being two in number containing three eighths of an acre bounded on the S by the new ditch and on all other sides by the old channel of the river. Wit: **Hamilton Pollard, Jeremiah (x) Pack.** Signed, **Reuben Gramling.** Witness oath, 30 Jan 1851: Signed, **Jeremiah Pollard** [Hamilton Pollard in magistrate's statement]. Registered the 4 Augst 1851.

p. 397. 18 Feb 1851. Deed of Conveyance. **Sarah Brown** of Spartanburg Dist, for $52 to me paid by **John Odam** of Spartanburg Dist, sold 82 acres, all that tract where I now live; bounded by **John Wheeler, William Ballenger** and others. Wit: **John Wheeler, James S. Wheeler.** Signed, **Sarah (x) Brown.** Witness oath, 1 Aug 1851: Signed, **Jno. Wheeler** to **R. Bowden** Exffo Mags. Registered the 4 day of August 1851.

p. 397-398. 13 Nov 1848. Deed of Gift. **Milly Duncan** of Spartanburg Dist, being desirous to divide certain property between and amongst my Several Children for the love and affection I have to them do give to my daughter **Permelia A. Wilkins** the tract on which I now live consisting of two separate tracts (1) 230 acres and (2) 25 acres, 250 acres in all; which land is valued to my daughter at $1,200 and on the N side of North Pacolet River, **Sarah Camp, Josiah Slucklins [Stucklin?]** line through its several Changes to **Seays,** formerly **Austells** corner, **Dodds & Hannon.** Wit: Test: **W.A. Hawkins, Gabrel Cannon.** Signed, **Milly Duncan.** Witness oath, 5 Jan 1849: Signed, **G. Cannon** to **Elias Wall** Mag. Registered the 4 August 1851.

p. 398-399. 8 April 1851. Deed of Conveyance. **A.C. Bomar** of Spartanburgh Dist, for $500 to me paid by **B.M. High** of Spartanburgh Dist, sold 7 acres on Brows Creek of North Tyger River including a Tan Yard and the house wherein **B.M. High** now lives and on said river. Wit: **Thomas**

K. Brice, W.A. Caldwell. Signed, **A.C. Bomar.** Witness oath, 12 April 1851: Signed, **W.A. Caldwell** to **J.C. Caldwell** Magistrate. Release of Dower, 20 Day of April 1851: Signed, **Emily S.** [or **L.**] **Bomar** to **J.C. Caldwell** Magistrate. Registered the 5 Sept 1850 [1851?].

p. 400-401. 6 Jan 1849. Deed of Conveyance. **John Stevens** of Spartanburgh Dist, for $148 to me paid by **Benjamin M. High** of Spartanburgh Dist, sold 18¾ acres near Timmons old field, a part of a tract conveyed from **Daniel & Jane Mullin** to **Harvey Finch**, from **Finch** to **Stevens**; on a road. Wit: **A.J. Pearson, John Snoddy Junr.** Signed, **John Stephens.** Witness oath, 6 Aug 1851: Signed, **A.J. Pearson** to **J.C. Caldwell** Mag. Release of Dower, 12 April 1851: Signed, **Lucinda (x) Stevens** to **J.C. Caldwell** Magistrate. Registered the 5 Sept 1851.

p. 401-402. 21 July 1851. Deed of Conveyance. **Balam Dempsey** of SC, for $10 to me paid by **William P. Dickson,** sold 159 acres on the waters of South Pacolet River, bounded by **Vernon,** Dargus Creek, Millses gap Road. I, said **Dempsey** warrant and defend 40 acres of the tract, a part of which lies upon both sides of the Mills gap Road; he also gives title to the entire 159 acres; land was granted to **Bailem Dempsey** 21st March 1848. Wit: **E.H. Coggin, William G. McDowell.** Signed, **Bailem (x) Dempsey.** Witness oath, 1 Aug 1851: Signed, **William G. McDowell** to **James Caldwell** Mag. S.D. Registered the 5 August 1851.

p. 403-404. 14 Dec 1850. Deed of Conveyance. Chatham Co., GA. **John W. Hutchings** of Chatham Co., GA, for $60 to me paid by **Edward W. Bucker** of Chatham Co., GA, Trustee for **Lucy T. Fleming,** wife of **Livingston Fleming,** sold 46¾ acres in Spartanburg Dist between the Saluda Gap Road and the Middle Tyger River; bounded by the S bank of the river, Saluda Gap Road, **Matthew Moore, Lucretia Robbins, Eunice Hutchings** and others; reference plat made by **James K. Dickson** D.S. August 20th 1850. Wit: **Robt. W. Christie, Jno. P. Thomas.** Signed, **John W. Hutchings.** Georgia. Witness oath, 5 May 1851: Signed, **John T. Thomas** to **Solomon Cohen.** to Cor ofllers for Georgia. Registered the 20th August 1851.

p. 404-405. 26 Aug 1851. Deed of Conveyance. **Henry Bishop** of Spartanburg Dist, for the natural love and affection I have for my beloved son **H.J. Bishop** and also for the labor, pains and care performed and done in my behalf and for my protection and maintainance by **H.J. Bishop** since his attaining to full age, and for $10 to me paid by **H.J. Bishop,** grant 224 acres on the waters of Standing Stone Branch, beginning at the mouth of Meadow Branch. Wit: **Dr. F.L. Parham, H.J. Rowland.** Signed, **Henry (x) Bishop.** Witness oath, 27 Aug 1851: Signed, **F.L. Parham** to **J.B. Tolleson.** Release of Dower, 4 Sept 1851: Signed, **Martha (x) Bishop** to **J.B. Tolleson** clk & mag Exoff. Registered the 27th Aug. 1851.

p. 406. 22 Aug 1851. Deed of Conveyance. **John Burnett** of Spartanburg Dist, for $400 to me paid by **George A. Fike** of Spartanburg Dist, sold 60 acres on the S side of Pacolet River; bounded by **Zechariah Cannon, Isaac Epting, Elias Burnett** and others. Wit: **James L. Pearson, Elias Burnett.** Signed, **John P. Burnett.** Witness oath, 6 Sept 1851: Signed, **Jas. L. Pearson** [magistrate not named]. Registered The 6th day Sept 1851. Written vertically in left hand margin: For Dower to this deed, see Book "YY," page 336.

p. 407. 10 May 1851. Deed of Conveyance. **William Burnett** of Spartanburg Dist, for the natural love and affection I have for my son **John Burnett**, have granted him [acres not mentioned] on the waters of Thomsons Creek, waters of Pacolet River; bounded by **William McDowell, Greenham Crowder,** formerly **H.J. Rowlad [Rowland?]**, binding on land surveyed for **Lenard Carden,** land surveyed for **Joseph Venable,** and two branches mentioned but not named. Wit: **S. Bullinton, Henry Wolf.** Signed, **William (x) Burnett.** Witness oath, 8 Sept 1851: Signed, **Henry Wolf** to **J.B. Tolleson** clk & mag Exoff. Registered 8 Sept 1851.

p. 408-409. 13 Sept 1851. Deed of Conveyance. **Jesse Cleveland** of Town of Spartanburg, for $594.67 to me paid by **George A. Fike** of Spartanburg Dist, sold a lot in the Town of Spartanburg; Beginning on the corner of a lot laid out to **Fielding Turner,** on the E side of Church Street, along Church Street to **Mr. Patton's** corner, to **F. Turner's** line containing 3 acres 9½ tenths. Wit: **Jesse M. Cannon, Jefferson Choice.** Signed, **Jesse Cleveland.** Witness oath, 13 Sept 1851: Signed, **Jesse M. Cannon** to **Jefferson Choice** N.P. & Exoff Mag. Release of Dower, 13 Sept 1851: Signed, **Mary Cleveland** to **Jefferson Choice** N.P. & Magistrate. Registered Sept 18th 1851.

p. 409-410. 4 Sept 1839. Sheriff's Titles. By a write of Fieri Facias issued out of the Court of Common pleas held for Spartanburg Dist, tested 12th Nov 1838, at the suit of **Westmoreland** and **Dickie,** ordered **A.C. Bomar,** Sheriff of Spartanburg Dist, to levy $33, damages and costs out of the lands, etc. of **David Tippins;** exposed to public auction 350 acres on Abners Creek, adjoining **Benjamin[?] Wilson** and others; sold for $40 to **Josiah Kilgore** of Greenville Dist, SC. Wit: **G.W. Bomar, David Anderson.** Signed, **A.C. Bomar** S.S.D. Registered 2nd Oct 1851.

p. 410-411. 26 Dec 1848. Deed of Conveyance. **Earle Clark** of Chester Dist, SC, for $265 to me paid by **Marion B.** and **R.L. Duncan** of Chester Dist, SC, sold 91 acres on the waters of Pacolet River; bounded by **Jake Griffin, Henry Littlejohn, Salathiel Littlejohn** and **James Littlejohn.** Wit: **Felix W. Littlejohn, Wm M. Wilkins.** Signed, **Earle Clark.** Assignment, 22 July 1850: I sign over my Claim to **M.B. Duncan** in the within deed for value Recd. Signed, **R.L. Duncan** to **J.M. Elford** Mag. Registered 19th Sept 1851.

p. 411-412. 25 Sept 1850. Deed of Conveyance. **Salathiel Littlejohn** and **Sarah** his wife, for $120 to us paid by **E. Webster** of Spartanburg Dist, sold 17 acres bounded by **John Wood's** old corner, a hill near the right side of the branch and my line. Wit: **Robertson Littlejohn, Obadiah Griffin.** Signed, **Salathiel Littlejohn, Sarahan Littlejohn.**
[This appears to belong with the **Earle Clark** to **Duncan** deed above: Personally appeared before me on the 17th of Sept 1851. **R.L. Duncan** and testified to the above. **J.M. Elford**]. Registered Sept 19th 1851.

p. 412-413. 6 April 1850. Deed of Conveyance. **William W. Torrence,** for $200 to me paid by **James Husky,** sold 64 acres, by computation, on Sarratts Creek of Broad River; bounded by **Sarratt.** Wit: **Berriman Humphries, D. Scruggs.** Signed, **William W. Torrence.** Witness oath, 7 Oct 1850: Signed, **Berriman Humphries** to **A. Bonner** Mag. Registered 6th Oct 1851.

p. 413. 18 Nov 1847. Deed of Conveyance. **William D. Weber** of Spartanburg Dist, for $70 to me paid by **James Parris**, sold 76 acres, by computation, lying on Horse Creek, the waters of Broad River. Wit: **Wilson (x) Scruggs, Jackson Byars**. Signed, **Wᵐ D. Weber**. Witness oath, 6 Sept 1848: Signed, **Jackson Byars** to W.H. Wilbanks Mag. Registered 6 Oct 1851.

p. 414. 20 Sept 1847. Deed of Conveyance. **Aaron Briges,** for $76.50 to me paid by **James Parris**, sold 76 acres by computation, on head waters of Horse Creek, waters of Broad River. Test: **Robert (x) Scruggs, William (x) Scruggs**. Witness oath, 26 July 1848: Signed, **Robert (x) Scruggs** to W.H. Wilbanks Mag. Registered 6ᵗʰ October 1851.

p. 414-415. 18 Jan 1850. Deed of Conveyance. **Wiley Littlejohn** of Union Dist, SC, for $800 to me paid by **Thomas H. Littlejohn** of Spartanburg Dist, sold 112 acres in Spartanburg and Union Dists, on Plumbtree branch the waters of Pacolet River; bounded on SE by **Wᵐ T. Nuckols,** NE by **Jesse Griffin** formerly **Josiah Sparks,** N by **Mrs. Wood's** land formerly **John Sparks,** SW by **William Wood's** land and another branch with a rock spring. Wit: **Obediah Griffin, G.T. Moore**. Signed, **Wiley Littlejohn**. Witness oath, 7 Aug 1851: Signed, **G.T. Moore** to William Lipscomb Mag. Registered 7ᵗʰ Oct 1851.

p. 416. 8 Sept 1851. Deed of Gift. Spartanburg Dist. **Jesse Griffin,** for the regard, good will and Affection I have for my son **Ignatious Griffin**, have given and forever quit all claim to 150 acres; all my lands not otherwise Conveyed and E of the dividing line of my lands, on **M.B. Duncan's** line, below the Spring, near the ridge Road and **Mrs. Wood's** line. Wit: **Thomas Littlejohn, Robertson Littlejohn**. Signed, **Jesse (x) Griffin**. Witness oath, 1 Oct 1851: Signed, **Robertson Littlejohn** to Wᵐ Lipscomb Mag. Registered the 7ᵗʰ October 1851.

p. 416-417. 8 Sept 1851. Deed of Gift. Spartanburg Dist. **Jesse Griffin**, for the good will, love and affection I have for my son **Obediah Griffin**, have given and forever quitting all Claim to all that portion of my lands lying W of a line commencing on **M.B. Duncan's** line, some distance below the Spring, near the ridge road, and on **Mrs. Wood's** line. Wit: **Thomas H. Littlejohn, Robertson Littlejohn**. Signed, **Jesse (x) Griffin**. Witness oath, 7 Oct 1851: Signed, **Robertson Littlejohn** to Wᵐ Lipscomb Mag. Registered the 7ᵗʰ October 1851.

p. 417-418. 27 Dec 1850. Deed of Conveyance. Spartanburg Dist. **E. Webster,** for $675 paid by **Marion B. Duncan** of Spartanburg Dist, sold 127 acres in Spartanburg and Union Districts; bounded by **John Moore's** old corner, **Duncan** and **Salathiel Littlejohn;** except ½ acre Round the Graves, which belongs to **Henry Littlejohn**. Attest: **R.L. Duncan, W.A. Hawkins**. Signed, **E. Webster**. Witness oath, 17 Sept 1851: Signed, **R.L. Duncan** to J.M. Elford mag. Registered the 7ᵗʰ October 1851.

p. 418-419. 8 Sept 1851. Deed of Conveyance. Spartanburg District. **Jesse Griffin,** for $200 paid and secured to me, sold to my son **Ignatious Griffin** all my lands purchased of **Josiah Sparks Sen.;** 100 acres on the waters of Pacolet River, bounded on the N by my own land, on the S by **Wᵐ T. Nuckolls,** E by **James Littlejohn,** and W by **Thomas H. Littlejohn**. Wit: **Thomas H. Littlejohn,**

Robertson Littlejohn. Signed, **Jesse (x) Griffin.** Witness oath, 1 Oct 1851: Signed, **Robertson Littlejohn** to **Wm Lipscomb**Mag. Registered October 7th 1850.

p. 419-420. 23 Aug 1851. Deed of Conveyance. Spartanburg Dist. **Elijah Logan,** for $400 to me paid by **J.P. Burnett,** sold 304 acres by computation, on Turner's fork of Thickety Creek, waters of Broad River. Test: **Esau Price, Carter Burnett.** Signed, **E.B. Logan.** Witness oath, 6 Oct 1851: Signed, **E. Price** to **A. Bonner** Mag. Release of Dower, 20 Sept 1851: Signed, **Patsy (x) Logan** to **A. Bonner** Mag. Registered October 7th 1851.

p. 420-421. 5 July 1851. Deed of Conveyance. **John Golightly** of Spartanburg Dist, for $400 to me paid by **Robert E. Cleveland** of the Village of Spartanburg, sold 154 acres on Peters Creek; bounded by **Bryant, Hines** and **Golightly's** other lands; should there be more land in the boundaries, it is to be paid for in proportion to the price and number of acres; and if there should turn out to be less than specified, the price is to be ratiably less. Wit: **Jefferson Choice, William Walker A.S.H.** Signed, **John Golightly.** Witness oath, 5 July 1851: Signed, **William Walker A.S.H.** to **Jefferson Choice** N.P. & Ex Off Magistrate. Registered 6 October 1851.

p. 421-422. 26 Aug 1851. Release. **H.J. Bishop** of Spartanburg Dist, for $10 to me paid, divers other good causes, give my Father **Henry Bishop** of Spartanburg Dist, and also unto my Mother **Mrs. Bishop,** the wife of said **Henry Bishop,** for and during their natural lives, and the survivor of them, all that tract [acres not given] where **Henry Bishop** now lives; for location refer to a Deed this day executed and delivered to me for the premises by the said **Henry Bishop.** Wit: **F.L. Parham, H.J. Rowland.** Signed, **H.J. Bishop.** Witness oath, 27 Aug 1851: Signed, **F.L. Parham** to **J.B. Tolleson** clk & mag Exoff. Registered October 7th 1851.

p. 422-423. 2 April 1851. Deed of Conveyance. **Solomon Bishop** of Spartanburg Dist, for $700 to me paid by **R.E. Cleveland** of the Town of Spartanburg, sold all that tract of land [acres not mentioned] on the waters of Shoaly Creek; bounded by the creek, **Willis,** the old ridge road, **Beannor[?], Miller** and **Sarah Owens.** Wit: **A.P. Brannon, Alberry Bishop, Louisa (x) Brannon.** Signed, **Solomon Bishop.** Release of Dower, 11 June 1851: Signed, **Celey (x) Bishop** to **Jefferson Choice** N.P. & Ex off Mag. Registered 4 October 1851.

p. 423-424. 7 Jan 1850. Deed of conveyance. **Joel Dean** of Floyd Co., GA, for $200 to me paid by **Joel W. Miller** of Spartanburg Dist, sold all my interest (being one half) to 230 acres, adjoining **Elizabeth Rogers** and others, which was sold as the property of **John Stephens,** at the suit of **Joel Hurt** for **James H. Hurt** and was purchased by **John Stroble** and he conveyed one half of said tract to me, by his deed of 9th February 1846. Wit: **G. Harris, Lecil Bearden.** Signed, **Joel Dean.** Release of Dower, 18 Sept 1850: Signed, **Eliza Dean** to **John Stroble Jr.** mag public. Registered 7th October 1851.

p. 424-425. 6 Sept 1851. Mortgage. **James G. Pearson** of Spartanburg Dist, is firmly bound unto **J.P. Burnett** for $107; for better securing the payment, sells and releases 140 acres on the S side of Cherokee Creek waters of Pacolet River; bounded on the E by **E.C. Lietner,** on the N by **Lewis**

Cannon, on the W by **H.H. Thomson,** and on the S by **John Linder;** known as the **M.C. Miller** tract and now cultivated by **J.P. Burnett.** Deed null and void if **Pearson** pays the debt. Wit: **Jefferson Choice, George A. Fike.** Signed, **Jas. G. Pearson, J.P. Burnett.** Witness oath, 6 Sept 1851: Signed, **George A. Fike** to **Jefferson Choice** N.P. & Ex off Magistrate.

p. 426. 5 April 1851. Deed of Conveyance. **John Martin** of Spartanburg Dist, for $300 to me paid by **Judge Edwards,** sold 158 acres on waters of Big and little Buck Creek and adjoining **Yarbour.** Wit: **J. Dewberry, Henry M. Turner.** Signed, **John Martin.** Witness oath, 3 Aug 1851: Signed, **Henry M. Turner** to **J.B. Tolleson** clk & mag Exoff. Registered 7th Oct 1851.

p. 427-428. 21 Feb 1851. Deed of Gift. **David Patterson** of Spartanburg Dist, for the natural Love and affection I have for my son **John L. Patterson** of Spartanburg Dist, release 112 acres on Pebers [Peters?] Creek; bounded by the Creek and **John D. Cannon.** Wit: **James Templeman, John W. Moore** [or **John Willoore**]. Signed, **David Patterson.** Release of Dower, 10 May 1851: Signed, **Ruth (x) Patterson** to **J.B. Tolleson** clk & mag Exoff. Registered October 8th 1851.

p. 428. 30 July 1850. Deed of Conveyance. Spartanburg Dist. **Simpson Bobo,** for $100 to me paid by **John Bomar,** sold 10 acres on Thickety Creek and said **Bomar;** a part of the **Hugh Moore** tract. Wit: **Jesse Hotes** [or **Holls**], **A.R. Simpson.** Witness oath, 2 Aug 1850: Signed, **A.R. Simpson** to **Wm Guthrie** Mag. Registered October 8th 1851.

p. 429. 20 Oct 1851. Deed of Conveyance. **H.H. Thomson** of Spartanburg Dist, for $500 to me secured to be paid by **Wm Carver** of Spartanburg Dist, sold 112 acres on Peters Creek; bounded on E side of creek and **John D. Cannon.** Wit: **Henry F. Evans, J.W. Tucker.** Signed, **H.H. Thomson.** Witness oath, 8 Oct 1851: Signed, **J.W. Tucker** to **J.B. Tolleson** clk & mag Exoff. Registered Oct. 8th 1851.

p. 430. 9 May 1836. Deed of Gift. **Peyton Simmons** of Spartanburg Dist, with the consent of **James W. Cooper, Jesse Cooper** and **Thomas Cooper,** all of Spartanburg Dist, have sold a Negro boy named **Prince,** said **Prince,** I give and sold to **J.W., Jesse** and **Thomas Cooper** with other Negroes on 26th May 1829; deed is recorded in the office of the Clerk of Court of Common pleas; I do give the proceeds or sale of **Prince** to the **Coopers** forever reserving to myself and my wife the use of said Negro during our lifetime.Test: **H.O. Golightly, Reuben Bowden.** Signed, **Peyton Simmons.** Witness oath, 4 Aug 1851: Signed, **R. Bowden** to **H. White** Mag. Registered Oct 8th 1851.

p. 430-431. 7 May 1838. Deed of Gift. **Peyton Simmons** of Spartanburg Dist, with the consent of **James W. Cooper, Jesse Cooper** and **Thomas Cooper,** all of Spartanburg Dist, have sold a Negro boy named **Prince,** said **Prince,** I give and sold to **J.W., Jesse** and **Thomas Cooper** with other Negroes on 26th May 1829; deed is recorded in the office of the Clerk Court of Common pleas; with the proceeds of **Prince** I have purchased two negroes, **George** about 11 years old and **Caroline** about about 12 years old, and her increase, which Negroes I give to the **Coopers,** forever reserving to myself and my wife the use of said Negros durng our lifetime.Wit: **J.B. Cleveland, Jehu Wells.**

Signed, **Peyton Simmons**. Witness oath, 4 Aug 1851: Signed, **J.B. Cleveland** to **H. White** Mag. Registered Oct 8th 1851.

p. 431-432. 16 Sept 1851. Deed of Conveyance. **Presley Brannon** of Spartanburg Dist, for an equal division of property purchased jointly, for $1 to me paid by **G.W. Royston** of Spartanburg Dist, sold 227 acres on Meadow Creek; bounded by **Harrison** and **Seay**. Wit: **H.F. Evans, J.W. Tucker**. Signed, **Presley Brannon**. Witness oath, 18 Sept 1851: Signed, **H.F. Evans** to **Elias Wall** Mag. Registered October 8th 1851.

p. 432-433. 17 July 1851. Deed of Conveyance. **John T. Kirby** of Spartanburg Dist, for $250 to me paid by **A.J. Daniel** of Spartanburg Dist, sold 5 acres in the Town of Spartanburg; beginning on **J.T. Kirby's** Corner on the Road, runs with the road to a small road, adjoining **Kirby**. Wit: **John N. Murry, Govan Mills**. Signed, **Jno. T. Kirby**. Witness oath, 25 July 1851: Signed, **J.N. Murry** to **J.B. Tolleson** Clk & Mag Ex off. Release of Dower, 25 July 1851: Signed, **P. Kirby [Patsy]** to **J.B. Tolleson,** Clk and Mag. Registered October 8th 1851.

p. 433-434. 8 Jan 1850. Deed of Conveyance. **Wilson Nesbitt** of Cherokee Co., AL, for $5 to me paid by **Robert Scruggs** of Spartanburg Dist, sold (1) 1,000 acres, land granted to **Daniel M'Clarin** 3 Jan 1803; on waters of Suck and Horn Creeks, waters of Broad River including a part of the Cowpens Battleground; bounded NE and NW by **Williams**, NW by __?__ and unknown, SW and W and N by **Bivins** when surveyed, SE by **M'Claren**. (2) 1,000 acres granted to **Daniel M'Claren**, on the waters of Island, Buck & Horn Creeks, including the Cowpens Battle ground by lines running SW by **Abbot's** land, NW by **Cantrel's**, NE and ENW and W by an old survey unknown as date of grant, and SE by **M'Claren** and other sides by **Williams**. Wit: **Wm Walker, J. Fitch Mallory**. Signed, **Wilson Nesbitt**. Witness oath, 4 Aug 1851: **Wm Walker** to **Elias Wall**, Mag. Registered October 8th 1851.

p. 434. 8 May 1848. Deed of Gift. Spartanburg Dist. **Sarah Waters**, now in presence of mind do of my own free will and pleasure, in Consequence of my Special love and esteem towards my youngest son, **Smith Lipscomb** now residing in Alabama, give him the right of a dark, Ball faced mare now owned by me, and purchased out of my own funds, name of the mare not now recollected, the same to be possessed by him at my death. Test: **N.P. Walker, Martha P. Walker**. Signed, **Sarah (x) Waters**. Registered October 8th 1851.

p. 434- 435. 8 May 1848. Deed of Conveyance. **G.W.H. Legg** of Spartanburg Dist, for $100 to me paid by **H.J. Dean** of Spartanburg Dist, sold 5 acres and 4 and a half Tenths acre in the Town of Spartanburg; Beginning on **Dean's** line, adjoining **Wm Walker**; represented by a plat made by **A.J. Camp** on the 30th Nov 1847, and part of a tract I purchased at the sale of real estate of **Richard Thomson**, Decd. Wit: **D.C. Judd, Joseph Foster**. Signed, **Geo. W.H. Legg**. Witness oath, 8 May 1848: Signed, **Joseph Foster** to **O.E. Edwards** N.P. & Mag. Ex Offico. Registered Oct 8th 1851.

p. 436-437. 16 Jan 1850. Deed of Conveyance. **Doct. A.W. Bivings** of Spartanburg Dist, for $85 to me paid or secured to be paid by **J.W. Quinn** of Spartanburg Dist, sold in the Village of

Spartanburg, one half the lot which I bought of **R.D. Owen** adjoining a lot of **B. Wofford**; bounded by the **Wofford** lot on Church Street, running half the distance of the line of the lot which **R.D. Owens** bought of **S. Bobo** and **S. Bobo's** lot. Wit: **Hiram McAbee, J. Belton Tolleson.** Signed, **A.W. Bivings.** Witness oath, 24 March 1851: **J.B. Tolleson** [signatures omitted]. Release of Dower, 11 Nov 1850: **Mrs. Elizabeth Bivings** to **J.B. Tolleson** Clk & Mag.

p. 437-438.   18 April 1844. Deed of Conveyance. **Z.J. Bates** of Spartanburg Dist, for $213 to me paid by **Clerrisca/Clerrica Bates** of Spartanburg Dist, sold 71 acres on the waters of Fair Forest on the N side of the creek; bounded by **Cooper**, [**Crow's**? or Cross the road?], **Barnet** and **Golightly.** Test: **Elizabeth H. Bates, Elvina A. Bates.** Signed, **Z.J. Bates.** Witness oath, 20 Sept 1851: Signed, **Elizabeth H. Bates** to **B.F. Bates** Mag. Ex Officio. Release of Dower, 8 Sept 1844: Signed, **Ibalina (x) Bates** [or **Jbalina**] to **B.F. Bates** Mag. Registered Oct 8th 1851.

p. 438-440.   6 Nov 1840. Sheriff's Titles. By writ of a fieri facias issued to **A.C. Bomar**, Sheriff of Spartanburg Dist, out of the Court of Common pleas, tested 20 November 1839, at the suit of **Thomas P. Brockman**; property of **Solomon Burnett** to be sold to levy $340, damages and costs; sold at public outcry, 130 acres adjoining **Thomas Wood** and others. Sold to **James M. Nesbitt** of Spartanburg Dist, for $290. Wit: **H.J. Dean, J. Tapp.** Signed, **A.C. Bomar.** Witness oath, 2 Sept 1850: **H.J. Dean** to [not filled in]. Release of Dower, 5 Jan 1848: Signed, **Sarah (x) Burnett** to **John Anderson** Magt S.D. Registered October 8th 1851.

p. 440-441.   17 Nov 1849. Sheriff's Titles. By writ of a fieri facias issued to **R.C. Poole**, Sheriff of Spartanburg Dist, out of the Court of Common Pleas, tested 11 March 1848, at the suit of **Jesse Cleveland** for **J.T. Kirby**; property of **J.N. Coventon** to be sold to levy $512.92, with interest, damages and costs; sold at public outcry, 150 acres on the camp for K. of horse Creek, and bounded by lands of **John Coventon** Decd, **Simpson Humphries, Jeremiah Cudd, Jacob Davis** and **George A. Fike.** Sold to **Zibion/Zibeon Cantrell** of Spartanburg Dist, for $100. Wit: **W.F. Covington, Jacob Davis.** Signed, **R.C. Poole.** Witness oath, 6 Oct 1851: Signed, **Jacob Davis** to **A. Bonner** Mag. Registered October 12th 1851.

p. 441.   12 Oct 1851. Deed of Title Claim. **Richard Gramling** of Spartanburg Dist, relinquish to **William Golightly,** all Claim or Title to a parcel of land beginning on a persimmon, where a Black Oak stood called for in my deed, thence about 200 yards in a NW direction to a dogwood, near where a White Oak Called for in my deed is believed to have stood, thence S to the River (S. Pacolett), thence down the river to the beginning. Wit: **John King, John (x) George.** Signed, **J. Richard Gramling.** Witness oath, 11 Sept 1851: Signed, **John (x) George** to **H.J. Dean** N.P.

p. 442.   25 Nov 1850. Deed of Conveyance. **James Selman** of Spartanburg Dist, for $75 to me paid by **James Tapp**, sold 280 acres on the waters of Pacolett River; bounded by **H.J. Dean, W[m] Adkins, H. King** and others. Wit: **Harvy Underwood, Nathan Walden.** Signed, **James Selman.** Witness oath, 13 Oct 1851: Signed, **Harvy Underwood** to **J.B. Tolleson** Clk & Mag Ex off. Registered October 13th 1851.

p. 442-443. 1 Oct 1849. Deed of Relinquishment. Marshal Co., Mississippi. **Edith Clayton,** Surviving wife of **Fielding Clayton** deceased, relinquish to **Mary Miles** if Spartanburg Dist, all my interest to that Tract of land, known as the **Smith** Tract, described in a deed made to **Mary Miles** by a letter of attorney Executed by **Fielding Clayton** to **Z.D. Bragg**, resting in him the authority to sell said land. Test: **Henry Moore, T.H. Smith.** Signed, **Edith (x) Clayton.** Marshal Co, Miss. Signed, **S.B. Clayton** Commissioner of Deed for SC in the State of Miss, certify that **Edith Clayton** Executed the above relinquishment of dower in my presence. 1 Oct 1849. Registered October 13th 1851.

p. 443-444. 2 Feb 1851. Deed of Conveyance. Russell Co., Alabama. **Isaac Adair** [or **Isack Addir**] and **N.B. Adair** his wife, for $196.87 paid to us by **Z.D. Bragg** of Spartanburg Dist; some 19 years ago sold all our interest in 105 acres, it being a part of a tract bequeathed to **E.W.** and **N.B. Farrow** by the late **Samuel Farrow** decd of Spartanburg Dist; bounded by Cedar Shoal Creek on the N, and W by **Z.D. Bragg**, and S by a part of the above bequeathed land. Wit: **R.B. Farrow, C.B. Farrow.** Signed, **Isaac Adair, Nancy B. Adair.** Witness oath, Spartanburg Dist, 7 June 1851: Signed, **R.B. Farrow** to **P.R. Bobo** Magst. The within deed is given now because the one that was previously given **Thomas F. Murphy** and **Isaak Adair** for the same land was found to be illegal. Release of Dower, 3 May 1851, Russell Co., Ala.: Signed, **Nancy B. Adair** to **Henry M. Crowder** J.P. Registered October 13th 1851.

p. 444-446. 28 Dec 1846. Deed. **W.W. Harris, Elizabeth Moss** and **Woodward Allen** and **Harriet Allen** his wife, all of Spartanburg Dist, for $278 to us paid by **Baily Lawson** of Union Dist, SC, sold 139 acres on the waters of [blank] and beginning on a corner formerly belonging to **William Ginnings (Sen)**, and on the W side of Black Stock Road, and runs with the road to **Phillip Oats** line, and lands formerly **John Stevens.** Test: **Hiram Mitchell, T.W. Wingo.** Signed, **W.W. Harris, Elizabeth Moss, Woodard Allen, Harriet Allen.** Witness oath, 12 Jan 1849: Signed, **T.W. Wingo** to **J.B. Tolleson** Clk & Mag Ex Offo. Release of Dower, [4 Jan 1847?, date and signature not recorded] **Elizabeth Harris.** Release of Dower, 4 Jan 1847: Signed, **Harriett Allen** to **J.W. Tucker.** Registered October 13th 1851.

p. 446-447. 5 March 1850. Sheriff's Titles. By writ of fieri Facias issued out of the Court of Common Pleas of Spartanburg Dist, tested 14 Nov 1842, at the suit of **W.G. Clark** and **D.B. Ross** Survivors, **W.G. Clark** Assignee; out of property of **J.Q. Sarratt**, ordered the sheriff to levy $65.09, with interest, damages and costs; Sheriff **R.C. Poole** sold 500 acres where **Samuel Sarratt** lived at the time of his decease; on the waters of Broad River adjoining **John Sarratt, Lasson H. Sarratt** and others. Premises sold at public outcry for $32, to **Wm G. Clark.** Wit: **L.C. Cooper, W.D. Cooper.** Signed, **R.C. Poole** S.S.D. Registered Oct 13th 1851.

p. 447-448. 16 April 1851. Deed of Conveyance. **John T. Kirby** of Spartanburg Dist, for $1,055 to me paid by **Abial Foster** of Spartanburg Dist, sold a 17 acre lot in the Village of Spartanburg, beginning on a street of twenty feet width between **A. Tolleson's** and said lot, cross a small branch, to **Kirby's** fence, and on a street between **H.H. Thomson** and **John T. Kirby.** Wit: **J.C. Caldwell, J.C. Z'nmerman.** Signed, **Jno. Kirby.** Witness oath, 16 April 1851: Signed, **J.C. Caldwell** to **J.B.**

Tolleson Clk & Mag Ex Off. Release of Dower, 25 July 1851: Signed, **P. Kirby** to **J.B. Tolleson** Clk & Mag Ex Off. Registered October 15th 1851.

p. 448-450. 18 Oct 1851. Deed of Conveyance. **James Hogan** of Spartanburg Dist, for $313.75 to me paid by **H.J. Dean** of Spartanburg Dist, sold 152 acres on the W bank of Blue pond Branch and W bank of Ellicks Creek; the land sold by **James Fisher** to **Henry M. Earle** and by **Eale**) to **James Hogan** and where **James Hogan** now lives. Wit: **M. Thompson (x) Hogan, John L. Pearson, James Caldwell.** Signed, **James Hogan.** Witness oath, 18 Oct 1851: Signed, **John L. Pearson** to **James Caldwell** Mag. S.D. Release of Dower, 18 Oct 1851: Signed, **Jane (x) Hogan** to **James Caldwell** Mag S.D. Registered October 18th 1851.

p. 450-451. 2 Nov 1846. Sherriff's Titles. On or about 3 March 1846, [omitted] petitioned the Court of Ordinary at Spartanburg Court house, setting forth that **Burkley Clifton** Departed this life intestate, owing 380 acres on the Enoree River; bounded by **Thomas Garrott, Isaac Lindsey, Mary Wofford, Jas. W. Durham, Garner Vaughn** and **M. Hastings;** prayed that division might be done; **Reuben Bowden,** Esq, Ordinary of Spartanburg Dist, ordered the land sold by the Sheriff in the 1st Monday in October; Sheriff **R.C. Poole,** on 5 Oct 1846, by public outcry, sold 133 acres to **R.S. Wright** for $200. Wit: **Hiram Bennett, James Brewton.** Signed, **R.C. Poole** S.S.D. Witness oath, 2 Sept 1850: Signed, **James Brewton** to **J.B. Tolleson** Clk & Mg Ex offo. Registered Oct 18th 1851.

p. 451-454. 20 May 1851. Deed of Conveyance. **James McMakin** and **Mary R. McMakin** of Spartanburg Dist, for $1,000 to us paid by **Mary Smith** of Charleston, SC, and to Survivor, and the Executor or administrator of the Survivor, for the purposes hereinafter expressed, sold 40 acres on Branches of the South fork of Tyger River and on the N side of the road leading to **David W. Moore's** factory; a part of Lot № 8; a plat more fully explains; In trust for the Sole and separate use and benefit of **Jennette Powell,** Wife of **Dr. J.B. Powell,** during her life free from the Control of her present or any future husband; if **Jennette Powell** does not occupy the land, to rent it out and pay over to **Jennette** for her sole use and benefit. At **Jennette's** death the property to be divided amongst her children. Wit: **Leroy Burnes, John Odam.** Signed, **James McMakin, Mary R. McMakin.** Witness oath, 20 Sept 1851: Signed, **Leroy Burns** to **B.F. Montgomery** M.S.D. Consent to act as Trustee, 20 July 1851: Signed, **Mary Smith** to **Ephraim Suber.** Release of Dower, Greenville Dist, 7 Aug 1851: Signed, **Mary R. McMakin** to **R.P. Goodlett** M.G.D. Registered October 21st 1851.

p. 454. 21 July 1831. Deed of Conveyance, Spartanburg Dist. **James Fisher Sen.** for $250 to me paid by **Henry M. Earle,** sold 200 acres on South Pacolet and Ellicks Creek and Blue pond Branch. Wit: **John J. Dodd, James Woodruff.** Signed, **James (x) Fisher.** Witness oath, 2 Jan 1832: Signed, **John J. Dodd** to ?.?. **Clement,** J.Q.

p. 455-456. 17 Oct 1851. Deed of Conveyance. **David Oshiels** of Spartanburg Dist, for $1,169 to me paid by **Andrew Pettit** of Spartanburg Dist, 334 acres beginning near the branch on **Ralph Williams** line; bounded by **John Williams, G.A. Smith, T. Shands,** a part of the tract where I, **David Oshiels,** now lives. Wit: **James Harrison, Young Osheals.** Signed, **David (x) Osheals.** Witness oath, 17 Oct 1851: Signed, **James Harrison** to **H. Wofford** Magst. Release of Dower, 25

October 1851: Signed, **Nancy (x) Oshields** to **Harvy Wofford** Magst. Registered October 21st 1851.

p. 456-457. 5 Nov 1851. Deed of Conveyance. **H.H. Thomson** of Spartanburg Dist, for $150 to me secured to be paid by **J. Henry Turner** of Spartanburg Dist, sold a 1½ acre lot on the W side of Tanyard Branch known as Lot Nº 13 in the **Poole** survey certified by **George Nichols.** Beginning on the N side of Greenville road on the lot I sold to **Haden Poole**; reserving a Street of thirty three feet on the line of **Bomar** and **Fry** whenever it may be laid out from the Greenville road, out by **Tucker's** lot at the Tan yard branch. Wit: **P.M. Wallace, H.F. Evans.** Signed, **H.H. Thomson.** Witness oath, 6 Nov 1851: Signed, **H.F. Evans** to **J.B. Tolleson** Clk & Mag Ex offo. Registered November 6th 1851.

p. 457-458. 26 Dec 1850. Apprenticeship. Spartanburg Dist. **John Miller Kirby** (age 13 years the 12th August last) hath put himself, with the consent and approbation of his mother, **Sarah Read,** doth voluntarily and his own free will and accord put himself apprentice unto **John Gossett Sen.**, to live and work with him int farm and do all other reasonable Business or employment that **John Gossett** may require until he becomes age 21 during which term the apprentice shall faithfully serve **John Gossett** and obey all lawful and reasonable commands. **John Gossett** obligates and binds himself to take good and faithful care of **John Miller Kirby**, and learn him and instruct him in farming, to furnish him with good holesome food and Clothing during apprenticeship, and further obligates himself to give one years Schooling and at the end of his apprenticeship to give **John Miller Kirby** a horse, Saddle and Bridle to be valued at $50; also to give him a good suit of clothes. Wit: **G.W.H. Legg**, Magistrate. Signed, **John Miller (x) Kirby, John (x) Gossett, Sarah (x) Read.** Witness oath, 6 Nov 1851: Signed, **G.W.H. Legg** to **J.B. Tolleson** Clk Mag Exoffo.

p. 458-459. 3 Nov 1851. Apprenticeship. Spartanburg Dist. **Marcus Turner** hath put himself and with the consent and approbation of **Nancy Turner** his mother doth voluntarily and of his own free will and accord put himself apprentice unto **James Fowler**, to learn his art Trade, and mystery of a Carriage maker and repairer, and after the manner of all Apprentice to serve **James Fowler** from this date and until he arrives at the age of 21 years, during which term the apprentice, his said Master shall faithfully serve, his secrets kept, his lawful commands every where obey, He shall do no damage to his master nor see it done by others without giving notice thereof to said master, shall not waste his goods, nor lend them unlawfully to other, nor contract matrimony within the term; at cards, dice nor any unlawful game he shall not play whereby his master may have damage. With his own goods nor the goods of others, without license from his master, Shall neither buy nor sell; he shall not absent himself day nor night from his said master's Service without his leave, nor haunt ale houses, Taverns or play houses, but in all things behave himself as a faithful apprentice ought to do during the said Term.   And **James Fowler** the Master shall use the utmost of his endeavours to Teach or cause to be taught or instruct the apprentice in the art of trade and mystery of Carriage maker and repairer, and procure and provide for him sufficient meat, drink, clothing, lodging and washing fitting for an apprentice, during the Term of his minority. And shall teach or cause to be taught the apprentice, the rudiments of a clear English Education; when the apprentice comes to full age, **James Fowler** shall give him a good and comfortable [set] of clothes and also pay him $25 in cash. Wit: **Geo. W.H. Legg**. Magistrate. Signed, **Marcus M. (x) Turner, Nancy T. (x) Turner, Jas. A. Fowler.** Witness oath, 5 Nov 1851: Signed, **G.W.H. Legg** to **J.B. Tolleson** Clk & Mag.

p. 459. 1 Nov 1851. Relinquishment of Dower. **Elizabeth Cannon**, wife of **James Cannon** to **John Linder.** Signed, **Elizabeth (x) Cannon** to **A. Bonner** Mag. Registered Nov 6th 1851.

p. 460-461. 18 Oct 1851. Deed of Conveyance. **James B. Glazier** of Spartanburg Dist, $268 to me paid by **John B. Archer** of Spartanburg Dist, sold 88 acres where I now live; on Rocky Branch, waters of Shoaly Creek, Boiling Springs Road and saw mill Road. Wit: **J.W. Wood, J.B. Tolleson.** Signed, **J.B. Glazier.** Witness oath, 6 Nov 1851: Signed, **J.W. Wood** to **J.B. Tolleson** Clk & Mag Ex offo. Release of Dower, 20 Oct 1851: Signed, **Mary E. (x) Glazier** to **J.B. Tolleson** Clk & Mag Ex offo. Registered Nov 6th 1851.

p. 461-462. 8 Nov 1851. Mortgage. **Robert White** bought from **Jacob Zimmerman** two adjoining tracts in Spartanburg District near the Cedar Springs. **Robert White** gave **Jacob Zimmerman** four sealed notes of $155 each, due one, two, three and four years from date with interest, total $620. For better securing payment of the notes, **White** conveys the land to **Zimmerman,** but null and void if payment is made. (1) 120 acres, bounded by the road; (2) the balance of the **Thomas Smith** tract of about 3 acres. Wit: **J.W. Tucker, Col. H.H. Thomson.** Signed, **Robert White.** Witness oath, 8 Nov 1851: Signed, **H.H. Thomson** to **J.B. Tolleson** Clk & Mag Ex offo.

p. 463-464. 8 Nov 1851. Deed of Conveyance. **Robert E. Cleveland** of Town of Spartanburg, for $462 to me paid by **James Dillard** of Spartanburg Dist, sold 132 acres bounded by **Bryant, Hix(?)** and **Golightly;** on the waters of Peters Creek, conveyed by deed dated 5 July 1851, to **Cleveland** by **John Golightly.** Wit: **A.W. Bivings, J.M. Dean.** Signed, **R.E. Cleveland.** Witness oath, 8 Nov 1851: Signed, **A.W. Bivings** to **Jefferson Choice** N.P. & Ex offo Mag. Release of Dower, 8 Nov 1851: Signed, **Elizabeth Cleveland** [**Elizabeth C. Cleveland** in magistrate's statement] to **Jefferson Choice** N.P & Mag. Registered November 8th 1851.

p. 464-465. 10 Nov 1851. Deed of Conveyance. **E.C. Lietner** of Spartanburg Dist, for $220 to me paid by **John T. Kirby** of Spartanburg Dist, sold 120 acres bounded by the Estate of **Richard Thomson, Thomas Wells** and others. Wit: **J.R. Poole, J.W. Wood.** Signed, **E.C. Lietner.** Witness oath, 10 Nov 1851: Signed, **J.W. Wood** to **J.B. Tolleson** Clk & Mag. Registered Nov 10th 1851.

p. 465-466. 10 Nov 1851. Deed of Conveyance. **J.T. Kirby** of Spartanburg Dist, for $220 to me paid by **E.C. Lietner** of Spartanburg Dist, sold (by virtue of power vested in me by **Frederick Harley,** as his mortgagee bearing date of record the 24th Nov 1843. See Book Y, page 313-314) 120 acres bounded by the Estate of **Richard Thomson, Thos. Wells,** and others. [Same description as the deed above, Lietner to Kirby]. Wit: **J.W. Wood, J.R. Poole.** Signed, **J.T. Kirby.** Witness oath, 10 Nov 1851: Signed, **J.W. Wood** to **J.B. Tolleson** Clk & Mag Ex offo. Registered Nov 10th 1851.

p. 466-467. 7 Nov 1851. Deed of Conveyance. **Wm D. McMakin** of Spartanburg Dist, for $300 to me paid by **Jacob Zimmerman** of Spartanburg Dist, sold 158 acres known as the **Kendrick** Tract; bounded by **Dantzler, John Poole, H. Rush(?)** and **Bowens Griffin.** Wit: **J.B. Cleveland, J.W. Webber.** Signed, **W.D. McMakin.** Witness oath, 8 Nov 1851: Signed, **J.W. Webber** to **J.B. Tolleson** Clk & Mag Ex offo. Registered Nov 10th 1851.

p. 467-468. 8 Nov 1851. Deed of Conveyance. **Jacob Zimmerman** of Spartanburg Dist, for $720 to me paid by **Robert White** of Spartanburg Dist, sold (1) 120 acres near Cedar Springs bounded by **Simmons** and a road; refer to a plat made by **W.W. Harris** on 8th Aug 1849, attached; (2) also the balance, about 3 acres, of the **Thomas Smith** tract which I have not sold, known as the Black Smith shop place formerly owned by **Thomas Smith** on the road leading from Cedar Springs to **Bivingsville.** Wit: **J.W. Tucker, H.H. Thomson.** Signed, **Jacob Zimmerman.** Release of Dower, 11 Nov 1851: Signed, **Mary Ann Zimmerman** to **J.B. Tolleson** Clk & Mag Ex offo. Registered November 10th 1851.

p. 468-469.   14 Nov 1843. Spartanburg Dist. **John Linder,** for $700 to me paid by **James A. MaKamson,** sold 271 acres on Thickety Creek; bounded by **Price, Smith, Clark,** a branch and Thickety Creek. Test: **David MaComson, John Oglesby.** Signed, **John Linder.** Witness oath, 1 Jan 1844: Signed, **David Macomson** to **H.G. Gaffney,** Mag. Release of Dower, 6 Oct 1851: Signed, **Louisa Linder** to **A. Bonner** Mag.   Registered November 10th 1851. In lower right hand corner: Taken out paid $1.00.

p. 469-471. 7 Sept 1847. Deed of Conveyance. **Henry Murph** of Spartanburg Dist, $1,500 to me paid by **Joel Ballenger** of Spartanburg Dist, sold 350 acres where **Ballenger** now lives, on Fairforest and Kelsoes Creek; beginning on a stone marked C.J., now **David Whetstone** corner, bounded by **Whetstone, Isaac Smith, Jno. Cook,** crosses the road not far from a branch which heads on Stony Nap, the edge of the longrounds, **David Golightly,** N bank of Fairforest where **Wm Smith's** original grant crosses the creek, **John Thomas,** S side Kelsoes Creek, **John Murph** and Thomsons Branch; a part of three tracts: One granted to **William Smith** originally, one to **Peter Smith,** and the third to **Giles Conel** and was conveyed to **Jane Smith,** now dead(?), by certain commissioners as her Dower in the Land Estate of **James Smith** Deceased. N.B. Before assigned 60 feet square including the Grave yard is excluded. Wit: **H. White, B.B. Foster, J. Zimmerman.** Signed, **Henry Murph.** Release of Dower, 7 Sept 1847: Signed, **Ann Murph** to **H.White.** Witness oath, 7 Sept 1847: Signed, **B.B. Foster** to **H. White** Mag. Registered Nov 10th 1851.

p. 471-472.   15 Nov 1851. Deed of Conveyance. **J.W.V. Hunt** of Spartanburg Dist, for $66.36 to me paid by **James Nesbitt** of Spartanburg Dist, sold all my interest (being one half) in 116 ares on Beaver dam Creek, the land willed by **R.M. Daniel** to my brother **Robert G. Hunt** and myself; bounded by lands of **John Bomar** and **James Nesbitt.** Wit: **J.B. Tolleson, William Hunt.** Signed **J.W.V. Hunt.** Witness oath, 15 Nov 1851: Signed, **W. Hunt** to **J.V. Trimmier** N.P. & Magistrate Ex officio. Registered November 16th 1851.

p. 472-473.   31 Oct 1851. Deed of Conveyance. **Alfred Tolleson** of Spartanburg Dist, for $1,510 to me paid by **Reuben Briant Jun.** of Spartanburg Dist, sold 436 acres on both sides of the road leading from Spartanburg to Union called the **Tolleson** old place; bounded by **Quinn** on the E, on South by **A. Mitchel** and **James Quinn,** on the South by **Cummins** and **Gazaway, Briant** on the W, by **Sprink(?)** on the N and by said **Reuben Briant** on the E. On a branch which is the dividing line betwixt **R. Briant** and **W.G. Briant.** Wit: **H.M. Kirby, R.C. Quinn.** Signed, **Alfred Tolleson.** Witness oath, 17 Nov 1851: Signed, **R.C. Quinn** to **J.B. Tolleson** Clk & Mag Ex offo. Release of

Dower, 13 Nov 1851: Signed, **Margaret Tolleson** to **J.B. Tolleson** Clk & Mag Ex offo.

p. 474-475. 31 Oct 1851. Deed of Conveyance. **Alfred Tolleson** of Spartanburg Dist, for $1,265 to me paid by **Wm G. Briant** of Spartanburg Dist, sold 375 acres on both sides of the main road to Spartanburg C.H.; bounded by **Cummings, Hammett, Whitbey(?)**, a branch to the fork of the branch and **Tolleson**'s spring branch. Wit: **H.M. Kirby, R.C. Quinn**. Signed, **Alfred Tolleson**. Witness oath, 17 Nov 1851: Signed, **R.C. Quinn**. Release of Dower, 13 Nov 1851: Signed, **Margaret Tolleson** to **J.B. Tolleson** Clk & Mag Ex offo. Registered November 16th 1851.

p. 475-476. 31 Oct 1851. Deed of Conveyance. **Wm G. Briant** of Spartanburg Dist, for $300 to me paid by **Alfred Tolleson** of Spartanburg Dist, sold two tracts purchased of **James D.? Briant** and **Terril Briant** containing 115 acres; the two tracts adjoining. The piece purchased from **James R. Briant** on Peters Creek, bound by **Thomson, James Dillard, Barnett**, the tract purchased of **Terril Briant** and near the main road. Wit: **H.M. Kirby, R.C. Quinn**. Signed, **W.G. Briant**. Witness oath, 17 Nov 1851: Signed, **R.C. Quinn** to **J.B. Tolleson** Clk & Mag Ex offo. Registered November 17th 1851.

p. 476-477. 3 Oct 1851. Deed of Conveyance. **William S. Morgan** of Spartanburg Dist, for $1,000 to me paid by **David Osheals** and **Young Osheals** of Spartanburg Dist, sold 237 acres where I now live; in Spartanburg and Greenville Districts on Jimmersons Mill Creek, waters of South Pacolet River; bound by the Greenville line, **Elias Dill** on the S, **Lewis Edwards** on the E, and **Campbell** and **Long** on the W. Wit: **R. Bowden, J.B. Tolleson**. Signed, **W.S. Morgan**. Witness oath, 17 Nov 1851: Signed, **R. Bowden** to **J.B. Tolleson** Clk & Mag Ex offo. Release of Dower, 6 Oct 1851: Signed, **Sintha (x) Morgan** [**Cintha** in Magistrate's statement]. Registered Nov 17th 1851.

p. 477-478. 23 Oct 1851. Deed of Conveyance. **R.C. Poole** and **Absalom Poole**, two of the Executors of the Will of **John Poole** Decd, of Spartanburg Dist, for $453 to us paid by **John M. Poole** of Spartanburg Dist, sold 124 acres on Lossons Fork known as lot N° 3, part of the real estate of **John Poole** Decd; bounded by lots N° 1 and 2 and S and N sides of Lossons Fork. Wit: **A.J.W. Land, John McKeough**. Signed, **R.C. Poole, A.N. Poole**, Executors. Witness oath, 24 Oct 1851: Signed, **A.J.W. Land** to **R. Bowden** Ordinary & Ex off mag. Registered November 17th 1851.

p. 479-480. 23 Oct 1851. Deed of Conveyance. **John M. Poole** and **Alexander N. Poole**, Executors of the Will of **John Poole** Decd, of Spartanburg Dist, for $1,501 to us paid by **R.C. Poole** of Spartanburg Dist, sold 74 acres on Pacolet River, whereon the Pacolet Springs is situated; Lot N° 1 of the Real Estate of **John Poole** Decd; bounded by Lots N° 2 and 3, **Mildred Patterson**, estate of **Edward Patterson** Decd, **Israel Willis** and one corner of **Wiley Willis's** land. Wit: **A.J.W. Land, John McKeough**. Witness oath, 24 Oct 1851: Signed, **A.J.W. Land** to **R. Bowden**, Ordinary Exoff Mag. Registered November 17th 1851.

p. 480-481. 23 Oct 1851. Deed of Conveyance. **R.C. Poole** and **John M. Poole**, two of the executors of the Will of **John Poole** Decd, of Spartanburg Dist, for $581 to us paid by **Absalom N. Poole** of Spartanburg Dist, sold 144 acres on Pacolet River, sold as Lot N° 2, part of the real estate of **John Poole** Decd; bounded by Lots Nº 1 and 3, S side of Pacolet River, and crossing the river above the Island and down the meanders of the river below the Island. Wit: **A.J.W. Land, John McKeough.** Signed, **R.C. Poole, John M. Poole**, Executors. Witness oath, 24 Oct 1851: Signed, **A.J.W. Land** to **R. Bowden**, Ordinary, Exoff Mag.   Registered Nov 17ᵗʰ 1851.

p. 481-482.   23 Oct 1851. Mortgage on Real Estate. **R.C. Poole** is liable to pay by two promissory notes to **John M. Poole** and **Absalom N. Poole** Executors of the Will of **John Poole** Decd, one note due to **Absalom N. Poole** $628.22 on 23 Oct 1852, the first annual payment on the notes of which $399.83 is due to the widow **Polly Poole,** and $228.39 is due to the legatees; and also the same sum of $628.22 for the second and last annual installment payable 23ʳᵈ Oct 1853 with interest, divided between the widow and legatees as in the 1ˢᵗ installment. The notes given for the balance of the purchase money for the 74 acres on Pacolet River whereon is situated the Pacolet Springs, sold as Lot Nº 1.Wit: **A.J.W. Land, John McKeough.** Signed **R.C. Poole.** Witness oath, 24 Oct 1851: Signed, **A.J.W. Land** to **R. Bowden**, Ordinary, Ex off Mag.

p. 483-484.   15 Feb 1844. Deed of Conveyance. **Thomas L. Bulow** of Charleston, SC, for $500 to me paid by **Nathaniel Gist** of Union Dist, SC, sold 2,690 acres in the Dist of Spartanburg on Branches of Broad and Pacolet Rivers, part of the tract originally granted to **James Steadman;** bounded by Sulphur Branch of Suck Creek, represented as plat A by a survey made by **Richard Thomson** 13 Oct 1839. Wit: **William Moore, Alexander Brown.** Signed, **Thomas L. Bulow.** Witness oath, 16 May 1844: Signed, **Wᵐ Moore** to **Stephen Kirby** Mag. Registered November 17ᵗʰ 1851.

p. 484-485.   8 Nov 1851. Deed of Conveyance. By the will of **David Dantzler** decd, he directed his lands &c. to be sold to the highest bidder. The undersigned had administered his estate with the will annexed. **Simpson Bobo,** by the authority given him by the will, and permission of the Ordinary of Spartanburg Dist, for $500 to me paid by **Wᵐ McMakin** of Spartanburg Dist, sold 342 acres on a branch of North Tyger River known as the **Spuer(?)** place; bounded by lands of **John Booker, Robert Gaines** and others represented by a plat by **James K. Dickson** 4ᵗʰ Sept 1847. Wit: **Landon Huett, David W. Moore.** Signed, **Simpson Bobo** Admr, Testament annexed of **D. Dantzler.** Witness oath, 17 Nov 1851: Signed, **David W. Moore** to **J.B. Tolleson** Clk & Mag Ex offo. Registered November 17ᵗʰ 1851.

p. 485-486.   4 Nov 1851. Deed of Conveyance. **L.M. Demcey** of Spartanburg Dist, for $106 to me paid by **J. Bankston Davis** of Spartanburg Dist, sold 150 acres on Branches of Alexanders Creek, waters of South Pacolet River; bounded by a road and S side of a little branch. Wit: **C.C. Lancaster, J.L. Pearson.** Signed, **L.M. (x) Demcey.** Witness oath, 13 Nov 1851: Signed, **C.C. Lancaster.** Release of Dower, 13 Nov 1851: Signed, **Jane (x) Demcey** to **James Caldwell** Mag. S.D. Registered Nov 17ᵗʰ 1851.

p. 486-487.   20 Oct 1851. Mortgage. **Wᵐ Carver** gave **H.H. Thomson** five notes of $100 each, payable annually, commencing on 25 Dec 1852, receiving interest from 25 Dec 1851, for land [acres not given] bought this day from **Thomson**. For better securing the payments, **Wᵐ Carver** deeds

H.H. Thomson the same land on Peters Creek which **Thomson** bought from **John L. Patterson,** reference Deed made by **Patterson** to **H.H. Thomson.** Wit: **Henry F. Evans, J.W. Tucker.** Signed, **Wm Carver.** Witness oath, 20 Nov 1851: Signed, **J. Wofford Tucker** to **J.B. Tolleson** Clk & Mag Ex offo. Register office 17 Nov 1851.

p. 488.   30 March 1851. Deed of Conveyance. **H.H. Thomson** of Spartanburg Dist, for $225 Secured to be paid by **Zachariah Cannon** of Spartanburg Dist, sold about 2 acres in the town of Spartanburg; Beginning on the W side of Greenville Street at the S corner of a cross street which is thirty feet wide, running with said street SW to a back street to **Dye's** corner, 15 feet reserved inside this line for a street, and I give 20 feet outside the line for the street. Wit: **Jesse M. Cannon, J.W. Tucker.** Signed, **H.H. Thomson.** Witness oath, 20 Nov 1851: Signed, **J.W. Tucker** to **J.B. Tolleson** Clk & Mag Ex offo.   Register office the 20 Nov 1851.

p. 489-490.   27 Nov 1850. Deed of Conveyance. **Felix W. Hill** of Greenville Dist, for $250 to me paid by **Julian Amanda Johnson** of Spartanburg Dist, sold 100 acres on the waters of Mottys [or Motlys or Mollys] creek; Beginning on a branch of Mollys creek where **Morris Loftis** line crosses the branch, on another branch and meandering of an old mill race and on old Blackstock road. Wit: **David Rudisel, Andrew A. Rudisel.** Signed, **F.W. Hill.** Witness oath, 4 Dec 1851: Signed, **David Rudisail** to **James Caldwell** Mag. S.D. Release of Dower, 7 Dec 1850: Signed, **Elizabeth Hill** to **James Caldwell** Mag S.D. Registered the 20 November 1851.

p. 490-491.   18 Nov 1851. Mortgage. **N.H. Waldrip,** in consideration that **S.B. Woodruff** has gone my security on two notes, one made payable to **William Hunter** of Laurence Dist, for $1,000, given 7 Nov 1850; the other payable to **Jordan Poole** of Greenville Dist, for $425, due 25 Dec 1851, given 12 Sept in the same year; and to secure a note of $419, which I owe to him myself given on 18 Nov 1851, all drawing interest; **Waldrip** deeds to **S.B. Woodruff,** 168 acres in the Dist of Spartanburgh on the waters of James Creek bounded by **A.P. Bobo, S.W. Tucker, J.S. Rogers,** and others; also 8 head of cattle, twenty head of hogs, 400 bushels of corn, 4,000 pounds of fodder, one bureau, one cupboard, two fether Beds, three bedstids, four tables, two pens of shucks & farming tools of all Kinds. It is agreed that **Woodruff** may sell perishable property to best advantage. Deed to be of no effect if **Waldrip** pays the debt. Wit: **J.B. Desheals, Wm A. Young.** Witness oath, 21 Nov 1851: Signed, **Wm A. Young** to **John H. Walker** Magistrate. Registered 21 Nov 1851.

p. 492.   23 Nov 1836. Deed of Conveyance. **Fielden Turner** of Spartanburg Dist, for $400 paid to him by **Carter Burnett Se^r,** sold 121 acres, a part of a tract granted to **Isaac Landsdale.** Attest: **Spencer Eaves, Carter Burnett Jun.** Signed, **Fielden Turner.** Witness oath, 22 Sept 1851: Signed, **C. Burnett** to **Joel Cannon** Mag.   Registered the 1 December 1851.

p. 493-494.   6 April 1850. Deed of Gift. **Carter Burnett** of Spartanburg Dist, for love and affection I bear to my son **John Burnett,** and that he agrees to discount $259.25 out of his distributive share of my real and personal estate at my Decease, sold 46 acres on the S side of Pacolet River; bounded by **Zachariah Cannon, George A. Fike** and others as a plat made out by **John Epting** D.S. will more fully describe; plat annexed to this deed. Wit: **John Epting, James A. Epting.** Signed, **Carter**

Burnett. Witness oath, 1 Dec 1851: Signed, **John Epton** to **J.B. Tolleson** Clk & Mag Ex offo. Release of Dower, 22 Sept 1851: Signed, **Jane (x) Burnett** to **Joel Cannon** Mag. Registered Dec 1st 1851. Original delivered to ~~ **G.A. Fike** 23 Nov 1855.

p. 494-495. 5 Nov 1851. Deed of Conveyance. The President and Directors of the Bank of the State of South Carolina for $216 to us paid by **Allison Clary** and **Lee Linder** of Spartanburg Dist, sold 72 acres, a part of a tract conveyed to the President and Directors by **R.C. Poole**, Sheriff of Spartanburg Dist, by deed dated 14th October 1847; on Prices Creek and bounded on the S by **Lee Linder,** on the W by Lands of the South Carolina Manufacturing Company, N claimed by **Allison Clary,** on E by **Lee Linder,** and is divided from the land claimed by **A. Clary** and a line drawn from a corner of lands formerly of the Estate of **Woods;** annexed is a plat by **P.Q. Camp** Deputy Surveyor. Wit: **Fisher Gardney** [or **Gadsden**], **C.S. Cogdell.** Witness oath, 7 Nov 1851: Signed, **C.S. Cogdell** to **Jno. D. Alexander** N.P. Registered December 1st 1851.

p. 495-497. 5 Nov 1851. Spartanburg Dist. Mortgage. **J. Henry Turner** has this day purchased of **H.H. Thomson**, a 1½ acre lot in the Town of Spartanburg, known as Lot N° 13 in a plat made for **Poole** and certified by **Geo. Nichols; Turner** gave **Thomson** three notes for $50 each due One, Two and Three years from date, with interest. For better security of payment of the notes **Turner** deeds the land to **Thomson;** deed is void if **Turner** pays the notes; reference to the deed **Thomson** this day gave me. Wit: **Dr. P.M. Wallace, H.F. Evans.** Signed, **J. Henry Turner.** Witness oath, 20 Nov 1851: Signed, **P.M. Wallace** to **J.B. Tolleson** Clk & Mag Ex off.

p. 497-498. 20 Nov 1847. Deed of Relinquishment. **Elizabeth Tippins** [or **Tippens**] of Anderson Dist, SC, this day released unto **David Tippins Jun.**, all my claim to two tracts in Spartanburg Dist; (1) known as the **McClain** [or **W.C. Clain**] tract; (2) where **William Tippens** formerly lived, on both sides of Abners Creek joining lands of **William Hendrix, Bennett Wilson** and others. Wit: **M.L. McCay, John Tippens.** Signed, **Elizabeth (x) Tippins.** Witness oath, 31 Dec 1851: Signed, **John Tippins** to **Mark Bennett**, Magt. Registered Dec 31st 1851.

p. 498-499. 8 Sept 1851. Deed of Conveyance. **Josiah Kilgore** for $75 to me paid by **David Tippens**, sold to **David Tippens** (son of **Benjamin**) all the right, title, interest and Estate which **David Tippens** (son of **William** Decd) had in 350 acres **William Tippens** Decd, owned on Abners Creek of Enoree; bounded by **Bennett Wilson** and others. The unclaimed Estate which said **David Tippens** had in said land conveyed to me by **A.C. Bomar**, Sheriff of Spartanburg Dist, 4th Sept 1839. Wit: **J.C. Kilgore, J.W.C. Mayfield.** Signed, **Josiah Kilgore.** Witness oath, 4 Oct 1851: Signed, **J.W.C. Mayfield** to **Mark Bennett** Magst. Registered Decr. 31st 1851.

p. 499-500. 18 Nov 1848. Deed of Conveyance. **John Tippens** of Spartanburg Dist, for $75 to me paid by **David** and **Pleasant Tippens** of Spartanburg Dist, sold one Sixth part of two tracts; (1) 202 acres formerly owed by **William Tippens** where he lived on Abners Creek; (2) 122½ acres being the **McClain** tract adjoining the other and once owned by **William Tippens** Decd; Bounded by **B. Wilson, Drummond, Hendrix** and others; one sixth share being the share of **Benjamin Tippens** that he conveyed to **Thomas P. Brockman.** Wit: **A.L. Sheppard, Tho. P. Brockman.** Signed, **John**

Tippens. Witness oath, Greenville Dist, 8 Nov 1851: Signed, **Tho. P. Brockman** to **Josiah Kilgore** M.G.D. Registered Decr 31st 1851.

p. 500-501. 9 Aug 1850. Deed of Conveyance. **Willis Lanford,** of Benton Co., Ala., for $300 to me paid by **Richard S. Woodruff** of Spartanburg Dist, sold 90 acres on the Branches of Buffalow Creek, waters of the Enoree River; bounded by a road, **Dean,** a corner formerly **Lewis Lanfords, Richard S. Woodruff,** the road to **Dickies** bridge and **Terry.** Wit: **P. Mason, James Mason.** Signed, **Willis Lanford.** Witness oath, 9 Aug 1850: Signed. **James Mason** to **Z. Lanford** Magst. Release of Dower, Benton Co., Ala., 3 Oct 1850: Signed, **Gincy (x) Lanford** to **Aaron D. Wilkins** J.P. Registered Decr 31st 1851.

p. 501-502. 24 July 1847. Deed of Conveyance. **R.W. Foster** and **Excey Foster** of Spartanburg Dist, for $300 to us paid by **James Nesbitt** of Spartanburg Dist, sold 225 acres on waters of Fairforest Creek; bounded by **Walden, Moses Foster.** Wit: **Silas Brewton, Elisha Ginnings.** Signed, **Excey Foster, R.W. Foster.** Witness oath, 30 Dec 1851: Signed, **Silas Brewton** to **Jonas Brewton** Mag. Release of Dower, 5 Jan 1851: Signed, **Elizabeth A. Foster** to **Jonas Brewton.** Registered December 31st 1851.

p. 502-504. 25 Oct 1851. Deed of Conveyance. **H.W.** [or **William H.**] **Burnett** of Spartanburg Dist, for $950 to me paid by **Alfred Dean** of Spartanburg Dist, sold 245 acres adjoining **H. Bennett, Garrison Green, T.P. Brockman,** &c. Wit: **James A. Anderson, W.R. Burnett.** Signed, **H.W. Burnett.** Witness oath, 25 Oct 1851: Signed, **James A. Anderson** to **Mark Bennett** Mag. Release of Dower, 25 Oct 1851: Signed, **Pernecy Burnett** to **Mark Bennett** mag. Registered January 1st 1852.

p. 504-505. 11 Jan 1849. Deed of Conveyance. **John Heatherington Senr.** of Spartanburg Dist, for the love and affection I bear to **Elias Johnson,** gave 128½ acres on the waters of Buck Creek; Beginning at the head of the old branch, bounded by **McElway** and **Elison.** Wit: **John Heatherington Junr., Jeremiah Giles.** Signed, **John Heatherington Sen.** Witness oath, 10 Nov 1851: Signed, **John Heatherington Jun.** to **P.N. Head** Mag. Registered January 1st 1852.

p. 505-506. 28 Jan 1818. Deed of Conveyance. **William Turpin,** merchant of Charleston, SC, for $150 to me paid by **Benjamin Greer,** sold all that tract of land by the original survey on Abners Creek in the District of Ninety Six containing 252 acres; Bounded NW on **David Qualls** land and on SE by **John Redman;** plat of the original grant annexed; surveyed for **William Wilson** on 11th April 1785; granted to **Augustus Mernik** on 5th Feb 1781. Recorded [blank] office Book R.R.R.R. page 171; by **Augustus Mirreck** Conveyed to **Wadsworth** and **Turpin** on the 24th March 1787; Recorded public Registers Office Book Z, no 5, page 25 to 28, and a quit claim deed from **Wadsworth** to **Turpin,** Recorded in Clerks office Laurens County, Book F, page 272, on 17th Feb 1798. Witness and signed at Charleston 28 Jan 1818: Wit: **David T. Cureton.** Signed, **William Turpin.** No date: Received of **Benjamin Greer** $150, and $9.50 in full for 11 months Interest on the same. Wit: **David T. Cureton, Joseph Greer.** Signed, **Will Turpin.** Witness oath, Laurens Dist, 22 Sept 1827: Signed, **Joseph Greer** to **Thomas Owens** J.P. Registered Jan 1st 1852.

p. 506-507.   1 Nov 1839. Deed of Conveyance. **Daniel J. Barnett** of Spartanburg Dist, for $750 paid by **Benjamin Greer** of Spartanburg Dist, sold 204 acres on the waters of Rocky field Creek, waters of Enoree River, where **Barnett** now lives; bounded by a branch, **John Glenn, B. Greer** and **W. Mayfield.** Wit: **James McClain, Tho. P. Brockman.** Signed, **D.J. Barnett.** Witness oath, 1 Nov 1839: Signed, **Tho. P. Brockman** to **J.W. Bradley,** J.Q.   Registered January 1st 1852.

p. 507-508.   23 Aug 1851. Deed of Conveyance. **John M. Hall** of Spartanburg Village, for $1,600 to me paid by **John Brown** of Spartanburg Dist, sold 223 acres on the waters of Lawsons fork Creek, known as part of the tract where **Ebal Williams** lived at the time of his death; bounded by lands now belonging to said **John Brown, Jefferson Bishop, Seynthia Lancaster** and **Bivings** and **Bennett;** the place now known as the **Polly Wood** plantation, and now occupied and cultivated by **John Fowler** as my tenant. Wit: **Wm C. Camp, A.A. James.** Signed, **John M. Hall.** Witness oath, 30 Dec 1851: Signed, **Wm C. Camp** to **J.B. Tolleson** Clk & Mag Ex offo. Registered January 1st 1852.

p. 508-510.   5 Jan 1852. Mortgage. On 3 Dec 1851, **William T. Wilkins** of Spartanburg Dist, made and executed his Bonds, one due 12 months after date for $1,000; another for $1,000 due 3 Dec 1853; all of which due and payable to **William Robbs** of Spartanburg Dist; for better securing the payments, **William Wilkins** sold to **William Robbs,** 300 acres on the waters of South Pacolett river where **Robbs** lives; adjoining lands of **Golightly, J. Green** and others. Wit: **J.V. Trimmier, P.S. Hunter.** Signed, **W.T. Wilkins.** Witness oath, 6 Jan 1852: Signed, **J.V. Trimmier** to **J.B. Tolleson** Clk & Mag Ex offo.

p. 510-511.   20 June 1843. Deed of Conveyance. **William Fergerson** of Spartanburg Dist, sells **John Heatherington,** a part of a tract surveyed for **William M. Williams Sr.** Decest, and made from him to his heirs being **Elizabeth Ferguson, Mary Ferguson** and **Jiny Ferguson,** now the property of **William Ferguson;** 35 acres on the Branches of Buck Creek. Wit: **John Ridings, Jane Heatherington.** Signed, **Wm Ferguson.** Witness oath, 6 Nov 1851: Signed, **John Riding** to **P.W. Head** Magst.   Registered Jan 6th 1852.

p. 511-512.   23 Oct 1851. Deed of Gift. **Claiborn D. Blanton** of Spartanburg Dist, for $160 paid by **Rebecca Dobbins** of Spartanburg Dist, sold 93 acres on the meder Branch, the waters of Island Creek. Wit: **Wm P. Cash, Benjamin (x) Cash.** Signed, **Claboun D. Blanton.** Witness oath, 8 Nov 1851: Signed, **William P. Cash** to **R. Scruggs** Mag. Release of Dower, 8 Nov 1851: Signed, **Jane (x) Blanton** to **R. Scruggs** Mag.   Registered January 6th 1852.

p. 513.   5 Dec 1851. Deed of Conveyance. **James N. Nolley** of Spartanburg Dist, for $500 to me paid by **William F. Tapp** of Spartanburg Dist, sold a 1 acre lot in the Village of Spartanburg, known as the **Rollens** Lot on Greenville Road near the Baptist Church. Wit: **Thos. P. Vernon, J.W. Ken.** Signed, **Jas. N. Nolley.** Witness oath, 5 Dec 1851: Signed, **Tho. O.P. Vernon** to **J.B. Tolleson** Clk & Mag Ex offo. Registered January 6th 1852.

p. 514-515.   4 Dec 1851. Deed of Conveyance. **John T. Kirby** of Spartanburg Dist, for $715 to me paid by **J.N. Nolley** of Spartanburg Dist, sold 39 ½ acres, a portion of what is known as the mill tract on Fairforest Creek, waters of Tyger River; bounded by **Daniel McHam,** on the Greenville Road and **Bullington.** Wit: **J. Gwinn Harris, J.B. Tolleson.** Signed, **Jno. Kirby.** Witness oath, 4 Dec 1851: Signed, **J. Gwinn Harris** to **J.B. Tolleson** Clk & Mag Ex offo. Release of Dower, 6 Jan 1852: Signed **P. Kirby** to **J.B. Tolleson** Clk & Mag Ex offo. Registered January 6th 1852.

p. 515-516. 5 Aug 1846. Deed of Conveyance. **Henry Wolf** of Spartanburg Dist, for $150 to me paid by **Caleb Kimbrel** of Spartanburg Dist, sold 60 acres, adjoining **Hugh Bishop, William Burnett** and others. Wit: **Elias Wall, Wesley Wall.** Signed, **Henry Wolf.** Witness oath, 6 May 1848: Signed, **Wesly Wall** to **Elias Wall** Magt. Release of Dower, 18 Dec 1847: Signed, **Martha (x) Wolf** to **Elias Wall** Magst. Registered. January 6th 1852.

p. 516-518. 15 Jan 1850. Deed of Conveyance. **Joseph Foster** of Spartanburg Dist, for $400 to me paid by **William Smith** of Spartanburg Dist, sold 426 acres, by estimation, on both sides of Beaver Dam Creek, a branch of South Pacolet River; one part includes the farm where **William Smith** now lives; Originally granted to **Abigail Tenaill** by patent dated Nov 5th 1771 for 150 acres; the other a part of Survey joining the same granted me by patent dated Nov 6th 1797 for 483 acres; reference the **Tournal** Conveyance thereunto belonging, will make the Title more fully appear. Wit: **R.W. Folger, D.C. Judd.** Signed, **Joseph Foster.** Witness oath, 6 May 1850: Signed, **D.C. Judd** to **James Caldwell** Magst. Release of Dower, 6 Jan 1850: Signed, **Minerva M. Foster** to **James Caldwell** Magst. Registered January 6th 1852. Original delivered to ~~ **William Smith.**

p. 518-519. 9 Jan 1852. Deed of Conveyance. **Lewis A. Green** of Spartanburg Dist, for $1,000 to me paid by **Tho. O.P. Vernon** of Spartanburg Dist, sold 1¼ acre in the Village of Spartanburg; bounded on N by **B. Wofford,** W by estate of **Thomson,** S by the Baptist Church Lot, E by **Mrs. A. Bomar's** Lot and street. Wit: **O.E. Edwards, Jno. Earle Bomar.** Signed, **L.A. Green.** Witness oath, 9 Jan 1852: Signed, **O.E. Edwards** to **J.B. Tolleson** Clk & Mag Ex offo. Release of Dower, 9 Jan 1852: Signed, **Charlotie(?) C. Green.** Registered January 9th 1852.

p. 519-520. 6 Jan 1852. Mortgage. **Alfred Brown** of Spartanburg Dist, this day purchased from **Calvin Foster,** two negroes named **Will** and **Mary** for which I am to pay $450 by the 25th of next December without interest. For better securing the sum of money, **Brown** reconveys, sells and mortgages both the negroes to **Calvin Foster**; deed void if **Brown** pays the debt when due. Test: **O.E. Edwards.** Signed, **Alfred Brown.** Witness oath, 6 Jan 1852: Signed, **O.E. Edwards** to **J.B. Tolleson** Clk & Mag Ex offo. Registered Jan 9th 1852.

p. 520-521. [no day] Jan 1852. Mortgage. **Jesse Hughey,** a free person of Colour, have this day purchased from **O.P. Edwards** a Cream mare for which I am to pay $30; for better security of the debt, **Hughey** Mortgages to **Edwards** 7 head of hogs, one Cow and the Cream mare, to be seized upon and sold whenever **Edwards** may think proper by his giving at least 15 days notice of said sale, and accounting to **Hughey** for any surplusage that may accrue from the sale. Deed void is debt is paid. Test: **J.B. Tolleson.** Signed, **Jesse (x) Hughey.** Witness oath, 12 Jan 1852: Signed, **J.B. Tolleson** to **J.V. Trimmier.** Registered January 9th 1852.

p.521-522. 8 Jan 1852. Deed of Conveyance. By the last will and Testament of **D. Dantzler** decd, has directed his Estate, real and personal, to be sold at public Sale. **Simpson Bobo,** administrator of Estate of **D. Dantzler,** with the will annexed, by order of the Ordianary , exposed them to sell; for $955 to me paid by **P.M. Wallace** of Spartanburg Dist, sold three lots on the Ridge between Lawsons fork, and Fairforest Creek, from three to five miles above Spartanburg C.H. near the Howard Gap Road, designated as Lots Nº 4, 5, and 6, containing 208¼ acres; plat attached. Wit: **Henry F. Evans, H.H. Mitchell.** Signed, **Simpson Bobbo,** Admr, will annexed of **D. Dantzler,** Decd. Witness oath, 9 Jan 1852: Signed, **Henry F. Evans** to **J.B. Tolleson** Clk & Mag Ex offo. Registered January 9th 1852.

p. 522-524. 28 Feb 1851. **Junius W. Thomson** on about the 1st day of Oct 1845, petitioned the Court of Equity against **H.H. Thomson, J.W. Thomson** and **J. Waddy Thomson,** for a Specific performance and partition of lands, all of which will more fully appear by reference to Bill filed; cause heard in chambers, Term in 1847 and land ordered to be sold; **Tho. O.P. Vernon** Esq Commissioner of the Court of Equity for Spartanburg Dist, on 16th & 17th Nov 1847, disposed of the lot to the highest bidder, **Robert Rollens** (who assigned his bid and interest to **Alfred Brown** on 17th Jan 1851, and **A. Brown** assigned his bid and interest to **Lewis A. Green** who paid $102 to **T.O.P. Vernon** for ¼ acre bounded on N by **B. Wofford,** on W by Lot the Estate of **Thomson,** S by the Baptist Church Lot, E by **Mrs. E. Bomar's** Lot and street. Wit: **R.C. Poole, W.C. Bennett.** Signed, **Tho. O.P. Vernon** C.E.S.D. Witness oath, 9th Jan 1852: Signed, **R.C. Poole** to **J.B. Tolleson** Clk & Mag Ex offo. Registered January 10th 1852.

524-525. 5 Aug 1851. Deed of Gift. **John Rogers** of Spartanburg Dist, for the natural love and affection which I bear to **William Simpson Rogers** of Spartanburg Dist, give [acres not given]; bounded by **H. Wofford,** the Factory road, to the mouth of the lane that leads to **Willis Rogers.** Wit: **William Moore, Jeremiah Wofford, E.W. Moore.** Signed, **John Rogers.** Witness oath, 12 Jan 1852: Signed, **Jeremiah Wofford** to **H. Wofford** Mag. Registered January 12th 1852. Original Delivered to ~~ [not filled in] Delivered and paid .75.

525-526. 15 Nov 1851. Deed of Gift. **John Keast** of Spartanburg Dist, for love and affection and $1 to me paid by **Robert M. Corbett** of Spartanburg Dist, released a lot in the Village of Spartanburg, a part of the lot I now live on, on the side next to **D.E. Dalton,** containing 16 yards on the Street and 50 yards in the back. Wit: **John B. Archer, Simpson Bobbo.** Signed, **John Keast.** Witness oath, 9 Jan 1852: Signed, **J.B. Archer** to **J.B. Tolleson** Clk & Mag Ex offo. Registered January 12th 1852. Delivered and paid.

p. 526-527. 6 Dec 1850. Deed of Conveyance. **H.H. Thomson** of Spartanburg Dist, for $600 secured to be paid by **Alfred Brown** of Spartanburg Dist, sold 91 acres on waters of Lawsons Fork, known as the **Crocker** tract, which was sold as part of the Estate of **Richard Thomson** Decd; bounded by S side of the road which leads from **Thomsons** Mills to **Well's.** Wit: **William Walker, J.B. Archer.** Signed, **H.H. Thomson.** Witness oath, 9 Jan 1852: Signed, **J.B. Archer** to **J.B. Tolleson** Clk & Mag Ex offo. Registered January 12th 1852.

p. 527-528. 13 Dec 1851. Mortgage. **Sealy Kelly** of Spartanburg Dist, for $504.45 to me paid by **John Davis** of Spartanburg Dist, sold about 160   acres where I now live; bounded by said **John Davis, Thos. P. Miles, Edward Kelly** and others. Wit: **John H. Walker, John Kelly.** Signed **Sealy** (her mark) **Kelly.** Witness oath, 13 Dec 1851: Signed, **John Kelly** to **John H. Walker** Magistrate. Registered January 12th 1852.

p. 528-530. Deed of Conveyance. **John P. Mclerath** of Coosa Co., Ala., for $370.50 to me in hand paid by **Thomas M. Hendrix** of Spartanburg Dist, sold 123½ acres on South Tyger River; bounded by S bank of the river, **N.J. McErath** and **Joel McVey.** Wit: **William W. Hendrix, N. McErath.** Signed, **John P. McErath.** Witness oath, 7th June 1851: Signed, **William W. Hendrix** to **Isham Wood** Mag. Release of Dower, Coosa Co., Ala, 13 March 1851: Signed, **Martha Mclerath** to **Stephen Hughes** Justice of the peace. Witness signature, Coosa Co., Ala., 13 March 1851: **Isaac W. Suttle** Judge of the Probate Court, 13 March 1851, certify that **Stephen T. Hughes Esq** whose genuine signature appears to the foregoing Signature of Dower is and was at the time of signing, Justice of the peace for said County. Signed, **J.W. Suttle** Judge of Probate. Registered January 12th 1852.

530. 3 Oct 1848. Deed of Gift. **S.R. Shelton** of Spartanburg Dist, for the love and affection I bear unto my friend and relation **Mary T.G. Sims,** daughter of **C.E. Sims** of Union Dist, SC, and divers other good and Sufficient causes, have this day given **Mary T.G. Sims,** all my interest to a certain negro slave called **Peter.** Wit: **J. Stark Sims, Ann C. Sims.** Signed, **S.R. Shelton.** Witness oath, 3 Oct 1848: Signed **J. Starks Sims** to **G.W.H. Legg,** magt. Registered January 12th 1851.

531. 20 Dec 1851. Deed of Conveyance. **Elijah Holtzclaw, Jun.** of Marshall Co., Miss., for $200 in hand paid by **George Holtzclaw Senr,** sold 100 acres in Spartanburg Dist, on which **Henry Jenkins** formerly lived, known and described as subdivision N° 5; on waters of Enoree River and Abners Creek. [No witness signatures], Signed, **Elijah Holtzclaw.** Witness oath, 20 Dec 1851: **George West** , a commissioner of the State of South Carolina in and for the State of of Mississippi, appointed by the Governor of SC to take the probate and acknowledgements of Deeds and on the 20th of Dec 1851. **Elijah Holtsclaw Junr,** acknowledges that he did sign and seal and deliver the same for the use and purposes therein mentioned. Signed, **Elijah Holtzclaw Jun.** Signed, **George West** Com. Registered January 12th 1852.

632-533. 14 May 1845. Deed of Conveyance. **R.W. Folger** of Spartanburg Dist, for $400, paid by **R.W. Folger** and **D.C. Judd,** of which firm I am one, sold a ½ acre lot in the Village of Spartanburg to **Folger** and **Judd,** merchants; bounded by **Dr. W.C. Bennett,** main street, a street which runs between **H.H. Thomson's** shop lot; purchased by **Folger** from **Richard Thomson** Decd, in his life time; which lot so purchased by me is to be improved according to a contract entered into by me with **Thomas L. Badget,** by the building of houses &c., at $1,365, $900 of which money is already advanced to **Badget** by the firm of **Folger** and **Judd** out of their store beside the $400; and therefore in order to renew an accounting of said firm on my separate part unnecessary, I make this conveyance thereby making said lot and future improvements a part and parcel of the stock in trade of said firm of **Folger** and **Judd.** Wit: **E.C. Lietner, James S. Cook.** Signed, **R.W. Folger.** Witness oath, 14 May 1845: Signed, **James S. Cook** to **E.C. Lietner** Notary Public. Release of Dower: 19 May 1846: Signed **C.L. Folger** to **E.C. Lietner**, N.P. (**Lietner's** statement says **J. Lucy** wife of **R.W. Folger**). Registered January 12th 1852.

p. 533-535.   19 May 1846. Deed of Conveyance. **R.W. Folger** and **D.C. Judd** of Spartanburg Dist, $400 to us paid by **Joseph Foster** and **D.C. Judd** of Spartanburg Dist, successors in merchandise of **Folger** and **Judd**, sold about ½ acres lot in the Village of Spartanburg; bounded by **Dr. W.C. Bennett's** lot, running with Main Street, to a street which runs between **H.H. Thomson's** Shop lot; same lot purchased by **R.W. Folger** from **Richard Thomson** Deceased, in his life time, which lot to be improved and became part and parcel of the Stock in trade in Merchandise of said **Foster** and **Judd**, Successors in Merchadise to **Folger** and **Judd**. Wit: **J.S. Cook, E.C. Lietner**. Signed, **R.W. Folger, D.C. Judd**. Witness oath, 16 Jan 1852: Signed, **E.C. Lietner** to **G.W.H. Legg**, Magst. Release of Dower, 19 May 1846: Signed, **C.L. Folger, Catherine F. Judd** to **E.C. Lietner**, N.P. Registered January 13th 1852.

p. 535-537.   16 Nov 1847. Deed of Conveyance. **Junius W. Thomson**, on or about the 1st day of Oct 1845, exhibited his Bill of Complaint in the Court of Equity at Spartanburg C.H., against **H.H. Thomson, J.M. Thomson**, and **J.W. Thomson**, praying for a Specific performance and partition of lands which will more fully appear by reference to the Bill files; case heard at June Term 1847 and the court decrees that the lands be sold at public auction; by order of the court, **Thomas O.P. Vernon** Esq, Commissioner of Court of Equity for Spartanburg Dist, on 16th and 17th of Nov 1847, sold 1½ acres for $113 to **David C. Judd** and **Joseph Foster**; in Town of Spartanburg, bounded on W by Wyatt Street, E by **Maj Henrys**, and S by the Presbyterian Lot and **Bennett's** and **Judd's** lots. Wit: **J.V. Trimmier, R. Bowden**. Signed, **Tho. O.P. Vernon**, C.E.S.D. Witness oath, 19 Jan 1852: Signed, **R. Bowden** to **J.B. Tolleson** Clk & Mag Ex offo. Registered January 14th 1852.

p. 537-538.   17 Jan 1846. Title Deed. **Junius W. Thomson**, on or about the 1st day of Oct 1845, exhibited his Bill of Complaint in the Court of Equity at Spartanburg C.H., against **H.H. Thomson, J.M. Thomson**, and **J.W. Thomson**, praying for a Specific performance and partition of lands which will more fully appear by reference to the Bill files; case heard at June Term 1847 and the court decrees that the lands be sold at public auction; by order of the court, **Thomas O.P. Vernon** Esq, Commissioner of Court of Equity for Spartanburg Dist, on 16th and 17th of Nov 1847, sold 1 and 46/100 acres in Town of Spartanburg for $68 to **Junius W. Thomson** and he afterward transferred his bid to **D.C. Judd** and **Joseph Foster**, land designated as Lots № 15 on Wyatt Street; bounded on W by Wyatt Street, on E by Mag. **Henry**, on S by lot marked № 14. Wit: **J.V. Trimmier, R. Bowden**. Signed, **Tho. O.P. Vernon** C.E.S.D. Witness oath, 19 Jan 1852: Signed, **R. Bowden** to **J.B. Tolleson** Clk & Mag Ex offo.   Registered Jan 19th 1852.

p. 539-540.   3 Nov 1851. Mortgage. Spartanburg Dist. **Andrew Pettit**, is indebted to **James M. Nesbitt** for $469 due 25th Dec 1853, which is to endemnify him in being his Security to **David Osheals** for the same sum of money. **Andrew** conveys to **James M. Nesbitt** 133 acres on waters of Cain Creek, bounded by **J.M. Nesbitt, Ebsworth Moore, William Moore, N. Vise, Kmuer[?or K. Moore?], A. Vise**. Wit: **R. Bowden, W**mson Seay. Signed, **Andrew Pettit**. Witness oath, 19 Jan

1852: Signed, **R. Bowden** to **J.B. Tolleson** Clk & Mag Ex offo.   Registered January 20th 1852.

p. 540-541.   14 Jan 1852. Deed of Conveyance. **Thomas B. Collins** of Spartanburg Town, for $600 to me paid by **Joseph Foster** and **D.C. Judd** of the firm of **Foster** and **Judd** of the Town of Spartanburg, sold 9 acres in the Town of Spartanburg; bounded by **Henry** line, N side of **Foster** road, crosses a branch; Wit: **Abiel Foster, Jas. W. Rogers.** Signed, **T.B. Collins.** Witness oath, 21 Jan 1852: Signed, **J.W. Rogers** to **J.B. Tolleson** Clk & Mag Ex offo.   Registered January 22nd 1852.

p. 541-542.   31 Oct 1851. Deed of Conveyance. **John Linder,** for $2,000 to me paid & secured to be paid by **Andres Floyd** of Spartanburg Dist, sold 546 acres on Walker's Branch, waters of Loysons fork of Pacolett river, 3 miles N of Spartanburg Court house on the road leading from the Court house to the Rolling mill of the So. Ca. Ma. Co, whereon I now live; bearing such shapes as are represented by a plat made by **A. Bonner** on the 7th May 1851; on **Wells'es** line. Wit: **R. Bowden, A. Bonnor.** Witness oath, 20 Jan 1852: Signed, **R. Bowden** to **J.B. Tolleson** Clk & Mag Ex offo. Release of Dower, 1 Nov 1851: Signed, **Louisa Linder** to **A. Bonner,** mag. Registered January 22nd 1852.

p. 543-544.   10 June 1850. Sheriff's Titles. Whereas, by 3 Tax executions issued by **D. Scruggs** Tax Collector for the District of Spartanburg, tested the 30th day of September 1849, at the suit of Spartanburg Dist, commanding me, **R.C. Poole** Sheriff of Spartanburg Dist, of the goods, chattels, lands and tenements of **Shands Golightly,** to levy $13.42 with costs and damages, I have seized 800 acres; bounded by **Archibald Kimbrell, Anderson Wingo** and others; and sold to **A. James McMakin** of Spartanburg Dist, for $142. Wit: **J.R. Poole, W.J. Poole.** Signed, **R.C. Poole.** Witness oath, 21 Jan 1852: Signed, **J.R. Poole** to **J.B. Tolleson** Clk & Mag Ex offo.   Registered January 21st 1852.

p. 544-546.   14 Oct 1847. Sheriff's Titles. By a writ of fieri Facias issued out of the Court of Common pleas of Dist of Charleston, Tested 3rd Dec 1845 at the suit of the President and Directors of the Bank of the State of SC, and against **Charles M. Furman.** Admr, debonis non, of **Abraham Markley** Decd; commanding **R.C. Poole,** Sheriff of Spartanburg Dist, that of the goods, Chattels, lands and tenements of **Abraham Markley** Decd, to levy $28,434 with damages and costs, seized 750 acres on Quinns Fork of Thickoty Creek, adjoining lands of S.C. Manufacturing Company, **William Wood** decd, **Lee Linder, John Byars** and others; and sold to the President and Directors of the Bank of the State of SC for $500. Wit: **J.B. Cottrell, J.R. Poole.** Signed, **R.C. Poole** Sher. Witness oath, 21 Jan 1842: **J.R. Poole** to **J.B. Tolleson** Clk & Mag Ex offo Registered January 22nd 1852.

p. 546-547.   5 May 1851. Deed of Conveyance. **Carter Burnett sen.** of Spartanburg Dist, sold [amount not mentioned] to **Isaac Eptin** of Spartanburg Dist, sold 145 acres on both sides of Cherokee Creek, one mile below **Martins** Springs; beginning at the mouth of **Carter Burnett's** lane, on the E side of old Green River road, **Elias** and **John Burnett's** corner and along **John Burnett's** line, on the Cherokee Creek at the mouth of Little Cherokee, with **Solomon Abbott's** line, to **Easler's** corner, widow **Setter's** line, near a spring, with **Lewis Cannon's** line, **Aron Burnett's** line, crossing the Green River road to **Zechariah Cannon's** line. Wit: **Alfred Brown, John Epton.**

Signed, **Carter Burnett**. Witness oath, 21 Jan 1852: Signed, **John Epton** to **J.B. Tolleson** Clk & Mag Ex offo.   Registered January 22nd 1852.

p. 547.   23 Dec 1851. Deed of Conveyance. **John Bomar Jr.** of Spartanburg Dist, for $250 which was paid to **G.W. Bomar** in 1843, have sold to **J.T. Kirby** of Spartanburg Dist, a 1½ acre Lot in the Village of Spartanburg, near and W of said **Kirby's** present dwelling on the W side of Laurens Road, bounded N by a cross street, W by **Jane Poole's** land, S by a lot which I sold **J.M.** and **T.J. Elford**, and E by the Laurence Road. Wit: **R. Bowden, J.B. Tolleson.** Signed, **John Bomar Jr.** Witness oath, 21 Jan 1852: Signed, **R. Bowden** to **J.B. Tolleson** Clk & Mag Ex offo.   Registered Jan 22nd 1852.

p.548-549.   22 Jan 1849. Deed of Conveyance. **Amaryllis Bomar, Jno. Earl Bomar, Thomas O.P. Vernon** and **Harriet C. Vernon** of Spartanburg Dist, for $400 to us paid by **John T. Kirby** of Spartanburg Dist, sold 96 acres beginning on **R. Thomson's** line; bounded by **M'Bee(?)** once **Bomar, J.T. Kirby** and others. Wit: **W.D.D. Poole, Thos. C. Poole.** Signed, **Amaryllis Bomar, John Earl Bomar, Tho. O.P. Vernon, H.C. Vernon.** Witness oath, 23 Jan 1852: Signed, **W.D.D. Poole** to **J.B. Tolleson** Clk & Mag Ex offo.   Registered January 23rd 1852.

p. 549-550.   31 Oct 1848. Deed of Conveyance. **Mahala Wood**, Executrix, **Isham Wood** and **J.W. Wood**, Executors, of the last Will and Testament of **William J. Wood** Decd, of Spartanburg Dist, for $502 to us paid by **James J. Greer** of Spartanburg Dist, sold 165 acres on Abners Creek, waters of Enoree River, beginning on Branch.Wit: **Benjamin B. Wood, Burrel J. Wood.** Signed, **Mehala Wood**, Executors, **Isham Wood, J.W. Wood.** Witness oath, 1 Nov 1851: Signed, **B.J. Wood** to **Mark Bennett** magistrate.   Registered January 23rd, 1852. Taken out paid .75.

p. 550-552.   27 Jan 1852. Mortgage. **James Farrow** is indebted to the President and Directors of the Bank of the State of SC, by a note due 15th Jan next for the sum of $410 with interest, it being a part of the purchase money for 500 acres in Spartanburg Dist, first granted to **Abraham Markley** and was recovered by the said Body corporate & Politic from **John Clements.** A more particular description may be seen from the deed from the bank to **James Farrow.** For better security of the payment of the note **Farrow** conveyed the deed to the bank officers; also, the deed to 14½ acres about 1¼ miles from the Town of Spartanburg Court House, the lot **Farrow** bought from **Revd. J.D. McCulloch**, by reference to whose deed a more particular description may be had. Deed void if **Farrow** pays the debt. Wit: **Govan Mills, H.H. Thomson.** Signed, **James Farrow.** Witness oath, 27 Jan 1852: Signed, **H.H. Thomson** to **J.B. Tolleson** Clk & Mag Ex offo.   Registered January 27th 1852,

p. 552-553.   15 Jan 1852. The President and Directors of the Bank of the State of SC, for $880 to us paid by **James Farrow** of Spartanburg Dist, sold 518 acres, a tract conveyed to the President and Directors by **R.C. Poole**, Sheriff of Spartanburg Dist, by deed of 14 Oct 1847, which tract is on fawn Branch and Branches of Lawsons Fork of Pacolet river; bounded by **Jefferson Rowland, John Clements, William Woody, W.W. Harris** and others; as surveyed by Dept. Surveyor **John Gibbs** under order of Court on the 27th Sept 1850. Bank defends and warrants against **Mrs. L.C. Markley** and her heirs, etc. Wit: **Fisher Gadden, C.S. Coydell.** The President and Directors of the Bank per **C.M. Furman,** President(?). Witness oath, 3 Jan 1852: Signed, **C.S. Coydell** to **Jno. D. Alexander** Not. Pub. Registered January 27th 1852.

p. 553-554. 24 Jan 1852. **Elizabeth Cowan** of Spartanburg Dist, for **R. Bowden** having paid off and discharged or assumed the payment and discharge of a Judgement and Execution against me in favor of **Dr. J.R. Bowden** for something over $50 and also said **R. Bowden** having agreed and undertaken to board(?) and protect me and Secure me the necessary board, Sustenance and lodging in his family during the remainder of my life; have given and sold to the said **R. Bowden** all my interest in the following Negro Slaves: a negro woman named **Rebecca** near about 45 years old, a negro woman named **Malinda** about 23 years old, and her 3 children **Stephen** about 7 years old, **Champion** about 7 years old and **Rebecca** about 2 years old; my right, title and interest in said negro slaves being for and during my life; also all my interest to all the house hold and kitchen furniture which I now have, hold and possess, which interest is absolute. Wit: **J.V. Trimmier.** Signed, **Elizabeth (x) Coan.** Witness oath, 25 Jan 1852: Signed, **J.V. Trimmier** to **J.B. Tolleson** Clk & Mag Ex offo. Registered January 27th 1852.

p. 554-555. 7 Nov 1851. Deed of Gift. **John C. Kimbrel** of Spartanburg Dist, for the love and good will that I have for Son **Caleb Kimbrel,** do give 140 acres where **Caleb Kimbrel** has a plantation binding on the lands the said **Caleb Kimbrel** now lives. Beginning on corner **William Burnett, Sab's** old corner, running SE on **Sab's** old line, **Hugh Bishop's** old corner, **Cartey's** line, a conditional line between **John C. Kimbrell** and **Caleb Kimbrell,** supposed to be **Crowder's** old corner, **Crowder's** old line. Wit: **Robert D. Gilbert, Richard Turner, Javous [or Javas] Kimbrel.** Signed, **John C. Kimbrel.** Witness oath, 26 Jan 1852: Signed, **Robert D. Gilbert** to **J.B. Tolleson** Clk & Mag Ex offo. Registered Jan 27th 1852.
[See grant to **Sabb** and **Lee** in Deed Book T, page 380]

p. 555-557. 26 Jan 1852. Deed of Conveyance. **John C. Kimbrell** of Spartanburg Dist, for $2,000 to me paid by **Caleb Kimbrell,** sold 800 acres where said **John C. Kimbrell** lately resided and parts of other tracts collected together in one grant; bounded by **Sab's [or Sabb]** old line, **Bennett's** old line, N bank of Thomson's Creek, Saphires branch, **Simpson Gilbert's** line, on the old road, near the pond field, a conditional corner betwixt **John C. Kimbrell** and **John J. Kimbrell, Matthew Seay's** line, westward down furnace road, persimmon branch, on a conditional line between **John C. Kimbrell** and **Caleb Kimbrell** on the old ridge road, supposed to be **Crowder's** corner and W along **Crowder's** line; together with a field called the **Hicks** tract which is Exhibited in this grant, on **Sims'es** line and **Clark.** Wit: **Robert D. Gilbert, Javaus Kimbrell, John (x) Kimbrell.** Signed, **John C. Kimbrell.** Witness oath, 26 Jan 1852: Signed, **Robert Gilbert** to **J.B. Tolleson** Clk & Mag Ex offo. Registered January 27th 1852.

p.557-558. 3 March 1851. Deed of Conveyance. **R.C. Poole** of Spartanburg Dist, for $1,000 to me paid by **John Brown** of Spartanburg Dist, sold 200 acres on Lawsons Fork Creek, bounded by **John Tuck, John S. Bishop, H.J. Bishop, John Hall** and others, a branch, E side of the Mills Gap Road, the corner of a tract formerly owned by **Edward Turner** and Lawsons Fork. Wit: **John Moore,**

H.C. Poole. Signed, R.C. Poole. Witness oath, [no day nor month] 1852: Signed, H.C. Poole to J.B. Tolleson Clk & Mag Ex offo.Release of Dower, 11 Nov 1851: Signed, Sibley Poole to J.B. Tolleson Clk & Mag Ex offo.   Registered January 27th 1852.

p. 559-560.   17 Jan 1852. Deed of Conveyance. Robert E. Cleveland of Spartanburg Dist, $1,000 to me paid by John Tuck of Spartanburg Dist, sold 380 acres on the waters of Shoaly Creek; bounded by Shoaly Creek, Wells, W side of the old ridge road, to the corner of Brannon's fence, the old original line, a conditional line between the parties, Miller, Sarah Owens. Wit: Jefferson Choice, James Bishop. Signed, R.E. Cleveland. Witness oath, [No day nor month] 1852: Signed, Jefferson Choice to J.B. Tolleson Clk & Mag Ex offo.   Release of Dower, 17 Jan 1852: Signed, Elizabeth Cleveland to J.B. Tolleson Clk & Mag Ex offo.   Registered January 27th 1852.

p. 560-562.   28 Jan 1852. Sheriff's Titles. By virtue of a writ of fieri facias issued out of the Court of Common pleas for Spartanburg Dist, tested the 27th August 1849 at the suit of Edwin White administrator, commanding J.R. Poole, Sheriff of Spartanburg Dist, to levy $73.31¼ and interest, damages and costs against the goods, chattels, lands and tenements of Matthew Seay; seized 300 acres bounded by John Clement, A. McAllester, N. Edwards and others, which was sold at public outcry on 4 August 1851 and purchased by A.M. Bivings, R.E. Cleveland and A.J. McMakin, who afterward transferred their bid to Mrs. Sarah Seay to the following portion of the land and directed me to make titles to her for the same; 100 acres bounded by J. Clement, it being the residence of the entire tract, sold and conveyed by me belonging to Matthew Seay known as his home plantation, after taking off said tract that portion conveyed by me to A.W. Bivings, R.E. Cleveland and A.J. McMakin, all of Spartanburg Dist, for $840. Wit: Jefferson Choice, J.B. Cleveland. Signed, J.R. Poole, Sh. Witness oath, 29 Jan 1852: Signed, J.B. Tolleson Clk & Mag Ex offo.   Registered January 29th 1852.

p. 562-565.   2 Sept 1850. Commissioner's Titles. Whereas Mrs. A. Bomar and John Earle Bomar, on or about the 25th April 1850, Exhibited their Bill of Complaint in the Court of Equity at Spartanburg C.H., against Tho. O.P. Vernon, and wife Harriet C. Vernon, praying for a partition of the real Estate of Elish Bomar deced, all will be more fully appear by reference to pleadings filed; and heard at June Term 1850, when the Court decreed the land should be sold at public auction; Tho. O.P. Vernon, as Commissioner of the Court, on the 2nd Sept 1850, sold said tract, 70½ acres, for $916 to H.H. Thomson; land on the road that leads to H.H. Thomson's plantation and on H.H. Thomson's line, Union Road, the main road leading to Spartanburg and cornering in the fork of the road leading to Glenns Springs and Union Court house, and along the road leading to Spartanburg C.H. to where the road starts from the main road and leads to H.H. Thomson's plantation; bounded by said H.H. Thomson and John Earle Bomar. Wit: J. Waddy Thomson, J.A. Walker. Signed, Tho. O.P. Vernon C.E.S.D. Witness oath, 29 Jan 1852: Signed, J.A. Walker to J.B. Tolleson Clk & Mag Ex offo.   Registered January 29th 1852.

p. 565-566.   6 Nov 1849. Deed of Conveyance. Jno. T. Kirby of Spartanburg Dist, $1,500 to me paid by H.H. Durant of Spartanburg Dist, sold (1) a ¾ acre lot on Church Street, the lot I purchased from Rev. A.W. Walker; Beginning on W.B. Seay's corner on Church Street. (2) a ¾ acre lot adjoining the above described lot joining on the SE lands of **H.H. Thomson,** N by the lot hereafter described, known as the **Boyd** lot, and W by Church Street; the lot I purchased from **J.W. Tucker** on 13th Nov 1847. (3) a lot adjoining the last described, beginning on the SW corner of the last described, on the parsonage alley to Church Street; the three lots being known as the **Walker, Tucker** and **Boyd** Lots. Wit: **P.M. Wallace, H.J. Evans.** Signed, **Jno. T. Kirby.** Witness oath, [no day/month] 1852: Signed, **H.J. Evans** to **J.B. Tolleson** Clk & Mag Ex offo.

 W.W. Boyd for $353.54 which was due and owing by me to **J.T. Kirby,** and to secure the payment, I give **Kirby** a mortgage of the last described lot on the 28th of March 1845 which is recorded in the Clerk's office in Book Z, page 12, by which mortgage I authorized **Kirby** on failure of payment to advertize twenty one days and sell for cash, which he did and at the sale he purchased at the sum of $250; **Kirby** since then sold the same to **Revd. H.H. Durant;** now in consideration of the above premises above set forth, I convey to **H.H. Durant** all my interest to the last within mentioned lot, the lot which I purchased from **R. Thomson** on 1st Oct 1844, all which will fully appear by reference to the deed from **R. Thomson.** Wit: **P.M. Wallace, H.J. Evans.** Signed, **W.W. Boyd.** Release of Dower, 6 Dec 1849: Signed, **H.A. Boyd** [In clerk's statement, **Adoline**] to **J.B. Tolleson** Clk & Mag Ex offo. Registered January 29th 1852.

p. 567-568. 26 Nov 1849. Deed of Conveyance. **H.H. Durant** of Spartanburg Dist, for $1,500 to me paid by **J.T. Kirby** of Spartanburg Dist, sold three tracts all in the Town of Spartanburg; (1) a ¾ acre lot on Church Street, the lot **John T. Kirby** purchased from **Rev. A.W. Walker,** Beginning on **W.B. Seay**'s corner, Church Street. (2) a ¾ acre lot adjoining the above described lot on the S, on the E by **H.H. Thomson,** N by the lot hereafter described known as the **Boyd** lot, and W by Church Street, the lot said **Kirby** purchased from **J.W. Tucker** 13th Nov 1847. (3) lot adjoining the last described lot, Beginning on the NW corner of the last described lot, the parsonage alley to Church Street; the three lots known as **Walker, Tucker** and **Boyd** lots which I purchased from **John T. Kirby** on the 6th Novr 1849. Wit: **C.W. Styles, H.J. Dean.** Signed, **H.H. Durant.** Witness oath, [noday/month] 1852: Signed, **H.J. Dean** to **J.B. Tolleson** Clk & Mag Ex offo. Release of Dower, 29 Nov 1849: Signed, **M.T. Durant** [clerk's statement says **Martha**] to **J.B. Tolleson** Clk & Mag Ex offo. Registered Jan. 29th 1852.

p. 568-570. 22 Jan 1850. Deed of Conveyance. Spartanburg Dist. **A.W. Bivings** for $241.50 paid to **E.C. Lietner** paid by **W.C. Bennett;** one half the purchase money for the within described tract of land; sold to **W.C. Bennett** of Spartanburg Dist, one moiety(?) in the entire tract of land conveyed to me by deed bearing date 1st January 1850 by **E.C. Leitner** containing 575 acres on **Polly Wood**'s branch, waters of Lawsons Fork; bounded by **Henry Bishop, Barney Bishop, Binson** and **Linly**(?). [**Little**(?) [See pages 384-385, this Deed Book]; had such shape as the plat annexed to **E.C. Lietner**'s deed to me, which plat was made out by **Jno. N. Barrellon** (DS) it being the same that was sold by **Jno. N. Barrellon** Atty **Dr. E.** and **Eliza C. Brailsford,** heirs at law of **William Moultue** to **D.W. Moore** and by **D.W. Moore** to **E.C. Lietner** and **Leitner** to myself. Wit: **J.W. Webber, J.B. Cleveland.** Signed, **A.W. Bivings.** Witness oath, 29 Jan 1852: Signed, **J.W. Webber** to **J.B. Tolleson** Clk & Mag Ex offo. Release of Dower, 4 Dec 1850: Signed, **Sarah Elizabeth Bivings** to **J.B. Tolleson** Clk & Mag Ex offo. Registered Jan 29th 1850.

p. 570-571. 6 Aug 1850. Mortgage. Spartanburg Dist. **Joseph Turner** has this day bought from **Nancy C. Golightly,** 100 acres on both sides of Holaston Creek, waters of South Pacolett; for which **Turner** has given **Nancy C. Golightly** four sealed notes, all for $43.75, each bearing interest from 1 Jan 1850, due one, two, three and four years; for better security for the payments, conveys to **N.C. Golightly,** 173 acres which she this day made me. Deed void if debt is paid. Wit: **William Walker**A.S.H., **C.T. Ragan.** Signed, **Joseph Turner.** Witness oath, 4 Dec 1850: Signed, **Wm Walker** A.S.H.to **J.B. Tolleson** Clk & Mag Ex offo. Registered Jan 29th 1852.

p. 572-573. 29 Jan 1852. Sheriff's Titles. Whereas **Anthony Pearson,** applicant, on or about the 5th day of March 1850, petitioned the Court of Ordinary at Spartanburg Court House, setting forth that **Thomas Pearson (Senir)** departed this life intestate on [no date filled in], in possession of 146 acres, on the waters of Bens Creek, bounded by **D. Anderson, J. Leonard** and others; that division yet remained to be made, which he prayed might be done. On the 12th day of July 1850, **R. Bowden** Esq. Ordinary of Spartanburg Dist, ordered that the land be sold by the Sheriff on the first Monday in August next. **J.R. Poole,** Sheriff, on 5 Aug 1850, sold at public outcry, to **William Hoy** for $367. Wit: **Jefferson Choice, J.W.Wood.** Signed, **J.R. Poole,** Sh. Witness oath, 29 January 1852: Signed, **Jefferson Choice** to **J.B. Tolleson** Clk & Mag Ex offo. Registered January 29th 1852.

p. 573-574. 30 Dec 1851. Mortgage. **David Zimmerman** of Spartanburg Dist, for the better security , the payment of $230.62 ½ to **John C. Zimmerman** of Spartanburg Dist, due him by note dated 30th Dec 1851, with interest, due the 1st May next; **David** mortgaged to **John C.** 145 and 2/10 acres, originally granted to **D. White** and **Henry Murph** on Kelseys Creek, and waters of Fair Forest; on the Spartanburg Road, near an old road, on **Whetstone**'s corner; deed void if payment is made. Wit: **David R. Zimmerman, Carter Burch.** Signed, **David Zimmerman.** [Witness of oath not filled in]. Registered January 30th 1852.

p. 574-575. 24 Nov 1849. Deed of Conveyance. **Thomas Garrett** of Spartanburg Dist, for $21 to me paid by **Ralph Right,** sold 5 acres. Wit: **John Anderson, James Anderson.** Signed, **Thomas (x) Garrett.** Witness oath, 22 Jan 1852: Signed, **John Anderson** to **R. Bowden** Ordinary & Ex off Mag. Registered Jan 30th 1852.

p. 575-576. 16 Dec 1831. Deed of Conveyance. Spartanburg Dist. **Lemuel Lucas** of Spartanburg Dist, $15 to me paid by **Thomas Prince** of Spartanburg Dist, sold 1 acre and 3 rods, on the S side of South Pacolett River, beginning on the bank of the river, bounded by **Thomas Prince.** Wit: **Joseph Smith, John C. Hoyt.** Signed, **Lemuel Lucas.** Witness oath, **John C. Hoyt** to **R.P. Goodlett,** mag. G.D. [mag. Greenville Dist]. Registered January 30th 1852. Taken out and paid.

p. 576-578. 27 Dec 1849. Deed of Conveyance. **John Baswell** of Spartanburg Dist, for $700 to me paid by **Richard Ballenger** of Spartanburg Dist, sold 319 acres on the ridge between Jimmy Creek and Middle Tyger River; Beginning on Nazareth road, to a stake in coal bed joining **J.A. Miller,** then by old road to **R. Ballenger**'s land, **McMellen**'s, **Dr. A.L. Moore**'s purchase. Wit: **J.J. Vernon, John S. Collens.** Signed, **John Baswell.** Release of Dower, 18 May 1850: Signed, **Matilda Baswell.** Witness oath, 2 Feb 1852: Signed, **J.S. Collens** to **J.B. Tolleson** Clk & mag Ex offo. Registered

January 30ᵗʰ 1852.

p. 578. 17 Jan 1845. Deed of Gift. **Andrew Foster** of Spartanburg Dist, for the Love and affection that I have and bear to my Daughter **Catharine Foster** of Spartanburg Dist, donate to her and her lawful heirs 62 ½ acres on Kelsoes Creek; bounded by **A. Foster, Harrisons Whites** [or **Harrison and White**], **Martin Otts**. To the said **Harriet** and her heirs. Wit: **Henry White, James M. Foster.** Signed, **Andrew Foster.** Witness oath, 17 Jan 1845: Signed, **James M. Foster** to **H. White** J.Q. Registered January 30ᵗʰ 1852.

p. 578-580. 23 Nov 1850. Deed of Conveyance. **Hugh Bishop** of Spartanburg Dist, for $250 to me paid by **Simpson Ginnings** of Spartanburg Dist, sold 160 acres, whereon I now live; on both sides of Burtons Branch, the waters of Lawsons Fork, a part of two tracts; Beginning on **Thomson's** line and with **Thomson's** line until it strikes **Mrs. Owens** line, along **Sarah Owens** line to Furnace Road and along the road to persimmon Branch, up the Branch to the head, along **J.C. Kimbrel's** line to a conditional corner made between **Lee Bishop** and **Hugh Bishop**, then down the drain to the Branch and **Thomson's** line to the beginning. Wit: **John Bishop, J.B. Tolleson.** Signed, **Hugh Bishop.** Witness oath, 3 Feb 1852: Signed, **J.B. Tolleson** to **John Bankston Davis** N.P. Ex offo mag. Release of Dower, 23 Nov 1850: Signed, **Permelia (x) Bishop** to **J.B. Tolleson** Clk & mag Ex offo. Registered January 30ᵗʰ 1850.

p. 580-581. 2 Feb 1852. Deed of Conveyance. **Hugh Bishop** of Greenville Dist, SC, for $350 to me paid by **Simpson Ginnings** of Spartanburg Dist, sold 218 acres whereon I formerly lived, which I purchased from **Aaron Bishop**; Beginning on the Furnace Road, to the spring on **Belchers** Still house Branch, down said Branch to **Conner's** Branch, with meanders of Conners Branch and up Furnace Road to the beginning. Wit: **Ransom Ginnings, J.W. Wood.** Signed, **Hugh Bishop.** Witness oath, 3 Feb 1852: Signed, **J.W. Wood** to **Jno. Bankston Davis**, N.P. Ex offo mag. Release of Dower, 2 Feb 1852: Signed, **Permilia (x) Bishop** to to **J.B. Tolleson** Clk & mag Ex offo. Registered January 30ᵗʰ 1852.

p. 581-582. 10 Oct 1851. Deed of Conveyance. Spartanburg Dist. **J.W. Burnett**, for $650 to me paid by **John Baswell**, sold 120 acres on Williams Creek. Wit: **Mat S. Moore, William Smith.** Signed, **J.W. Burnett.** Witness oath, Signed, **Mat S. Moore** to **Mark Bennett** Magst. Release of Dower, 20 Oct 1851: Signed, **Julian (x) Burnett** to **Mark Bennett** Magistrate. Registered January 30ᵗʰ 1852.

p. 583-584. 29 Dec 1851. Deed of Conveyance. **John Wingo Sen.** of Spartanburg Dist, for $1,140 to me paid by **John W. Wingo Jun.** of Spartanburg Dist, sold 350 acres, Beginning in a Cross roads; bounded by **A.J. Wingo, W.G. High**, a branch and the meanders of **Wingo's** spring branch; To **John W. Wingo** forever, Excepting about ¾ of an acre which is reserved as a family Burrying place including the present grave yard in the center of said Burrying ground. Wit: **William Moore, A.J. Wingo.** Signed, **John Wingo.** Witness oath, 2 Feb 1852: Signed, **William Moore** to **Elias Wall** magistrate. Registered February 2ⁿᵈ 1852.

p. 584-585. 1 March 1851. Deed of Conveyance. **Mary Linder** of Spartanburg Dist, for $240 to me paid or secured to be paid, sold **Reuben Bowden** of Spartanburg Dist, a lot in the Village of Spartanburg; bounded on the N by Main Street, E by **H. Houlshouser's** lot, on the S by Land of **H.H. Thomson** and on the W by **Jefferson Choice** and whereon **Jefferson Choice** now resides; The said Town lot known and distinguished from others as the **Ellison** House & place; purchased jointly by myself, said **R. Bowden, John Linder** and others at the sale of real Estate of **Lee Linder** Decd; my interest in the premises being one fifth part of the whole. Wit: **Simp Linder, Elifus Linder.** Signed, **Mary Linder.** Witness oath, 24 March 1851: Signed, **Elifus Linder** to to **J.B. Tolleson** Clk & mag Ex offo.   Registered Feb 2nd 1852.

p. 585-586. 4 Feb 1852. Mortgage. Twelve months after date, I promise to pay **J.W. Tucker** $250, money borrowed today, with Interest from date. Wit: **H.F. Evans**. Signed, **A.G.W. Land.** For better security of the above note **A.G.W. Land** mortgaged to **J.W. Tucker**, the 1 acre lot whereon **Land** now lives; bounded by **John S. Brown** on the NW and by a street on the E, another street on the W; house near the Baptist Church in the Town of Spartanburg, reserving to myself the use and possession until default of payment. Test: **H.F. Evans, Samuel M. Littlejohn.** Signed, **A.G.W. Land.** Witness oath, 4 Feb 1852: Signed, **Sm. M. Littlejohn** to **J.M. Elford** Mag.   Registered February 4th 1852. Taken out not paid [fee?].

p. 586.   9 Jan 1852. Deed of Conveyance. **William Parris** of Spartanburg Dist, for $150 which is to be deducted out of the share falling to **David Parris** my son out of my Estate at my decease, I have released unto **David Parris** 155 acres on Branches of Buck Creek, Waters of Pacolett River; bounded by **Jackson, Henderson, Thomas, Gest** and others. Wit: **J.W. Wood, William Ezell.** Signed, **Wm Parris.** Witness oath, 4 Feb 1852: Signed, **J.W. Wood** to to **J.B. Tolleson** Clk & mag Ex offo.   Registered Feb 4th 1852.

p. 587.   9 Jan 1852. Deed of Conveyance. **William Parris** of Spartanburg Dist, for $150 which is to be deducted from the share of **Abram** [or **Abraham**] **Parris** in my estate at my decease, release unto **Abram Parris** my Son, 126 acres on Branches of Buck Creek, waters of Pacolett River, adjoining lands of **Henry Parris, David Parris** and **Hammett**. Wit: **J.W. Wood, William Ezell.** Signed, **Wm Parris.** Witness oath, 4 Feb 1852: Signed, **J.W. Wood** to to **J.B. Tolleson** Clk & mag Ex offo.   Registered February 4th 1852.

p. 588.   9 Jan 1852. Deed of Conveyance. **William Parris** of Spartanburg Dist, for $150 to be deducted out of the distributive share of my Son **Henry Parris** of my real and personal Estate at my decease, release 131 acres on Branches of Buck Creek, waters of Pacolett River, adjoining lands of **Abram Parris, Jackson, Henderson** and others, on the road leading from **Henry Parris** to **Abram Parris**. Wit: **J.W. Wood, William Ezell.** Signed, **Wm Parris.** Witness oath, 4 Feb 1852: Signed, **J.W. Wood** to to **J.B. Tolleson** Clk & mag Ex offo.   Registered February 4th 1852.

p. 589. 11 March 1846. Deed of Conveyance. **George Nicholls** of Spartanburg Dist, $94 to me paid by **J.W. Tucker** of Spartanburg Dist, sold a ¾ acre lot in Spartanburg Village on what is called Church Street, adjoining lots now owned by or occupied, on the S by **Rev. A.W. Walker,** on the N by **W.W. Boyd,** on the E by lands owned by **Richard Thomson** Decd, and on the W by the public Street. Wit: **J.B. Tolleson, Willam F. Tester.** Signed, **G. Nicholls.** Witness oath, 5 Feb 1852: Signed, **J.B. Tolleson** to **J.V. Trimmier** N.P. Exoffo. Registered February 5th 1852.

p. 590-591. 5 Aug 1850. Mortgage. Whereas, **B.E. Wofford** filed his Bill 5 Feb 1850 against **Absolem Hasting** and others praying for the sale of land mortgaged to **S. Bobo** and the said **B.E. Wofford,** reference the pleadings filed in the case; the cause heard at June Term 1850, it was agreed that tract should be sold by the Commissioner of Equity, and was sold 5 Aug 1850, by **Thos.O.P. Vernon,** by a Bond of $470, secured by **R.S. Wright** and **J.P. Wofford,** to the said **Thos. O.P. Vernon.** Wit: **A. McCallister, John J. Miller.** Signed, **Tho. O.P. Vernon,** C.E.S.D., **R.S. Wright.** Statement of witness of oath not filled in. Registered Feb 9th 1852.

p. 591-592. 27 May 1851. Deed of Conveyance. **J.W. Tucker** of the Town of Spartanburg, for $62.50 to me paid by **Dr. A.W. Bivings** of the same place, sold all my Claim in a ½ acre lot below the Baptist Church in the Town of Spartanburg, which we, **A.W. Bivings** and myself purchased jointly from **Patric O.Shancy;** reference deed made by said **Shancy.** Wit: **Henry F. Evans, Jas. T. Wofford.** Signed, **J.W. Tucker.** Witness oath, 5 Feb 1852: Signed, **Henry F. Evans** to **T.B. Tolleson** Clk & Mag Ex offo. Release of Dower, 8 Feb 1852: Signed, **Emily A. Tucker** to **T.B. Tolleson** Clk & Mag Ex offo. Registered February 9th 1852.

p. 592-594. 9 Feb 1852. Mortgage. **E.L. Huggens** [or **Huggin**] is indebted to **H.H. Thomson** for $100 with interest from 1st Feb 1850 by four Single Bills; due One, Two, Three and four years from date; for better securing the payments, **Huggens** conveys to **H.H. Thomson,** a lot of 3 acres which I bought from **Thomson** 30th April 1851; Beginning on the SW corner of **Tewell's** Lot on a new street and bounded by **Peyton Turner** and N side of a branch. Wit: **J.B. Archer, F. Turner.** Signed, **E.L. Huggens.** Witness oath, 9 Feb 1852: Signed, **J.B. Archer** to to **T.B. Tolleson** Clk & Mag Ex offo. Registered Feb 9th 1852.

p. 594-595. [No date]. Spartanburg Dist. Mortgage. **A.J. Ginnings** for and consideration of my having this day given my [omitted] to **Hiram McAbee** for $30 dated this day and I am dependant on said **Hiram McAbee** for all my provisions that will support my family next year and for the purpose of Securing to him the note of $30 and all that I may owe him for provisions for my Support for the next year, I have this day Sold and mortgaged to **Hiram McAbee** one blind bay mare, one yoke of oxen and cart, 6 head of hogs, one Cow and Calf, all the corn fodder and Shucks that I now have, and further mortgage all the Corn fodder Cotton Oats and Wheat, that I may make next year or so much as will pay the note of $30, and all the account that he may have against me for the years provisions or otherwise. Mortgage void if **Ginnings** pays the note, interest and all debts by 1st Oct 1852. Wit: **J.B. Tolleson, John McKeogh.** Signed, **A.J. (x) Ginnings.** Witness oath, 7th Feb 1852: Signed, **J.B. Tolleson** to **R. Bowden** Ordinary & Ex off mag. Registered Feb 9th 1852.

p. 595-596. 3 Nov 1851. Deed of Conveyance. **Robert Dobson** of Spartanburg Dist, for $200 to me paid by **David T. Smith** of Spartanburg Dist, sold 245 acres remaining (after taking out 100 acres mentioned below) on the head waters of Wolf Creek, waters of North Pacolett River; bounded by the state line, comprising the whole of said tract, excepting 100 acres heretofore sold by **Robert** to **Randolph Wood;** reference to the deed made by **Dobson** to **Wood.** Wit: **Jas. N. Nolly, R.L. Bowden.** Release of Dower, 1 Dec 1851: Signed, **Rebecca (x) Dobson** to **James Caldwell** Mag. S.D. Witness oath, 6 Feb1852: Signed, **R.L. Bowden** to to **T.B. Tolleson** Clk & Mag Ex offo. Registered 11ᵗʰ Feb 1852.

p. 597- 598.   20 Feb 1851. Deed of Conveyance. **Elizabeth Linder** of Spartanburg Dist, for $200 to me paid by **James Philips** of Spartanburg Dist, sold 150 acres bounded by **Gray's** old line, S side of Pacolet River, **Poole's** Survey, **William Pettit** and **Henry Pettit's** spring branch.Wit: **William P. Pettit. W.W. Pettit.** Signed, **Elizabeth (x) Linder.** Witness oath, 23 Jan 1852: Signed, **William P. Pettit** to **William Lipscomb.** Registered February 11ᵗʰ 1852.

p. 598-599.   2 Feb 1852. Deed of Conveyance. **Daniel McHam** of Spartanburg Dist for $500 to me paid **O.E. Edwards** of Spartanburg Dist, sold 130 acres on the waters of Fair forest Creek; bounded by **Daniel McHam, James Tapp Sr., R. Bowden, Ben Sellers** and others; a plat accompanying the deed made 28ᵗʰ Jan 1852; 108 acres called the **Bomar** Tract, and 22 acres, a part of a tract formerly belonging to **John T. Kirby,** whole amount 130 acres. **Daniel McHam** also gives absolute right and title to a waggon way along my line from **Ben Sattes** Spring Branch to the Greenville Road from the afore said tract of land. Wit: **William A. Todd, J.T. Holt.** Witness oath, 2 Feb 1852: Signed, **Wᵐ A. Todd** to **J.V. Trimmier** mag Ex offo. Release of Dower, 10 Feb 1852: Signed, **Kesire (x) McHam** to to **T.B. Tolleson** Clk & Mag Ex offo.   Registered Feb 11ᵗʰ 1852.

p. 599-601.   3 Dec 1851. Deed of Conveyance. **John T. Kirby** of Spartanburg Dist, for Seventy Hundred Sixty Dollars [$7,060] to me paid by **Daniel McHam** of Spartanburg Dist, sold 76 acres on Fairforest Creek; bounded by **J.N. Nolley,** the millpond, a branch, **Tapp** and **McHam's** corner, **Miss Sellers,** with Greenville Road to where it intersects the disputed line; more fully explained by a plat annexed. Wit: **J.B. Tolleson, Joseph Foster.** Signed, **Jno. T. Kirby.** Witness oath, 9 Jan 1852: Signed, **Joseph Foster** to to **T.B. Tolleson** Clk & Mag Ex offo.   Release of Dower, 9 Jan 1852: [not signed, Magistrate's statement says **P. Kirby**]   Registered February 11ᵗʰ 1852.

p. 601-602.   6 Aug 1849. Commissioner's Titles. Whereas **Edin White** on or about the 18ᵗʰ April 1849 Exhibited his Bill of Complaint, in the Court of Equity at Spartanburg Ct. Ho., against **Owen White, James White** and others, praying for a partition of the lands belonging to the Estate of **Daniel White** Decd, reference to pleadings filed; the case came to be heard in Court at June Term 1849, when the Court decreed that the lands should be sold; **Thos. O.P. Vernon,** Commissioner of the Court of Equity, sold at public outcry 6ᵗʰ August 1849, for $50 to **George W. Royster,** 33 acres, platted and numbered Nº 1, and bounded by road, lot Nº 5, **W. Harris, G.W. Royster** and **William Dodd.** Wit: **William Petty, H.A. Johnson.** Signed, **Tho. O.P. Vernon,** C.E.S.D. Witness oath, 12 Feb 1852: Signed, **Wᵐ Petty** to **R. Bowden,** Ordinary & Ex offo mag. Registered Feb 12ᵗʰ 1852.

p. 603-604.   7 Oct 1851. Deed of further assurance. **William Guthrie** of Spartanburg Dist, for $250 to me paid by **John W. Webber** of the Town of Spartanburg, sold 93 acres, by computation, on Rocky Fork of Thickety Creek; the land conveyed by **Guthrie** to **John W. Webber** by deed dated

October 10th, 1842, for which I make this deed of further assurance. Wit: **Jefferson Choice, E.L. Huggin.** Signed, **William Guthrie.** Witness oath, 7 Oct 1851: Signed, **E.L. Huggin** to **Jefferson Choice**N.P. & Exofficio mag. Release of Dower, 7 Oct 1851: Signed, **Clementine (x) Guthrie.** Registered Feb 14th 1852.

p. 604-606.   18 Feb 1852. Commissioner's Titles. Whereas **Thomas Brian** and wife **Narcissa Brian.** on or about 8th September 1851, Exhibited their Bill of Complaint in the Court of Equity at Spartanburg Court House, against **Harriet Camp** & others, praying for a partition of the real Estate of **James Camp** Decd, which will more fully appear by reference to the proceedings on file; heard at Court in Chambers in 1852, and decreed that the Real Estate described in the findings and in the plat made by **John Bankston Davis,** should be sold at public auction by **Tho. O.P. Vernon,** Commissioner;   and was sold to **Peyton S. Hunter** for $3,000; land on North Pacolet River bounded by North Carolina line, **Col. Wilkies** field, North Pacolet River by a mineral spring, **William T. Wilkins, William Chapman;** 419 acres comprising the whole of the real estate and hereby conveyed as original in the decretal order above referred to, without any warrantee of Titles of that portion in dispute and as denoted by the Red lines on the Plat, but with a warrantee of Titles of all the balance containing 419 acres and bounded by said **P.S. Hunter, Col. William Wilkins, William T. Wilkins, Joseph Stricklin, William Chapman** and the Estate of **Jesse Cleveland** Decd. Wit: **J.V. Trimmier, H. Hicks.** Signed, **Tho. O.P. Vernon** C.E.S.D. Witness oath, 19 Feb 1852: Signed, **J.V. Trimmier** to to **T.B. Tolleson** Clk & Mag Ex offo.   Registered Feb 19th 1852.

p. 606-607.   20 Feb 1852. Mortgage. **Thomas Taylor** of Spartanburg Dist, in consideration that **Samuel McCravy** has this day become my security upon a sealed note as Bond for the payment of $600 with interest twelve months after date, to **J.W. Tucker.** For better securing **Samuel McCravey,** and holding him harmless from said debt, **Taylor** mortgages 215 acres where **Taylor** lives; bounded by **Samuel McCravey** and **Asa Smith** on the W, by said **McCravey** on the S, on the E by **Dr. J. Winsmith** and others; reserving to myself the use and possession of said land until default of payment. Wit: **A. Brawley, G.W. Royston.** Signed, **Thomas (x) Taylor.** Witness oath, 20 Feb 1852: Signed, **A. Brawley** to **J.W. Tucker** N.P.   Registered 21st February 1852.

p. 607-608.   20 Feb 1852. Deed of Gift. **John Keast** of the Town of Spartanburg, for natural love and affection which I have for my grand Son **Jabez Bunting Corbett,** of the Town of Spartanburg, release a lot in Town near Church Street and near the lot where I now live; bounded on the W by **Robert Corbett's** lot, on the N and E by **Daniel Dalton's** lot, on the S by my own lot; Lot is 20 yards in length and 16 yards in width. Wit: **Dr. P.M. Wallace, Henry F. Evans.** Signed, **John Keast.** Witness oath, 20 Feb 1852: Signed, **P.M. Wallace** to **J.W. Tucker** N.P.   Registered Feb 21st 1852.

p. 608-610.   21 Feb 1852. Mortgage. **William D. McMakin** has this day given three Single Bills to **H.H. Thomson** and **J. Waddy Thomson,** for $300 each with interest from 13th Dec last, due on 1st Feb 1853 - 1854 - & 1855, being the purchase money for a ½ acre Lot this day bought of them in the Town of Spartanburg. For better securing payment of the debt, **McMakin** conveys to the **Thomsons,** the ½ acre lot beginning on **J.W. Thomson's** corner of main Street, part of the lot which

H.H. Thomson and **J. Waddy Thomson** bought at the sale of their father's Estate. Wit: **Govan Mills, J.B. Archer**. Signed, **W.D. McMakin**. Witness oath, 24 Feb 1852: Signed, **J.B. Archer** to to **T.B. Tolleson** Clk & Mag Ex offo. Registered Feb 24th 1852.

p. 610-611.   22 July 1851. Spartanburg Dist. **Wilson Wingo**, for $500 to me paid by **Fanny Cannon** of Greenville Dist, sold 143 acres on the S side of the Middle fork of Tyger River, bounded by the river as the water now runs in the Old Channel and Ditches, **Edward Smith** and others. Wit: **James K. Dickson, William F. Tate**. Signed, **Wilson Wingo**. Witness oath, 20 Sept 1851: Signed, **William F. Tate** to **B.F. Montgomery** M.S.D. Release of Dower, 21 Oct 1851: Signed, **Mary A. Wingo** to **B.F. Montgomery** M.S.D.   Registered Feb 21st 1852.   Original deliver to ~ **James K. Dickson** 8th March 1853.

p. 611-613.   19 Feb 1852. Deed of Conveyance. **David W. Moore** of Spartanburg Dist, for $260 to me paid by **O.E. Edwards** of Spartanburg Dist, sold 104 acres on both sides of Howard Gap Road, three miles N of Spartanburg Court House, lately purchased of one **Davidson** of York Dist, So.Ca.; Beginning near **W.W. Harris** line, it being a corner of the **Windsor** and **Davidson** grant, on line of said grant to **Dr. W.C. Bennett's** line. Wit: **J.V. Trimmier, James F.V. Legg**. Signed, **David W. Moore**. Witness oath, 20 Feb 1852: **J.V. Trimmier** to **H.J. Dean** N.P. & Ex offo. Release of Dower, 21 Feb 1852: Signed, **Mary C. Moore** to **Simpson Bobo** Not Pub. Registered February 21st 1852.

p. 613-614.   9 July 1847. Deed of Conveyance. **John Crocker** of Spartanburg Dist, in consideration of **Francis Mulligan** and **Susan [or Susanna] Mulligan**, his wife of Spartanburg Dist, Deeding to me all their Interest in a tract of land adjoining the Tract hereby conveyed, and also $1 to me paid by **Francis Mulligan** and **Susanna Mulligan**, I release 133 acres on the N side of Richland Creek; Beginning on **James Gore's** corner at the mouth of the big Branch on Richland Creek, on **Richard Thomson**'s old line, now **Dr. Boyd's**, adjoining **William A. Poole, Elisha Pool** and **Simeon Crocker**. Wit: **P. Quinn Camp, G. Nicholls**. Signed, **John Crocker**. Witness oath, 21 Feb 1852: Signed, **P. Quinn Camp** to to **J.B. Tolleson** Clk & Mag Ex offo.   Registered Feb 21st 1852.

p. 614-616.   7 May 1851. Deed of Conveyance. York Dist, SC. **Charles W. Davidson** of York Dist, for $103 to me paid by **David W. Moore** of Spartanburg Dist, sold 103 acres on a branch of Chinquepin waters of Lawsons fork, and on both sides of Howard Gap Road, part of a tract originally granted to **John Windsor** and [blank]; bounded by lands now belonging to **Drs. Bivings** and **Bennett** on the N, on the W and S the heirs of **David Dantzler**, on the E by **W.W. Harris'** lands, on **Moultry's** line and on a line that was set up some years past as a division between **Windsor** and myself. Wit: **William Alexander, John W. Davidson**. Signed, **C.W. (x) Davidson**. Witness oath, York Dist, 7 May 1851: Signed, **William Alexander** to **James Moore** magst. Release of Dower, York Dist, 7 May 1851: Signed, **Lucinda Davidson** to **James Moore** magst. Registered Feb 21st 1852.

p. 616-617.   6 Feb 1837. Deed of Conveyance. **William Clark,** for $150 to me paid by **Tobias Bright,** sold a tract of land on the waters of South Tyger; bounded SE by **John Baswell,** SW by **Joel**

McVey, NW by **Calvin Bright** and NE & NW by **William Hendrix** and **J.T. Smith**. Wit: **Samuel Otterson, H.J. Dean**. Signed, **William Clark**. Witness oath, 6 Feb 1837: Signed, **Samuel Otterson** to **H.J. Dean** J.P. Release of Dower, 18 Feb 1837: Signed, **Anna Clark** [J.Q.'s statement says **Ann**] to **Joseph Camp**, J.Q. Registered February 28th 1852.

p. 617.   6 Feb 1852. Assignment. $73.33 Due **John S. Finch** value received. Signed, **Larkin Ballenger**. Spartanburg Dist. For better securing the payment of the above note and also for the better securing another note for $56.75 bearing date 31st Jan 1852, and signed by myself and **Henry M. Ballenger**; I hereby assign to **John S. Finch** all my interest in the estate of **Luvey Cothran** both real and personal until the said notes shall be paid, the remainder to be my own. Wit: **J.W. Tucker**. Signed, **Larkin Ballenger**.

p. 618.   15 Oct 1850. Deed of Conveyance. **Wiley D. Wood** of Spartanburg Dist, for $164.25 to me paid by **B.K. Vaughn** of Spartanburg Dist, sold 50 acres bounded by **Henry Smith, W.D. Wood, Gilfred Mason** and **Williams**. Wit: **J. Staggs, John Odam**. Signed, **W.D. Wood**. Witness oath, 17 June 1851: Signed, **John Odam** to **B.F. Montgomery** M.S.D. Registered Feb 28th 1852.

p. 619-620.   27 Aug 1845. Deed of Conveyance. **William Robbs** of Spartanburg Dist, for $475 to me paid by **E.P. Clement** of Spartanburg Dist, sold 150 acres whereon **William D. Underwood** now lives; on the waters of South Pacolet River on the S side of river, beginning at the bridge and running S with the meanders of the road; bounded by **Clark** and **Hammett**. Wit: **David Ramsey, James McDowell**. Signed, **William Robbs**. Witness oath, 2 March 1852: Signed, **David Ramsey** to **Elias Wall** magst. Release of Dower, 24 May 1851: Signed, **Malinda (x) Robbs** to **Elias Wall** Magst. Registered Mar 2nd 1852.

p. 620-621.   15 March 1847. Deed of Conveyance. **Thomas Hammett** of Spartanburg Dist, for $800 to me paid by **E.P. Clements** of Spartanburg Dist, sold 155 acres on South Pacolett river on the S side; on the road leading from the Waggon road on the top of the hill near where **E.P. Clement** lives to **Mose's, Moses Foster's** corner and **Thomas Hammett**. Wit: **Matthew West, Benjamin Clark**. Signed, **Thomas Hammett**. Witness oath, 15 March 1847: Signed, **Benjamin Clark** to **William H. Chapman** mag. Release of Dower, 15 March 1847: Signed, **Lucy Hammett** to **W.H. Chapman** Magst. Registered March 2nd 1852.

p. 621-622.   23 Oct 1848. Deed of Conveyance. **John Stroble Jr.** of Spartanburg Dist, for $100 to me paid by **J.W. Miller** of Spartanburg Dist, sold all my interest, being one fourth, in 230 acres which was sold by **Geo. Nicholls** Sheriff of Spartanburg Dist, on the first Monday in June 1843, as the property of **John Stephens**, at the suit of **Joel Hurt** for **James H. Hurt** vs **E. Stephens** and **John Stephens**. Wit: **S.W. Williams, William Lavin**. Signed, **John Stroble Jr.**
Stroble & Miller vs **George Knight**; **Stroble & Miller** vs **Harrison Knight**: For value received I do hereby transfer unto **Joel W. Miller** all my interest to the above named Execution, 23 Oct 1848. Signed, **John Stroble**. Witness oath, 3 March 1852: Signed, **S.W. Williams** to **Z. Lanford** magt. Registered March 3rd 1852.

p. 622-623.   1 Nov 1848. Deed of Conveyance. **John Lindsey** of Spartanburg Dist, for $1,200 to me paid by **Jeremiah Lindsey** of Spartanburg Dist, 6 acres in a corner between **William P. Brown** and myself; bounded on SE by **William P. Brown** as also on the NE, and on the W by my land, the old **Thompson** line and the corner between **William P. Brown** and **Goforth's** line. Wit: **William P. Brown, H.J. Thomson**. Witness oath, 1 March 1852: Signed, **H.J. Thomson** to **A. Bonner** Mag. Registered March 3rd 1852.

p. 623-624.   2 March 1852. Deed of Conveyance. **Reuben Briant Jun.** of Spartanburg Dist, for $1,687.50 to me paid or secured to be paid by **James Wood, William Littlejohn** and **William Norris** all of Union Dist, SC, sold 375 acres deeded to me by **Alfred Tolleson** called the **Tolleson** land in Spartanburg Dist, on both sides of Union Road; Beginning on said **Reubin Briant's** corner near the road, then on **Stephen Kirby's** line, on the Branch, **Amy Michel's** line, **James Quinn's** Still house, **Gazaway Briant's** corner, on the road at said **P. [R.?] Briant's** line, to **Shrink's** land, then along said **R. Briant's** line to the beginning. Wit: **James Scott, John Petty**. Signed, **Reuben Briant Jun.** Witness oath, 2 March 1852: Signed, **John Petty** to **B.F. Bates** Mag Exofocio. Release of Dower, 18 Feb 1852: Signed, **Sarah C. (x) Briant** to **B.F. Bates** N.P. & mag Exoffo. Registered March 3rd 1852.

p. 625.   7 Sept 1848. Deed of Conveyance. **Robert Stacy** of Spartanburg Dist, for $125 to me paid by **James Ellis** of Spartanburg Dist, sold 50 acres on a branch, waters of Cherokee Creek; on meanders of the branch to **Ellis** Spring branch. Attest: **M.C. Stacy, Absalem (x) Ellis**. Signed, **Robert (x) Stacy**. Witness oath, 7 Oct 1850: Signed, **Abner (x) Ellis** to **A. Bonner** Magt. Registered March 3rd 1852.

p. 626-627.   5 Jan 1852. Deed of Conveyance. **John Tuck** of Spartanburg Dist, for $605 to me paid by **W.J. Tuck** of Spartanburg Dist, sold 3 parcels on Lawsons Fork and Shoaly Creek Waters of Pacolet river. (1) 105 acres, Beginning on Lawsons Fork Creek, the corner made between myself and **William Tuck** on our division line, then near the Saw mill pond, measurement along the Mills Gap road. (2) 28 acres Beginning on **Brown's** line near Lawsons Fork, runs with **Brown's** line to **Tuck's** corner, then on the N bank of said Creek. (3) 18 acres of which I do convey all my interest of said land and Mill which is one half. First tract bounded by **William Tuck, John Willis** and others; Second tract bounded by **William Tuck, John Brown** and **John Bishop**. Wit: **J.W. Wood, Francis James Mangleburg**. Signed, **John Tuck**. (The aforesaid Deed does not include the lot where the School house stands, So long as School may be kept up at said place; and I do except twenty feet square where there is two small graves near the Dwelling house. Wit: **J.W. Wood, F.J. Mangleburg**. Signed, **John Tuck**.) Witness oath, 2 March 1852: [not filled in]. Registered March 3rd 1852.

p. 627-628.   19 Feb 1852. Deed of Conveyance. **Miner Lipscomb** and **Nancy M. Lipscomb**, his wife, of Jackson Co., Georgia, for $468 to me paid by **John H. Lipscomb** of Spartanburg Dist, sold 78 acres known Lot N° 3 belonging to the Estate of **David Lipscomb** Decd, laid off by the Commissioners in that Case; lying on the waters of Little Thickety; Beginning near the corner of **Tempy Wilkins**, apple orchard on the right hand side as you go from the Gin - on the old line to a crook in the road, **Hopkins** corner, to **J.H. Lipscomb**'s corner, **Nathan Littlejohn**'s line to **Tempy Wilkin**'s corner. Wit: **J.W. Tucker, P.M. Wallace.** Signed, **Miner Lipscomb, Nancy M. (x) Lipscomb.** Witness oath, 8 March 1852: Signed, **J.W. Tucker** to to **J.B. Tolleson** Clk & Mag Ex offo. Release of Dower, 19 Feb 1852: Signed, **Nancy M. (x) Lipscomb** to **J.W. Tucker** N.P. Registered March 8th 1852.

p. 629-630. 2 Jan 1852. Deed of Conveyance. **Harvy Wofford** and **Benjamin Wofford**, Executors of **Rev. B. Wofford** deceased of Spartanburg Dist, ofr $150 to us paid by **William M. Foster** of Spartanburg Dist, sold a lot, supposed to be 2 acres, in the Town of Spartanburg; Beginning at the NW corner of **James Low**'s lot now occupied by **John S. Brown**, fronting on a Street, along said street to **A. Templeman**'s corner, then W to a corner on a cross street along **J.M. Tucker**'s line, then S along street to the W corner of **James Low**'s lot, then with **Low**'s (or **Brown**'s) to the beginning. Wit: **Henry F. Evans, J.W. Tucker.** Signed, **Harvy Wofford, Benj. Wofford.** Witness oath, 8 March 1852: Signed, **Henry F. Evins** to to **J.B. Tolleson** Clk & Mag Ex offo. Registered March 8th 1852.

p. 630-631. 9 March 1852. Spartanburg Dist. Mortgage. **Nancy Bomar**, daughter of **John Bomar Sen.** Deceased, this day sold to **Andrew P. Caldwell** all of my interest in my Father's Real Estate, and a Negro girl named **Emily**, one bed Stead, Bed and furniture, one chest, one candle stand, and one Side Saddle, for $445.The condition of the above Sale is such that whereas **A.P. Caldwell** entered as my Surety for $445 payable to the administration of **John Bomar Sen.** Deceased. If **Nancy Bomar** shall pay the aforesaid sum and Exhonerate **A.P. Caldwell** from the burden of Securityship. Then the above Sale be null and void. Wit: **Thomas J. Bomar, P.C. Caldwell.** Signed, **Nancy Bomar.** Witness oath, 10 March 1852: Signed, **P.C. Caldwell** to **J.C. Caldwell** Magistrate. Registered March 10th 1852.

p. 631.   26 Feb 1852. Spartanburg Dist. Mortgage. **Newton Darby**, of Union Dist, SC, in consideration of my debtedness upon a note this day given to **Stephen Darby** of Newberry Dist, SC, sold a negro slave named **Catharine**, together with her future increase. Provided and it is expressly agreed that if said **Newton Darby** shall pay **Stephen Darby** on or before 27th Feb 1852 the full and Just sum of $570.55, and interest, this conveyance is to cease and be void. Witness: **W. Hance, S.F. Vance.** Signed, **Newton Darby.** Witness oath, 5 March 1852: Signed, **S.F. Vance** to **W.B. Henderson** M.S.D.   Registered March 10th 1852. Original Delivered to **Stephen Darby** 13 April 1853.

p. 632. 1 Jan 1852. Deed of Conveyance. **Abram Brock** of Spartanburg Dist, for $85 to me paid by **John Vehawn** of Spartanburg Dist, sold 119 acres on head branches of Lossons fork Creek; on E bank of a creek and on **Turpin**'s line; a part of a tract originally granted to **Abram Brock** on 29th Nov 1848. Wit: **Elias (x) Stone, William Gowen, John Bankston Davis.** Signed, **A. Brock.** Witness oath, 19 Feb 1852: Signed, **Jno. Bankston Davis** to **James Caldwell** Mag. S.D. Registered March 10th 1852.

p. 633. 13 Feb 1852. Spartanburg Dist. Affidavit to Deed, **A.C. Bomar**, Sheriff, to **Josiah Kilgore.**

Personally appeared before me **David Anderson** and made oath that he saw **A.C. Bomar** Sheriff, sign, seal and deliver the within deed of Titles for the uses and purposes therein contained and that **G.W. Bomar** together with himself in the presence of each other witnessed the due Execution thereof; Sworn to before me this 13ᵗʰ day of February 1852. Signed, **David Anderson** to **Jefferson Choice**, N.P. & Exoff magistrate. Registered March 10ᵗʰ 1852. The above affidavit belongs to deed recorded on page 409, Same Book. BB.

p. 633-634. 25 Jan 1849. Deed of Conveyance. **Jesse Leatherwood** of Spartanburg Dist, for $600 to me paid by **John Beason** of Spartanburg Dist, sold 102 acres in Spartanburg Dist. Stake by bares(?), S bank of a creek, road and shoal mentioned. Wit: **Ephraim Drummond, James Leatherwood.** Signed, **Jesse Leatherwood.** Witness oath, 25 Jan 1849: Signed, **Ephraim Drummond** to **Z. Lanford** Magst. Release of Dower, 25 Jan 1849: Signed, **Zelotty (x) Leatherwood** to **Z. Lanford** Magst. Registered March 10ᵗʰ 1852.

p. 635-636. 10 Jan 1851. Deed of Conveyance. **John Williams** of Spartanburg Dist, for $600 to me paid by **Robert R. Williams** of Spartanburg Dist, sold 225 acres on both sides of Cane Creek Waters of Tyger River; bounded by **Ralph Williams, H. Wofford, John Davis, R.R. Williams** and **G.A. Smith.** Warrants all Except about 2 acres around the meeting house, including the spring unto **R.R. Williams.** Wit: **John Osheals, Allen T. Cooksey.** Signed, **John Williams.** Witness oath, 18 Jan 1851: Signed, **John Osheals** to **H. Wofford** mag. Registered March 10ᵗʰ 1852.

p. 636-637. 15 March 1852. Mortgage. **Mary Ann Sellers** and **Bennett Sellers** are indebted to **H.H. Thomson** for $43.62 ½ with interest on a Sealed note. For better Security of the payment of the debt, **Mary Ann & Bennett Sellers** convey to **H.H. Thomson** 127 acres near the forest Creek, the land bought from **John Poole. Mary Ann & Bennett Sellers** to occupy the premises until default of payment. Wit: **R.E. Cleveland, Jefferson Choice.** Signed, **Mary Ann (x) Sellers, Bennett (x) Sellers.** Witness oath, 26 March 1852: Signed, **Jefferson Choice** to to **J.B. Tolleson** Clk & Mag Ex offo. Registered March 26ᵗʰ 1852.

p. 638-639. 23 March 1852. Deed of Conveyance. **Mahala Wood,** Executrix, and **Isham Wood** and **J.W. Wood,** Executors of the last Will and Testament of **William J. Wood** Deceased of Spartanburg Dist, $398 to us paid or secured by **Burrel J. Wood** of Spartanburg Dist, sold 140 acres on Rockyfield Creek, waters of Enoree River; bounded by the Creek, a road and **B.B. Wood.** Wit: **B.B. Wood, W.J. Wood.** Signed, **Mahala Wood, Isham Wood, J.W. Wood.** Witness oath, 23 March 1852: Signed, **Benjamin B. Wood** to **Isham Wood** Mag. S.D. Registered March 26ᵗʰ 1852.

p.639-640. 18 March 1852. Deed of Conveyance. **Simpson Low** of Spartanburg Dist, for $550 to me paid by **Langdon Huett** [or **Hewitt**], sold all my interest in 131½ acres known as the **Wardsworth** land, part of the land that **Hiram Mitchell** bought of **Messrs. Vernon** and **Mitchell,** on the waters of Fairforest Creek and on both sides of Camp Branch; all my interest will more fully appear by reference to the proceedings in the Court of Equity in the case of **Vernon** and **Mitchell** against the heirs of **William Benson** Decd. Land beginning at the road W of Camp Branch, along said road, crossing Camp branch and to the beginning. Wit: **R.E. Cleveland, J.W. Wood.** Signed,

Simpson Low. Witness oath, **J.W. Wood** to to **J.B. Tolleson** Clk & Mag Ex offo.   Release of Dower, 18 March 1852: Signed, **Rebecca Low** to to **J.B. Tolleson** Clk & Mag Ex offo.   Registered March 30th 1852.

p. 640-642.   29 Aug 1851. Commissioner's Titles. Whereas **Samuel Lipscomb** and **William E.S. Lipscomb,** on or about 12 Nov 1850 Exhibited their Bill of Complaint in the Court of Equity at Spartanburg C.H., against **Elizabeth Littlejohn, John L. Littlejohn** and others, praying for a partition of the real Estate of **Frances Littlejohn** decd, all will more fully appear by reference to pleadings files; the cause being heard before the court at Chambers in 1850, and the court decreed that the plats numbering 1 & 3 should be sold at public outcry by the Commissioner, (decretal order in the registry of the said court); **Thos. O.P. Vernon**, Commissioner, for $501 paid to him by **Thomas Lipscomb**, sold 99 acres; on a spring branch, Goucher Creek, as appears from [plat?] of **John Epting** D.S. Wit: **William Lipscomb, Edward Lipscomb.**   Signed, **Tho. O.P. Vernon** C.E.S.D.   Witness oath, 2 March 1852: Signed, **Edward Lipscomb** to **William Lipscomb** Magst. Registered March 30th 1852.

End of Book BB

INDEX

177

179

189

191

194

196

197

198

206

207

210

212

215

216

222

226

227

228

229

230

233

234

237